Shakespeare and European Politics

Shakespeare and European Politics

Edited by
Dirk Delabastita, Jozef De Vos,
and Paul Franssen

With a Foreword by Ton Hoenselaars

Newark: University of Delaware Press

© 2008 by Rosemont Publishing & Printing Corp.

All rights reserved. Authorization to photocopy items for internal or personal use, or the internal or personal use of specific clients, is granted by the copyright owner, provided that a base fee of $10.00, plus eight cents per page, per copy is paid directly to the Copyright Clearance Center, 222 Rosewood Drive, Danvers, Massachusetts 01923. [978-0-87413-004-1/08 $10.00 + 8¢ pp, pc.]

Other than as indicated in the foregoing, this book may not be reproduced, in whole or in part, in any form (except as permitted by Sections 107 and 108 of the U.S. Copyright Law, and except for brief quotes appearing in reviews in the public press).

Associated University Presses
2010 Eastpark Boulevard
Cranbury, NJ 08512

The paper used in this publication meets the requirements of the American National Standard for Permanence of Paper for Printed Library Materials Z39.48-1984.

Library of Congress Cataloging-in-Publication Data

Shakespeare and European politics / edited by Dirk Delabastita, Jozef de Vos, and Paul Franssen ; with a foreword by Ton Hoenselaars.
   p. cm.
   A selection of papers from the international conference Shakespeare and European Politics, hosted in Utrecht in December 2003 by the universities of Utrecht, Namur, and Ghent, in conjunction with the Shakespeare Society of the Low Countries.
   Includes bibliographical references and index.
   ISBN 978-0-87413-004-1 (alk. paper)
   1. Shakespeare, William, 1564–1616—Appreciation—Europe—Congresses. 2. Politics and literature—Europe—Congresses. 3. Shakespeare, William, 1564–1616—Stage history—Europe—Congresses. 4. Shakespeare, William, 1564–1616—Translations—History and criticism—Congresses. 5. Shakespeare, William, 1564–1616—Criticism and interpretation—History—Congresses. 6. Shakespeare, William, 1564–1616—Influence—Congresses. 7. Europe—In literature—Congresses. I. Delabastita, Dirk. II. Vos, Jozef de, 1945– III. Franssen, Paul, 1955–
PR2971.E85S5 2008
822.3'3—dc22
                                                                          2007033043

PRINTED IN THE UNITED STATES OF AMERICA

Contents

Foreword Ton Hoenselaars	9
General Introduction	13

Part I: Geography, History, and Politics

Introduction John Drakakis	31
Making Shakespeare National Joep Leerssen	36
Twenty-three Skidoo: Bringing Home the Bard Terence Hawkes	56
"Here in Vienna": The Setting of *Measure for Measure* and the Political Semiology of Shakespeare's Europe Roderick J. Lyall	74
Shakespeare, Joyce, and the Politics of European Traditions Raphaël Ingelbien	90

Part II: Politics and/on the Stage

Introduction Dennis Kennedy	105
Shakespeare, Napoleon, and Juan de Grimaldi: Cultural Politics and French Troops in Spain Clara Calvo	109
Coriolanus in France from 1933 to 1977: Two Extreme Interpretations Isabelle Schwartz-Gastine	124
Der Merchant von Velence: *The Merchant of Venice* in London, Berlin, and Budapest during World War II Zoltán Márkus	143
Measuring the "Most Cheerful Barrack": Shakespeare's	

Measure for Measure in Hungary under the Kádár Regime
(1964–85)   158
VERONIKA SCHANDL

Feminist Movement and the Balance of Power in John
Cranko's Ballet *The Taming of the Shrew* (Stuttgart, 1969)   169
NANCY ISENBERG

Rewriting Shakespeare: Bertolt Brecht, Heiner Müller, and
the Politics of Performance   179
LAWRENCE GUNTNER

Hybridization: A New Trend in German Shakespeare
Productions   196
WILHELM HORTMANN

Part III: The Politics of Criticism

Introduction   215
MANFRED PFISTER

Groundlings, Gallants, Grocers: Shakespeare's Elizabethan
Audience and the Political Agendas of Shakespeare Criticism   220
BETTINA BOECKER

Hamlet and Modernism: T. S. Eliot and G. Wilson Knight   234
JANET CLARE

"What dost thou think 'tis worth?": *Timon of Athens* and
Politics as a Nonreligious Religion   246
ANTONELLA PIAZZA

Reeducating Germany: BBC Shakespeare 1945   255
ANDREAS HÖFELE

Part IV: Translating Politics, Politicizing Translation

Introduction   281
RUI CARVALHO HOMEM

Translating Europe into Your England   286
DOMINIQUE GOY-BLANQUET

Conservatism and Liberalism in the Four Spanish Renderings
of Ducis's *Hamlet*   304
ÁNGEL-LUIS PUJANTE and KEITH GREGOR

Prokofiev's *Romeo and Juliet* and Socialist Realism: A Case
Study in Intersemiotic Translation   318
KAREN BENNETT

The Smithy of the Soul: Shakespeare, Translation, and Identity Michael Cronin	329
Anthologies, Translations, and European Identities Dirk Delabastita	343
Notes on Contributors	369
Index of Names	374

Foreword
Ton Hoenselaars

Over the past decade and a half, a growing contingent of scholars has come to focus on "European Shakespeare," studying the formative role of the playwright and his work in the constitution of the Continent's sense of identity. These scholars have studied Shakespeare's own work, but also the countless European cultures that went into the shaping of it, as well as the afterlives that the plays, the poems, and the life of their author subsequently inspired in Britain and across the Continent. These scholars' devotion has yielded a range of fine articles, books, conferences, and essay collections, addressing these themes from a variety of angles.

The distinctive feature of this new collection of essays—carefully designed and edited by Dirk Delabastita, Jozef De Vos, and Paul Franssen—is that it approaches Shakespearean culture across Europe from a specifically political angle. It looks at the ways in which events like the Reformation and its political consequences may help us reinterpret the man and his plays, but it also addresses the ways in which altogether less conspicuous ideologies permeate all appropriations of Shakespeare and his work to the present day, in stage or screen adaptations of the plays and the poems, in the many translations produced on the multilingual European continent since time immemorial, in appropriations of the Shakespearean heritage by popular culture, and in scholarly readings of Shakespeare and theoretical reflections on such academic practice.

Shakespeare and European Politics creates an awareness of the complexity of the subject matter as it ventures into largely unexplored terrain in an attempt to enhance our appreciation of the isolated events and political tendencies that had a bearing on what Shakespeare meant by Europe and, in addition, to reveal how Europe has meant and continues to mean by Shakespeare. With their primary focus on the intercultural dynamics of Shakespeare, the researchers presented here position Shakespeare at a vital point on the sliding scale from local, regional, and national to universal, world, and global manifestations of the Bard.

This collection enhances our appreciation of political Shakespeare and the ideology of appropriation in a broader European context, as it moves all the way from the divisive religious struggles of the sixteenth century to the recent attack on the Twin Towers, taking in its stride Shakespeare's idiosyncratic rise to fame in Spain through French mediation in the Age of Napoleon, the playwright's varying fortunes during the politically volatile 1930s, some rather unexpected European representations of Shylock in World War II, the BBC's reeducating program for postwar Germany with a pivotal role reserved for Shakespeare, Communism's paradoxically creative rule, and the absorption of Shakespeare in the recent debate over European cultural values as various constitutional documents for a European Union (EU) were in the process of being ratified.

Shakespeare and European Politics also marks a further advance for the academic discipline itself, as it reflects rather seriously on the no less political and ideological implications of the rapidly expanding field known as "European Shakespeare" to its adherents, and as "EU Shakespeare" to some of its skeptics. When the trumpet call for "European Shakespeare" as a distinct research area was first sounded in the early 1990s (notably at the 1990 Antwerp "European Shakespeares" conference devoted to eighteenth- and nineteenth-century translations), English-speaking scholars from the Stratford side of the Channel were still conspicuously absent. However, anyone perusing the publications of the conferences that followed in 1992 (Sofia, Bulgaria), 1999 (Murcia, Spain), and 2001 (Basle, Switzerland), will agree that, in the course of the years, the tide has been turning. *Shakespeare and European Politics*, therefore, presents the work of a large number of distinguished scholars from both sides of the Channel and beyond, and one is happy to learn that they represent only a fraction of the ever-expanding European Shakespeare research network. Likewise, anyone perusing these essays—including the editors' informed and impassioned introduction (which reads like a manifesto), flanked by theoretical reflections on European Shakespeare from critics including Joep Leerssen, Terence Hawkes, and John Drakakis—must acknowledge that this new research area, which, like any other, had teething troubles all its own, has rapidly developed a solid basis for future research.

This collection elegantly posits that European Shakespeare is not the factual account of just so many Shakespearean events that took place once upon a time in Europe. With poise, too, it argues that European Shakespeare is not simply the ideal of a European band of brothers fighting for an unclaimed space somewhere between Anglo-American and Global Shakespeare studies. The editors, and with them the contributors, believe that European Shakespeare is a vital site of cultural exchange best brought into focus simultaneously from inside out and outside in. It is the challenge as well as the duty not merely of European scholars but of scholars worldwide to occupy themselves with the complex cultural and political trajectory that ranges all the way from the Greeks and the Romans, via the life of Shakespeare himself, and the dissemination of the Stratfordian lore across the Old Continent and the New World, to the postcolonial discussion around the globe that has come to mobilize the Bard for its complex counterdiscourse.

Clearly, one of the major achievements of *Shakespeare and European Politics* is the deft way in which it responds to those skeptics who frown on the ideology behind a project that puts center stage a continent whose past expansionist endeavors explain how, until quite recently, it enjoyed such a powerful presence worldwide. As Delabastita, De Vos, and Franssen in their general introduction state with as much emphasis as justification, the essays in this collection do not spring from "a spirit of self-complacent Eurocentrism, let alone Europhilia." And the international cast of contributors demonstrates beyond a doubt that "[i]nsofar as Eurocentrism plays a role in it at all, it is as an object of study." Shakespeare's Europe stretched from Britain to the Balkans, from Porto to St. Petersburg. European Shakespeare is a worldwide affair.

General Introduction

This book offers a selection of papers prepared for the international conference on *Shakespeare and European Politics*, which was hosted in Utrecht in December 2003 by the universities of Utrecht, Namur, and Ghent, in conjunction with the Shakespeare Society of the Low Countries.[1] The initiative for this conference had been taken two years earlier at the 2001 Basle conference, whose proceedings have recently been published as *Shifting the Scene: Shakespeare in European Culture.*[2] The Basle conference itself followed in the wake of comparable meetings organized in the 1990s in Antwerp ("European Shakespeares"), Sofia ("Shakespeare in the New Europe"), and Murcia ("Four Hundred Years of Shakespeare in Europe").[3] Meanwhile, the Utrecht event has in its turn already been followed up by a successful international conference on "Shakespeare in Europe: History and Memory" held in Krakow in November 2005.

This thumbnail sketch of the background may suffice to suggest how this book grew out of a broader scholarly interest that has been gathering momentum over the past fifteen years or so around the study of "European," "international," and "foreign" Shakespeares, or of "Shakespeare without his language."[4] The internationalization of Shakespeare, not always but often involving his un-Englishing,[5] started during the author's lifetime, but many of the facts and implications of this process are only now becoming fully visible to the critical eye of Shakespearean scholarship. This may be the case because Shakespearean criticism is itself at last shedding its long customary Anglo-American bias, in what may perhaps be regarded as an academic articulation of the globalizing trend, which for better or for worse also characterizes the media, science and technology, industry, trade, banking, violence, and violence control.

None of this is intended to suddenly erase the "Englishness" of Shakespeare and to trade it for new "European" or "global" identities, as if it sufficed merely to replace one myth by a more convenient or trendy one. The challenge is much more profound. These very "English," "European," "universal," and other national and international identities, myths, and constituencies need to be scrutinized—

with due acknowledgment of their often elusive complexity and their dynamic interdependence—in terms of both how they have shaped perceptions of Shakespeare and how they have themselves been inspired by Shakespearean images.

Such a project indeed requires that Anglocentric and insular attitudes be jettisoned, but the scholars themselves need to remain on board. As is demonstrated by the presence between the covers of this book of some of the most prominent Anglo-American Shakespearean critics, the idea is not to cut out native British Shakespearean scholars and their Anglophone non-British cousins, but rather to bring about an integration of "native" and "overseas" scholars in a collective research effort that matches the cosmopolitanism, multilingualism, multiculturalism, and the sheer geographical dimensions of the domain to which that effort is directed, namely, the European and then the worldwide spread of Shakespeare—allegedly the pearl in the imperial crown of the English language—in a world of linguistic and cultural diversity where globalizing action causes antiglobalizing reaction, and where the inadequacies of international structures provoke nationalistic responses, and vice versa, in the never-ending dialectics of human history. In some cases, modes of Shakespeare reception coincided with the boundaries of the emerging nation-states; in others they transcended narrow frontiers; but in all, a Pan-European perspective, and sometimes even a global perspective, is invited. Terence Hawkes's contribution, for instance, takes its starting point in England and its territorial ambitions in Britain, Ireland, and France, but it also draws in the Middle East, the United States, and in a sense the entire world, in its discussion of the ultimate consequences of the ideal of a "national home," promoted with the aid of Shakespeare's works.

As we write these lines, the European Union is going through one of its worst patches ever in its young political history. The member states are at loggerheads over the Union's future budget policies, the proposed text for a European constitution is meeting with widespread indifference or even rejection, debates about expanding the Union are getting more polarized, the divisive effect of the Iraq crisis continues to make itself felt, and the rival bids between London and Paris for the 2012 Olympic Games are causing some real unpleasantness. For those who need reminding, Europe's politics are not and have never been stable or homogeneous. With its many divisions, permanently shifting borders, and problematic self-definition, Europe is hardly a coherent concept or reality, and that is not even counting the complications that ensued when Europe started to export itself, first tentatively and soon more aggressively, in the colonial era, which started roughly during the age of Shakespeare. It is with a full awareness of all this, and not in a spirit of self-complacent Eurocentrism, let alone Europhilia, that the contributors to this book address the European theme that has brought them together. Insofar as Eurocentrism plays a role in it at all, it is as an object of study.

Central to our purpose is the way in which, over the past four centuries, Shakespeare has played a role of significance within a "European" context, particularly where it concerned a series of political events and developments. The book will thus explore the multiple uses of Shakespeare in political propaganda in times of war and peace, as well as the more subtle manner in which ideologies have permeated readings, performances, adaptations, pedagogical applications, translations, and other "appropriations" of his plays. The following papers speak, among other things, of the early modern wars of religion, Napoleonic expansionism, the emergence of the "nation" during the late-eighteenth and nineteenth centuries, world wars, Fascism and Communism, European unification during the 1990s, the attacks of 9/11, *and* of a Shakespeare whose lasting but mutable relevance can never, it seems, be entirely divorced from such developments.

～

Shakespeare's work did not engage only with English or British culture and society, but was part and parcel of the European context. Continental European literature, in translation or in the original, forms a sizable proportion of his acknowledged sources, and many of his plays, in particular the comedies, are set on the Continent, in locations that would have had reverberations of their own during the period. Conversely, from an early age onward, Shakespeare's works and reputation traveled abroad, mainly to the European continent, where they gradually established themselves as powerful cultural and political signifiers. In that process, Shakespeare was often given a new language to speak, while plots, characters, and genres went through a complex metamorphosis. What has long been regarded essentially as "loss" may equally be read, in cultural terms, as "gain": as a "sea-change / into something rich and strange." A better understanding of this process, through which "Shakespeare" and "European Politics" alike become more legible in each other's light, will be the main business of this book.

We have subdivided the essays into four sections, each of which is headed by an introduction. The first section, introduced by John Drakakis, brings together essays that explore the nexus between space, history, and politics, and raise questions of home and ownership. Some of the papers in this section are written from the reverse angle of the Bard's afterlife. They touch on Shakespearean refractions as diverse as philology, theater history, Shakespearean cults, and James Joyce's recycling of *Hamlet* in his *Ulysses.*

The perspective of Shakespeare's reception is the main focus of the three following sections, each of which concentrates on one specific reception mode. Thus, the second section, "Politics and/on the Stage," headed by Dennis Kennedy's introduction, zooms in on a number of significant moments in Shakespeare's stage history across Europe to investigate their political resonance.

The third section, "The Politics of Criticism," introduced by Manfred Pfister, shows how careful reading between the lines will reveal ideological pressures at work behind Shakespearean criticism even in what are allegedly its most academic, historical, or formalistic modes. One case study included here reveals rather more overtly propagandistic forms of criticism, broadcast by the BBC in postwar Germany.

The fourth and final section, "Translating Politics, Politicizing Translation," prefaced by Rui Carvalho Homem, presents a range of quite diverse case studies showing how translation, no less than criticism or performance, can be a revealing form of political intervention, and not just the equivalence-seeking "technical" operation of matching words, syntax, intentions, or effects, which it is all too often mistakenly reduced to.

Most papers included here approach the issue of the political and European dimensions of Shakespeare's plays from a retrospective viewpoint, showing how later generations have understood Shakespeare through the prism of their contemporary experience, or how Shakespeare's plays have offered them a prism through which to consider and understand their contemporary experience of culture and politics. The history of these multiple refractions and reflections is particularly revealing, but also prone to throw up very thorny questions.

One such question concerns the borders between nations, even continents, which invariably turn out to be relative and problematic matters, also where the reception of Shakespeare is concerned. The history of the Jewish people and its way of dealing with *The Merchant of Venice* is a case in point. As Dror Abend-David has reminded us in his recent study on the latter subject (a study that on several points echoes Zoltán Márkus's essay included here on wartime performances of *The Merchant* in London, Berlin and Budapest), European borders are utterly incapable of containing or figuring the history of the Jewish people, and of its engagement with Shakespeare's famous play.[6] Until the creation of Israel in 1948, efforts to create a modern Jewish culture had no solid territorial basis, unlike most other cultural projects that have recruited Shakespeare for their culture-building or nation-building purposes. This becomes particularly evident in the second chapter of Abend-David's book, which focuses on Yiddish translations and adaptations of *The Merchant* and which describes how Shakespeare's work entered the repertoire of an expanding Yiddish theater as it became an important part of the Jewish community not only in Europe, but in urban centers such as Montreal, New York, and Buenos Aires as well.

The case of *The Merchant* highlights a second problem with equally glaring clarity—how difficult it has become for Shakespeare to speak to us "directly," "innocently," in a "nonpolitical" manner. As Abend-David's book and other studies of Shakespeare and the Jews have shown, the multiple contexts and ideological viewpoints of the reception history of *The Merchant of Venice* have not failed to generate multiple Shylocks.[7] In more recent times, Shakespeare's Jewish moneylender has variously been "translated" into a banker, a soldier, a Palestinian refugee, or a Jewish terrorist; we see him appear in settings as widely different as a Nazi concentration camp, the Sinai desert, and a corporate office. In one individual rewriting of the play, Philip Roth's 1993 novel *Operation Shylock: A Confession*, no fewer than five different Shylocks appear, including a spokesman for Palestinian Arabs complaining about Israeli oppression. But where in this myriad of representations is the "real" Shylock? Where is "the Jew / that Shakespeare drew"?[8] Every representation of Shakespeare's protean Jew is bound to be a partial one that shows the fingerprints of its maker and the traces of the political circumstances of its making. Crucially, history before, during, and after the Holocaust has raised the political stakes to an often intolerably extreme pitch of ethical urgency. Therefore the question of how to translate or represent Shakespeare's Jew can no longer be just an issue of philological accuracy, historical authenticity, or aesthetic merit only. Not surprisingly, this is also the underlying thesis of Zoltán Márkus's paper included here.

A similar line of argument could be developed for other plays and their reception history, perhaps most significantly for *The Tempest*, which presents some interesting analogies with the case of *The Merchant*. Compare, for example, the ways in which both plays end up blurring or questioning our conventional boundaries of "European politics" (Jewry and colonialism); or the iconic, even mythical status acquired by those enigmatic and ambivalent characters in both plays (Shylock and Caliban) who, perhaps despite the author's intentions, have progressively moved to the thematic and ideological center of either play, where they are at the mysterious heart of the unspeakable violence that the respective plays evoke behind the veil of romance.

The difficulty we have just touched upon—that of finding a direct way to Shakespeare, or a neutral perspective that can save our understanding of the Elizabethan world from being distorted by contemporary political sensitivities and concerns—is central to Bettina Boecker's contribution to this volume. Boecker discusses the social composition of Shakespeare's original audience, an issue that has semantic implications (e.g., were Shakespeare's spectators and readers, or at least some of them, erudite and sophisticated enough to grasp more complex meanings?) as well as aesthetic ones (e.g., may some scenes or characters be understood as "concessions" to his audience's overall lack of refinement?). Boecker's focus, however, is not on the actual sociological makeup of Shakespeare's audience but on historical reconstructions of this issue across the ages, in Europe and beyond. Explicit statements, as well as implicit assumptions about groundlings or wits, turn out to display great variations that never fail to reflect the scholar's ideological position or social utopia. The historical "facts" of Shakespeare's audience become all the more elusive, of course, leaving one wondering if a value-free shortcut to them may be found. More generally, this raises the question of an ideological bias underlying *any* form of Shakespeare criticism—including the more recent criticism, which always has a way of looking more "natural" to us; including even the kind of metacriticism that we are practicing here and that self-flatteringly likes to situate itself on a safe epistemological higher ground. Manfred Pfister, in his introduction to section 3, rightly notes the need for a new "New Historicism" to be "applied to the circulation of political energies in our own criticism" or for "a hermeneutics whose circular loops would not stop short at our own critical metadiscourses."

Rod Lyall is not deterred by such methodological difficulties in the exercise in geopolitical semiotics that he offers in his reading of *Measure for Measure*. Lyall teases out the meanings and values—the political subtexts—associated with the emphatic and somewhat curious choice of Vienna as the setting for this play. This involves the discussion of European politics and religion in the late Elizabethan and early Jacobean periods and leads the author to consider the textual genesis of the play. But Lyall duly realizes that the rippling effects of political allusion and allegory defy exact or uniform measurement. Answering the concerns expressed in Boecker's paper, he concedes the "highly variable states of awareness of the religious and cultural politics of central Europe" of Shakespeare's audience, arguing that "for some at least" the intertextual-political echoes he recognizes in the play would have been audible and meaningful. Many of these echoes were rumblings of the religious wars between Reformers and

Roman Catholics that so troubled Renaissance Europe. Other papers also hint at the importance of religion in the definition of what is "right" and "wrong" and of what separates "us" from "them." The frame of reference can extend as far as Judaism and Islam (see Zoltán Márkus's aforementioned essay, or that of Terence Hawkes) or even Buddhism (see Piazza's essay on G. Wilson Knight's criticism), or, as in Lyall's paper, confine itself to the historically more familiar Protestant-Catholic axis (see the contribution by Ingelbien on Joyce's *Hamlet*).

Like Lyall's essay, Dominique Goy-Blanquet's paper, "Translating Europe into Your England," takes us back directly to Renaissance England, even to pre-Shakespearean drama, in a discussion of George Gascoigne's translation of Euripides' *Jocasta,* which was actually based on an intermediate Italian text made by one Lodovico Dolce, itself probably derived from a Latin version. Gascoigne's play reveals many "Shakespearean" ingredients, and it is a tempting hypothesis to assume that Shakespeare would have been influenced by it. What is particularly significant about Gascoigne's play and its critical afterlife from a political perspective is the large-scale English blindness to its many-layered continental sources. The demands of national literary pride apparently make it easier to picture "foreign" Shakespeare as a genius bound to conquer the world than as an author who may himself have been at the receiving end of a sequence of foreign, European influences.

Much of this can be made to cohere with the argument of Michael Cronin's wide-ranging essay on Shakespeare, translation, and identity, which deals with Renaissance notions about language, eloquence, and civility, and the possibly destabilizing effects of translation that occur when nationalism begins to export itself through colonial expansion. Cronin explores this theme mainly by a reading of representations of otherness, (dis)loyalty, and translation in two of the history plays, *2 Henry VI* (Jack Cade) and *Henry V* (Fluellen, Jamy, Macmorris). Cronin thus offers us a politically sensitive reading not of the translation *of* Shakespeare, but of translation *in* Shakespeare.

If we continue to read this volume along chronological lines, it next transports us to the late-eighteenth and nineteenth centuries. Joep Leerssen's paper "Making Shakespeare National" critically examines the uses that were made of Shakespeare, especially in Germany and England, in the context of the rise and articulation of their "national literatures." Behind the antiquarian interest, philological work, and various (English) editorial or (German) translational projects that mobilized Shakespeare for this purpose, one can see the twin mechanisms of nationalizing the past and inventing traditions at work.

The contexts elucidating the rise of European nationalisms in the nineteenth century include the dominance of French eighteenth-century taste and the European aspirations of Napoleon's rule. This is where both Clara Calvo's paper on Shakespeare in Napoleonic Spain and Ángel-Luis Pujante and Keith Gregor's discussion of political dimensions of Spanish translations of Ducis's *Hamlet* weave themselves into the fabric of implicit story lines of this collection. Marshaling detailed historical evidence to back her claims, Calvo demonstrates the impact of the French military presence and cultural hegemony on theatrical life in Spain's great cities in the early decades of the nineteenth century. Along with the success of Italian Shakespearean operas, it was French mediation (the Ducis adaptations, Talma's famous performances) that accounts for the Spanish discovery of Shakespeare, first as a cultural icon, then as a playwright: "Shakespeare arrived in Spain partly with the aid of Napoleon." Gregor and Pujante pursue this story line by homing in on one of Ducis's Shakespearean adaptations, namely his *Hamlet,* which spawned no fewer than four different Spanish translations within fifty-five years after its publication in French in 1770. As the authors demonstrate, the lexical modulations and interventions in the plot that come to light in a mutual comparison of these versions lend themselves to interpretation in terms of contemporary political upheavals and the translators' loyalties and sympathies.

The bulk of the remaining papers deal with twentieth-century politics. Terence Hawkes's contribution spans nearly the entire century, and even spills over into the twenty-first century, though it has its starting point in one precise moment in time: Saturday, April 23, 1932, the day that saw the simultaneous inauguration of two major Shakespearean monuments, one on either side of the Atlantic: the Folger Shakespeare Library in Washington DC, and the Shakespeare Memorial Theatre in Stratford-upon-Avon. But then, both events turn out to play their part in so many biographical and historical story lines, in so many patterns of quotation and allusion, and so many possible analogies, that they cannot possibly contain their own significance. A recurrent theme and motive in Hawkes's narrative is that of "home." What is the true home of Shakespeare? But also: how to create a national home for the Jewish people? The actor playing Prince Hal during the Stratford opening season ended up more than thirty years later serving on MI6 in Jerusalem during the terrorism-plagued, violent end of British rule in Palestine. The question of finding legitimate homes for all in the Middle East remains as topical today as ever it was. Hawkes's ingenious linking of "4/23" (the birth and celebration of Shakespeare, and everything he has been made to stand for) and "9/11" (the bombing of the World Trade Center, and how it has affected today's world) may appear to hinge on a string of eerie coincidences, but they quite powerfully bring to mind the complicities between "Shakespeare," "England," and international politics.

The early decades of the twentieth century saw many artists, critics, and intellectuals engaged in the search for a modernist aesthetics and sometimes finding refuge in the autonomy of the work of art, at a time when mutually hostile totalitarian ideologies were consolidating and expanding their influence in the buildup to the tragic clashes of World War II. This is the background for Raphaël Ingelbien's contribution on "Shakespeare, Joyce, and the Politics of European Traditions" and for two of the papers in section 3, devoted to the politics of criticism: "*Hamlet* and Modernism: T. S. Eliot and G. Wilson Knight," by Janet Clare, and "'What dost thou think 'tis worth?': *Timon of Athens* and Politics as a Nonreligious Religion" by Antonella Piazza. Clare shares her interest in *Hamlet*, T. S. Eliot, and the question of Shakespeare's Englishness with Ingelbien, that in G. Wilson Knight and Nietzsche with Piazza; in this way, these three papers enter into a complex configuration of mutual references, at the heart of which is the tension between the professed modernist insistence on the text's absolute autonomy and the unavoidability of a sense of social belonging, moral order, and/or historical destiny.

At the end of the day, the political leanings of modernists usually tended to the conservative side of the ideological spectrum and they often remained latent. In other quarters and in a far less civilized manner, varieties of Fascism and organized anti-Semitism were at the same time rearing their ugly heads and, as is amply documented by two of the papers from the performance section, this phenomenon was not restricted to Nazi Germany only. Isabelle Schwartz-Gastine's essay on *Coriolanus* in France demonstrates how the 1933–34 staging of this Roman tragedy at the Comédie-Française played into the cards of extreme right-wing politics and led to violent riots in the streets of Paris. Zoltán Márkus's contribution on *The Merchant of Venice* in London, Berlin, and Budapest during World War II lays bare a disturbing streak of anti-Semitism in the Old Vic's production of *The Merchant* in 1943, whereas in Hungary, where anti-Semitism had become something of an official policy, the Budapest wartime production managed to project a more positive and thus "subversive" image of Shylock than local circumstances might have led one to expect.

Staying within the same time window, Karen Bennett's essay on "Prokofiev's *Romeo and Juliet* and Socialist Realism" reminds us of the Stalinist brand of totalitarianism in the Soviet Union, which was in its own way every bit as sinister and repressive as Nazism. Prokofiev not only had to cope with the intrinsic challenge of transubstantiating Shakespeare's famous tragedy of ill-fated love into the language of music and envisaged movement; whatever his personal beliefs and intentions may have been, he also had to make sure to remain on the right side of the artistic orthodoxies of socialist realism. Difficult as it may have been for the composer to walk this tightrope, it turns out to be just as hard for the later historian to get behind the silences and the state-controlled ideological smokescreens for a glimpse of the deeper whys and hows of the creative process.

With the grim prospect of European Fascism looming ever larger in a wider context of spiritual malaise and economic crisis, a fair number of artists in the West in the 1930s came to reject the modernist aesthetic in favor of *une littérature engagée.* Or, as was famously the case with Bertolt Brecht and one generation later with Heiner Müller, they tried to wed the modernist sense of formal experiment and innovation with what is believed to be an authentic socialist political project. This provides the subject for Lawrence Guntner's essay on Brecht, Müller, and Shakespeare.

Set roughly within the same spatiotemporal parameters, in "Reeducating Germany: BBC Shakespeare 1945," Andreas Höfele contemplates the smoking ruins—not least the moral ones—of postwar Germany and explains how Shakespeare's universal genius and modern radio technology were simultaneously harnessed in the context of a British pacification and reeducation project. Not surprisingly, perhaps, among the characters given the floor in the German BBC radio program in question, we find Hamlet and Shylock.

Veronika Schandl, too, deals with the aftermath of World War II in her essay on the fate of *Measure for Measure* in Communist Hungary. The Cold War strongly boosted the use of Shakespeare for ideological purposes, which in the Eastern bloc often involved the use of topicalizing political allegory on either side of the official state doctrine, with degrees of subtlety or explicitness depending on the orthodoxy or dissidence of the views expressed, as well as on the degree of expressive freedom tolerated. The rich tradition of Hungarian productions of *Measure for Measure* in the two decades or so leading up to the implosion of official Communism reflects all the shifts and variations of the period.

Postwar ideological contestation also occurred in the West, but not all of it took the standoff between capitalism and Marxism as its main frame of ideological reference. Sexual politics is one of those other battlegrounds, and Nancy Isenberg looks at one dimension and one example of its growing impact on Shakespeare's reception in her case study on John Cranko's ballet production of *The Taming of the*

Shrew (Stuttgart, 1969). The case of John Cranko invites comparison with Karen Bennett's paper on Prokofiev's *Romeo and Juliet* (which, interestingly, was choreographed by John Cranko as well, in Venice in 1958). However, where Bennett focuses on the music, Isenberg is concerned with choreography, and the contexts and the kinds of politics behind either ballet are entirely different as well.

When the Berlin Wall came down in 1989, Europe seems to have entered an era where explicit ideology had to make room for the free cultural play of an increasingly globalized market economy. The consumer demanded instant and momentary gratification; ideological narratives with a wider time span or with universal aspirations receded into the background. These factors have combined with the growing physical and intellectual mobility of today's generation to create a perfect breeding ground for "hybrid" Shakespeares, in which spatial, temporal, cultural, linguistic, and/or stylistic heterogeneity and interbreeding become something like a new norm. Wilhelm Hortmann ponders this fashion in his critical essay on "hybridization" in German Shakespeare productions. Some form of hybridization and hence the inevitable loss of any supposed Shakespearean "purity" characterize any act of reading and rewriting, in the sense that we cannot help viewing the past through our knowledge and experience of the present (hence Hawkes's "presentism"). There is not a single essay in this collection that could not be invoked somehow to underpin this view, and it is a truth that Wilhelm Hortmann himself readily acknowledges. Hybridizing Shakespeare productions, he argues, may actually be a welcome development inasmuch as they are "mutually enhancing" for the cultures that meet and interpenetrate in the theatrical event. But for Hortmann there are other forms of hybridization in the theatrical aesthetic of several current German Shakespearean productions that are deeply problematic because they merely reveal lack of vision and superficial eclecticism.

Europe is not only the geographical and imaginative space where these and other developments have taken place; it is also itself engaged in a Utopian project, that of the political integration of its states in a framework that is supposed to reflect its identity and should guarantee internal peace, at last, and prosperity for all. The twin themes of "politics *in* Europe" and "the politics *of* Europe" are the focus of Dirk Delabastita's essay that concludes this collection: "Anthologies, Translations, and European Identities." This piece brings the book full circle as it revisits, on a Pan-European scale, some of the issues that Joep Leerssen raised at the level of individual European states in the first essay: can Shakespeare be regarded as a "European" author, and, what are the complexities that arise when the anthologist or the critic tries to construct a European literary identity out of linguistic and cultural diversity? The European flag with all its literary stars turns out to have been waved on more than one occasion to serve less than Pan-European causes. Delabastita explores the case of a recent French-language anthology of European literature, which shows that the days of Ducis and Napoleon (as evoked in the papers by Calvo and by Pujante and Gregor, for instance)—days when French could confidently claim to be the voice of culture for all of Europe—are not completely over, or at least not in the nostalgic longings of some.

In the middle of the nineteenth century, there were plans to erect a one-hundred-foot-tall Shakespeare monument in London, designed by a Signor Chardigni.[9] Like the Statue of Liberty, it was to be hollow, made of cast iron, and resting on a pedestal. Inside, there would be space for a small library containing Shakespeare's works, some bas-reliefs representing the most important scenes from the plays, smaller statues of Queen Victoria and Prince Albert, and busts of some of the author's eminent contemporaries. Most importantly, there would be a winding staircase leading up to the statue's eyes, each approximately two feet in diameter, from which the spectator was to have a wonderful view of London. The monument was never built; yet in a number of ways it would have been a marvelously apt symbol for the concerns of this book. Shakespeare is himself a monument, to the erection of which also continentals, like Signor Chardigni, have contributed. He is not only a landmark that can be spotted from afar; but if we bother to ascend the winding staircase up to his head, we can look at the world through his eyes; or at least we think so, for of course it is our own eyes that show us London, Europe, the world. It is we, too, who fill up the hollow space inside him with the idols of our own time.

In the library of his works, in the bas-reliefs of prominent scenes from his plays, we might have found apt phrases and images to speak of events that, as Terence Hawkes suggests in this volume, have come to be expressed by numbers in our digital age: not just 4/23 and 9/11, but also more recently 11/3 (Madrid) and 7/7 (London). Having been declared an honorary Muslim by *Al Jazeera*, who better than Shakespeare to comment on the atrocities committed in the name of Islam, some of them right underneath the projected statue's nose?[10] On the issue of terrorists' dependency on the Western news media, he might well have commented: "The fault, dear Brutus, is not in our stars, but in ourselves."[11] Even Shakespeare's best-worn cliché, Hamlet's delicately poised soliloquy "To be or not to be," which may be about the "canons against self-slaughter," about killing the enemy, or about both simultaneously, has unexpectedly gained a new relevance for the contemporary world, which is waiting to be exploited by some theater production. Clearly, political appropriations of Shakespeare have not yet come to an end; his wisdom extends—or more properly, can be extended—to developments that might well have amazed him.

Acknowledgments

The editors would like to thank all those who have contributed to the success of the Utrecht conference and to the achievement of this volume, including the various speakers and authors. We gratefully acknowledge the generous funding we received from the universities of Ghent, Namur, and Utrecht, and from the following organizations: ACUME, the European Thematic Network for Cultural Memory in European Countries; IVT, the Foreign Language Institute of the Utrecht Faculty of Arts; the Huizinga Research Institute and Graduate School of Cultural History; NWO, the Netherlands Organization for Scientific Research; Netherlands Society for English Studies; OGC, Research Institute for History and Culture, Utrecht University; the Royal Netherlands Academy of Arts and Sciences (KNAW); and the Shakespeare Society of the Low Countries.

Kristine Steenbergh (Utrecht) deserves a special mention for being such a remarkably efficient and obliging conference assistant. Ton Hoenselaars (Utrecht), who amiably accepted to write the foreword for this book, was the conference's "prime mover" and co-organizer, and he never stopped for one moment being a source of inspiration and energy.

Notes

1. Politics in Europe has often been enacted or decided on the battlefield. The Utrecht conference had a double seminar on war and Shakespeare. A selection of papers on this specific subtheme have found their way into a separate volume: Ros King and Paul Franssen, eds., *Shakespeare and War* (Houndmills, Basingstoke: Palgrave [forthcoming]).

2. Ladina Bezzola Lambert and Balz Engler, eds., *Shifting the Scene: Shakespeare in European Culture* (Newark: University of Delaware Press, 2004).

3. Dirk Delabastita and Lieven D'hulst, eds., *European Shakespeares: Translating Shakespeare in the Romantic Age* (Amsterdam: John Benjamins, 1993); Michael Hattaway, Boika Sokolova, and Derek Roper, eds., *Shakespeare in the New Europe* (Sheffield: Sheffield University Press, 1994); Ángel-Luis Pujante and Ton Hoenselaars, eds., *Four Hundred Years of Shakespeare in Europe* (Newark: University of Delaware Press / London: Associated University Presses, 2003). See also, in the latter volume, Ton Hoenselaars, "Bibliography: Shakespeare in European Culture," 241–59. The

Murcia conference further generated *More European Shakespeares,* a special issue of *Cuadernos de Filología Inglesa* 7:1 (2001), guest-edited by Keith Gregor and Ángel-Luis Pujante.

4. The phrase is Dennis Kennedy's. Kennedy's research in particular has been instrumental in unlocking the worldwide dimension; his key publications include *Foreign Shakespeare: Contemporary Performance* (Cambridge: Cambridge University Press, 1993).

5. For a recent survey of the translation of Shakespeare, see Ton Hoenselaars, ed., *Shakespeare and the Language of Translation,* the Arden Shakespeare (London: Thomson Learning, 2004).

6. Dror Abend-David, *"Scorned My Nation": A Comparison of Translations of* The Merchant of Venice *into German, Hebrew, and Yiddish* (New York: Peter Lang, 2003).

7. See, for instance, John Gross, *Shylock: A Legend and its Legacy* (New York: Simon and Schuster, 1992).

8. This phrase has been attributed to Alexander Pope. See Abend-David, *Scorned My Nation,* 2 and 11n.

9. Information on these plans is detailed in the *Algemeene Konst- en Letterbode* 30 (July 29, 1854): 250. This Dutch periodical in turn quotes as its source the *Journal of the Society of Arts,* July 14, 1854.

10. "Was Shakespeare a Muslim?" commenting on the 2003 Globe season on Shakespeare and Islam. See http://www.aljazeera.com/cgi-bin/review/article_full_story.asp?service_id=5835.

11. John W. Whitehead used this quote in a column, to suggest that we should turn off our television sets to frustrate terrorists hungry for media attention. See http://www.rutherford.org/articles_db/commentary.asp?record_id=347.

Shakespeare and European Politics

I
Geography, History, and Politics

Introduction
John Drakakis

IN LES MAYFIELD'S 2001 FILM *AMERICAN OUTLAWS*, THE OUTLAW Frank James quotes from Berowne's speech at 4.3.299–304 of Shakespeare's *Love's Labour's Lost*:

> From women's eyes this doctrine I derive:
> They are the ground, the books, the academes,
> From whence doth spring the true Promethean fire.
> Why, universal plodding poisons up
> The nimble spirits in the arteries,
> As motion and long during action tires
> The sinewy vigour of the traveller.
>
> (4.3.299–304)

This is a seemingly inappropriate response to a railroad's attempt to drive the James family from their land, but Shakespeare is invoked because he is a "European" writer. At this moment in the film, two versions of the "American Dream"—individual freedom, and the power vested in money and articulated as "progress"—oppose each other, and a "European" Shakespeare is invoked as a means of legitimizing the communal traditional values of a rural society, against those of an urban industrial culture that threatens to sever the connection between Europe and the American South. The film is full of contradictions, and it obscures and sentimentalizes the racist premise upon which the American Civil War was fought. But its opportunistic deployment of one of the less well known of Shakespeare's texts, and one that, in part, addresses a nationalist agenda, focuses a debate about the possession of "Shakespeare" as a cultural icon. What is there in Shakespeare that permits him to be easily appropriated into the category of *Weltliteratur*, and that makes of his writings a type of cultural capital to which non-English societies feel the need to stake a claim?

The following four papers, by Joep Leerssen, Terence Hawkes, Roderick Lyall, and Raphaël Ingelbien, all address various aspects of this question and some of its implications. Joep Leerssen's paper, "Making Shakespeare National," focuses on the very process of the European struggle for possession of Shakespeare's texts and suggests some of the reasons why it is Shakespeare, and not Cervantes or Camões, who has been appropriated in this way. It is Leerssen's contention that Shakespeare occupies this position because he stands "at the threshold of modernity and fixed individuality," and that in the case of late nineteenth- and early twentieth-century German appropriations, they were dependent upon a "German *moral* identity for Shakespeare over and against his bio-bibliographical Englishness." Of course, "Englishness" refers not to what Leerssen calls a "factual nationality," but rather to a "functional nationality," a concept that facilitates the construction of a national identity, and that can transform debt into ownership: "the fact that Germany *owes* Shakespeare is transmuted into the claim that Germany *owns* Shakespeare." This argument derives part of its force from the sense of a "universal" Shakespeare, whose cultural capital extends across national boundaries: a form of *global* Shakespeare, if you will, whose influence upon national identity is of a clearly constructivist kind. Any nationality can lay claim to Shakespeare as the instrument of its own self-definition, since all that is required is access to the means of disseminating texts, the very print culture that Benedict Anderson has drawn to our attention in his book *Imagined Communities: Reflections on the Origin and Spread of Nationalism* (1983) as the precondition for the construction of a national consciousness. The German choice of Shakespeare as an exemplary phenomenon, claims Leerssen, derives from the desire to break free of the influence of "French-classicist court culture." It was also entangled in what Leerssen describes as the evolution of a "philological nationalism" that could identify common linguistic origins and that could, thereby, lay claim to cultural traditions that were "anthropological" and "ethnic-tribal." There are some difficulties with this formulation of the problem insofar as Leerssen conflates formal and literary antagonisms and political oppositions. Moreover, we need also to think in a little more detail about what precisely is at stake in the desire to transform a Warwickshire dramatist into a figure of "world literature." Leerssen opts for categorizations such as factual and functional nationality. But what needs further detailed development is some sense of the ways in which a Shakespeare *core*—to use a formulation advanced by Franco Moretti—confronted with a "system *of variations*" engages with "the reality of difference" on a transnational scale.[1]

This intriguing inroad into the evolution of a "European" (or more particularly, a German) Shakespeare and the succession of "myths" through which it passed is nicely augmented by Terence Hawkes's wonderfully provocative account of the simultaneous international celebration of two institutions, and the subsequent reimportation of a Shakespeare who has already traversed national boundaries. "Twenty-three Skidoo: Bringing Home the Bard" juxtaposes the setting up of the Shakespeare Memorial Theatre in Stratford and the inauguration of the Folger Shakespeare Library in Washington DC, on April 23, 1932, the "official" date of Shakespeare's birthday. He argues that the date 4/23 has been as momentous for Anglo-American culture as 9/11 has recently become for North American politics, and that such defining moments are of crucial significance in the cultural history of the two nations. The position is perhaps a little more complicated than in the case of German culture, since North America and Great Britain are effectively two cultures separated by a single language. Parallel to the claims of Lessing and Schlegel in Germany in the eighteenth- and nineteenth centuries, as Michael Bristol has ably shown in his *Shakespeare's America, America's Shakespeare,* was that of Ralph Waldo Emerson, for whom Shakespeare "wrote the text of modern life; the text of manners: he drew the man of England and Europe; the father of the man in America."[2] It would be difficult to know where exactly to place Emerson's claim: is he appealing to etymological or political roots, or to that very universality with which Shakespeare has become invested? For Hawkes, the love affair between England and North America in the early twentieth century, exemplified in the constitutional crisis occasioned by the events surrounding the abdication of King Edward VIII, is crystallized in the inaugural production at Stratford-upon-Avon of *1 Henry IV,* which Edward attended as Prince of Wales. Hawkes is quite brilliant at teasing out unexpected connections between diverse historical details that pull us in different directions, as the progress of Gyles Isham from the role of Prince Hal to one of the progenitors of the state of Israel after 1946 indicates. The image of one Prince of Wales (the future Edward VIII) watching another (Gyles Isham as Prince Hal), and both in some senses fulfilling roles as conduits for significant moments in the culture and history of a Britain whose own boundaries had already become porous, may appear to confirm that home is where the art is, although its origins, as well as its destiny, are invariably elsewhere. This is the paper that Terence Hawkes was destined to deliver, as he intercalates, in the manner of a fully paid-up, card-carrying presentist, his own autobiography, which exactly mirrors the state of the present Shakespeare Memorial Theatre. Moments and monuments come and go, but the decline of Professor Hawkes's own Western elevation is an image that will remain with Shakespeareans the world over well into the twenty-first century. He will, doubtless, after this admission, be deluged with global offers of medication.

Roderick Lyall's paper, "'Here in Vienna': The Setting of *Measure for Measure* and the Political Semiology of Shakespeare's Europe," offers a different emphasis insofar as it proposes to unravel a Shakespearean perspective on the Europe that this play represents. Lyall invokes John Gillies' deployment of Vico's phrase "poetic geography" to explain the dramatist's imaginative perception of geographic space as setting, and he wonders why, when a number of Shakespeare's plays are given Italian settings, *Measure for Measure* is set in Vienna. In order to answer this question he posits a historical context that furnishes an appropriate supply of meanings. While managing judiciously to avoid too close an engagement with the debate about Shakespeare's own religious leanings, Lyall proposes that the interest in Austria generally, and in Vienna in particular, may have derived from the perception that it was on this geographical terrain that a conflict between a dominant Protestant population and a Counter-Reformation minority was being fought out. This is a new speculation, the consequence, in part, of viewing Shakespeare from a European scholarly perspective. Lyall rehearses the familiar arguments against the extreme nature of Angelo's puritanism, and he appears to suggest that in the Duke's rejection of "rigorism," which we are invited to approve, the play's dominant sympathies are with the Duke's implied Catholicism. Whether we need to go this far is an open question, just as it is difficult to know just how sympathetic we are expected to be to the Duke's own position. But the even larger question that Lyall poses, with admirable lucidity, is the extent to which the process of generating meanings (both in Shakespeare's own case, and in the case of the modern scholar) is itself a transnational matter that extends well beyond questions of ownership.

The final paper in this section, Raphaël Ingelbien's "Shakespeare, Joyce, and the Politics of European Traditions" extends the debate in another, no less provocative, direction. Ingelbien begins from the proposition that Shakespeare's texts fulfill the function of a colonizing influence in relation to Irish culture, and that in his deployment of quotations from the Shakespeare canon in *Ulysses,* James Joyce seeks to reassess their presence "in the light of European cultural politics." His concern is to draw out the extent to which Joyce's engagement with Shakespeare and with English culture generally was influenced by ideas of Europe. He foregrounds Joyce's own "subversive ridicule" as a weapon in freeing himself from English cultural domination. But—and this is an important caveat—Ingelbien draws attention to the deployment of Shakespeare's *Hamlet* in Joyce's novel in a way that clearly does not imply the marginal nature of English culture. This, he argues, undercuts any claim that an easy distinction can be made between English and European culture on the evidence of Joyce's novel, just as it blurs the boundaries between "postcolonial parody and the modernist conjuring of classical authority." Ingelbien is quite right to want to tease out the politics of quotation here, and Joyce is a suitable case for treatment precisely *because* of his mendicant bypassing of England in favor of Paris. But his argument raises a larger question concerning the "identity" that various cultures fashion for "Shakespeare." In the essay to which I referred earlier, Franco Moretti notes that "studying how forms vary, you discover how symbolic *power* varies from place to place."[3] He distinguishes between two models: "that of 'the tree' with its tentacular roots that branch out from culture to culture and whose growth comes under the auspices of comparative philology, and 'the wave' that obliterates all boundaries, observ[ing] uniformity engulfing an initial diversity."[4] He goes on to argue, pursuing the metaphor a stage further, that "[t]rees need geographical *discontinuity* (in order to branch off from each other, languages must first be separated in space, just like animal species); waves dislike barriers, and thrive on geographical *continuity* [. . .]. Trees and branches are what nation-states cling to; waves are what markets do."[5] Each of these four papers prompts us to ask the question: is Shakespeare a tree or a wave? Comparative cultural analysis would suggest the former, but the universalizing, not to say the globalizing of "Shakespeare" tends toward the latter.

Notes

1. Franco Moretti, "Conjectures on World Literature," *New Left Review* 1 (Jan.–Feb. 2000): 64.
2. Michael Bristol, *Shakespeare's America, America's Shakespeare* (London: Routledge, 1990), 125.
3. Moretti, "Conjectures on World Literature," 66.
4. Ibid., 67.
5. Ibid.

Making Shakespeare National
Joep Leerssen

Introduction: Factual versus Functional Nationality

EUROPEAN LITERARY HISTORY IS FULL OF CONTESTED HEIRLOOMS. The *Edda* has been claimed as part of a "national" heritage by Norwegian, Danish, and Icelandic critics; Slavic cultures contest each other's titles to Saints Cyril and Method; French, German, and Dutch/Flemish philologists have crossed swords over the primacy of various chivalric romance-themes and over the question as to whose version of the animal fable of Reynard the Fox was the authentic one.

Such quarrels peaked in the nationalism-ridden nineteenth and twentieth centuries. They projected contemporary, national categories back into an inchoate and scarcely documented medieval period—a period when literary themes, stories, and motifs floated freely across a preprint practice of adaptation and recycling; when individuals identified more with their church, their lord, or their liege than with their language or "nation"; before vernacular languages and language-areas had crystallized into the patterns with which we are familiar nowadays. To subject, as nineteenth-century philologists did, texts and themes from those bygone centuries to contemporary claims of "national appurtenance" was a gigantic, chauvinism-induced exercise in anachronism.

In one case, however, the contest involves not some anonymous or semilegendary material from the dark Middle Ages, but an individual author, known by name and *oeuvre,* from the canon of printed European letters: William Shakespeare. To be sure, Shakespeare's life is still beset by "medieval"-style problems of identity and authorship: it is so ill documented that his individuality is blurred at the edges. This allowed for the William Ireland forgeries of the eighteenth century. It has also made debate possible about the "real" authorship of his plays: Shakespeare has continued to attract speculative theories about his authorship, from the famous Baconian craze to the Oxfordian theory and, more marginally, the recent "gendered" variation raising the standard of Mary Sidney.

Yet, despite the elusive indeterminacy of the signifier "Shakespeare" (a lack of personal individuation that the Bard shares with medieval anonymi rather than with Cervantes or Camões), this author stands at the threshold of modernity and fixed individuality. And one thing that is obvious beyond question is his nationality, which is fixed within the parameters of modern nation- and state-formation. Whatever the bandwidth of uncertainty that the paucity of documentary evidence allows, the country he lived in, the history he identified with, the literary and theatrical system he was involved in, and the language he wrote in are all so unmistakably and indisputably English as to foreclose any further debate on that topic.

Nevertheless, the Englishness of even this Shakespeare has been disputed. In particular, and notoriously, claims have been raised to make him German. These attempts peaked in the opening decades of the twentieth century, and are probably best illustrated by the names of Gerhard Hauptmann and Friedrich Gundolf. Hauptmann himself, speaking to the *Deutsche Shakespeare-Gesellschaft* (and it is deeply meaningful, in this context, that this was the first such society formed in Europe) in the dark year 1915, when Anglo-German relations were mired in the trenches of the Great War, advanced a German *moral* identity for Shakespeare over and against his bio-bibliographical Englishness: "No nation, not even England, has earned a greater claim on Shakespeare than Germany. Shakespeare's characters are part of our world, his spirit has become one with ours, and although he has been born and lies buried in England, it is in Germany that he truly lives."[1] Such sentiments are in line with the arguments unfolded in Friedrich Gundolf's notorious classic *Shakespeare und der deutsche Geist* (1911). Gundolf's and Hauptmann's rhetoric opposes Shakespeare's bio-bibliographical prima facie Englishness on two grounds: (a) Shakespeare's spiritual and cultural greatness transcends narrowly national boundaries or English exclusiveness; and (b) his impact in, particularly, Germany has been such that functionally he has played a formative role in the growth of German literature, forms part of it. As a result, though German literature does not *own* Shakespeare, Shakespeare *belongs* to it. This allows Germans to say that Shakespeare is "theirs," much as descendants can use the possessive pronoun when speaking of "their" ancestor, subjects when speaking of "their" monarch, fans when speaking of "their" football team.

Debt becomes claim: the fact that Germany *owes* Shakespeare is transmuted into the claim that Germany *owns* Shakespeare.[2] Shakespeare's factual nationality is none other than English; his functional nationality can just as well be German.

Literary Nationality: A Concept in Need of Historicization

The implications and ramifications of such "functional nationality" arguments can lead into various directions. There is, to be begin with, Gundolf's own approach, which looks at the qualities of Shakespeare's work, and the question of how and why these exercised such a very particular appeal to German literary sensibilities at a formative period of German literary history. (Such questions can be addressed with greater or smaller degrees of national essentialism.)

Furthermore, it is possible to place the history of Shakespeare's German reception in the historical context of nineteenth-century politics. As we know, German authors like Lessing and Herder had looked to English letters, and to Shakespeare in particular, as a possible alternative for the oppressive hegemony of French-style classicism; shared anti-French sentiment had been strengthened in the Napoleonic years; early-Victorian England came to celebrate its "Saxon," Germanic roots, and the marriage between Victoria and Albert did much to cement a sense of close kinship between the two "cousin-nations." This relationship soured, initially in Britain, with the rise of German imperialism after 1870. German imperial ambitions and growing military power led to apprehensions expressed in a spate of anti-German fear-mongering "invasion novels."[3] The 1890s saw a growing cultural and political rapprochement between Britain and France, culminating in the entente cordiale of 1904. When French, German, and British armies faced each other in Flanders a century after Napoleon, the Hate Triangle had switched polarity. At Waterloo, a French empire faced a British-Prussian alliance; at Verdun, a German empire faced a British-French alliance. Added irony: whereas the growth of anti-German feeling after 1870 in Britain seems to have increased suddenly and steeply, the German Gründerzeit had been much more reluctant to abandon Germany's accustomed Anglophilia, partly at least because of the German cult of Shakespeare (witness the fact that the first European Shakespeare society had been founded in, precisely, Germany, in 1864, and celebrated its jubilee in the fateful year of 1914).[4] This gives the sentiments of Gundolf and Hauptmann their additional poignancy.

I want to address an underlying issue. Whether factual or functional, the concept of nationality in literary discussions went through far-reaching changes at precisely the time that Shakespeare was discovered and appropriated in Germany, and these changes, historically important though they are, have not yet received sufficient attention from literary historians. Literary history has not yet developed a sense of "conceptual history," of *Begriffsgeschichte,* a historicization of the conceptual apparatus with which we describe the world and its changes.[5] If Shakespeare, in his Englishness, is positioned vis-à-vis German literature, does the word "German" mean the same thing for Gundolf as it did for Lessing? Are the terms and parameters of the interaction constant throughout the nineteenth century?

What I want to argue is that long-term processes of literary exchange, such as the long and intense German preoccupation with Shakespeare, present a variable geometry in which not only the exchange itself is part of a historical dynamics, but where the conceptual parameters of the exchange are themselves shifting their position and meaning over time. What constitutes a "literature" (let alone a "national literature," like an English or a German one); what constitutes a literary genius of transnational importance (like Shakespeare): these underlying parameters and attitudes are the shifting sands in which we have to chart the emergence of Shakespeare's German "functional nationality."

This requires some extra specification. Let me, to begin with, make explicit our generally current, implicit, and often naive mode of viewing national literatures. It assumes that literatures have a nationality, that the reception of Shakespeare in German literature is a qualitatively different process from the reception of Schiller in Germany or the reception of Shakespeare in England. Our mental template is more or less as follows: European literature is naturally divided into different national traditions, by and large distinguished as such on the basis of their respective languages. Each of these European literatures has a more or less autonomous history and canon. The German canon includes Hölderlin and Handke, the English canon includes Dryden and Dickens. These nationally canonical figureheads may in the second instance manage to gain canonicity abroad, through translations into foreign languages—much as highly talented football players, from nationally leading teams and in the national team, may score internationally, by winning international tournaments and obtaining transfers to foreign teams. In this "national league" template of literature, the "great" authors who gain international fame are like international football stars: the Pelés, Cruyffs, Maradonas, and Beckhams of literature. In such a template, the World Cup of literature would be something like the Nobel Prize.

This assumption is (or has been until recently) so transparently self-evident that it has only rarely been queried.[6] It has, of course, been refined by the rise of approaches like polysystem theory and, more recently, theories of cultural transfer;[7] the rise of hermeneutically inspired approaches in literary studies has likewise helped to combat the anachronisms of national-literary essentialism; but there is still room for a more persistent application of the imagological insight that national identity in literature, and also the national identity *of* literature, is fundamentally a construct, not a given: not something that categorically determines the course of literary history, but something that is articulated within the course of literary history.[8]

Nationality in literature is, in short, a *variable.* Its variation patterns are slow, take place in a *longue durée* dynamics and may therefore fail to be registered (and indeed not be very meaningful) in the analysis of short-term literary phenomena. But in the analysis of long-term literary processes this variability has to be taken into account lest we fall victim to anachronism—the sort of anachronism of Ludwig Eckhart, when he marked the foundation of the Deutsche Shakespeare-Gesellschaft in 1864 with a published lecture on *Lessing und das erste deutsche Nationaltheater in Hamburg,*[9] implicitly claiming continuity from Lessing's invocation of Shakespeare in the 1780s to the German Shakespeare festivities of 1864. The German preoccupation with Shakespeare is, however, precisely such a long-term process that its underlying terms of reference must be recalibrated for conceptual changes that occurred during its period of historical activity.

Prenational Shakespeare

The "football league" template of literary nationality—we may call it, less flippantly, the "national paradigm"—is some two hundred years old. It emerged precisely in the decades when the German reception of Shakespeare gathered steam: between 1800 and 1830. This implies, conversely, that a national paradigm in literature was by and large absent, or only embryonically present, before 1800. That certainly was the case in the Middle Ages. The various medieval vernaculars had no literary or national status in the modern sense: themes and motifs migrated across a heterogeneous, polyglossic European landscape. This is the reason that the appurtenance of medieval texts (*matière de Bretagne,* Carolingian cycles, animal fables) and authors (Marie de France, Henric van Veldeke) is in many cases so nationally unspecific, even though such indeterminacy has been filtered out by nationally slanted literary histories of the last two hundred years. Who is familiar, nowadays, with the fact that the earliest version of Marco Polo's travel account is in a French dialect?

With the simultaneous rise of print culture and the modern state system, we see a process of stratification and crystallization set in.

Even so, the literary canon remained by and large nationally aspecific. That goes without saying for the canonical works of classical antiquity, theology, and philosophy. It also means that names like Dante, Tasso, Camões, and Cervantes belong to an older, undifferentiated sense of "literature"-at-large. Indeed, the very word literature is originally an abstract, uncountable *singulare tantum* like "milk" or "smoke." As Jorge Luis Borges succinctly phrased the classical outlook: "According to the classical view, the plurality of men and of periods is accidental; literature is always in the singular."[10] To be sure, subdivisions in "literature" were possible and were made, predominantly, between the literature of "the ancients" and of "the moderns" (i.e., post-Renaissance Europe). But to a significant extent, a universalist, undifferentiated concept of literature, with a single, anational canon current in a "Republic of Letters," maintained itself well into the eighteenth century. This anational or prenational canon, strongly dominated by classical or classicist values, is the one that initially facilitated Shakespeare's European fame.

THE NATIONAL DIFFRACTION OF THE EUROPEAN CANON

What we must trace from this starting position onward is, then, a growing national diffraction: the rise and articulation of national literatures. The various factors that set this process going need not specifically concern us here: Giambattista Vico's ideas about an anthropology of cultural specificity, Herder's philosophy defining human culture specifically in its diversity, specifically in ethnic ("national") terms; a growing taste for primitivism, surrounding also the "discovery" of Ossianic remains in Scotland.[11]

All this influenced both the status of Shakespeare and the literary system in Germany. Shakespeare, who heretofore had been criticized for his lapses (by neo-Aristotelian standards) in dramatic bienséance, from ca. 1760 onward acquired the reputation of an "original genius"—a quality he shared with Homer and Ossian.[12] "Original" meant that such literary geniuses formed an origin, a point of departure. They had learned their literary mastery from no established conventions; they were the primary creators and instigators and, as such, worked with a freshness that their later imitators and successors could only envy, never equal.

Accordingly we see, among late-Enlightenment critics, a growing preoccupation with the *beginnings* of literature. Much as Enlightenment philosophers debated the origins of language, so too do we see critical debates, by Hugh Blair and others, concerning the origins of literature. The status of archaic texts like the Old Testament, Homer, and Ossian acquired fresh interest in this capacity: as "Big Bang" moments where one sees the incipience of a literary tradition, a starting point from which subsequent history unfurls. That such archaic texts tended to be written in the High Style, and followed the register that, in new critical phraseology, was now known as *Sublime,* seemed no more than fitting for such originary masterpieces.[13]

Shakespeare's status and reputation, as Godfather of English literature, profited from this new critical-philological approach. And it is as such that he came into the purview of German critics like Lessing, who felt that *their* literature had, until now, been a damp squib, fizzling under French-style hegemony, in need of a Big Bang of its own.

German Calls for a "National" Theater, 1780–1800

Much has been written about the German calls for a national literature in the late eighteenth century, the dissatisfaction with Gottsched-style classicism-by-numbers, and the tendency to look away from France in search of more suitable examples to emulate. The process was a complex one and mingled social and ethnic sentiment. Elite conventions in culture and literature were resented and rejected both because they were snobbish and disdainful vis-à-vis the main body of German society, and because they were French-derived, and, as such, alien to the main body of German society. The "main body of society" was called, in late-eighteenth-century parlance, the *nation,* and its tastes and preoccupations were accordingly called *national.* It is important to realize that the concept of a *national literature* in this ancien régime context was more foregroundedly sociological than ethnic in its purport.

Thus, if Lessing sarcastically mentions, in 1768, the quixotic idea "of giving to the Germans a national theatre" (and dismissing that idea, dear, of course, to his own heart, "because we Germans are not yet a nation"),[14] he discusses a moral, social, and literary problem, rather than an ethnic one: Germany *does* need a theater for the main mass of the population at large, in the cities, outside the aristocratic courts; but that population is as yet an inchoate, unconnected, and disparate aggregate, and can only follow foreign (French) taste. Following Lessing, early calls for a national theater or a national literature seem to imply that what German society needs is a *public sphere,* in Habermas's sense of the term: a forum for social concourse and opinion-forming, an intellectual space for egalitarian exchange of and communal reflection on matters of common importance.[15] Habermas sees the emergence of such a public sphere as a vital precondition for the rise of a democratic, civil society, locates it in the seventeenth and eighteenth centuries in the English coffeehouses, the French salons, the German benevolent societies, and, to a significant extent, in and around the theaters. After all, the term "public opinion" first arises in seventeenth-century poetics and refers initially to the taste of the theater going *public*.[16] Thus, the need for a national theater, as expressed by intellectuals like Lessing and Schiller, can be read as a desire to have something like a German public sphere, a public opinion, a common bonding agent for society apart from the suzerainty of lords and princes. This, at least, is how I read Schiller's 1784 essay on "The stage as a moral institution":

> I cannot overlook the great influence which a good firmly established theater would have on the nation's spirit. That national spirit I define as the similarity and concord of its opinions and proclivities in matters where other nations think and feel differently. Only through a theater is it possible to effect such concord to a high degree, because theater moves through the entire field of human knowledge, takes in all situations of life and shines into all corners of the heart; it unites all ranks and classes of society and has free access to the mind and to the heart. . . . if we saw the day when we have a national theater, then we would become a nation. What else was it that forged Greece into a unity? What was it that pulled the Greeks to its theater? Nothing other than the public-mindedness of their plays, their Greek spirit, the great, overwhelming interest of the state and of the better part of humanity.[17]

If Lessing states, as early as 1759, his doubt that French-style theater is suited to the German mentality,[18] he does, to be sure, argue from cultural essentialism; but the main thrust of the German turn to Shakespeare is a sociocultural one. German literature needs a fresh start, away from French-classicist court culture: a public-minded culture for the people-at-large; and Shakespeare, original genius that he was, is a suitable example for such a fresh departure.

In support of this view, I may point out that Shakespeare was not the only godfather-figure that German critics and literati sought out in these decades: another one was, significantly, Ossian, another Original Genius, another sublime literary figurehead who came from outside the threadbare classical-classicist tradition. The early German reception of Shakespeare meshes with the early German reception of Ossian, which has recently been admirably charted by Wolf Gerhard Schmidt.[19] Ossian and Shakespeare apparently both appealed to an emerging literature in search of an identity and agenda. Herder and young Goethe (in *Werther*) turned with gusto to Macpherson's mournful Caledonian foghorn; indeed we may hazard the conjecture that only as Ossian's appeal began to pall in the 1770s and 1780s, was his function taken over by Shakespeare.

Schlegel's Translation Project and its 1800–20 Hiatus

It is against this background that we must see the great German interest in Shakespeare of the 1790s, exemplified in the translation undertaken by August Wilhelm Schlegel in 1789. Schlegel continued this work throughout the 1790s, and gained fresh inspiration from the "theatrical" passages in Goethe's *Wilhelm Meister* of 1795. The culmination point came in 1801, when seventeen pieces from the Shakespeare corpus were published, in the translation by him and Ludwig Tieck. And then the project lapsed. It was, indeed, wholly abandoned by Schlegel, and was only completed in the 1820s through the sole efforts of Tieck.[20] Thus, Schlegel's translation project seems to indicate the high-water mark of early German Shakespeare interest, and, shortly after 1800, also a tidal turn in that process. That turn, I contend, has to do with a shift in the critical sense as to what constitutes a "national" literature.

What changed after 1800? One possibility may be that, much as Shakespeare had ousted Ossian as the father figure for an emerging literature, so too Shakespeare himself was ousted by another one again: in this case, possibly and briefly, Calderón. Schlegel's own translation career seems indeed to take a Spanish turn in these years. Tieck, his close collaborator, had in 1799 published his translation of Cervantes's *Don Quixote,* and Schlegel himself published, in 1803, his translation of *Schauspiele von Don Pedro Calderón de la Barca,* followed in 1804 by the *Blumensträusse italienischer, spanischer und portugiesischer Poesie.* In his *Vorlesungen über dramatische Kunst und Literatur* of 1809, Schlegel indeed put Shakespeare and Calderón side by side as eminently *national* playwrights—but in a new sense of the word. National here means: grown from its own traditions, without admixture from foreign, let alone classical-cosmopolitan, standards. What Schlegel praises most highly is that English and Spanish literature moved from the Middle Ages into the sixteenth and the seventeenth centuries without passing under the yoke of Renaissance neo-Aristotelianism, drawing on their own country's historical themes and motifs, and maintaining, as it were, a cultural autarky. It is as such that he praises the great theater of England and Spain as being properly "national," that is, sheltered and aloof from cosmopolitanism.

This stance must be seen in its own historical context. Between

1800 and 1810, Britain and Spain were the two countries most forcefully resisting Napoleonic rule in Europe—one as a maritime empire, the other as a restive country nominally brought under French rule but in reality engaged in ongoing insurrection. To the bitterly anti-French and anti-Napoleonic German authors of these Romantic decades, they must have presented a powerful anti-French ideal. Germans were living in French client states under direct or indirect French hegemony; cultural activists and philosophers like Jahn, Arndt, and Fichte were beginning to formulate the idea that cultural mixtures and multicultural empires were decadent and abhorrent, and that Germany should, against Napoleonic rule, draw moral strength from its un-Romanized, purely Germanic traditions. Even the Germanist scholar Jacob Grimm, who had no sympathy for any Romance language or culture, published an anthology of ancient Spanish texts, and Spain, after centuries of vilification known as the *leyenda negra*, earned European sympathy for its anti-Napoleonic stalwartness and the long-standing self-enclosed isomorphy of its cultural traditions.[21]

There is, possibly, another reason why Shakespeare, in the period 1800–20, had to compete with Spanish role models. Heinrich Heine, himself a believer in Enlightenment ideals as put into practice by Napoleon, castigated the national navel-gazing of anti-Napoleonic Romantics in Germany. It was, in his view, obscurantist, harking back to the papist, benighted, feudal Middle Ages. That was what the Romantic School stood for, and in that agenda, so Heine argued, the monkishness of Spanish examples fit better than the humanism of Shakespeare:

> The translation of Shakespeare, who already smiles into our own modern time with Protestant clarity, was only intended for polemical purposes which it would lead too far to discuss here. Moreover, Mr. A. W. Schlegel undertook this translation before people had really enthused themselves all the way back into the Middle Ages. Later, when this had happened, it was Calderón who came to be translated, and praised far more than Shakespeare: he offered the clearest imprint of medieval poetry, especially in its two main aspects, chivalry and monkishness. The pious comedies of the Castilian priest-poet, whose poetical flowers are sprinkled with holy water and smoked with ecclesiastical incense, came to be imitated in all their saintly grandeur, all their sacerdotal pomp, all their blessed madness.[22]

Archaism and Medievalism: The Philological Turn

Heine's notion that German Romanticism came increasingly close to a reactionary nostalgia for the pre-Reformation Middle Ages is obviously aimed at the impact of Catholic authors like De Maistre, Goerres, and the converted Friedrich Schlegel, and their influence even on Protestant authors like Tieck and Uhland. Even so, Heine is right in signaling an increasing archaism and medievalist nostalgia in German letters, which we can trace from the abolition of the Holy Roman Empire in 1806 onward.

However, the more meaningful shift in literary attitudes had set in a decade or so earlier, with the famous Homeric controversy around F. A. Wolff. The upshot of this debate was a widespread acceptance that Homer had not been a single, individual genius, but rather a gathering point for preexisting demotic, oral traditions of a heroic nature. It was, in other words, the overthrow of the "Big Bang" theory of the Original Genius. Literatures did not begin with a solitary, titanic figurehead, but slowly coalesced out of popular traditions. The true literary heritage of a nation was not the exclusive product of solitary authors, but rather an organically grown and collectively owned complex of themes, motifs, memories, and tales. The beginnings of literature, like the beginnings of language and law, were collective, tribal, and indeed (there's that word again) *national.*

The word *national,* in other words, shifted its meaning drastically in critical parlance. Whereas with Schiller it had referred to a society, a social body, and whereas Schlegel had used it to refer to self-enclosed cultural isomorphy from medieval into modern times, *national* now came to refer to an anthropological, ethnic-tribal tradition. The roots of language and literature reached back into a tribal collectivity, like fairy tales or the great anonymous texts of the early-medieval European vernaculars. Truly *national* were texts like the *Nibelungenlied,* the *Chanson de Roland,* and *Beowulf.* Significantly, all these texts were, in these precise years, retrieved from oblivion and published to great effect.[23]

The first publication of the *Nibelungenlied,* by Friedrich von der Hagen (1807), is a case in point. It carried with it a vehemently moral-political preface urging Germans, at the nadir of their political fortunes, to look to their moral-literary heritage for inspiration. Jacob Grimm, in a review, praised, if not the edition, then at least the "excellence of this national epic," and Wilhelm Grimm, in another review, pointed out (albeit with some sour-grapes begrudgerism) that "the nation is to be given its epic and offer poets the opportunity of creating a national drama." One year later, Jacob Grimm published an essay (*Gedanken, wie sich die Sagen zur Poesie und Geschichte verhalten*) formulating his collectivist-organizist notion that such "national epics" as the *Nibelungenlied* are not the product of a single author, but of a nation-at-large, and that they "write themselves."

All this marks an enormous swing away from the sort of literary nationality that we saw propounded by Schiller. A new, philological view gained ground, bolstered by the new insights of comparative linguistics, according to which each language has its own historical and anthropological trajectory, marking off the community of its speakers as a nation and expressing that nation's worldview and experiences in its own literature. And in each case, literary ethnogenesis is held to move from oral-collective mythological material to the poetic celebration of a common historical experience or heroic crisis. Collective, anonymous, archaic, pure within the tribal-ethnic ambience that it articulates: such is the "national epic" which Grimm sees as the fountainhead of each separate literature. (And in the process, the word "literature" has now become countable, for in this paradigm there are as many separate literatures as there are languages and nations.)

German Philological Nationalism, *Beowulf,* Shakespeare

In this philologically led climate, German literature was placed under the auspices of its own ethnic antecedents rather than foreign geniuses. After Von der Hagen's *Nibelungen* edition, the folksong collection *Des Knaben Wunderhorn* by Arnim and Brentano, and the Grimms' collection of folktales (all of them published under Napoleonic rule, in 1807, 1805–8, and 1812 respectively), German literature, led by its *Germanisten,* began to edit its forgotten antecedents: the medieval *Minnesänger* and Romance poets.[24] Kleist celebrated Germanic chieftains like Arminius the Cheruscan in his anti-French propaganda piece *Die Hermannsschlacht* of 1810, initiating a form of German national theater that was to lead to Wagner's Ring cycle—a *national* theatre that would have made Schiller stare in wonder. Germany was to emulate the Spanishness of Calderón and the Englishness of Shakespeare by connecting its modern literature back to its own, long-neglected, pre-Renaissance, medieval traditions. People "enthused themselves back into the Middle Ages," as Heine put it, with a vengeance. Original geniuses of foreign provenance need not apply.

Goethe himself saw this process of the ethnic nationalization of German literature with marked reservations. The notion that "each nation feels it necessary for its self-esteem to possess a national epic" is mentioned by him with considerable sarcasm.[25] He gave a masterly piece of insightful criticism in his *Shakespeare und kein Ende* of 1813–15, at the height of national enthusiasm in Germany, in which he pointed out that Shakespeare transmuted the tragic conflict of the ancients (between what the protagonist should do and what he does, *sollen* vs. *vollbringen*) into a modern one (between what the protagonist wants to do and what he does, *wollen* vs. *vollbringen*). Eventually he went so far as to denounce both romanticism ("Classical is what is healthy, and romantic what is sick," in the *Maximen und Reflexionen* of 1829) and the very notion of national literature: "I see increasingly that poetry is a common possession of humankind, and that it appears everywhere and in all periods in hundreds upon hundreds of people . . . if we Germans do not turn our gaze beyond the narrow circle of our own environment, we will all too easily end up in pedantic obscurity . . . National literature does not mean much these days, the time has come for world literature."[26]

But old Goethe was by then a solitary presence on his own Mount Olympus, the lower slopes of which had been settled by Teutons and Goths. By the 1830s, German literature was indeed introspectively cultivating and celebrating its own nativism. The ongoing appreciation of Shakespeare now invoked a newfangled, philological argument: that of Germanic, Anglo-Saxon kinship.

German philologists in the wake of Grimm were fond of stressing that the English as a nation all descended from emigrated Germanic tribes (Angles, Saxons) and that in philological-anthropological terms their early literature was in fact an insular offshoot of the complex of the literature of the German tribes. With the help of such Greater-German arguments, philologists laid claim to texts like the *Beowulf* epic.[27] In the tendentious phraseology of Ludwig Ettmüller (1840): "The *Song of Beowulf* [*Beowulflied*] is extremely important in various respects. In the first place, it offers us a clear idea of the state of German popular poetry in the period before Charlemagne; moreover, it gives us information about many aspects of public and private life among the north-Germanic tribes during the Great Migration of Peoples; and finally it gives incontrovertible proof of the continuity between myth and historical saga."[28] The self-aggrandizing philology of this generation of *Germanisten* worked principally on the elasticity of the concept of "German" or *deutsch*. In the narrower sense (as in the Grimms' *Deutsches Wörterbuch*), it referred to the (High-)German language and its speakers and roots; in the wider sense (as in Jacob Grimm's *Deutsche Grammatik*), it referred to all Germanic languages and dialects, including Dutch/Flemish, Frisian, and even Danish and Anglo-Saxon. Thus, by claiming a given text such as *Beowulf* as *deutsch* or "Germanic" in the wider sense, a phraseological door was opened for *Germanisten* representing the "core element" of the German(ic) sphere to lay claim to it. The highly respected Karl Simrock (popularizer of the Grimm school of *Germanistik,* and the man whose modernizations and text editions were a great source of inspiration to Wagner) could testify, in his *Beowulf: Das älteste deutsche Epos* (1859) to his project of "spanning a thousand-year-old separation and once again to obtain for this tale, which emigrated along with the Anglo-Saxons, a rightful, native's place in our midst. If I failed to get any closer to this goal than my predecessors have done, then this can only be due to my own shortcomings, *not* to any notion that this ancient poem might be alien to us."[29] On what basis can such an agenda proceed? Simrock spells it out. The actual *language* or concrete provenance of a given text is incidental. The substance of a text is its underlying "Mythus," its "material." If a given text can be shown to rest on the underpinnings of a given ethnic, anthropological, mythological, or narrative tradition, then those roots determine its real appurtenance: "As others before me have pointed out, *Beowulf,* for all that it has been transmitted into the Anglo-Saxon language, is in its foundations a German poem. What is more, my comments will serve to prove that the underlying myth is a German one which has left manifold traces among us. All the greater was my desire to re-appropriate this text to our language."[30] What matters, in short, is not author or language, but material, *Stoff:* the Grimm-inspired Germanisten used texts for *Stoffgeschichte,* analyzed texts purely in order to tease out their archaic, tribal-anthropological provenance and mythical substrata. It amounted to an *etymology* of texts; and if the text's etymology was Germanic, then the text was German. This appropriation-through-*Stoffgeschichte* was one of the main factors sparking off the aforementioned, numerous conflicts concerning multilingual textual traditions (Roland, Reynard the Fox, etc.). Those conflicts form one of the more fascinating, though underexplored, aspects of nineteenth-century literary history. Suffice it here to point out how very different this philological idea of literary nationality was from the attitudes of the Sturm und Drang and the Weimarer Klassik.

In the mid-nineteenth century, we can see the philological approach feeding into the German reception of Shakespeare as well. The selfsame Karl Simrock furnishes an example, and the procedure is as may have been expected: Shakespeare is stripped of unphilological incidental details such as individuality or verbal concreteness, and reduced to the underlying *Stoff:* the mythological themes and collective-unconscious remembrances and source-traditions. These constitute the true identity of Shakespeare and are set forth in a book entitled *Die Quellen des Shakespeare in Novellen, Märchen, und*

Sagen (The Sources of Shakespeare in Romances, Folktales, and Sagas.)[31]

Repercussions

This philological nationalization of Shakespeare echoed back to England itself. The great adept of German thought in English letters, Thomas Carlyle, had read Schlegel's *Lectures on Dramatic Poetry*, and misinterpreted them to some extent. Where Schlegel had praised the authenticity of Shakespeare, his homegrown, self-made quality, his reliance on native sources, Carlyle read this to mean that Shakespeare (especially in the history plays and foremost in *Henry V*) had produced something like a *national epic*—a phrase not used (as far as I am aware) by Schlegel in this context, and certainly not in the philological sense as current, since 1807, around Grimm, Von der Hagen, and Simrock—as a heroic expression of the national-collective experience. This is what Carlyle wrote in *On Heroes and Hero-worship* (1840):

> August Wilhelm Schlegel has a remark on [Shakespeare's] Historical Plays, *Henry Fifth* and the others, which is worth remembering. He calls them a kind of National Epic. Marlborough, you recollect, said, he knew no English History but what he had learned from Shakespeare. There are really, if we look to it, few as memorable Histories. The great salient points are admirably seized; all rounds itself off, into a kind of rhythmic coherence; it is, as Schlegel says, epic;—as indeed all delineation by a great thinker will be.... That battle of Agincourt strikes me as one of the most perfect things, in its sort, we anywhere have of Shakespeare's.... There is a noble Patriotism in it ... A true English heart breathes, calm and strong, through the whole business; not boisterous, protrusive; all the better for that. There is a sound in it like the ring of steel. This man too had a right stroke in him, had it come to that![32]

Henry V as a prototype of Kleist's *Hermannsschlacht?* By 1840, in Carlyle's treatment, Shakespeare has been well and truly nationalized; not through the prima facie evidence of his bio-bibliographical anchoring, but on the basis of more quasi-anthropological arguments concerning the quality of his patriotism and his imagination. This will set the tone for further debates about Shakespeare's "Englishness." Matthew Arnold, for instance, was to argue in the 1860s that Shakespeare is most "English" because his work incorporates, alongside its "Anglo-Saxon" sense of practicality and realism, Celtic elements of fantasy and otherworldly irrationalism (Puck, Cymbeline, Lear). This

Celtic admixture distinguishes him, in exemplary "English" fashion, from the pure, unalleviated Teutonism of continental Germanic traditions.[33]

In a further instance of cross-European literary flux and reflux,[34] this status of Shakespeare as being the exemplary poet expressing the collective imagination and experience of his nation is exported throughout Europe, where new, marginalized cultural traditions claim literary presence by each starting a "national" theater in line with their image of a "national-epic" Shakespeare à la Carlyle. What had been attempted in a different, ancien-régime dispensation by Goethe and Schiller *(Götz von Berlichingen,* 1774; *Wilhelm Tell,* 1804) became an agenda for literary/theatrical nationalism, which we can trace from Italy (Manzoni's *Il conte di Carmagnola,* 1820) to central and eastern Europe (Popović's *Miloš Obilić,* 1825; Pushkin's *Boris Godunov,* 1831; Hollí's *Swatopluk,* 1833). The rise of national opera and the rise of national theaters in the later century all fall under the shadow of a nationalized Shakespeare.

The philology-driven process of Shakespeare's characterological nationalization in the nineteenth century gives him a curiously double status: on the one hand, he belongs to the world at large, as one of the literary giants of the older, classical canon (alongside Homer, Virgil, Cervantes, and Dante), who can be appropriated by any nation that acknowledges itself inspired by them; on the other hand, he becomes the jealously guarded, because not uncontested, property of England specifically. His anonymity, in this context, becomes an asset: he is not an egregious individual, but rather an English Everyman, a disembodied ideal type of "the English imagination." In the process, his regional Stratford identity is stressed as never before, in line with the contemporary tradition from George Eliot to Thomas Hardy, which sees the timeless, transhistorical, and essential England located precisely in the rural counties and county towns.[35] It is as such, as a nonindividual, a *type,* moving from the Cotswolds to London, that someone like Carlyle can claim Shakespeare most strenuously for "England":

> Well; this is our poor Warwickshire peasant, who rose to be manager of a Playhouse, so that he could live without begging . . . consider what this Shakspeare has actually become among us. Which would we not give up rather than the Stratford peasant? There is no regiment of highest Dignitaries that we would sell him for. He is the grandest thing we have yet done. For our honour among foreign nations, as an ornament to our English Household, what item is there that we would not surrender rather than him? Consider now, if they asked us, Will you give up your Indian

Empire or your Shakspeare, you English; never have had any Indian Empire, or never have had any Shakspeare? Really it were a grave question. Official persons would answer doubtless in official language; but we, for our part too, should not we be forced to answer: Indian Empire will go, at any rate, some day; but this Shakspeare does not go, he lasts forever with us; we cannot give up our Shakspeare![36]

NOTES

This text is based on two separate lectures: one for the conference "Shakespeare and European Politics" held at Utrecht in December 2003, the other for the conference "Goethe, Schiller, Shakespeare: Drei Weimarer Klassiker," held by the Deutsche Shakespeare-Gesellschaft at Weimar in April 2004. I am grateful to the organizers of both conferences for giving me a place in their programs and an occasion to elaborate my thoughts on the topic. For feedback on ideas and concrete information, I am indebted to Ton Hoenselaars.

1. *Shakespeare-Jahrbuch* 51 (1915): 7–12. In the original: Es gibt kein Volk, auch das englische nicht, das sich ein Anrecht wie das deutsche auf Shakespeare erworben hätte. Shakespeares Gestalten sind ein Teil unserer Welt, seine Seele ist eins mit der unseren geworden, und wenn er in England geboren und begraben ist, so ist doch Deutschland das Land, wo er wahrhaft lebt.

2. Much work has been done on the German reception history of Shakespeare, which is, indeed, one of the weightier topics in European literary history. I mention only: *The Reception of Shakespeare in Eighteenth-Century France and Germany*, special issue of *Michigan Germanic Studies* 15.2 (1989), ed. Kenneth E. Larson and Hansjoerg R. Schelle; Simon Williams, *Shakespeare on the German Stage, 1586–1914* (Cambridge: Cambridge University Press, 2004); and Wilhelm Hortmann, *Shakespeare on the German Stage* (Cambridge: Cambridge University Press, 1998).

3. Generally on that process, see Peter E. Firchow, *The Death of the German Cousin: Variations on a Literary Stereotype, 1890–1920* (Lewisburg, PA: Bucknell University Press, 1986).

4. Cf. Klaus Vondung, ed., *Das wilhelminische Bildungsbürgertum: Zur Sozialgeschichte seiner Ideen* (Göttingen: Vandenhoeck und Ruprecht, 1976).

5. Cf. Gunter Scholz, ed., *Die Interdisziplinarität der Begriffsgeschichte* (Hamburg: Meiner, 2000).

6. One of the first comparatists to do so with systematic rigidity was Hugo Dyserinck, in the chapter "Die Nationalliteratur als komparatistisches Problem," in his *Komparatistik: Eine Einführung* (Bonn: Bouvier, 1977), 90–102, which firmly maintains the primacy of the linguistic medium as the fundamental taxonomical criterion in literature and distinguishes linguistic appurtenance from "nationality." Dyserinck goes so far as to reject the very concept of "national literature" (German, French, or English) in favor of the more neutral phraseology of a (German-language, French-language, or English-language) "single literature."

7. See José Lambert, "L'éternelle question des frontières: Littératures nationales et systèmes littéraires," in *Langue, Dialecte, Littérature: Études romanes à la mémoire de Hugo Plomteux*, ed. Christian Angelet et al. (Leuven: Leuven University Press, 1983), 355–70; my own "Literatuur op de landkaart: Taal, territorium en culturele identiteit," *Forum der Letteren* 34.1 (1993): 16–28.

8. On imagology as applied to literary taxonomy, see, again, the work of Hugo

Dyserinck, "Die Problematik der Nationalität aus der Sicht der Vergleichenden Literaturwissenschaft," in *Geschichte, Politik und ihre Didaktik* 6 (1989; special issue on *Entstehung und Bewahrung einer Nation—Ein Thema der Gesellschaftsgeschichte?*): 61–72.

9. *Lessing und das erste deutsche Nationaltheater in Hamburg: Eine deutsche Gabe zur Shakspeare-Feier* (Hamburg: Boyes & Geisler, 1864).

10. My translation, from the essay "La postulación de la realidad" (1930), in Borges's *Prosa Completa*, 5 vols. (Barcelona: Bruguera, 1980), 1:157. In the original: Para el concepto clásico, la pluralidad de los hombres y de los tiempos es accesoria, la literatura es siempre una sola.

11. See my "Ossian and the Rise of Literary Historicism," in *The Reception of Ossian in Europe,* ed. Howard Gaskill (London: Continuum, 2004), 109–25.

12. Best-known example: William Duff's *Essay on Original Genius* (1767). See Roy Harvey Pearce, "The Eighteenth-Century Scottish Primitivists: Some Reconsiderations," *ELH* 12 (1945): 203–20; Margaret Mary Rubel, *Savage and Barbarian: Historical Attitudes in the Criticism of Homer and Ossian* (Amsterdam: Koninklijke Nederlandse Akademie van Wetenschappen, 1978).

13. Despite the new, postmodern interest in the Sublime, the standard work for eighteenth-century critical theories is still Samuel H. Monk, *The Sublime: A Study of Critical Theories in Eighteenth-Century England* (New York: Modern Language Association of America, 1935).

14. My translation, from the famous phrase in the final section of the *Hamburgische Dramaturgie,* mentioning "den gutherzigen Einfall, den Deutschen ein Nationaltheater zu verschaffen, weil wir Deutsche noch keine Nation sind!"

15. Jürgen Habermas, *Strukturwandel der Öffentlichkeit* (Frankfurt: Suhrkamp, 1962).

16. Gérard Genette thus cites Rapin's *Poétique* of 1662, and comments that this "opinion of the public, real or presumed, corresponds fairly precisely to what nowadays we would call an 'ideology'," astutely linking the theater as an opinion-making concourse to what Habermas would see as the germ of a public sphere. "Vraisemblance et motivation," in Genette, *Figures II: Essais* (Paris: Seuil, 1969), 71–100. (In the original: cette "opinion du public," réelle ou supposée, correspond assez précisément à ce qu'on nommerait aujourd'hui une idéologie; my translation.)

17. Friedrich Schiller, *Die Schaubühne als eine moralische Anstalt betrachtet* (lecture read in Mannheim, 1784; my translation). In the original: Unmöglich kann ich hier den grossen Einfluss übergehen, den eine gute stehende Bühne auf den Geist der Nation haben würde. Nationalgeist eines Volks nenne ich die Ähnlichkeit und Übereinstimmung seiner Meinungen und Neigungen bei Gegenständen, worüber eine andere Nation anders meint und empfindet. Nur der Schaubühne ist es möglich, diese Übereinstimmung in einem hohen Grad zu bewirken, weil sie das ganze Gebiet des menschlichen Lebens durchwandert, alle Situationen des Lebens erschöpft und in alle Winkel des Herzens hinunter leuchtet; weil sie alle Stände und Klassen in sich vereinigt und den gebahntesten Weg zum Verstand und zum Herzen hat . . . wenn wir es erlebten, eine Nationalbühne zu haben, so würden wir auch eine Nation. Was kettete Griechenland so fest aneinander? Was zog das Volk so unwiderstehlich nach seiner Bühne? Nichts anders als der vaterländische Inhalt der Stücke, der griechische Geist, das grosse überwältigende Interesse, des Staats, der besseren Menschheit, das in denselbigen athmete. I have chosen not to translate Schiller's *vaterländisch* as "patriotic" because I want to safeguard his text from retroprojective anachronism. The word "patriotic" (*vaterländisch*) in these decades had no national-chauvinist overtones whatsoever, and referred only to a civic-minded interest in the well-being of

society at large. See Franco Venturi, *Utopia and Reform in the Enlightenment* (Cambridge: Cambridge University Press, 1971), and Maurizio Viroli, *For Love of Country: An Essay on Patriotism and Nationalism* (Oxford: Clarendon Press, 1995). Similarly, the term *Nationalgeist* as used by Schiller should by no means be confused with later coinages such as *Volksgeist;* it means "public climate, public spirit." In his Jena lecture on the legislators of ancient Greece, Solon and Lycurgus, Schiller praises Spartan society for inculcating such a public spirit and uses terms like *vaterländisch* and *Nationalgeist* to describe it: alle Handlungen wurden dadurch öffentliche Handlungen. Unter den Augen der Nation reifte die Jugend heran und verblühte das Alter. Unaufhörlich hatte der Spartaner Sparta vor Augen und Sparta ihn. Er war Zeuge von allem, und alles war Zeuge seines Lebens. Die Ruhmbegierde erhielt einen immerwährenden Sporn, der Nationalgeist eine unaufhörliche Nahrung; die Idee von Vaterland und vaterländischem Interesse verwuchs mit dem innersten Leben aller seiner Bürger.

18. ob dieses französisierende Theater der deutschen Denkungsart angemessen sei oder nicht. *Briefe, der neuesten Literatur betreffend,* nr. 17. It is significant that all these initiatives toward a cultural "public sphere" came from urban centers with a strong civic tradition: Hamburg, Riga, Frankfurt, Mannheim.

19. Wolf Gerhard Schmidt, *"Homer des Nordens" und "Mutter der Romantik": James Macphersons Ossian und seine Rezeption in der deutschsprachigen Literatur,* 4 vols. (Berlin: De Gruyter, 2004).

20. More details in Ken Larson, "The Origins of the 'Schlegel-Tieck' Shakespeare in the 1820s," *German Quarterly* 60 (1987): 19–37.

21. See my "Literary Historicism: Romanticism, Philologists, and the Presence of the Past," *Modern Language Quarterly* 65.2 (2004): 221–43.

22. *Die romantische Schule,* ed. Helga Weidmann (Stuttgart: Reclam, 1976), 26; my translation. In the original: Die Übersetzung des Shakespeares, der . . . schon protestantisch klar in unsere moderne Zeit hereinlächelt, war nur zu polemischen Zwecken bestimmt, deren Besprechung hier zu weitläufig wäre. Auch wurde diese Übersetzung von Herrn A. W. Schlegel unternommen zu einer Zeit, als man sich noch nicht ganz ins Mittelalter zurück enthusiasmiert hatte. Später, als dies geschah, ward der Calderon übersetzt und weit über den Shakespeare angepriesen; denn bei jenem fand man die Poesie des Mittelalters am reinsten ausgeprägt, und zwar in ihren beiden Hauptmomenten, Rittertum und Mönchstum. Die frommen Komödien des kastilianischen Priesterdichters, dessen poetischen Blumen mit Weihwasser besprengt und kirchlich geräuchert sind, wurden jetzt nachgebildet, mit all ihrer heiligen Grandezza, mit all ihrem sazerdotalen Luxus, mit all ihrer gebenedeiten Tollheit.

23. See, generally, my *Nationaal denken in Europa: Een cultuurhistorische schets* (Amsterdam: Amsterdam University Press, 1999).

24. On the nationalist incipience of *Germanistik, Nationalismus in Germanistik und Dichtung: Dokumentation des Germanistentages in München vom 17. bis 22. Oktober 1966,* ed. Benno von Wiese and Rudolf Henß (Berlin: Schmidt, 1967); Ulrich Wyss, *Die wilde Philologie: Jacob Grimm und der Historismus* (München: Beck, 1979); Frank Fürbeth et al., eds., *Zur Geschichte und Problematik der Nationalphilologien in Europa: 150 Jahre Erste Germanistenversammlung in Frankfurt am Main (1846–1996)* (Tübingen: Niemeyer, 1999).

25. Jede Nation, wenn sie für irgend etwas gelten will, muss eine Epopöe besitzen. *Dichtung und Wahrheit,* 2:7. My translation.

26. Conversations, as recorded by Eckermann for January 31 and July 15, 1827. Johann Peter Eckermann, *Gespräche mit Goethe in den letzten Jahren seines Lebens,* ed. by H. H. Houben (Wiesbaden: Brockhaus, 1959), 174, 199, 153. My translation.

27. See generally Thomas A. Shippey and Andreas Haarder, eds., *Beowulf: The Critical Heritage* (London: Routledge, 1998).

28. Ludwig Ettmüller, trans., *Beowulf: Heldengedicht des achten Jahrhunderts zum ersten Male aus dem angelsächsischen in das Neuhochdeutsche stabreimend übersetzt* (Zürich, 1840), 1. In the original: Das Beowulflied ist in verschiedener Hinsicht äusserst wichtig. Zuerst gewährt es uns eine klare Vorstellung von der Beschaffenheit der deutsche Volksdichtung in der Zeit vor Karl dem Grossen; dann giebt es uns Aufschluss über so manche Gestaltung des öffentlichen und häuslichen Lebens nordgermanischer Stämme zur Zeit der Völkerwanderung; endlich liefert es den, wie mich dünkt, unwiderlegbaren Beweis von der Verschmelzung reiner Mythe mit geschichtlicher Sage, ja von dem völligen Übertritt jener in diese. My translation. Note the sliding terminology, also dear to Grimm, between *deutsch* and *germanisch;* note the periodization (one may as well place *Beowulf* in the chronology of the Han Dynasty as in that of Charlemagne), and the dissolution of literature into the concerns of tribal-national ethnography and anthropology.

29. Karl Simrock, trans., *Beowulf: Das älteste deutsche Epos* (Stuttgart 1859), iii–iv. In the original: eine tausendjährige Kluft zu überbrücken und dieser mit Angeln und Sachsen ausgewanderten Dichtung neues Heimatrecht bei uns erwerben zu können. Wenn ich diesem Ziele nicht näher gekommen bin als meine Vorgänger, so lag es gewiss nur an meinem Ungeschick, nicht daran, dass das uralte Lied uns zu ferne steht. My translation.

30. Ibid. In the original: Dass der Beowulf, obwohl in angelsächsischer Sprache überliefert, doch seiner Grundlage nach ein deutsches Gedicht sei, ist schon von Andern ausgesprochen. Die beigegebenen Erläuterungen gehen überdies noch auf den Nachweis aus, dass der Mythus ein deutscher ist, der noch vielfache Spuren bei uns hinterlassen hat. Um so mehr lag es mir am Herzen, das Gedicht unserer Sprache wieder anzueignen. My translation.

31. The first edition appeared as early as 1831 under the threefold authorship of Theodor Echtermeyer, Ludwig Henschel, and Karl Simrock. In the second edition, 1872, Simrock put himself forward as the main author.

32. Thomas Carlyle, *Of Heroes and Hero-worship* (London: Fraser, 1841), lecture 3 ("The Hero as Poet").

33. Matthew Arnold, *On the Study of Celtic Literature* (London: Smith, Elder, 1867). See also my "Englishness, Ethnicity and Matthew Arnold," *European Journal of English Studies* 10 (2006): 63–80.

34. Witness the fact that Carlyle's celebration of the "hero-poet" is plagiarized in Gundolf's essay "Dichter und Helden" (originally in *Jahrbuch für die geistige Bewegung,* 1 (1912), more extensively reprinted in the collection *Dichter und Helden* (Heidelberg: Weiss, 1921, 23–58). Of course, Gundolf's work, especially in this vein, is deeply imbued with the poetical elitism of the circle of adepts around Stefan George.

35. Günther Blaicher, *Merry England: Zur Bedeutung und Funktion eines englischen Autostereotyps* (Tübingen: Narr, 2000); Catherine Brace, "Finding England Everywhere: Regional Identity and the Construction of National Identity, 1890–1940," *Ecumene* 6.1 (1999): 90–109; David Matless, *Landscape and Englishness* (London: Reaktion, 1998).

36. Carlyle, *Of Heroes and Hero-worship,* lecture 3 ("The Hero as Poet").

Twenty-three Skidoo: Bringing Home the Bard

Terence Hawkes

Twenty-third

THIS IS THE PAPER I WAS BORN TO GIVE.

Nowadays, a number of ominous dates seem to punctuate our lives: the most fearful example is probably "9/11." But what draws us together on this occasion perhaps suggests another one, no less fateful and almost equal in impact. In the American styling, it would be 4/23, in the British one, 23/4: the 23rd of April. That date—Shakespeare's birthday—surely ranks as the defining binary opposite of the one that commemorates the attack on the World Trade Center buildings in New York. If 9/11 signals death and destruction on one side of the Atlantic, 4/23 (or 23/4) indicates birth and creation on the other. So if we needed a symbol, or a logo, for our concerns here and now in Utrecht, that simple number "23" would do it. For us, it must be the date of dates, the calendar's crescendo: a quality somehow captured in a vivid American slang phrase of the 1920s—I'd even propose it as our conference motto—"Twenty-three Skidoo."[1]

It is appropriate to cite the American and the British versions of the 23rd of April side by side, because my initial focus is going to be on a particular occurrence of that date, in a particular year, in each of those countries. The year was 1932. In the course of it, Shakespeare's birthday was marked by two significant events, three thousand miles apart. In the United States on Saturday, April 23, 1932, the Folger Shakespeare Library was officially opened in Washington DC. In Britain, the same Saturday, in the same year, the opening of the new Shakespeare Memorial Theatre (now known as the Royal Shakespeare Theatre) in Stratford-upon-Avon occurred.

O To Be in England

The foundation stone of the new theater had been laid some three years earlier, in 1929, as the first stage of the project to replace its predecessor, destroyed by fire in 1926. Indeed, in 1929, with full municipal ceremony, a huge company of be-aproned Stratford Freemasons, symbolic trowels dutifully raised on high, had approved the stone's placing with the solemn Masonic injunction "so mote it be!"[2] And now, in 1932, so indeed it was.

To some surprise, a woman, Elizabeth Scott, had won the architectural competition for the building. Her design had managed to combine modernity with the reverence demanded by a national institution. In fact, as part of its report on the opening ceremonies, the *Times* carried an editorial on "Shakespeare's England" confirming that, as its name indicates, the Shakespeare Memorial Theatre would stand, primarily, as a memorial to England's most prestigious son and the Englishness he represents. No observer could fail to recognize that totemic function, for, as one of them commented, in Stratford the theater lies "midway between Shakespeare's birth and burial places, a few hundred yards from either; and Stratford lies at the centre of England."[3]

Predictably, the theater's structure took resolute account of its role as worldwide proclaimer of Englishness. The same observer points out that "[t]he shape of the Theatre resembles a giant horn, and is so designed that the players can be heard in all parts of the stage, with the sound distributed evenly throughout the auditorium."[4]

The commitment to health, truth, and enlightenment appropriate to such an imperial project extended even to its audience's creature comforts. The new theater, an advertisement announced, was "equipped with Dunlopillo cellular cushion rubber seating"—a feature reliably claimed to be both "germ and vermin proof" and "antiseptic by nature." Grateful spectators would discover that the rubber "gives gently whenever pressure is applied" and "on removal of weight it springs back instantly to its original shape and all possibility of sagging is eliminated."[5]

No doubt the opening ceremonies on April 23 put such promises sternly to the test when it came to items such as the actress Lillah MacCarthy's recitation of a monumentally awful poem by the poet laureate John Masefield. But then, shortly after 2:00 PM, came the redemptive arrival of the occasion's chief guest: none other than the heir to the British throne, His Royal Highness Edward, Albert, Christian, George, Andrew, Patrick, David, son of King George V, later briefly to become King Edward VIII, and at the time universally known as the Prince of Wales. With characteristic panache, the prince descended literally *ex machina*, from the heavens, landing his aircraft alongside the river Avon to the cheers of what one historian calculated as "some forty thousand people, drawn from all parts of the world."[6] His purpose was clear, his manner resolute, and his speech carefully tuned to the occasion. He began by stressing Shakespeare's Englishness: "Shakespeare was, above all things, an Englishman. He loved his country with a great and passionate love, and his magic verse not only breathes the air of the countryside, the air of our long, still summer afternoons, but strikes back into the very heart of our history, with all its pageantry and daring . . ." However, he was also quick to point out that although the Bard's appeal is in the first instance to his fellow countrymen, his standing as a "great world figure" ensures that its range is far broader than that: "his genius is yet universal, and evokes the homage of the men of all nations. What is equally important, he speaks as significantly for the man-in-the-street as he does for the student, so that, in a double sense, he may be described as a universal poet."[7] In the face of such claims, it is perhaps necessary to establish that what confronts us here is nothing more alarming than common-or-garden—if industrial-strength—Prince of Wales-speak. Certainly, that office's most recent incumbent, Prince Charles, tends to deploy a similarly extravagant idiom. Introducing a volume of his favorite Shakespeare passages, Charles has even observed that although the Bard remains English to the core, his concern with the "essential truths about the meaning and significance of life" means that "his message . . . is a universal, timeless one." Shakespeare, he concludes, is "not just our poet, but the world's."[8]

The major implication of such princely discourse seems straightforward enough. All mankind is really, after all and when it comes to the push, English. Leaving aside the most obvious shortcomings of this thesis—especially with regard to Europe—it remains nevertheless a particularly helpful proposal when you want to claim that the Bard's generalized, portable, one-size-fits-all "Englishness" signals the sort of common ancestorship that enables him to speak to and for Americans. In 1932, at Stratford, the prince made no bones about that: "The ships that sailed westwards had not set forth in any numbers before Shakespeare's time and therefore the world's master-dramatist is historically as well as spiritually, to be numbered among the ancestors common to the two English-speaking peoples."[9] Then, as a man might whose manifest destiny was not only to foster but indeed to own the very language of those peoples, the King's English, the prince descended from the platform, accepted a large golden key, and to the strains of a local band playing "God Bless the Prince of Wales," opened the theater's doors and took his seat in the stalls.

Meanwhile, on the same day, on the other side of the Atlantic, Joseph Quincy Adams, the director of the new Folger Shakespeare Library in Washington DC, readied himself to speak at that institution's inauguration. Not surprisingly, a similar atmosphere prevailed. Since the library, like the theater, had been designed as a sort of holy sepulchre wherein the essence of the dead Bard would be preserved, there was every reason to claim that the dusty corner of a foreign field that was currently 201 E. Capitol Street would from now on house the richer dust of an essentialized Englishness. Better still, its presence in that building—no doubt equally "germ and vermin proof," if not "antiseptic by nature"—would help in a vital job of prophylaxis. It would act as a barrier against contamination from what Adams darkly terms "the forces of immigration." For in certain quarters in 1932 America, incomers from middle and southern Europe seemed to constitute, as he chillingly puts it, "a menace to the preservation of our long-established English civilisation."[10]

Home from Home

Back in Stratford, the throng had already been subjected to a torrent of speeches, including a remarkable effort by Stanley Baldwin. Ever the stage Englishman, the British ex-prime minister not only offered his own solution to the mystery of the Bard's second-best bed but, like the prince, went on to speak glowingly of the English way of life as a goal to which the rest of the world ought, if it were sensible, to aspire. And then, as if reinforcing in advance the note that was about to be struck in Washington, his speech moved to what must surely rank as a remarkable climax: "Before I sit down, I want to address a few words particularly on this day to our many American friends who have come here to join in our festival—["cheers" reported the *Times*]—and I say to them from my heart—'Welcome— home.'"[11] Of course, it is not altogether inappropriate, in a ceremony marking Shakespeare's own return to Stratford, for the term "home" to be generously deployed. Nonetheless, a proposal made to Americans that Britain, nay England, is where their roots finally, conclusively lie, and that whatever darker "forces of immigration" may be in play, Shakespeare can therefore stand as their distinctive "homeboy," obviously implies a much grander vision.[12] Indeed, it quickly becomes clear that a complex notion of "home" and of "Englishness" has been closely woven into the texture of this occasion. Whatever the ambitions of Stratford's masons, it functions as one of the most solid foundation stones—at least in ideological terms—on which the Shakespeare Memorial Theatre rests. When it comes to the Bard, apparently, home is where the art is. So mote it be.

Home and Away

And on April 23, 1932, so indeed it was. The play chosen as the initial production at the new theater was *Henry IV Part 1*, with *Part 2* to be given that evening.[13] It is chastening to report that, in the event, a certain amount of sagging did seem to characterize what the critics termed a "slightly listless" performance.[14] But more interesting is the extent to which, looked at in terms of the agenda on which the occasion evidently insists, the play immediately starts to focus on the issues both of Englishness and of "home."

In fact, its opening lines—and thus the first Shakespearean words spoken in the new theater—home in sharply and literally on *Blut und Boden*. "No more the thirsty entrance of this soil / Shall daub her lips with her own children's blood" (1.1.6–7), proclaims the King. "Shaken" and "wan with care" we may be, but nevertheless we stand, he tells us, on newly coherent, and decidedly native ground. This, emphatically, is home turf. "Trenching war" no longer violates English fields, "armèd hoofs" no longer trample English flowers, the "furious close of civil butchery" no longer results in English dismemberment, physical or national. A hard-won homogeneity prevails. From now on, "All of one nature, of one substance bred," English "homeboys" will, "in mutual well-beseeming ranks / March all one way, and be no more opposed." By contrast, any "short-winded accents of new broils" will smack only of "stronds afar remote." The opposition between "home" and "abroad," us and them, our soil and that of remoter "stronds"—the very basis, that is, of what we would now recognize as the nation-state—could scarcely be more strongly drawn (1.1.1–18).

Needless to say, these polarities will turn out, as they must, to be mutually defining. The price of "home" is always "abroad." Both concepts not only depend on one another; each brings the other into existence. We can only be "us" as long as our enemies obligingly operate as "them." Inevitably, we become—to a degree—what we oppose, so that what unfolds here is an Englishness almost *determined* by the Welshness, the Scottishness, the Irishness, or even the Frenchness that challenges it.

And there are further complications. Where the first part of *Henry IV* initially proposes peace, unity, and coherent national identity at home as the prerequisites for war and adventures abroad, it gradually and disturbingly becomes clear, as the cycle unfolds, that the reverse is also true. War and adventures abroad are the prerequisites for peace, unity, and national identity at home. It is the battle against the French that generates and sustains Henry V's notion of an English "home" as the redemptive soil from which a Ulysses-like return generates new, vibrant life: "He that outlives this day and comes safe home / Will stand a tiptoe when this day is named" (4.3.41–42). Fittingly, the alliance at the end of that play between the homespun English king and the exotic French princess climaxes in a proposal for a home life defined and reinforced by its commitment to military intervention abroad: "Shall not thou and I," says Henry, "between Saint Denis and Saint George, compound a boy, half French, half English, that shall go to Constantinople and take the Turk by the beard? Shall we not?" (5.2.204–7).

Cross-purposes

History seems broadly, and sadly, to confirm the potency of such projects and it is entirely characteristic that their gaze should be directed Eastward. From the eleventh century on, in Europe, the deployment of armed expeditions to the Holy Land, particularly to Jerusalem, operates as a vital instrument of national ideology. In fact, the single European enterprise virtually guaranteed to promote unity and a sense of nationhood at home was always—as perhaps it remains—the Crusade against the infidel abroad.[15]

In *1 Henry IV,* crusades obsess the King from the first. The goal to be pursued "in stronds afar remote" is of course "the sepulchre of Christ" in Jerusalem,[16] and well into the play's second part, civil strife is described, almost in passing, as the main obstacle to that larger scheme: "were these inward wars once out of hand, / We would, dear lords, unto the Holy Land" (*2 Henry IV,* 3.1.107–8). But the project turns out to be mired in the usual paradox. In effect, the Crusades abroad form part of Henry's *domestic* policy, for these foreign adventures not only intensify, they vitally determine, the notion of "home." The King is explicit about their role as reinforcers of Englishness:

> Forthwith a power of English shall we levy,
> Whose arms were moulded in their mothers' womb
> To chase these pagans in those holy fields
> Over whose acres walk'd those blessed feet . . .
> (*1 Henry IV,* 1.1.22–25)

In short, the road to the Holy Land leads directly to as well as from English shores. As Avraham Oz tells us, the accession of the Tudor dynasty "almost exactly coincides with the printing of the first realistic map of Jerusalem," and that suggests a concern with identification, even bonding, as much as with topographical accuracy. Certainly, in British culture, a continuous link between the Holy City and the "pastures green" of an English homeland persists well up to and beyond the poetry of William Blake.[17] So it is entirely appropriate as well as ironic that Bolingbroke should finally meet his death in the "Jerusalem Chamber" of his English palace (4.5.233–40).[18]

Most importantly, by the time of Shakespeare's history plays, it is clear that the notion of "home" had started to acquire additional, complicating dimensions. Thus, while in *Richard II* John of Gaunt describes England traditionally enough as

> . . . this teeming womb of royal kings,
> Fear'd by their breed and famous by their birth,
> Renownèd for their deeds as far from home,
> For Christian service and true chivalry,
> As is the sepulchre in stubborn Jewry,
> Of the world's ransom, Blessed Mary's son
>
> (2.1.51–56)

he bolsters his case by weaving together two related myths. First, that England, the "royal throne of kings," is a separate and distinct entity: an island, no less, a solitary "precious stone" set alone "in the silver sea"—a remarkable fiction that persists to the present day in some quarters. Second, that its unique singularity not only links this "sceptred isle" with the Holy City: it also justifies a wholesale transformation in status whereby a self-limiting and solidly grounded homeland of *Blut und Boden* ("This blessed plot, this earth . . .") effortlessly expands—in the space of one line—to become a full-fledged, coherent, and definitively named political state: "this earth, this realm, this England."[19]

Two Princes

As with the opening ceremony of the theater, it is hardly surprising that the idea of "home" should pervade the play chosen in 1932 to welcome its author back to his Stratford birthplace. The focus in *1 Henry IV* on Prince Hal as a Prodigal Son who binds his life to an arc of recovery and redemption is unmistakable: the pulse of an ancient commitment to return "home" beats insistently beneath the Ulysses-like cunning that cloaks it:

> So when this loose behaviour I throw off,
> And pay the debt I never promisèd,
> By how much better than my word I am,
> By so much shall I falsify men's hopes;
> And like bright metal on a sullen ground,
> My reformation, glitt'ring o'er my fault,
> Shall show more goodly and attract more eyes
> Than that which hath no foil to set it off.
> I'll so offend, to make offence a skill,
> Redeeming time when men think least I will.
>
> (1.2.203–12)

But, listen carefully, and we can surely also hear something else in these lines that hints at the development I have mentioned. It is the sound of an ironclad statecraft pushing urgently through the softer, more yielding textures of affection and the ties of friendship that we associate with the concept of "home." This, if you like, is the Prince of Wales's music: a signature tune that subtly informs the playing rhythm of *1 Henry IV*, as each domestic scene of a prince unbuttoned and "at home" among his friends is regularly followed—even trumped—by one in which policy and affairs of state direct and restrict him, en route to his "reformation," his final donning of the crown, and his ultimate assumption of the "lineal honour" (*2 Henry IV*, 4.5.45). While Falstaff wallows in the bibulous pleasures of Shallow's Gloucester home, Hal makes a sterner commitment in the presence of the Lord Chief Justice whereby his youthful "tide of blood" will in future flow toward a more "formal majesty" (*2 Henry IV*, 5.2.129, 133). This rhythmic swiveling between polarities eventually reaches its climax, of course, in the rejection of Falstaff: that moment when concerns of state finally and fully emerge, cruelly drawn, "like bright metal," glittering, honed, and unforgiving from the sheath of hearth and home.

The impact of all that in the new Shakespeare Memorial Theatre in Stratford on April 23, 1932, must have been considerable. Apart from anything else, the building seemed to have become worryingly cluttered with Princes of Wales. The miniature play in act 2, in which Falstaff and Hal confront each other, generates no less than three of them: Hal himself; the Hal he then "plays" to Falstaff's King; and, most memorably, Falstaff's imitation of Hal—all present onstage at the same time. The next scene immediately brings in the startling figure of another, self-proclaimed Prince of Wales, Owain Glyn Dwr, who causes the number to rise disconcertingly to four. If we add the figure of a fifth, the actual Prince of Wales, the future Edward VIII seated in the audience, then we might be forgiven for thinking that the theater was in real danger of being overrun by them.[20]

To concentrate our attention for the moment on two of the five—the virtual prince on the stage and the actual one in the audience—is immediately to realize that, in the play's terms, they have a certain amount in common. Both sensed a poor "fit" between their private lives and the roles that public life had landed them with. Both were given to consorting with commoners, even to going disguised among them. Both generated scandal and sympathy as a result. Both had early on resolved to forsake pleasure and embrace duty, to accept the transition from "homeboy" to supreme officer of the state as progress toward a final marriage in which personal inclination willingly subordinates itself to historical necessity—a consummation marked in the play by Hal's curious echoing of the marriage-vow just as he promises to divorce himself from Falstaff: "I do, I will" (*1 Henry IV*, 2.4.475). Unfortunately, when the time came for the prince in the audience to say "I do," the consequences proved—as they have in the case of his successor—to be rather more dire.

The private life of the twentieth-century Prince of Wales was always regarded by his father, King George V, with a certain amount of suspicion, so that part of the prince's response to a play featuring a madcap heir to the throne and his disapproving parent must have been a growing sense of *de te fabula narratur*. If ever a story concerned *him*, this one did. But, unlike Hal, he managed no redemptive return. The prince's eventual and notorious decision to marry the divorced American woman, Mrs. Wallis Simpson, signally failed to "make offence a skill / Redeeming time when men think least I will." Quite the reverse. Only four years later, that liaison would lead to a crucial domestic and political upheaval, and the first abdication in British history since Richard II.

Essentially, the marriage seemed to elevate inward and intimate "home" concerns above and beyond the exterior demands of the state. In the radio broadcast that Stanley Baldwin's cabinet would later prevent him from delivering, the modern Prince of Wales had wanted to make, he tells us, "an appeal to the hearth and the home."[21] He had intended to say of Mrs Simpson, "Without her, I have been a very lonely man. With her, I shall have a home and all the companionship and mutual sympathy and understanding which married life can bring."[22] And in his actual abdication broadcast, he insisted on comparing his own situation with that of the brother who would take his place as King George VI, saying "he has one matchless blessing, enjoyed by so many of you, and not bestowed on me—a happy home with his wife and children . . ."[23]

But, in this context, that sort of sentimentality was more hindrance than help, for the prince and his fellow members of the British nation-state were living in disastrous times. In truth, Edward VIII's accession to the throne, and his short reign, marked the end of an era. He was the last king of Britain to progress through the mighty British Empire while all its diverse parts were still in place.[24] In 1932, there were already unmistakable signs that the imperial theme was, if not over, then approaching the point of final skedaddle. In the summer before the opening of the Memorial Theatre, the depression had hit Britain with its greatest force. There were hunger marches and street demonstrations. There was a disastrous run on the pound. The Labour government had virtually collapsed, and in August 1931 a National Government had been formed under Ramsay Macdonald. In September, in an unheard-of development, elements in the British Atlantic fleet mutinied at Invergordon. Then, six days later, with the country still reeling from that news, the government announced that it had abandoned the gold standard. As the prince himself put it, "For a dreadful moment one had the feeling that the foundations of British power were being swept away."[25]

INTO BATTLE

A Disneyfied "happy home" was scarcely an adequate response to such a situation. And, as things turned out for the Duke and Duchess of Windsor, as the prince and his bride became, it was in any case never really in the cards. For although their subsequent lifestyle makes it difficult to think of them as "homeless," that is exactly the condition spectacularly signaled by the couple's later restlessness: a well-heeled nomadic foxtrot to the dying fall of an empire's decline. However passionate their involvement, however much it seemed positively to endorse the idea of family ties between the United States and Britain, none of the consolations of either home or state ever finally embraced them. In the circumstances, that prince's confrontation, across the footlights, with a stage Prince of Wales whose trajectory moved in quite the opposite direction, takes on the sort of ironic coloring that has always been history's most piquant gift.

The career of the actor who played Prince Hal in that Stratford season seems to confirm it. He was one of those Englishmen whose absolute centrality in respect of his own culture almost persuades you that this is the part he was born to play. His name was Gyles Isham. On the death of his father (the worryingly named Sir Vere Isham), he would become Sir Gyles Isham, the 12th Baronet, heir to a title created in 1627.

Unlike the royal misfit watching him from the stalls, Isham could not have been more "at home," more rooted in and part of the *Blut und Boden* of the England of that day. The family name is of Saxon origin. Sir Gyles's own history of his home—the country retreat of Lamport Hall, Northamptonshire, less than fifty miles from Stratford—cites genealogical evidence in support of the claim that, of all the families in the district, the Ishams are "the only one which takes its surname from lands in the county" and that they have "dwelt therein longer than any other of the landed houses." John Isham, citizen and mercer of London, had purchased the house in 1560.[26] His son, Thomas Isham (died 1605) could have been present at the original production of *1 Henry IV* in London in 1598. Indeed, the bust of Sir Justinian Isham, the 5th Baronet, in the Isham Chapel of All Hallows Church in Lamport, is said to be the work of the Flemish sculptor Peter Scheemakers who in 1741 had carved the Shakespeare monument in Westminster Abbey.[27] And, over the years, the blood of the Ishams duly flowed not only in the veins of many eminent British lawyers, courtiers, and politicians, but also in those of the family's American branches, which included Thomas Jefferson and Robert E. Lee.[28] Baldwin's "Welcome—home" was not idly conceived.

Born in 1903, at Lamport, Gyles Isham received as prestigious an English education as you can get, attending Rugby school and Magdalen College Oxford. A "star" of the Oxford University Dramatic Society (OUDS), he played Hamlet there, and became the society's president in 1925. In 1926, he was elected president of the Oxford Union. He then began work as a professional actor, playing leading Shakespeare roles at the Old Vic in London in 1929–30, where his popularity rivaled that of John Gielgud. After performing at Stratford in 1931 and 1932, he made his way to Hollywood, appearing in a number of films, including the 1935 MGM production of *Anna Karenina* with Greta Garbo and Fredric March.

In 1939, on the outbreak of war, Isham returned home and, quickly commissioned, served in Egypt with the Eighth Army. In 1941, he succeeded to the title while on active service in Libya.[29] In 1943–44 he was with the Intelligence unit (MI5) at HQ Ninth Army and later at the War Office. Then, suddenly, he found himself hurled into that conflict whose complexities and implications still penetrate and influence our time more subtly than any other. No doubt his stage father of 1932, the Crusade-besotted pagan-chasing Henry IV, would have been delighted. For in September 1945, Gyles Isham was posted to the place that constituted the lynchpin of Henry's notion of "home": none other than the heart of "stubborn Jewry" itself—Jerusalem.

Holy City

The central issue at stake in that place and at that time was a massive political problem largely of British making. It had to do with the aspirations of the Jewish people and, inevitably, with the question of "home." In 1917, as part of what became famously known as the Balfour Declaration, the British Foreign Secretary, Arthur Balfour, had declared that "His Majesty's Government view with favour the establishment in Palestine of a national home for the Jewish people, and will use their best endeavours to facilitate the achievement of this object . . ."[30] Now those chickens were coming home to roost. "Welcome—home" may have played well as a slogan promoting the bonding of Britain and the United States in Stratford in 1932. But by 1945, any unity between them on the question of what "home" meant in political terms was badly strained. As the war in Europe came to an end, the standing of the Jewish people in Palestine became, as one historian puts it, "a major source of conflict between the two leading English speaking nations." This increased as the Cold War, with the beginning of the U.S. peacetime military commitment to Europe, began to take hold.[31] Sensing a major shift in power from Britain to the United States, the active elements of Zionism, with David Ben Gurion at their head, began to apply pressure less in London and more in Washington.[32]

The impact of that change of emphasis was, and remains, considerable.[33] For whatever shades of meaning were finally at stake in it, the upshot was that, by the end of 1944, a new form of Zionism—latent in the old—was enabled, as a result, to emerge. In the words of one historian, it felt itself "no longer content with Palestine as a national home in which Jews could settle. There had to be a Jewish state."[34] That change, drawing out of the comfortable notion of "home"—or unsheathing "like bright metal" from it—the glittering, honed, and unforgiving imperatives of a political formation, signals a massive philosophical and historical shift. Geared to the decisive migration of power from one side of the Atlantic to the other, mocking, to some degree, its prototype in Shakespeare's history plays, it generates, for all of us, one of the most challenging political situations we face.[35]

In 1945, perhaps clinging to an older notion of "home," the British prime minister, Clement Atlee, had resolved to continue the restrictions on Jewish immigration to Palestine imposed in 1939. But after what had happened in Europe, this could only seem a betrayal of the principles of the Balfour Declaration. Accordingly, a number of militant Zionist organizations stepped up a program of violent opposition to the British mandate.[36] Between them, they set the Holy Land ablaze in what amounted to an extremely dirty war.[37] Palestine became for all sides a kind of laboratory in which modern notions and methods of terrorism were tested and developed. Both Jewish and Arab groups engaged in bombings, assassinations, torture, and abduction on an unprecedented scale, and the British responded with cruel antiterrorist tactics of their own. Needless to say, the secret intelligence services MI5 and MI6 found themselves heavily involved.[38] But the results were not encouraging. This, says Stephen Dorril, was "the blackest page in MI6's post-war history."[39] Lord Altrincham, British Minister in the Middle East, later admitted that "[t]he primary cause of our failure in Palestine was the failure of our intelligence service."[40] By late 1946 the senior representative of MI5 in Palestine had been transferred to MI6 in Jerusalem. His name was Sir Gyles Isham.[41]

On July 22, 1946, the most appalling terrorist act of the whole campaign took place. A bomb planted in the King David Hotel in Jerusalem exploded, killing ninety-one people.[42] Since the building housed prominent elements of the British Military Headquarters, the Criminal Investigation Department, and presumably central sections of MI5 and MI6, its destruction was a major disaster. The impact on morale and public opinion in Britain was enormous. You might even call it the British 9/11. Certainly, it marked the end of British rule in Palestine, the collapse of the project of a "national home" for the Jewish people, and the beginning of something quite different. Later the same year, with the rank of lieutenant colonel in MI6—and with the sound of that explosion perhaps still ringing in his ears—Sir Gyles Isham left the army and returned to England.[43]

Home Sweet Home

I have argued that the dates 9/11 and 4/23 are both significant to us in that the destruction of a monument to one way of life in New York, and the construction of a monument to another in Stratford-upon-Avon, both demand in their different ways that we focus on the values that each event embodies. I have suggested that their relationship to our concerns here becomes particularly evident when, following a first principle of the critical stance that has come to be called presentism, we are willing—or in my case anxious—to look at the earlier one in terms brought into prominence and given new significance by the later.[44] This permits us—perhaps scandalously—to revise our representation of them: to salvage from the appalling events in New York some mitigating sense of their capacity nevertheless to initiate a certain reading of history and, with that, of Shakespeare's history plays: one that discerns in those texts a tentative engagement with early modern representations of the concept of "home."

It is of course ironic that the production of *1 Henry IV* at Stratford in 1932 should feature as its Prince Hal a player who subsequently found himself entangled in the process that, generating the modern state of Israel, places itself unavoidably at the center of the tensions that spawned the tragedy of 9/11. But it would be a mistake to dismiss it as *merely* ironic, if that means we must forego the interpretative opportunity such a conjunction affords. For the irony it involves not only flows unstoppably back into the events at Stratford in 1932, coloring how we perceive them and modifying, here and now, our sense of what they signify, but also, as irony must, points to layers and shades of implication suddenly available within the plays that subtly challenge, change, and add to our sense of what they are able to tell us. If it is always and only the present that makes the past speak, it speaks always and only to—and about—ourselves.

I have said that Gyles Isham was born to play one Prince of Wales on that occasion, and I have implied that another—the future Edward VIII—was in a sense born uncomprehendingly to watch him. And in claiming that the careers of both show us broad aspects of that era's concerns and presuppositions, I have argued, as a fully paid-up presentist, that Shakespeare's play not only yields itself readily to the agenda those concerns and presuppositions set, it also helps us—post-9/11—to discern their implications for a Europe currently pondering its own possible future as a unified state drawn from an array of hitherto disparate "homes," as well as for a United States now obsessed with what it significantly calls "Homeland Security."

I have also said that I was born to give this paper, but my reasons for that are more personal. Less than a month after the opening of the Shakespeare Memorial Theatre at Stratford in 1932, a mere twenty miles away, in a suburb of Birmingham, I too first saw the light of day. We are of an age, that theatre and I. And so, when I hear tell of the problems that currently afflict it—it crumbles, it leaks, its western elevation leaves much to be desired—I am seized, like the Prince of Wales on the 23rd of April, with a sense of *de te fabula narratur*. I crumble, I leak, my western elevation has seen better days.

But if I wanted to pinpoint a more heartening message transmitted by that construction, its inauguration, and the subsequent careers of the two Princes of Wales who took part in it, to say nothing of myself, here, in the present, as I stand before you, I would not have to look far for an appropriate apothegm. Since our concern has been with buildings, you will not be surprised to learn that it is to be found literally inscribed on one. I am referring to the Isham family motto, proclaimed for all to see, in chillingly large letters, above the frontage of the family home of Lamport Hall. Set into the very fabric of a handsome country house, bleakly self-righteous yet blithely self-subverting, it is a fine example of the disconcerting ironies that always lurk within what the English like to dispense as eternal verities. IN THINGS TRANSITORY RESTETH NO GLORY, it thunders. What makes those words fit to be emblazoned on any replacement of the theater at Stratford, intoned at any celebration of Shakespeare's birthday, or even invoked in any academic paper that presumes to address both, is surely not just the fact that they neatly turn mere bricks and mortar into what we critical theorists deftly term a text. It is also the possibility that the hint they contain of our inevitable oblivion offers one of the greatest home truths of all. Appropriately, its consoling presentism finds a sympathetic echo in the racy transatlantic phrase with which we began: our new motto—"Twenty-three Skidoo."

Notes

1. "Twenty-three skidoo" was widely employed in the United States in the early twentieth century. In general terms it signifies an abrupt "that's it," "it is over," "let's go," and could be invoked in a whole range of dismissive contexts that—certainly to me—seem to capture something of the impatient brashness of the 1920s. Explanations of its origins abound, but these remain finally mysterious. Presumably, "skidoo" derives from "skedaddle," meaning to scuttle off or scurry rapidly away. "Twenty-three" is more difficult to account for. One of the most acceptable theories suggests that it was part of a number code originally used by telegraphers, whereby "30" meant "message concluded," "73" meant "best wishes," and so on, and "23" is said to have meant something like "end of the transmission." See the discussion in Eric Partridge, *Dictionary of Catch Phrases* (London: Routledge, 1977).

2. This is the Masonic form of "Amen."

3. G. A. Jellicoe A. R. I. B. A., *The Shakespeare Memorial Theatre, Stratford-upon-Avon* (London: Ernest Benn, 1933), 41.

4. Ibid., 74.

5. Ibid., advertisement at end of text.

6. A. K. Chesterton, *Brave Enterprise: A History of the Shakespeare Memorial Theatre, Stratford-upon-Avon* (London: J. Miles, 1934), 49–52.

7. Ibid., 52–53.

8. H.R.H. the Prince of Wales, *The Prince's Choice: A Personal Selection from Shakespeare with an Introduction by the Prince of Wales* (London: Hodder & Stoughton, 1995), 5.

9. Chesterton, *Brave Enterprise*, 54.

10. Quoted in Michael D. Bristol, *Shakespeare's America, America's Shakespeare* (New York: Routledge, 1990), 79. Bristol's discussion of the matter is incisive; see 79–90. Dismaying as this sounds, we should remember that an American identification with and commitment to "English civilization" had existed well before these celebrations, and continued to do so well beyond them, spurred by the Second World War and, perhaps, by the Cold War that ensued. Writing to Charles Seymour, president of Yale University in the late 1940s, Dean William C. De Vane spoke in support of the development of the new subject to be called American Studies at Yale in terms that saw the same feature as an asset to be preserved when confronting the menace of Communism: "No one who has lived or traveled extensively in our country or even flown from New York to San Francisco can fail to appreciate the magnificence and variety of the land. The imaginative mind inevitably thinks of the superb English stock which first settled and consolidated our Eastern seaboard. . . . One comes to a new appreciation of what we are and what we have done, and one is better prepared to face the dangers and hoarse disputes of our own time." Quoted in Michael Holzman, "The Ideological Origins of American Studies at Yale," *American Studies* 40, no. 2 (Summer 1999): 71–99.

11. *Times*, April 25, 1932, 16.

12. No doubt Andrew Mellon, an honored guest, appreciated it. Despite a recent hounding in the House of Representatives for alleged "high crimes and misdemeanors" as Secretary of the Treasury, he might even have felt relieved to find himself attending the ceremony—"home-free" as it were—as US ambassador.

13. The BBC also promised a "special studio performance of Shakespeare's *Henry V* adapted for broadcasting by Mr. Peter Cresswell" (*Times*, April 23, 1932, 3) to be transmitted later that day.

14. Details of the performance noted in Ruth Ellis, *The Shakespeare Memorial Theatre* (London: Winchester Publications Ltd., 1948), 68–71.

15. See Karen Armstrong, *Holy War: The Crusades and their Impact on Today's World* (London: Macmillan, 1988; New York: Anchor Books, 2nd rev. ed., 2001), 412.

16. Ibid., 59.

17. See Avraham Oz's groundbreaking essay, "Nation and Place in Shakespeare: The Case of Jerusalem as a National Desire in Early Modern English Drama," in *Post-Colonial Shakespeares,* ed. Ania Loomba and Martin Orkin, 98–116 (New York: Routledge, 1998): 103. See also his general conclusion, 106.

18. The historical Bolingbroke was even capable of substituting Danzig or Vilnius for the Holy City when it suited him, so an ideological connection between Jerusalem and London posed no problem. See Oz, "Nation and Place," 106.

19. Ibid., 108. A similar deployment of ideological counters is discernible in later national fantasies involving the supposed visit of the Lamb of God to British shores, the divine treading of those feet in ancient time on England's green and pleasant land, and his—and our—acceptance of destiny's consequent burden: the building of a new sepulchre and a new state; an English "new Jerusalem" among the dark satanic mills. See above, note 17. The modern British Conservative Party has, of course, long since adopted the musical setting of William Blake's poem *Jerusalem* as its anthem.

20. Predictably perhaps, the play, and in particular these scenes, are a favorite of princes. See H.R.H. the Prince of Wales, *The Prince's Choice*, 101–8. Meanwhile, we must make no bones about what that prodigality "says" on the stage. Father–son, King of Britain–Prince of Wales, the repeated emphasis on these relationships functions as nothing less than a crucial staking out of familial and political ground, the careful shoring up of ancient and inherited relationships, the mapping of essential structures of authority and inheritance fundamental to the maintenance of a national identity, and the welding together of a national British "home."

21. See H.R.H. the Duke of Windsor, *A King's Story* (1951; London: Prion Books, 1998), 361.
22. Reported in the *Guardian*, January 30, 2003, 12.
23. H.R.H. the Duke of Windsor, *A King's Story*, 413. According to the Duke, these words were in fact contributed to his speech by Winston Churchill, but they presumably embodied the Duke's sentiment and met with his approval. See 409.
24. Ibid., 211.
25. Ibid., 245.
26. When he died in 1595, he was buried in the chancel of All Hallows Church in the village.
27. See Gyles Isham, *The Isham Chapel of the Church of All Hallows, Lamport, Northamptonshire, Rugby* (Rugby: George Over, 1965), 3–4 and 9.
28. Gyles Isham, *Lamport Hall* (Derby: English Life Publications, 1974), 1, 22–24. Oddly enough, for one who played the Prince of Wales, and since we speak of "homes," Isham had Welsh blood. His opposition to Owain Glyndwr in the play may thus have required a certain degree of acting against inheritance. He was connected, through his mother, with the Vaughan family, so that among his forebears is the "Silurist" Welsh poet, Henry Vaughan (1621–95), born at Newton-upon-Usk, Breconshire. I deduce this from Noel Annan's complicated essay "The Intellectual Aristocracy" in his *The Dons: Mentors, Eccentrics and Geniuses* (London: HarperCollins, 1999, 2000), 327–28. See also Gyles Isham, *The Isham Chapel*, 9.
29. His elder brother had been killed in the First World War.
30. Interestingly, the Declaration went on: "it being clearly understood that nothing shall be done which may prejudice the civil and religious rights of existing non-Jewish communities in Palestine, or the rights and political status enjoyed by Jews in any other country." See Nigel West, *The Friends: Britain's Post-War Secret Intelligence Operations* (London: Weidenfeld and Nicolson, 1988), 29.
31. Ritchie Ovendale, *Britain, the United States, and the End of the Palestine Mandate, 1942–48*, the Royal Historical Society, Studies in History 57 (Woodbridge, Suffolk: Boydell Press, 1989), 2.
32. Ibid., 8.
33. The first draft of the Balfour Declaration in 1917 had stated that "His Majesty's Government accepts the principle that Palestine should be reconstituted as the national home of the Jewish people" and President Woodrow Wilson had endorsed this version. In the cabinet, however, Alfred Lord Milner rephrased this as "the establishment of a home for the Jewish people in Palestine." Wilson hesitated to give this public approval and the United States did not officially endorse the Balfour Declaration (with its "establishment in Palestine of a national home for the Jewish people") until 1922—adding at the same time a caveat that "nothing shall be done which may prejudice the civil and religious rights of Christians and all other non-Jewish communities in Palestine, and that the holy places and religious buildings and sites in Palestine shall be adequately protected." See Ovendale, *Britain*, 3–4.
34. Ovendale, *Britain*, 37.
35. Ibid., 37–40.
36. The main groups involved were the Haganah, the military wing of the Jewish Agency for Palestine, Irgun Zvai Leumi, a semi-independent Jewish underground organization, and the Stern Gang, a terrorist group (organized by Avraham Stern and aided by the fledgling MOSSAD).
37. The assassination of Lord Moyne in Cairo is a specific example. See Nigel West, *The Friends*, 30.
38. Hitherto, Palestine had not been a primary MI6 concern (the so-called "Atlee

doctrine" had placed it and its Defence Security Office within the sphere of MI5). But under the Foreign Secretary Ernest Bevin, the Defence Security Officers (DSOs) in Jerusalem included a number of cross-posted MI6 officers (DSOs were generally regular soldiers who made contact with local police overseas and reported back to Overseas Control in London). See Nigel West, *MI5: British Security Service Operations, 1909–45* (London: Bodley Head, 1981), 139.

39. See Stephen Dorril, *MI6: Fifty Years of Special Operations* (London: Fourth Estate, 2000, 2001), 549.

40. Quoted by West, *MI15*, 29. As Stephen Dorril confirms, "MI6 was engaged in a real war of attrition with the Zionists, and it paid a heavy price." According to Dorril, the effort to stem Jewish immigration marks the first example of the British Foreign Secretary Ernest Bevin's support for MI6 special operations. Dorril, *MI6*, 344, 543.

41. Dorril, *MI6*, 344. See also David A. Charters, *The British Army and Jewish Insurgency in Palestine, 1945–47* (London: Macmillan, 1989), 86. In 1946, Isham found himself directing a staff of eight to ten intelligence officers at DSO headquarters in Jerusalem. The office's chief task was counterintelligence. As the "local station" of MI5, it maintained a close liaison with police and army intelligence, and was responsible for the security of British personnel, installations, and information. Earlier in the war, Isham had been at the War Office in London (see Charters, *The British Army*, 91 and 280).

42. The official tally was 28 Britons, 41 Arabs, 17 Jews, and 5 others.

43. He retired to his family seat in Northamptonshire and stood, unsuccessfully, for Parliament in the Kettering Division in 1950. In 1958, he became High Sheriff of Northamptonshire. He made valuable and learned contributions to local history. In 1968, the discovery that dry rot had infected Lamport Hall enforced a move to the village rectory. Nonetheless, perhaps recognizing that—in Britain at least—we now inhabited a postimperial world in which the notion of "home" concerned itself with the domestic, intensely localized sphere, he devoted the rest of his life to the Hall's restoration. He died in 1976. Lamport Hall is now a thriving tourist attraction. Sir Gyles's photograph is in the National Portrait Gallery.

44. The term "presentism" is admirably discussed and placed in an illuminating context in Hugh Grady, *Shakespeare, Machiavelli and Montaigne: Power and Subjectivity from Richard II to Hamlet* (Oxford: Oxford University Press, 2002), 1–25. See also my *Shakespeare in the Present* (London: Routledge, 2002), 2–5, 61–65. For a detailed critique, see Edward Pechter, "What's Wrong with Literature?" *Textual Practice* 17.3 (2003): 505–26, and R. Headlam Wells, "Historicism and 'Presentism' in Early Modern Studies," *Cambridge Quarterly* 29.1 (2000): 37–60. See also Wells's *Shakespeare on Masculinity* (Cambridge: Cambridge University Press, 2000), 207–18. For a more positive account see Ewan Fernie, "Shakespeare and the Prospect of Presentism," *Shakespeare Survey* 58 (2005): 169–84. For overviews, see Helen Moore, "Present and Correct," *Times Literary Supplement*, August 15, 2003, 22, and Marshall Brown, "Literature in Time," *MLQ* 65 (2004): 1–5 and the Introduction to Hugh Grady and Terence Hawkes, eds., *Presentist Shakespeares* (New York: Routledge, 2006), 1–5.

"Here in Vienna": The Setting of *Measure for Measure* and the Political Semiology of Shakespeare's Europe

Roderick J. Lyall

THE SEMIOLOGY OF LOCATION HAS OF LATE BECOME AN IMPORTANT preoccupation in Shakespeare studies. In his landmark study *Shakespeare and the Geography of Distance* (1994), John Gillies used Vico's concept of "poetic geography" as a way of bringing together the new approaches to the world that accompanied the early modern exploration of territories beyond the boundaries of Europe and the development of scientific cartography that accompanied it into dialogue with the presence of an imagined Other on the Elizabethan and Jacobean stage.[1] Gillies's concerns are primarily with Shakespeare's conception of the lands beyond Europe and with such marginal spaces as the Mediterranean, but the questions that he poses (what did the sixteenth-century discourse of geography contribute to Shakespeare's own, and his audience's, sense of location? How is the exotic figured on the Shakespearean stage, and with what cultural significances?) are, of course, applicable in principle to any setting with which the early modern dramatist takes his viewers beyond the limits of their own immediate experience. The significations of Shakespeare's Italian settings have received a good deal of attention, and the ideological freight carried by Venice in particular has been extensively explored; here, too, in the context of *The Merchant of Venice,* Gillies's approach yields valuable new insights.[2] But apart from these two categories there is a third: a fairly small number of plays in which Shakespeare employs a non-Italian continental location. These include *Love's Labour's Lost,* with its structural opposition of Navarre and France; *Hamlet,* where the Danish location is interestingly placed between at least two and perhaps three other signifiers (Wittenberg, Paris, and, perhaps, England); *All's Well That Ends Well,* in which Roussillon and Paris provide an axis against which Padua marks the contrast; *The Winter's Tale,* where Bohemia is used structurally to contrast with

Sicily; and, I will be arguing—for the point is now controversial—*Measure for Measure*. I do not, I should perhaps add, regard *Twelfth Night* as belonging in this category, since if Illyria is anywhere, it is presumably part of that Venetian sphere of influence on the eastern Adriatic coast, which makes it effectively Italian.

Let us consider for a moment the case of *Love's Labour's Lost*. Putting a king of Navarre on the stage in around 1594, it is fairly widely agreed, could scarcely avoid making at least some members of the contemporary audience think of Henry IV of France, who had succeeded to the French throne in 1589 and who had caused a considerable political stir in 1593 by abjuring his Protestantism and becoming a Catholic. Shakespeare seems to lead us away from the identification by pointedly calling his king Ferdinand, but on the other hand the names of his courtiers clearly evoke specific members of the French aristocracy: the Duc de Biron, the Duc de Longueville, and the Duc de Mayenne. Is this mere exoticism for its own sake, the Navarrese court no more a point on the Ortelian map than the curiously dislocated forest of Arden (Arden? Ardennes? Eden?) in *As You Like It*? Does the amatory and intellectual confrontation of Navarre and France, in which the French ladies and their egregious chaperon Boyet consistently outthink and outfeel their painfully undergraduate opponents, have any cultural or ideological significance beyond itself? Should the masterly theatrical stroke of Marcadé's entrance and announcement—the moment, it seems to me, at which Shakespeare fully matures as a dramatist—be invested with any political subtext beyond its irreversible disruption of plot and genre? The Shakespearean audience must have possessed a great range of awareness of contemporary French politics, so that "Navarre" might have been for many as empty a signifier as "Abkhazia" is for many of us, a name we have heard in a political context but cannot really do anything with, while for others it probably evoked much more precise associations of ideological confrontation and doctrinal betrayal. We have no record of a court performance of the play, but the setting might, perhaps, have generated more of a frisson among some members of such an audience than it would before a wider public in the theater. The elusiveness of Shakespeare's management of all this defies clear answers: we may or may not feel that G. R. Hibbard's assertions that "[t]he King is, in some respects, Henry of Navarre" and that "the Princess of France is and is not Marguerite de Valois" tip the balance too far in favor of topical identifications, but it is difficult to dissent from Henry Woudhuysen's observation, that "if [Shakespeare] seemed to be alluding to current history . . . his version of it is far from straightforward."[3] The play of significances created by such locations can be an extremely complex process, rewarding to explore but offering no ultimate solution.

Locating *Measure for Measure*

In the opening scenes of *Measure for Measure,* Shakespeare is at some pains to tell us where we are. To the Duke's rather general references to the "nature of our people, / Our city's institutions, and the term / For common justice" (1.1.9–11), Escalus replies by nominating Angelo in explicitly local terms: "If any *in Vienna* be of worth . . ." (22), and soon afterward the Duke himself repeats the name in his charge to Angelo:

> Mortality and mercy in Vienna
> Live in thy tongue and heart.
>
> (44–45)[4]

In each of the two following scenes, moreover, Vienna is again explicitly named, as if to ensure that there is no uncertainty on the point, and in scene 1.3 the central European context is expanded a little as the Duke explains his situation and Angelo's perception of it to Friar Thomas:

> I have delivered to Lord Angelo,
> A man of stricture and firm abstinence,
> My absolute power and place here in Vienna,
> And he supposes me travelled to Poland—
> For so I have strewed it in the common ear,
> And so it is received.
>
> (12–17)

If there is less direct emphasis on the Viennese location for much of the rest of the play (although, as we will see, there are some less direct reminders of where we are), the point returns in act 5, with even the phrase "here in Vienna" being repeated by the Duke at 5.1.313 ("my business in this state made me a looker-on here in Vienna"). Is this a foregrounded choice on Shakespeare's part, or is the setting a trivial, insignificant detail, or even the consequence, as Gary Taylor has argued in an important recent paper, of revision, probably by Thomas Middleton for the King's Men around 1621, away from an original setting in the Italian city of Ferrara?[5]

Taylor's argument is essentially twofold: that the version of *Measure for Measure* written by Shakespeare in 1604 was set in Ferrara rather than Vienna; and that the Viennese location was substituted, probably by Middleton, in 1621. Vienna would have meant "almost nothing" to an audience in 1604, he claims, and the supposed association of the play with the visit of Ulric, Duke of Holstein to the English court at the time of its first recorded performance is a wholly unconvincing explanation of the choice of location.[6] Ferrara, on the other hand, was an Italian city with well-established associations on the Elizabethan stage, while the papal seizure of the city in 1598 after the death of its last d'Este duke gave it a topicality that Vienna did not have; Middleton's *The Phoenix*, performed at court in February 1604 and anticipating the disguised-duke motif of *Measure for Measure*, includes a Duke of Ferrara and his disguised son. The later substitution of the Austrian capital, at a moment when the King of Hungary's attack on Vienna was a matter of intense diplomatic and general interest, was facilitated by the metrical similarity of the two place names: "Of all the possible locations of the story told in *Measure for Measure*, in all the known sources," Taylor asserts, "Ferrara is the only one with the same metrical structure as Vienna."[7]

Together with John Jowett, Taylor first argued for a Middletonian revision some ten years ago,[8] and a key element in that argument is the passage that opens scene 1.2 and that anticipates the cover story that the Duke will later describe to Friar Thomas:

> *Lucio.* If the Duke, with the other dukes, come not to composition with the King of Hungary, why then all the dukes fall upon the King.
> *1 Gentleman.* Heaven grant us its peace, but not the King of Hungary's.

The suspicion that the scene between Lucio, the two gentlemen, and Mistress Overdone was not written by Shakespeare, and that there is evidence here of some process of revision dates back to Dover Wilson's New Shakespeare edition of 1922; Jowett and Taylor have now concluded that the political situation referred to is that of 1621, when Gabor Bethlen (who was actually prince of Transylvania but was apparently known in England as king of Hungary) was on the verge of attacking Vienna. It follows from this persuasive argument that no conclusions can be drawn from the passage about Shakespeare's original intentions, but does it follow that the Viennese setting itself should be regarded as suspect? Taylor's skepticism about the similarity between the political issues surrounding the Duke of Holstein's mission to England and those so lightly sketched in the play is well founded; but the other references to Vienna in the opening and closing scenes of the play remain, and the suggestion that they were originally to Ferrara is purely conjectural. As Taylor himself acknowledges, this concentration of allusion—suggesting that Shakespeare did not want the audience to miss his choice of location, whatever it originally was—is fairly unusual in the canon. If an Italian city was the default setting for that audience, why did it matter so much that they knew they were in Ferrara? Was Shakespeare, like Middleton in *The Phoenix* and Marston in *Parasitaster,* alluding to Ferrara as "a warning of what could happen to England if it did not keep up its guard," or is his referent more theatrical than political, imitating the location as well as the plot of these rival pieces? That *Measure for Measure* participates in a current craze for disguised-ruler plays is clear enough, but the sheer insistence on where we are remains puzzling, and seems easier to explain if the setting is somehow counterintuitive, unexpected, and therefore needing reinforcement. There are, moreover, other references in the play that seem to suppose a central European context. We have already noted the Duke's supposed journey to Poland in scene 1.3; to this we can add the statement that Barnardine is "A Bohemian born" (4.2.113)—although it is possible, as Jowett has suggested, that this, too, is a Middletonian touch. Since the Provost's remark occurs in a prose passage, the substitution would have been easy enough, but this too remains conjectural. A further indication can be found in 3.2, where Lucio reports on speculation about the Duke's whereabouts: "Some say he is with the Emperor of Russia; other some he is in Rome" (79–80).

If the setting is Vienna, then these two equally remote locations make perfect sense; we would again have to conclude that Middleton had tampered with the text here if we were to accept the hypothesis that Shakespeare's version of the play was set in Ferrara. Does it not seem more logical to conclude that the references to Poland, Bohemia, and Russia were all in the 1604 text, and that it was only the specific allusion to the "King of Hungary" that Middleton added in 1621?

Let us, then, consider a possible middle position: that Taylor is right about the "King of Hungary and the Dukes" passage in 1.2 and that it was added by Middleton in 1621 as a topical allusion, but that it was inserted into a play that was already located in Vienna. Given that Austria was an unfamiliar setting, as uncommon as Navarre or Bohemia, there must have been reasons for the choice, reasons that explain the dramatist's apparent determination that we will take the point. The fact that the version of the story in Cinthio's *Hecatommithi* is set in Innsbruck may well be relevant to Shakespeare's choice, but even if we could be sure that he knew this version, the fact by itself would not explain either his decision to retain an Austrian setting or his preference for Vienna over Innsbruck. Manfred Draudt has argued, developing a suggestion by Gunnar Sjögren, that the key lies in George Whetstone's setting of his *Promos and Cassandra* in a city called "Iulio," which might plausibly be taken to be the Roman Juliobona, that is, Vienna.[9] The coincidence is striking, and perhaps Shakespeare was indeed aware that "Iulio" could be identified with the Austrian capital.

Significances of Vienna

It is nevertheless true that neither Shakespeare nor his audience can be assumed to have known much about what was, in 1604, a provincial German city. As is often remarked, the emperor Rudolf II had moved his capital to Prague from 1583, and although some vestiges of the city's former glory remained (not least the remarkably rich Hofbibliothek, presided over by the Flemish humanist Hugo Blotius, to whom we shall return in a moment), it was now little more than the capital of Lower Austria and the residence of its archduke. It was, however, also an important source of information about developments in the constant depredations of the Turks along western Christendom's eastern frontier; in 1602, when the danger was at one of its peaks, the dispatches Cecil received from Venice, sometimes on an almost weekly basis, consistently included news about the conflict in Transylvania and Hungary, mostly deriving from "letters from Vienna." Taylor is therefore justified in suggesting that the Ottoman threat would have been the most natural association for *Measure for Measure*'s Viennese setting, and in pointing out that the play is remarkably silent about this potential link. But it is, on the other hand, irrelevant to Shakespeare's concerns here; that *Othello*—probably nearest to *Measure for Measure* in the chronology of the canon—is particularly dense in such references is scarcely surprising, given the play's themes.[10]

There is, moreover, another possible set of associations for Shakespeare's Vienna, less widely recognized in early seventeenth-century England, but of much greater potential interest for this play. Austria was at this period an important site of religious conflict, in which the proponents of the Counter-Reformation were engaged in a crucial struggle with a large and influential Protestant minority. Rudolf II appears to have adopted an ambivalent attitude toward the Evangelical faction, fueled in part by his increasing antipapalism, but he rescinded the tolerant policies of his father, Maximilian II, prohibiting Protestant worship in Vienna and ordering the expulsion of the Lutheran ministers.[11] Despite the opposition of many leading Austrian noblemen, the grip of the Protestants on Vienna was broken, and the city was officially re-Catholicized in 1585. A key figure in this project was Melchior Khlesl, whose counterreforming zeal is evident from soon after his conversion to Catholicism in 1573 and was well established by the time he was appointed provost of St. Stephen's, Vienna, in 1579. After Rudolf quit Vienna for Prague, however, Khlesl found an even more sympathetic environment under the emperor's brothers Ernst (until 1593) and then Matthias, and his position became ever stronger in the course of the 1590s. An imperial councillor from 1585, he became administrator of Wiener Neustadt in 1588, of Vienna itself in 1595, and bishop in 1598. In Lower Austria he was by the turn of the century by far the most powerful figure apart from the archduke himself, and he played a critical role in ensuring that, whatever the emperor's own ambivalence, Hapsburg Austria became resolutely Catholic. From 1598, moreover, the Counter-Reformation in Lower Austria was guided by the archduke Ferdinand (the future emperor Ferdinand II), whose enthusiasm was, if anything, even greater than that of his uncles Ernst and Matthias.[12]

It is important to realize that there was a great deal more to the Counter-Reformation enterprise than the repression of Protestantism. From the outset, Khlesl evinces great concern about the internal reform of the institutions and practices of the Church, an issue on which he initially found himself frustrated by the laxness of the secular arm; "as far as the reformation of the clergy in Austria is concerned," he wrote to Wilhelm V, Duke of Bavaria in July 1581, "many are frightened, no-one wants to offend anyone else, and there is furthermore a great deal of freedom, and everyone does as he pleases."[13] Lay indiscipline was also an important Counter-Reformation theme: the Council of Trent had issued a number of decrees on marriage and related issues, declaring in the decree Tametsi of 1563, for example, that marriage was only valid where vows were exchanged before witnesses, including the priest before whom the couple had announced their intention to marry—a principle that is evidently violated by Claudio and Juliet in *Measure for Measure,* who by Claudio's own admission "the denunciation lack / Of outward order."[14] Some indication of how close such reforming zeal could come to the views of Calvinists is evident from the Bohemian program launched in 1626 under Ferdinand's authority by his councillor William Lamormaini, which promoted serious (though unspecified) punishments under secular law for such offenses as adultery, fornication, or marriage outside the ecclesiastical laws. In Hapsburg Vienna, then, the same issues of sexual regulation that concerned English Protestants were debated under the auspices of sweeping Catholic reform.

Is it conceivable that Shakespeare could have known anything about all this, and is it likely that he would have been interested? Although it is true, as we have already noted, that most dispatches from central Europe were concerned with the Ottoman threat, there are a few indications that the issue of toleration and persecution was not wholly ignored. The Scottish informant Duncan Anderson, for example, writing to the principal English agent in the region, Stephen Lesieur, from Prague on September 11, 1604, reported that "[m]ost evident tokens doe appeare on great troubles to . . . stur for matters of Religion in all those provinces, and landes, which are [im]mediatly subiected to ye Emperour."[15]

A more general account, and perhaps a more significant one for our purposes, can be found in Sir Edwin Sandys's *Relation of the state of religion*, a work that was published by Simon Waterson in 1605 but that can be seen—from the evidence of manuscript notes in the British Library copy (shelfmark C.28.f.8) and from the later 1629 edition—to have been completed in Paris before April 9, 1599, in fact as a report on current religious affairs on the Continent for Archbishop Whitgift. Waterson's edition was evidently unauthorized, which suggests that copies were circulating in manuscript form between Sandys's return to England later that year and the publication of Waterson's edition.[16] The text provides a valuable insight into a well-informed, widely traveled contemporary's view of continental religious affairs around the turn of the century, for Sandys covered much of the Continent during a six-year sojourn abroad. "Touching *Germanie*," Sandys says,

> I have seene an olde estimate of it by such as fauoured the Papacy, that in the beginning [the empire] of *Ferdinand*, there was not one twelfth part remayning Catholike, which now in [any] vnderstanding must needs be otherwise. For comprehending in it *Bohemia* with his appurtenances, I should think that neere a sixt part were devoted that way, their number beeing increased, and perhaps doubled since that time, by the sedulitie of many of the Prelates and [one] other great Prince, the Duke of *Bavaria*, who vsing the advantage of the *Interim* on their part, have forced those Protestantes which were in their States to quitt, eyther Religion or goods and Countrey. The same hath beene attempted by the Arch-Dukes of *Austria*, and in some places, as in their Country of *[T]iroll*, effected. But in *Austria* it selfe not so, wherein the number of Protestants exceedes and is fearefull to their opposites, though the exercise of the [reformed] religion is [there nowhere allowed and wholely restrained] in some of the chiefe Cities, as *Vienna*, but the most part of the country [people] are of it, so are halfe the nobility.[17]

This remarkably circumstantial account confirms some aspects of Taylor's argument: Sandys evidently regards Austria—and, indeed,

Bohemia—as part of Germany, but on the other hand he puts Austrian affairs in a quite different context from that of the Turkish threat which is allegedly the central feature of English awareness of central Europe at the end of the sixteenth century. The archdukes in question here are presumably Ernst and Matthias, and their uncle Ferdinand, who had successfully suppressed Protestantism in the Tyrol between 1566 and 1595.[18] Sandys is here summarizing the course of events over a considerable period, but it is clear that he sees Austria as a site of sectarian conflict, and Vienna as a city in which the practice of Protestantism is suppressed, despite the fact that there remained a Lutheran majority in much of the Viennese hinterland.

Perhaps a more likely potential source of intelligence about Vienna and about central European political affairs more generally was the indefatigable traveler Sir Henry Wotton, who had actually resided in the city for seven months between November 1590 and April 1591, lodging with the Hofbibliothekar Hugo Blotius: his letters written to Edward, Lord Zouche during this period contain a good deal of information about current political matters, the dangers of walking in the Viennese streets at night, and one extraordinary detail about the archduke Matthias: "that which I have often heard the Dutch say, that our Queen was in some mind toward him, and swore him her servant by order of her Garter, is merely false, for I find that he travelled England disguisedly, and concealed his state there; which, since my departure from your Honour, was objected unto me as a point of wisdom in him, to be able to deceive a whole nation."[19]

Eventually returning to England in 1595, Wotton entered the Middle Temple and the household of the Earl of Essex, taking responsibility for intelligence regarding Italy, Germany, Transylvania, and Poland; he departed for Italy shortly before the Earl's fall, visiting Scotland in 1602 to inform James VI of a possible assassination attempt, and eventually coming back to England on the king's accession, rapidly receiving a knighthood, and then, in July 1604, departing for Venice as ambassador, an appointment celebrated by his close friend Donne.[20] If anyone is likely to have been a conduit for information about affairs in Austria, it is Wotton; his wide circle of continental acquaintances included many with a lively interest in such questions, and in an undated memorandum that found its way into Cecil's hands, and that Logan Pearsall Smith conjecturally dates to December 1594, he names the Baron von Friedesheim, a leading Austrian Protestant who had put him up when he first arrived in Vienna, as the one "from whom I have best occasion to hear of those parts."[21] As Paul Hammer has noted, this memorandum was almost certainly written for Essex, and "must have been one of Wotton's earliest services" for his new employer.[22] His literary connections in London certainly gave him opportunity to communicate with a dramatist such as Shakespeare, and we know from the fringe involvement of the Chamberlain's Men in the Essex plot of 1601 that there were connections between the Earl's circle and Shakespeare's company.[23]

In Vienna, furthermore, Wotton had come into contact with a remarkable group of men who had been attempting to find a way of resolving the doctrinal conflicts of their age. At the center of this circle was Blotius, Wotton's host and the imperial librarian, whose reform of the library under the irenic emperor Maximilian II (1564–76) has recently been interpreted as evidence of his search for "a program that could unite the continent."[24] Together with the physician Johannes Crato, the soldier and military theoretician Lazarus von Schwendi, and the artist Jacopo Strada, Blotius had labored within the space created by Maximilian's comparatively tolerant policies to counter the dangerous process of confessionalization; but their efforts had been brought to an abrupt end by the emperor's death, the relocation of the imperial capital in Prague, and the emergence of a more repressive regime under Rudolf II's brothers and their favorite Khlesl. As Howard Louthan notes, the Vienna in which Wotton stayed in 1590–91 was a very different place from that which had existed fifteen years earlier,[25] but the fact that he resided with Blotius must surely indicate that he heard something of the irenic idealism that contrasted so strongly with the policies that were now in force.

The Religious Politics of *Measure for Measure*

To what degree might any of this be seen as relevant to *Measure for Measure*? The Catholicism of the play's setting is obvious enough: Vienna is a city in which friars are commonplace, and in which the Poor Clares maintain a house. This would, of course, be as suitable to an Italian location as to a Viennese one, but it is nevertheless a central feature of the text. That Isabella is a postulant is the first thing we hear about her, and our first glimpse of her is her interrogation of one of the sisters about the strictness of their discipline. And however problematic the Duke's impersonation of a friar may be—and it has come to be seen as very problematic indeed—the religious practice that he pursues is one that is unmistakably Catholic. Even Angelo seems to fit fairly naturally within this setting: ordering the execution of Claudio, he instructs the provost to "Bring him his confessor, let him be prepared" (2.1.35), and while this may partly be a dramaturgical device to create a space for the Duke-as-friar, its assumptions are of

Catholic pastoral care. More remarkably, perhaps, the Duke later tells Claudio, spinning an improbable tale about the innocence of Angelo's intentions toward Isabella, that "I am confessor to Angelo and I know this to be true" (3.1.164–65). We are by this time becoming used to the Duke's capacity for improvisation and downright untruth, but the fact that he expects Claudio to accept this claim, and that Shakespeare expects the audience to accept his acceptance of it, is surely at odds with the notion of Angelo as self-evidently a fully paid-up, card-carrying Puritan.

Angelo's puritanism has long been a key topic in discussion of the play, dating back at least as far as Hermann Ulrici's *Shakespeare's Dramatische Kunst* (1847), and strongly propagated a century later by D. J. McGinn's influential essay on "The Precise Angelo" (1948).[26] Recent critics generally—although far from unanimously—accept the identification: for Anthony Gash, for example, "Angelo . . . is the real thing, a legally trained and theologically literate member of the Puritan movement."[27] That Angelo is puritanical is beyond question, but is he, or is he unequivocally, a Puritan? It is difficult to deny the associations of his preciseness with Puritan attitudes, and his insistence upon the letter of the law and his initial conviction of his own sanctity are equally pointers in that direction. It is even possible to agree with Debora Kuller Shuger's recent argument, developed in a book-length study of the play, that "*Measure for Measure* stages a counter-narrative to the Puritan vision of Christian politics."[28] But as Shuger herself acknowledges, "sexual regulation was not an exclusively Platonic-Puritan concern,"[29] and while she bases her analysis on a wide range of theological texts from Augustine and Aquinas to Bucer and Whitgift, she does not consider the possible relevance of a Counter-Reformation context.

To say this is not to deny that the issues of license and social control, of outward probity and private lust, would have had an immediate contemporary and local resonance for Shakespeare's audience. Vienna (or Ferrara) is, of course, in important respects London, the disorderly houses of its suburbs a displaced version of those that could be found a tankard's throw from the theater in which the play's public performances occurred—and the presence of such standard comic turns as Elbow, Froth, Pompey, and Mistress Overdone can leave us in no doubt about the fact. But the exotic locations of Elizabethan and Jacobean drama characteristically set up a kind of double vision: we both recognize our own world *and* see it transformed in place and time. The "mechanicals" of *A Midsummer Night's Dream* are manifestly English yokels transported into a crypto-classical Athenian wood, and we have no difficulty in keeping the two frames of reference equally in focus. The integration goes further in *Measure for Measure;* the imaginative distance between London and Vienna is compressed by the tight thematic concentration upon related cases of sexual disorder and differing approaches to its management. If Angelo has many of the characteristics of the "Court Puritan," the Catholicism of the Viennese setting tacitly invites us to generalize our understanding of his attitudes and his behavior.

It is a commonplace of criticism of *Measure for Measure* that Angelo and Isabella are very similar figures, united in their repression of their sexuality. As a prospective Poor Clare Isabella can scarcely be portrayed as a Puritan in the Elizabethan sense, no matter how double our vision may be; rather, it seems to me, we should regard both characters as "rigorists" in their attitudes toward the punishment of sexual offenses. If anything, it is Isabella who remains more consistent in her rejection of sexual license, beginning her suit to Angelo with the memorable assertion that

> There is a vice that most I do abhor,
> And most desire should meet the blow of justice,
>
> (2.2.30–31)

declaring in understandable horror at Angelo's proposition that "More than our brother is our chastity" (2.4.186), and rejecting Claudio's miserable appeals with an accusation of virtual incest (3.1.136–51). It is, indeed, precisely this "saintliness" that, by his own acknowledgment, triggers Angelo's desire, and in some respects Isabella even maintains it into her final speech, insisting that "My brother had but justice, / In that he did the thing for which he died" (5.1.441–42). Only in her very last words of all does she succumb to the kind of casuistry that Angelo, ironically, has employed in attempting to seduce her:

> For Angelo,
> His act did not o'ertake his bad intent,
> And must be buried but as an intent
> That perished by the way. Thoughts are no subjects,
> Intents but merely thoughts.
>
> (443–47)

Considering that at this moment Isabella is still under the impression that Angelo has had Claudio executed despite believing that he has had his way with her, this is a remarkable piece of special pleading, and one wonders whether her concentration on the uncompleted nature of "his act" does not reflect a continuing and unhealthy fixation upon the sexual. Her plea for mercy, on the other hand, is clearly what the Duke has been working towards, and it represents the ultimate triumph of his rather more latitudinarian approach to justice over the forces of rigorism.

He has achieved this, we should observe, by theatrically assuming a rigorist position himself: scene 5.1 is peppered with his demands for enforcement of the law, egging Escalus and Angelo on and then taking the role of Judge Dread onto his own shoulders, insisting upon "An Angelo for Claudio, death for death" (402). Even Isabella's submission seems at first to fail to bring him round: "Your suit's unprofitable. Stand up, I say" (448).

Only when he has completed the revelation of the living Claudio does he embark upon his round of pardons, enacting a regime of reconciliation that contrasts powerfully with both the rigorism he has fought so successfully and the permissiveness that he recanted at the beginning of the play. The way in which he fits both punishment and reward to specific cases may leave a number of unresolved questions—why does he allude in his final speech to his role as Mariana's confessor and what, above all, are we to make of his near-proposal to Isabella?—but it is the fulfillment of the casuistry that he practiced as Friar Lodowick, and it aims at a social reconciliation that conforms to the highest ideals of penitential governance.[30] Whether we see this in terms of the debate between Anglicans and Puritans in England or in a wider European context, which, I have been arguing, the Viennese setting invites, there can be no doubt that it is rigorism that the play invites us to join the Duke in rejecting.

Conclusion

Summarizing their 1993 study of the Folio text of *Measure for Measure*, Jowett and Taylor rightly emphasize the comparative modesty of their claims:

> Acceptance of the evidence for posthumous adaptation in *Measure for Measure* entails only five emendations of the Folio text: omission of TLN 1169–96 (4.1.0–24), transposition of the Duke's two soliloquies (TLN 1746–67 and 1834–9), omission of TLN 96–174 (1.2.0–116), alteration of the entrance direction and adjacent dialogue at TLN 205 and 207, and omission of "*Julietta*" from the direction at TLN 2875. These are, of course, major emendations, and we do not advocate them lightly. In each case we merely propose to solve a substantial problem which has troubled previous scholars, scholars who never dreamt that Thomas Middleton might in 1621 have adapted Shakespeare's play.[31]

They go on, indeed, to report that a comprehensive review of the rest of the play has yielded "little else in the text which justifies suspicion, and nothing which could justify editorial intervention."[32] It is, I find, precisely this caution, this working through textual problems that previous editors and critics have observed but were unable to resolve that makes their case so persuasive. The stylometric evidence for Middleton's hand in the opening passage of scene 1.2 is strong, and if subsequent research has yielded a specific source for the "King of Hungary" passage, then the association of those lines with the political situation in 1621 may be considered as good as proved. This argument, then, has the merit of proceeding from the inside outward, identifying textual problems and seeking solutions that are grounded in the inconsistencies of the text itself. Taylor's Ferrara thesis, it seems to me, reverses that process, commencing with extratextual considerations such as the cultural semiotics of "Vienna" in the first years of James's reign and drawing from these an entirely speculative series of emendations that the text itself in no way demands.

What I have been attempting to do in the above discussion is to confront the issues of location raised by the text of *Measure for Measure* as Jowett and Taylor left it in 1993. If that involves a Viennese setting, then what was the full range of ideological signification that might have been available to Shakespeare's audience, in their highly variable states of awareness of the religious and cultural politics of central Europe? For some at least, I have suggested, that may have been a good deal richer than Taylor now believes, and bringing those specifically Counter-Reformation associations to the text in turn enriches our understanding of the conflicts that are at the play's heart. There are rigorists everywhere, and whether they are hypocrites like Angelo or committed virgins like Isabella, their moral view is relentlessly subverted by the casuistical ingenuity of the Duke and the inescapable realities of human nature as it is mirrored by Viennese society.

Notes

1. John Gillies, *Shakespeare and the Geography of Distance* (Cambridge: Cambridge University Press, 1994).

2. See, for example, Murray J. Levith, *Shakespeare's Italian Settings and Plays* (Basingstoke: Macmillan, 1989); *Shakespeare's Italy: Functions of Italian Locations in Renaissance Drama*, ed. Michele Marrapodi, A. J. Hoenselaars, Marcello Cappuzzo, and L. Falzon Santucci, 2nd ed. (Manchester and New York: Manchester University Press, 1997); Graham Holderness, Nick Potter, and John Turner, *Shakespeare: The*

Play of History (Basingstoke: Macmillan, 1987), 157–209; Gillies, *Geography of Distance,* 64–68.

3. *Love's Labour's Lost,* ed. G. R. Hibbard (Oxford: Oxford University Press, 1990), 49–50; *Love's Labour's Lost,* Arden Shakespeare, ed. H. R. Woudhuysen (London: Nelson, 1998), 68. Woudhuysen's remark alludes to Hugh M. Richmond, "Shakespeare's Navarre," *HLQ* 43 (1978–79): 193–216.

4. *Measure for Measure,* ed. Brian Gibbons (Cambridge: Cambridge University Press, 1991), 80–82; all references to the text are based on this edition.

5. Gary Taylor, "Shakespeare's Mediterranean: *Measure for Measure,*" in *Shakespeare and the Mediterranean,* ed. Tom Clayton, Susan Brock, and Vicente Forés, 243–69 (Newark: University of Delaware Press, 2004).

6. Holstein, Taylor argues, would scarcely have been recruiting for the emperor since he is known to have criticized James's decision to make peace with Spain; but he does not consider the possibility that as a committed Protestant he was seeking to raise troops for Istvan Bocskai's resistance to the Hapsburgs.

7. Taylor, "Shakespeare's Mediterranean," 255.

8. John Jowett and Gary Taylor, "With New Additions: Theatrical Interpolation in *Measure for Measure,*" in *Shakespeare Reshaped, 1606–1623* (Oxford: Clarendon Press, 1993), 186–226.

9. Gunnar Sjögren, "The Setting of *Measure for Measure,*" *Revue de Littérature Comparée* 35 (1961): 25–39; Manfred Draudt, "Das Wien- und Österreichbild Shakespeares," *Shakespeare Jahrbuch West* (1993): 123–24. Draudt further connects Shakespeare's retention of this location with the progress of the Counter-Reformation in Austria, though in less detail than the argument that follows here.

10. The contrast with *Othello* is cited by Taylor as one argument for an original non-Viennese setting, "Shakespeare's Mediterranean," 245.

11. For an account of this process, see Grete Mecenseffy, *Geschichte des Protestantismus in Österreich* (Cologne: Hermann Böhlaus, 1956), 82–86.

12. On Ferdinand's career as a Counter-Reformer, see Robert Bireley, "Ferdinand II, Founder of the Habsburg Monarchy," in *Crown, Church and Estates: Central European Politics in the Sixteenth and Seventeenth Centuries,* ed. R. J. W. Evans and T. V. Thomas, 226–44 (Basingstoke: Macmillan, 1991).

13. My translation. The original: "[W]as die reformation dess cleri per Austriam belandgt, ist meniglich erschrockhen, niemants will den andern belaidigen, daneben ist grosse freihait, und thueth ein jeder was im wollgfellig;" Khlesl to Wilhelm V of Bavaria, July 31, 1581; quoted in V. Bibl, "Klesls Briefe an Herzog Wilhelm V von Baiern," *Mitteilungen des Institut für Österreichische Geschichtsforschung* 21 (1900): 654–55.

14. On the impact of the Counter-Reformation on Catholic attitudes and legislation with respect to sexual matters, see Merry E. Wiesner-Hanks, *Christianity and Sexuality in the Early Modern World* (New York: Routledge, 2000), 102–40.

15. TNA, SP80/2, fol. 313r.

16. See James Ellison, "*Measure for Measure* and the Executions of Catholics in 1604," *ELR* 33 (2003): 61–62, where it is suggested that a copy may have come into the hands of the Earl of Southampton. Ellison does not take up the specific reference to Vienna in Sandys's text, and although he touches on the implications of the setting, he does not pursue the Counter-Reformation dimension, reading the play rather as a response to the persecution of Catholics in England in the summer of 1604.

17. Sir Edwin Sandys, *A Relation of the State of Religion* (London: Simon Waterson, 1605), sig. Q3r-v.

18. Mecenseffy, *Protestantismus in Österreich,* 66–67.

19. *The Life and Letters of Sir Henry Wotton,* ed. Logan Pearsall Smith (Oxford: Clarendon Press, 1907), 1: 244–45; Wotton adds that Matthias is "of all the brothers . . . as Catholic as any of them, but not so hot in it as Ernestus." Pearsall Smith's version of Wotton's letters from Vienna is avowedly incomplete, omitting several letters and extended passages from the rest (including much of the "newsletter" material); for the complete texts, see *Reliquiae Wottonianae,* 4th ed. (London: For Benjamin Tooke and Thomas Sawbridge, 1685).

20. For Wotton's career, see *Life and Letters,* 1:1–225; on his connection with Essex, see Paul E. J. Hammer, *The Polarisation of Elizabethan Politics: The Political Career of Robert Devereux, 2nd Earl of Essex, 1585–1597* (Cambridge: Cambridge University Press, 1999), 183.

21. *Life and Letters,* 1:301.

22. Hammer, *Polarisation,* 183n179.

23. E. A. J. Honigmann, indeed, goes so far as to claim that "[a]s a follower of the Earl of Southampton, Shakespeare must be seen as a member of the Essex circle," in *Myriad-minded Shakespeare: Essays on the Tragedies, Problem Comedies and Shakespeare the Man,* 2nd ed. (Basingstoke: Macmillan, 1998), 7.

24. Howard Louthan, *The Quest for Compromise: Peacemakers in Counter-Reformation Vienna* (Cambridge: Cambridge University Press, 1997), 84.

25. Ibid., 157–59.

26. D. J. McGinn, "The Precise Angelo," in *Joseph Quincy Adams Memorial Studies* (1948), 129–39. For a crisp overview of the development of the idea up to the 1960s, see Ernst Schanzer, *The Problem Plays of Shakespeare* (London: Routledge, 1963), 86–87.

27. Anthony Gash, "Shakespeare, Carnival and the Sacred: *The Winter's Tale* and *Measure for Measure,*" in *Shakespeare and Carnival: After Bakhtin,* ed. Ronald Knowles, 177–210 (Basingstoke: Macmillan, 1998), 199.

28. Debora Kuller Shuger, *Political Theologies in Shakespeare's England: The Sacred and the State in* Measure for Measure (Basingstoke: Palgrave, 2001), 48.

29. Shuger, *Political Theologies,* 36. On the sixteenth-century English debate about fornication, see Martin Ingram, *Church Courts, Sex and Marriage in England, 1570–1640* (Cambridge: Cambridge University Press, 1987), 150–67.

30. See Shuger, *Political Theologies,* 131–34.

31. Jowett and Taylor, "With New Additions," 231.

32. Ibid., 232.

Shakespeare, Joyce, and the Politics of European Traditions

Raphaël Ingelbien

LIKE ALL ASPECTS OF *ULYSSES*, JOYCE'S ALLUSIONS TO *HAMLET* have prompted a multitude of conflicting interpretations. This is not just due to an indeterminacy inherent in Joyce's high-modernist aesthetics. The perception of Joyce's use of Shakespeare has followed the broader paradigm shifts that have affected the study of Irish modernism over the last century. Those changes have also had consequences for Joyce's and Shakespeare's respective places in various canons of European literature. Since the process by which such canons are defined often has a political dimension, my aim in tracing those shifts will be to call attention to the concomitant roles that Shakespeare and Joyce have been made to play in the creation of European cultural identities. That Joyce himself was concerned with such questions may seem obvious, but the rediscovery of a political Joyce over the past two decades has distorted both our view of his original reception as a modernist author and our understanding of his engagement with Shakespeare. A reassessment of the Shakespearean presence in *Ulysses* in the light of European cultural politics thus seems overdue. Indeed, such a reading will show that the postcolonial reappropriation of Joyce as an Irish author has more in common with a certain modernist agenda than it cares to admit, and that these affinities reveal reductive definitions of both Shakespeare and Europe.

THE CHANGING FACE OF SHAKESPEARE IN JOYCE CRITICISM

Joyce's numerous references to *Hamlet* in *Ulysses* did not attract much commentary among Joyce's first readers. When the controversies surrounding Joyce's bold experimentalism and his perceived obscenity finally prompted T. S. Eliot to defend Joyce, he did so by drawing attention to the ordering principle of the novel: Eliot famously singled out the parallels with Homer's *Odyssey* to define

Joyce's "mythical method," apparently setting the tone for subsequent New Critical, formalist, and structuralist readings of *Ulysses*.[1] When these later turned their attention to Shakespearean allusions in Joyce's text, they largely approached those references as yet another illustration of the ordering method that Eliot had discerned in the novel's Homeric structure. In such analyses, Joyce's Shakespearean intertext was yet another structuring device, on a par with Homer's *Odyssey*. A careful decoding of echoes of *Hamlet* in *Ulysses* could impose some degree of meaningful order on the chaos of the text, and help establish the true nature of Stephen's and Bloom's wanderings and eventual meeting.[2] Not surprisingly, disagreement persisted about the import of specific Shakespearean parallels, but there was a broad, tacit agreement on the status of Joyce's use of *Hamlet* among scholars. Only those who regarded *Ulysses* as a gigantic hoax scoffed at the seriousness with which the learned commentators of modernist art pursued allusion-hunting (whether Homeric or Shakespearean).

When the return to history and context in literary criticism displaced formalist and New Critical approaches, Joyce's allusions were thoroughly reassessed. The cosmopolitan aesthete was replaced by the exile who remained imaginatively immersed in Irish culture, and a new emphasis on Joyce's nationalist credentials qualified the picture of the apolitical exile.[3] As a consequence, the various intertexts of *Ulysses* each became fraught with specific cultural and political resonance. The combined rise of Irish and postcolonial studies meant that the Shakespearean presence in *Ulysses* underwent a dramatic critical revision. In postcolonial readings of Joyce's novel, *Hamlet* was no longer a structuring intertext: as a major text in the canon of the English colonizer, it was a cultural icon that invited defacement, subversion, and/or strategic appropriation at the hands of Ireland's foremost postcolonial genius. Joyce's use of Shakespeare then began to be analyzed as part of a struggle between the Irish artist trying to forge the "uncreated conscience of [his] race" and the towering presence at the heart of English literary culture.[4] Recent debates in Joyce criticism have often centered on the (post)colonial dimension of Joyce's relation to England. What has largely remained unexamined is the role that certain ideas of Europe have been made to play in the analysis of Joyce's engagement with English culture, and Shakespeare in particular. A new look at Joyce's use of *Hamlet* in *Ulysses* is probably the best way to explore how Joyce criticism, both old and new, has sometimes reified and instrumentalized Europe in order to score political points. Shakespeare is indeed a critical blind spot in the Europe that was constructed in the process.

The Irish relation to Shakespeare is necessarily ambiguous. In many ways, it conforms to the broader pattern of postcolonial responses to Shakespeare's work. The canon is rewritten to highlight and rehabilitate the figure of the colonized: Caliban's identities thus include an Irish passport; one example occurs in *Ulysses* when Stephen links the colonization of Ireland and of the New World by mentioning "Patsy Caliban, our American cousin."[5] Less obvious figures were also enlisted: Yeats turned Richard II into an honorary Celt, and was also drawn to a "pre-modern, carnivalesque vitality": "elements which survived in Shakespeare's plays, and which seemed to intersect, in suggestive ways, with the folk life of rural Ireland."[6] In *Ulysses,* Stephen insists that Shakespeare's work is pervaded by the "note of banishment, banishment from the heart, banishment from home" (272)—a typically Irish theme, although it is not quite clear whether Stephen means these notes to mirror the collective experience of the dispossessed in Ireland or Stephen's own increasing alienation from his Irish background.[7] However, the recruitment of "Patrick W. Shakespeare" (383) to the Irish cause is also parodied in *Ulysses,* as in the episode where Eglinton wonders if Shakespeare himself was ever "made . . . out to be an Irishman" (254). Yeats's example, on the other hand, also provides a stark warning to those who would draw too much inspiration from the Bard while rewriting him: Yeats's declaration that he "owed [his] soul to Shakespeare" has also been adduced as an example of the "pathology of literary Unionism," an unhealthy infatuation with the culture of the colonizer that postcolonial Ireland must disown.[8] In the postcolonial paradigm, the appropriation of Shakespeare must imply a considerable degree of subversion or resistance on the part of Irish writers. Joyce in particular is seen as pursuing precisely such a strategy. According to two recent studies of *Ulysses,* Shakespeare must now be seen as "the national poet of the English empire Joyce so resented," a cultural icon whom Joyce deliberately turned into "a red, white and blue Shakespeare."[9]

Compared with *The Tempest* or *Othello* (two minor intertexts in *Ulysses*), *Hamlet* is certainly a play that offers little purchase to those who would rewrite or appropriate it for postcolonial ends. It includes little in the way of exotic others in need of rehabilitation. Connections with a Celtic or Gaelic mind or theme are far from obvious. The folk, carnivalesque elements so dear to an Irish critic like Declan Kiberd are not foregrounded—indeed, the fool has been dead for some years, and the play was written after the departure of Will Kemp from the Lord Chamberlain's Men heralded a more highbrow approach to comic elements in Shakespeare's work.[10] The protagonist, far from exemplifying premodern energies, is an emblematic figure who has constantly inspired Western modernity. Faced with such apparently unpromising material, the main strategies available to the postcolonial artist would thus seem to be radical subversion, mockery, or defacement—and the treatment meted out to Shakespeare's tragedy may sometimes incline us to think that this was Joyce's intent. The first references to *Hamlet* in Joyce's text certainly set a peculiar tone. Buck Mulligan jokily warns Stephen's companions about the theory that Stephen will later be expounding: "Wait till you hear him on Hamlet" (18); "It's quite simple. He proves by algebra that Hamlet's grandson is Shakespeare's grandfather and that he himself is the ghost of his own father." Haines, the well-meaning but dimwitted Englishman, is actually intrigued: "What? Haines said, beginning to point at Stephen. He himself?" (21). Stephen's theory, which takes up most of the "Scylla and Charibdis" chapter, will be only slightly less extravagant than Mulligan makes out. Shakespeare himself will become, among other things, "a rich country gentleman . . . with a coat of arms and landed estate at Stratford and a house in Ireland yard, a capitalist shareholder, a tithe farmer" (261), and is thus derided in the same way as other icons of English literature, like "Lawn Tennyson" (259). The new critical emphasis on Joyce's subversive ridicule provides an updated version of the theory that his allusions are a leg-pull, but the joke now has a clear political edge. Seamus Deane argues that through Stephen's reckless hermeneutic exercise, Joyce is actually cutting the colonizer's culture down to size: "Shakespeare is not an overbearing presence in *Ulysses* because the context is always placing him in a pattern of popularization, quotation, insult, biographical extravagance and humour."[11]

Whose Europe? Whose Shakespeare?

As the intertextual games of *Ulysses* get reinterpreted as postcolonial strategies, Joyce's relation to European models is also seen in a new light, that is, mostly as a critique of the insularity of the English colonizer's culture. Joyce's Europhilia, in other words, becomes the flip side of the Anglophobia that makes him want to explode the English novel—a form that some Irish critics deride as intensely parochial and out of touch with the European mainstream.[12] Joyce, in this reading, was concerned to free Irish literature from its English limitations and connect it with a European culture where Ireland would have pride of place. Joyce's writings and career contain much that would confirm this view. Joyce left Ireland to wander over mainland Europe, but the English metropolis seems never to have been an option for him. Most of the literary models he championed were continental writers, so that his canon implicitly bypasses England. When Joyce criticized the Abbey Theatre for its incipient parochialism, he advocated Ibsen as a correcting influence that would put Irish drama on the world map. Joyce's early writings on drama also testify to his bias, for if Ibsen's plays embody his dramatic ideals, Shakespeare falls short of them: "it was the power of the Shakespearean clique that dealt the deathblow to the already dying drama. Shakespeare was, before all, a literary artist"; for Joyce, Shakespeare was not drama, but rather "literature in dialogue."[13] Whether Joyce's use of *Hamlet* in *Ulysses* is informed by a similar critique, however, is quite another matter.

Ulysses is certainly a product of Joyce's lasting obsession with Ireland during his continental exile. The novel is also rife with signs of Joyce's European erudition, and it placed the Irishman Joyce at the forefront of European modernist aesthetics. The postcolonial reading of *Ulysses* thus insists that the novel represents the homecoming of Ireland into a European tradition from which it had been severed by English oppression: Joyce is seen as a leading representative of those "Irish thinkers" who, in order to escape from the provincialism of English traditions, "turned to Europe, and beyond, as they had done so often in previous centuries." They thus rediscovered the "European dimension of Gaelic culture."[14] For Seamus Deane, Joyce places Stephen's aspirations in "a wide European context which, by virtue of its Catholic overtones, and by virtue of its literary tradition, is uniform with the young man's experience."[15] In this light, Joyce's own admiration for the European novel can be seen as part of an Irish postcolonial (and sectarian) project, since his model Flaubert, one critic informs us, "was also a Catholic."[16] This European tradition, however, is a highly debatable construct: Irish postcolonial criticism actually recycles a high-modernist definition of the "mind of Europe" in which classical antiquity, medieval philosophy, and (Catholic) Christianity are central.

This version of Europe had indeed been the shibboleth of Eliot's and Pound's brand of modernism. It has become usual to consider Eliot's famous essay *"Ulysses,* Order and Myth" as a seminal intervention that depoliticized Joyce as it co-opted him into the canon of a cosmopolitan modernism. This "elevation of an Irish-Catholic colonial writer like Joyce into the pantheon of the Modernist greats" is now considered as "rather insidious,"[17] but to blame Eliot for initiating a formalist neglect of Joyce's politics is rather disingenuous. In fact, Eliot's reading of Joyce was also political: it fitted in all too well with his own relentless promotion of a European literature that was classical, Latinate, and Catholic, and with his wish to subvert the English traditions of Northern, Protestant, and Romantic literature—an agenda that may be uncomfortably close to that of current postcolonial writing on Joyce. That criticism's insistence on the backwardness and parochialism of the English novel is of a piece with Eliot's observation that "the novel is a form which will no longer serve." Eliot's comments on Joyce did not just concentrate on the use of myth to control the chaos of contemporary history: it also insisted on the classical nature of Joyce's project. For Eliot, "doing the best one can with the material at hand" was one way of "being classical," and Joyce did precisely this by drawing parallels between Ireland and Greek antiquity. Eliot's focus on the Homeric parallels in *Ulysses* was, implicitly at least, a statement on what he saw as Joyce's significance in the European canon: since "the blood-stream of European literature is Latin and Greek," Joyce's use of the *Odyssey* obviously needed to be foregrounded.[18]

Eliot, by contrast, made no mention of Joyce's Shakespearean allusions. From a purely structural point of view, Shakespeare was a less noticeable part of the "scaffolding" that Joyce had used to build the chapters of *Ulysses,* which goes some way toward explaining Eliot's silence on that point. But Eliot's decision not to draw attention to the pervasive presence of allusions to Shakespeare, and to *Hamlet* in particular, may also be in keeping with his view of Shakespeare's place within European traditions. According to Eliot, Shakespeare, for all his undoubted importance, was not really a classic.[19] Most infamously, Eliot dismissed *Hamlet* as an "artistic failure," the impact of which could only be explained by a Romantic (and, implicitly, Germanic) propensity to identify with its protagonist, as was evidenced by Coleridge and Goethe.[20] Read in this light, Prufrock's outburst "No, I am not Prince Hamlet" is not just an example of modernist antiheroics: it also signals Eliot's desire to extricate himself from a late Romantic fascination with Shakespeare, mediated by Eliot's early Anglophile model Laforgue and the latter's infatuation with German transcendentalism.[21] Eliot's Shakespeare criticism often betrays a similar cultural agenda: although he declared that "Dante and Shakespeare divide the modern world between them," he insisted that Dante was a better model and "safer to follow," since Dante's language was still the product of a unified (and Latinate) European culture. And if *Hamlet* was an artistic failure, Shakespeare's "most assured artistic success" was "*Coriolanus* . . . with *Antony and Cleopatra*": Eliot's preference for Shakespeare's Roman plays is often noticeable in his discussions of the Bard, *Titus Andronicus* being the only (and unsurprising) exception.[22] *The Waste Land*, finally, only used echoes from the plays as part of a "Shakespeherian Rag" floating among the debris of Western culture.[23] If order was to be imposed on that chaos, it would have to come from other and, for Eliot, more orthodox sources of cultural authority than Shakespeare's works.

England and English culture (and indeed much of Shakespeare) were largely marginal to the European mind that Eliot tried to define: only if it followed the precepts of Eliotic modernism would English literature be able to overcome its Protestant, Anglo-Saxon insularity and join a European mainstream that was mostly Greek, Latin, and Catholic—and, in some cases, Irish. This reactionary version of European culture lives on in different guises; the rhetoric of Joyce criticism is one of them. Like the ultranationalist citizen in *Ulysses,* the strain of Joyce scholarship that insists on Joyce's subversion of Shakespeare effectively excludes England from Europe:

> —The European family, says J.J. . . .
> —They're not European, says the citizen. I was in Europe with Kevin Egan of Paris. You wouldn't see a trace of them or their language anywhere in Europe except in a *cabinet d'aisance.* (421)

And yet, Joyce's own contribution to the definition of that European culture was actually as ambiguous as it was crucial. His scholastic cast of mind and his fascination with the structuring power of Catholic theology were clearly appreciated by Eliot, even as Stephen's *Non Serviam* in *Portrait of the Artist as a Young Man* indicated the gulf between both modernist writers. Stephen may have lost his Catholic faith, but he nevertheless pays it the compliment of calling it "an absurdity which is logical and coherent," in the same way that Eliot commended Dante for his attachment to a "coherent traditional system of dogma and morals like the Catholic: it stands apart, for understanding and assent, even without belief, from the single individual who propounds it."[24] Joyce's supposed role in the development of a mythical method based on parallels between contemporary reality and classical texts further ensured that his work became central to the European modernist tradition of which Eliot was the self-styled spokesman. *Ulysses* remains its defining moment; in Eliot's famous words, it is "the book to which we are all indebted and from which none of us can escape."[25] At the same time, Joyce's affinities with this European modernism are literally superficial: his apparent commitment to the formal principles of modernist aesthetics is indeed matched by his rejection of the ideologies inherent in classical order and Catholicism.

Ulysses also testifies to this tension in Joyce's work; and the tension can be traced in his use of intertexts. Although some Dantean allusions can be found in *Ulysses,* Shakespeare is by far the bigger presence. Joyce seems to have disagreed with Eliot about the respective merits of Shakespeare and Dante. When asked which book he would take with him to a desert island, Joyce answered, "I should hesitate between Dante and Shakespeare, but not for long. The Englishman is richer and would get my vote."[26] Homer's *Odyssey,* of course, remains the most conspicuous intertext of *Ulysses:* Eliot focused on it in his influential reading, and the diagram Joyce gave to Stuart Gilbert established it as the main structuring principle of the novel. Yet *Ulysses* is also a joke at the expense of Celtic revivalists who likened Ireland to ancient Greece, and who are explicitly ridiculed at the end of the "Scylla and Charibdis" chapter (277–78).[27] *Ulysses* also deflates the impersonal heroism of Homer's epic. If it gives *Ulysses* its form, European antiquity is also derided by the contents of Joyce's novel. *Hamlet,* by contrast, is not openly touted as a model for *Ulysses,* but any reading of the text makes clear that the pattern of allusions to Shakespeare's tragedy is quite extensive—indeed, even postcolonial critics sometimes inadvertently suggest that it may be more crucial than Homer for an understanding of the novel.[28] This pervasive presence greatly complicates any claim that Joyce is inserting himself in a European tradition where English culture is marginal. Joyce's use of Shakespeare in *Ulysses* actually blurs any easy distinction between English and European cultures, or between postcolonial parody and the modernist conjuring of classical authority. Shakespeare, in other words, simply proves too large to be assigned a single role in the European cultural politics of modernism.

In one respect, Joyce is indulging in an extended, subversive romp through Shakespeare's *Hamlet.* Stephen's biographical reading of the play, which he expounds in a deadpan manner to his assorted companions, reads like a brilliant spoof that casts Shakespeare as the ghost, ordering his (dead) son Haml/net to avenge his cuckold father: Ann Hathaway, who has been fooling around with Shakespeare's brothers, is the adulterous figure behind Gertrude (235–80). At times, the parody takes on a clear political dimension and appears to denounce Shakespeare's complicity with English colonial violence: "Not for nothing was he a butcher's son wielding the sledded poleaxe and spitting in his palm . . . Khaki Hamlets don't hesitate to shoot" (239–40).

On the other hand, Stephen's outlandish theories are not just typical of postcolonial subversiveness. They are also indebted to a late-Victorian tradition in which the Shakespeare canon was read—with various degrees of seriousness—in the light of biographical speculation about the author. This means that Joyce's relation to contemporary English culture is less simple than postcolonial readings suggest, especially since he was increasingly part of an Anglophone (and not just Irish) diaspora on the Continent.[29] Moreover, it can be argued that Joyce's wide-ranging familiarity with Shakespeare criticism has implications for the so-called European dimension of *Ulysses* as well. In Trieste, Joyce had lectured on Shakespeare to European audiences, and would probably have tried to establish connections with European literature. While preparing those lectures, Joyce read the work of the Danish critic Georg Brandes.[30] Stephen's biographical method owes something to Brandes, who insisted on the link between Shakespeare's art and the Bard's life. But another key aspect of Brandes's influence is that the Danish writer did much to analyze Shakespeare in the context of European Renaissance humanism. Thus, in *Ulysses*, Shakespeare is not simply an English colonizer or, as Mr Deasy reminds Stephen, "a poet but an Englishman too" (37). Shakespeare was also a key figure in European cultural exchanges: he was "made in Germany . . . as the champion French polisher of Italian scandals" (263).

Such references still point to a humorous treatment of Shakespeare and of the biographical speculation that surrounded his work. Through Stephen, Joyce may parody Brandes as much as he uses him.[31] But at the same time, the insistence on Shakespeare as an individual allows Joyce to counterbalance and disrupt the novel's impersonality—the very aspect that the modernist, classical reading of *Ulysses* emphasized through its focus on Homeric, transindividual patterns. *Ulysses* itself can also be read as a plea for the importance of the individual life in the face of those same transpersonal forces. *Ulysses*—as its very title indicates—is partly about cutting Homeric epics down to the human size of their individual heroes. Seen in this light, Shakespeare's work, and *Hamlet* in particular, acquire a more exemplary role: they provide modern figures with which characters can identify or be identified, with various degrees of extravagance to be sure, but with less violence than is done to Homer. Indeed, while parallels with the *Odyssey* have to be detected by readers, Joyce's characters can actually be aware of their resemblance to Shakespeare and his tragic hero. And if the author's presence in Shakespeare's plays is a question that will not go away, the same is true of *Ulysses*. Joyce's modernist masterpiece is also a record of his own personal obsessions, including the kind of marital jealousy that is projected onto *Hamlet*. As Richard Ellmann noted, "in middle life Joyce celebrated not the 'lofty impersonal power' of the artist, but the intimate tie between work and life": if Stephen does not believe his own biographical reading of *Hamlet*, there are indications that Joyce took biographical analyses of the Shakespeare canon more seriously than his own protagonist.[32]

Canonical Identities: Joyce's Bloom, Bloom's Shakespeare, Shakespeare's Europe

Stephen may poke fun at *Hamlet,* but his own erratic behavior clearly suggests that he also reads himself into the Danish prince. Like Hamlet, Stephen is dressed in mourning black throughout the novel, as is Joyce's other protagonist Leopold Bloom.[33] If Stephen's remarks on *Hamlet* in the "Scylla and Charibdis" chapter have provided much ammunition for a postcolonial reading of Joyce's relation to Shakespeare, the Shakespearean dimension of Bloom reminds us that the Bard is put to many more uses in *Ulysses.* Joyce's homme moyen sensuel is not as mighty an intellect as Dedalus junior: his library is scantier and definitely less highbrow, but it does contain "Shakespeare's *Works* (dark crimson morocco, gold-tooled)" (832). Far from attacking Shakespeare (who, like him, lost a young son, and is painted as a cuckold), Bloom sees Shakespeare's face as "sympathetic," "human," and "intelligent" (120). When Stephen and Bloom make their way back home together, Bloom defers to Stephen's superior knowledge of Shakespeare, but Stephen does not bother to contradict Bloom when the latter refers to Shakespeare as "our national poet" (733). Even though one may be tempted to adjudicate between both characters' responses to Shakespeare, it is also worth remembering that when Bloom and Stephen stare together into a mirror (the "mirror up to nature") in the "Circe" episode, *"the face of William Shakespeare, beardless, appears there, rigid in facial paralysis, crowned by the reflection of the reindeer antlered hatrack in the hall"* (671). This synthesis of Joyce's two protagonists is itself humorous rather than grandly Shakespearean, but the vision of an antlered Shakespeare also leads back to the haunting, eminently personal theme of marital jealousy that is central to Joyce's novel and to the reading of *Hamlet* it proposes.

My aim is not to argue that Shakespeare only functions in *Ulysses* as the chief source of a humanist individualism that would be Joyce's sole or central message. Such a reading would be possible, as was shown by the nemesis of Eliotic modernism, Harold Bloom. Focusing on the character of Leopold Bloom ("Poldy," in whom he discerns a "Shakespearean inwardness") instead of the "more or less Dantesque Stephen," the author of *The Western Canon* makes out a case for a heterodox Joyce who creates Shakespeare in the image of his ultimate antihero: a "secular" Shakespeare, "replacing Scripture with the writings of common humanity."[34] Harold Bloom's reading is also the polar opposite of postcolonial interpretations that insist on Irish resentment of the English canon. In his own splendid Bardolatry, he of course neglects the elements of parody and subversion that are undeniably present in *Ulysses,* and that sometimes imply a form of politically motivated iconoclasm on the part of Stephen Dedalus. Yet some of those very parodies also place Shakespeare firmly in a European tradition of humanist individualism that is at odds with the "mind of Europe" defined by other modernists, and more recently by Irish postcolonial criticism. It may well be that in *Ulysses,* Joyce more than ever defined himself and his art as Irish and European (although the author of *The Western Canon* might suggest that even the second term is too parochial). But Joyce also insists that Shakespeare, and the cultures that Shakespeare helped to define, are part of that Europe—warts and all. Eliotic and postcolonial readings of Joyce have worked hard to exclude English legacies from European culture, but excluding Shakespeare remains an insuperable challenge. Other Anglophobes have attempted to do just this: "Charles De Gaulle was asked in an interview once: 'Are there three or four authors who are Europe to you?' He said immediately, without hesitating, 'Of course, Dante, Goethe, Chateaubriand.' The astonished interviewer said: 'What, Monsieur? No Shakespeare?' And the icy smile came: 'You asked me about Europe.'"[35] George Steiner, another influential scholar of modernism, quotes this anecdote as a revealing comment on what constitutes European cultural identity. The main contention of this essay, however, has been that Joyce, the greatest and most European novelist Ireland has produced, would have begged to differ with his modernist readers, postcolonial critics, and Charles de Gaulle about Shakespeare's importance to European culture.

Notes

1. T. S. Eliot, *"Ulysses,* Order and Myth," in *Selected Prose of T. S. Eliot,* ed. Frank Kermode (New York: Farrar, Straus and Giroux, 1975), 175–79.

2. See, for instance, William Schutte's *Joyce and Shakespeare: A Study in the Meaning of "Ulysses"* (New York: Yale University Press, 1957), and Richard Ellmann's *The Consciousness of Joyce* (London: Faber and Faber, 1977), where Ellmann examines complementarities between Joyce's Homeric and Shakespearean intertexts.

3. See Emer Nolan, *Joyce and Nationalism* (London: Routledge, 1995), and Seamus Deane's "Joyce and Nationalism," in his *Celtic Revivals* (London: Faber and Faber, 1985), 92–107.

4. *The Essential James Joyce,* ed. Harry Levin (London: Grafton, 1977), 365.

5. James Joyce, *Ulysses* (London: Penguin, 1992), 263. Hereafter cited parenthetically in the text.

6. See Mark Thornton Burnett and Ramona Wray, eds., *Shakespeare and Ireland* (London: Macmillan, 1997), and more particularly David J. Baker's "Where is Ireland in *The Tempest?*" 68–88. For Yeats's uses of Shakespeare, see Declan Kiberd, *Inventing Ireland* (London: Vintage, 1996), 269 and 274.

7. In his introduction to *Ulysses*, Declan Kiberd sees Stephen's reference to "the note of banishment" as an attempt to construct a "Celtic Shakespeare" (lxxi), but in *Inventing Ireland* Kiberd appears to interpret it as an allusion to Stephen's own exile (349). Len Platt links Stephen's theory to an Irish Catholic sense of dispossession at the hands of Anglo-Ireland; see his *Joyce and the Anglo-Irish* (Amsterdam: Rodopi, 1998), 84.

8. Seamus Deane, *Heroic Styles* (Derry: Field Day, 1984), 10.

9. Vincent Cheng, *Joyce, Race, and Empire* (Cambridge: Cambridge University Press, 1995), 14; Len Platt, *Joyce and the Anglo-Irish*, 82.

10. Richard Helgerson, *Forms of Nationhood: The Elizabethan Writing of England* (Chicago: Chicago University Press, 1992), 215–45. Conversely, it is true that *Hamlet* has sometimes been read in terms of Bakhtinian carnival, but such readings focus on elements of parody, punning, and metatheater in the play, and say little about popular energies. See Phyllis Grofain, "Towards a Theory of Play and the Carnivalesque in *Hamlet*," in *Shakespeare and Carnival: After Bakhtin*, ed. Ronald Knowles (London: Macmillan, 1998), 152–76.

11. Deane, *Celtic Revivals*, 88.

12. Deane writes that "the innate provincialism of the English novel deprived it of a consciousness of itself as part of a greater European culture" (*Celtic Revivals*, 76–77).

13. James Joyce, *The Critical Writings*, ed. Ellsworth Mason and Richard Ellmann (New York: Viking Press, 1959), 39.

14. Kiberd, *Inventing Ireland*, 161 and 158.

15. Deane, *Celtic Revivals*, 81. See also his broader discussion of the European novel (76–83). Deane alludes to Thomas Mann's attachment to a "European culture which is based on classical antiquity and Christianity" (78).

16. Platt, *Joyce and the Anglo-Irish*, 33.

17. Cheng, *Joyce, Race, and Empire*, 2. Len Platt also writes that Eliot's "remark about Joyce using myth to impose aesthetic order on the chaos of contemporary reality has influenced formalist accounts of Homeric correspondence in *Ulysses*" (*Joyce and the Anglo-Irish*, 103).

18. *Selected Prose of T. S. Eliot*, 177 and 130.

19. See his essay "What is a Classic," in *Selected Prose of T. S. Eliot*, 115–30.

20. "Hamlet," in *Selected Prose of T. S. Eliot*, 45–49.

21. T. S. Eliot, *Collected Poems, 1909–1962* (London: Faber, 1974), 17. For an analysis of Eliot's critique of Laforgue's transcendental leanings, see Ron Schuchard, *Eliot's Dark Angel* (Oxford: Oxford University Press, 1999), 84–85.

22. *Selected Prose of T. S. Eliot*, 227, 217, 230, 208–9, 47.

23. T. S. Eliot, *Collected Poems*, 67. What Seamus Deane sees as Joyce's strategy of "popularization, quotation, insult" of the Shakespearean canon (see above) is much in evidence in *The Waste Land*.

24. *The Essential James Joyce*, 358; *Selected Prose of T. S. Eliot*, 222.

25. *Selected Prose of T. S. Eliot*, 175.

26. Quoted by Frank Budgen in *James Joyce and the Making of "Ulysses"* (Oxford: Oxford University Press, 1972), 184.

27. Some postcolonial critics are also alert to this, particularly Platt in *Joyce and the Anglo-Irish*, 99–127.

28. See Deane, *Celtic Revivals*, 104.

29. See Richard Brown, "'Shakespeare Explained': James Joyce's Shakespeare," in *Shakespeare and Ireland*, 91–113.

30. Unfortunately, the texts of Joyce's lectures have not survived. But for a discussion of their significance and impact, see Brown, "'Shakespeare Explained': James Joyce's Shakespeare," 97–99. For Joyce's reading of Brandes, see Schutte, *Joyce and Shakespeare*, 157.

31. For suggestions of a parody of Brandes in Stephen's theories, see Colin MacCabe, "The Voice of Esau," in *James Joyce: New Perspectives*, ed. Colin MacCabe (Brighton: Harvester Press, 1982), 115.

32. Ellmann, *The Consciousness of Joyce*, 48.

33. This was noted by Alexander Welsh in *Hamlet in his Modern Guises* (Princeton: Princeton University Press, 2001), 167.

34. Harold Bloom, *The Western Canon* (New York: Riverhead, 1994), 389, 388, 385.

35. Quoted by George Steiner in "Culture, the Price You Pay," in *States of Mind: Dialogues with Contemporary Thinkers*, ed. Richard Kearney (New York: New York University Press, 1995), 82.

II
Politics and/on the Stage

Introduction
Dennis Kennedy

ALL THEATER TOUCHES ON POLITICS ON SOME LEVEL, IF ONLY because it takes place in groups and deals with human affairs. In Shakespeare, with so many of the texts representing political crisis, it is difficult to ignore the relationship of character to matters of state or the intrusions of power in ordinary life; the polis may not be in the foreground at every production of *As You Like It* but is usually somewhere about, in another part of the forest. This has been explicitly the case in continental Europe, where one of the most notable marks of Shakespeare production has been an overt concern with the contemporary consequence the plays can be made to bear, what Robert Weimann a generation ago called the difference between "past significance and present meaning."[1] While the British tradition has often obscured (and sometimes tried to deny) the politics of and in performance, the opposite tended to be the case abroad. From the time of his first major exportation in the later eighteenth century, Shakespeare in Europe has frequently been invested with social awareness. This is not to say that the work has always been yoked to the oxen of government or driven blindly into partisan fields, but it is reasonable to conclude that the harsh upheavals of the modern age on the Continent offered opportunities for European Shakespeare to be more readily engaged with the ideological issues.

The essays in this section, despite their varied topics and intellectual interests, tend to suggest that continental history created a Shakespeare considerably different from that seen in his homeland. Clara Calvo deals with the relationship between the theater and the Napoleonic occupation of Spain, drawing out the cultural politics of Shakespeare's introduction and success in Madrid, Barcelona, and Seville in the early nineteenth century. Isabelle Schwarz-Gastine moves us to the twentieth century with two French productions of *Coriolanus*, the notorious first one at the Comédie-Française prompting conflicts over a Fascist interpretation of the text. That was in 1933, the year Hitler was made chancellor of Germany, when it would have been difficult to ignore politics in public discussion in France, especially with Shakespeare's most insistently political play. Yet a few months before, William Bridges-Adams had staged *Coriolanus* at the Shakespeare Memorial Theatre in Stratford for the dramatist's birthday, deliberately avoiding political overtones. Aware of the potential for partisan assertion, the director reacted as a "custodian of eternal values," thinking it "shockingly improper" when an artist "turns his stage into a platform and takes sides in the temporal issues that divide us."[2] Moving to the period of the war itself, Zoltán Márkus treats the relationship between performance and ideology in the extremity of discord, as he considers the most socially sensitive of the plays, *The Merchant of Venice,* in productions in London, Berlin, and Budapest from 1940 to 1942.

After the defeat of Fascism, the desire for political and social stability was frustrated by the tensions of the Cold War in a divided Europe. Though these tensions were frequently exaggerated by the two superpowers for domestic reasons, the threat of mutual assured destruction was real enough to have a significant effect on many aspects of cultural production. Indeed, the greatest influence on Shakespeare performance in those years, Jan Kott's *Shakespeare Our Contemporary,* published and translated in the early 1960s, was very much about the failure of ideology, prompted by the domination of Eastern Europe by the Soviet Union, its counterinsurgent invasion of Hungary in 1956, and the general effect of the Stalinist regime in Poland. Veronika Schandl's essay on *Measure for Measure* in Hungary shows how significant the division of Europe remained with regard to Shakespeare well into the 1980s in the Eastern bloc. We might think of other productions that commented on the controlled politics of the area, such as the Moscow *Hamlet*s by Nikolai Okhlopkov (1953) and Yuri Lyubimov (1971). But the anxiety of the age could be seen west of the divide as well, as in the Brechtian versions of the history plays presented by Roger Planchon in Lyon (*Henry IV,* 1957) and even by Peter Hall in Stratford (*The Wars of the Roses,* 1963–64). The decades in the middle of the Cold War saw a vast rise in public funding for the arts on both sides of the Iron Curtain, a cultural arms race born out of geopolitics that considerably augmented the number and availability of Shakespeare performances.

Lawrence Guntner's essay on Brecht and Heiner Müller shows some of the ways in which this played out in the German Democratic Republic, the hottest nation in the Cold War. Its two great playwright-directors, both committed Socialists, nevertheless struggled with the retrograde policies of the Communist Party. Brecht knew that classic texts such as Shakespeare's were of value to the present only to the extent that the present could redefine them. "I think we can change Shakespeare if we can change him," he famously said—that is, if we have the skill for the job.[3] Brecht's question was always the same: does Shakespeare contain something we can adapt with conviction? Müller went a step further, seeing in Shakespeare not a "contemporary" in Kott's terms, which would be an impossible denial of the force of history, but rather material for radical reworking that dislocated the text. In Müller's view *Hamlet* no longer has value for us, yet we refuse to let it go; we are left trying to make sense out of the wreck of European civilization it helped form. Guntner quotes one of Müller's most revealing statements: "A dictatorship is more colorful than a democracy for a dramatist. Shakespeare is unthinkable in a democracy." Thus Shakespeare continues to have value because, following a Marxist method, his plays can reveal (or can be made to reveal) the hidden struggles of power. The more hidden those struggles are, Müller implied, the more use we have for Shakespeare.

But political approaches to the plays need not concern governmental agency or hegemonic dominance or what Guntner calls "a vision of history as performance." Nancy Isenberg reminds us how sexual politics were increasingly important in the era with her look at John Cranko's ballet version of *The Taming of the Shrew*, first seen in Stuttgart in 1969. Cranko, a South African who worked throughout Europe, also choreographed Prokofiev's *Romeo and Juliet* and a version of *The Tempest* (*Quatre images*, music by Debussy). His work was normally uninterested in the political, yet faced with the gender difficulties in *The Shrew* he managed to create a female role of power and authority that has been attractive to a number of ballet companies around the world.

This departure from direct politics is a reminder that the relationship of Shakespeare to Europe began to change significantly around the end of the 1970s, as the West moved beyond the worst fears of the Cold War and became more concerned with personal satisfaction, global tourism, and an accompanying interculturalism. The three productions by Ariane Mnouchkine in Paris in the early 1980s were among the main signs of change, overtly denying Kottian contemporary relevance in Shakespeare and relying instead on distance and an aesthetic borrowed from Asian theatrical forms. The growing interest in Shakespeare in Japan, China, and Ibero-America has stretched the social and political meanings of the plays further, especially when productions from far away have been transported back to Britain. Wilhelm Hortmann's essay on "hybridization" in recent German performance, which concludes this section, shows how travel, blending, and self-conscious appropriation of history, popular culture, and foreign manners have challenged the traditional postwar view of the place of politics in the theater. As usual, the fact that Shakespeare's work can manage such diverse and extreme construal says more about us, and our struggles with the terrifying consequences of modernity, than it says about that long-dead playwright.

Notes

1. Robert Weimann, "Shakespeare on the Modern Stage: Past Significance and Present Meaning," *Shakespeare Survey* 20 (1967): 113–20.

2. William Bridges-Adams, *Looking at a Play* (London: Phoenix House, 1947), 32. See my *Looking at Shakespeare,* 2nd ed. (Cambridge: Cambridge University Press, 2001), 126–27.

3. Ich denke, wir können Shakespeare ändern, wenn wir ihn ändern können, Bertolt Brecht, "Die Dialektik auf dem Theater," in *Gesammelte Werke* (Frankfurt am Main: Suhrkamp, 1967), xvi: 879; my translation.

Shakespeare, Napoleon, and Juan de Grimaldi: Cultural Politics and French Troops in Spain

Clara Calvo

THE ROLE PLAYED BY SHAKESPEARE IN THE CULTURAL INFLUENCE France exerted on Spain from the eighteenth century till long after the War of Independence runs deep, and its map has not been fully drawn. It is well known that Shakespeare's plays first reached the Spanish stage through translations of French adaptations by Jean-François Ducis (1733–1816) and that the first great success of a Shakespeare play on Spanish soil—*Otelo,* in 1802—was due to the influence of French acting and the Parisian theatrical world on Isidoro Máiquez, a Spanish actor who owed his successful career a good deal to his training with the well-known French actor François-Joseph Talma in Paris.[1] Most critical commentary on Shakespeare by Spanish men of letters during the late eighteenth and early nineteenth centuries reproduced neoclassical objections to Shakespearean drama disseminated by French authors since Voltaire. Clearly, in its beginnings, translation, performance, and criticism of Shakespeare in Spain seems little more than an echo of the French cultural presence. In this paper I intend to revisit the case and complete the map of cultural influences by considering the appearance of Shakespeare as a cultural icon and translated author in Spain in contexts specifically defined by the arrival of French armies in time of war.[2]

SHAKESPEARE AND NAPOLEON IN SPAIN

Shakespeare arrived in Spain partly with the aid of Napoleon. *Hamlet* (1772), *Othello* (1802), *Romeo and Juliet* (1803), and *Macbeth* (1803) had preceded him on the Spanish stage in the shape of translations of French adaptations by Ducis, but Shakespeare—as playwright and dramatic character—entered Spain in 1810, when the French troops which had occupied Barcelona celebrated Napoleon's birthday on August 15 by reopening the theaters. Barcelona had been occupied by Napoleon's army on February 13, 1808, and the theaters had been closed for two years until Napoleon was honored in 1810 with a production for which the choice fell on Alexandre Duval's *La pièce à l'étude, ou Shakespeare amoureux*.[3] After this day, the theaters in Barcelona remained in business. A French company put on plays from August 15, 1810, till June 13, 1811, all of them plays in French by French authors,[4] including a performance of Ducis's adaptation of Shakespeare's *Othello* in 1811 (see appendix 1 at the end of this essay). Although French troops stayed in Barcelona until May 1814, a Spanish company began to perform plays in Spanish after June 1811.

During the French occupation of Barcelona, theatrical performances were intended to achieve two wartime aims: entertaining the inactive Napoleonic troops garrisoned in the city and reasserting French national identity by means of French culture. Drama is thus presented as an *agent civilisateur:* the invaders bring culture, social éclat, and the air of peacetime activity to a part of Spain that effectively belonged to the Napoleonic empire after the occupation. The exact reasons that led the French authorities to choose a play featuring Shakespeare as hero to attain these strategic and propagandistic objectives in the midst of the Spanish War of Independence (1808–14) are difficult to pin down. Perhaps they simply chose a play that was available in the theatrical company's repertory or they wished to provide the troops with a play that had already been a success in Paris and whose title role had been taken by Talma, the greatest French actor of his age, in 1804.[5] In any case, for the study of the European reception of Shakespeare, the choice of this play to honor Napoleon's birthday shows that Shakespeare the icon, and not simply Shakespeare the body of dramatic works, was easily appropriated with a political and ideological motive in the very early stages of Shakespearean reception in a European country.

Having arrived in Spain as the main character of a play with Napoleon's army, Shakespeare returned to Spanish theaters, this time to Madrid, as a result of a second French invasion of Spain less than fifteen years later. In 1823, the 100,000 Sons of St. Louis, a French army under the command of the Duke of Angoulême, came in aid of King Ferdinand VII, with the backing of King Louis XVIII and the Holy Alliance, to put an end to three years of revolutionary experiment and constitutional government initiated in 1820 by Rafael de Riego and other Spanish liberal army officers. One of the French soldiers who came along with this repressive force decided to stay in Madrid and revitalize its decaying stage. Juan de Grimaldi (Jean-Marie Grimaldi, 1796–1872) took under his charge the two most important Madrid playhouses, the Príncipe and the Cruz. As impresario, stage director, and playwright, he went on to exert a considerable influence on Spanish cultural and theatrical life between 1823 and 1836.[6] Initially, his purpose when taking over the Príncipe was to make a profit providing Italian opera and plays in French for both the foreign army and the Spanish French-speaking elite,[7] but he soon put together a company of Spanish actors who began to perform plays in Spanish early in 1824. As the director of the most important company of actors in Madrid, he had a say in what plays were staged, and he was "concerned with the repertory" because he saw that "the theatrical repertory was not being enriched with new plays fast enough to meet the demands of a daily (and on holidays, twice daily) performance schedule."[8] Grimaldi's influence, however, reached further, as he became a friend and mentor to a whole generation of Spanish writers, translators, and "refundidores" (i.e., those who adapted classical drama and foreign plays), who met at the Príncipe coffee shop, known as the "Parnasillo," or "little Parnassus." He is known to have encouraged two young writers, Bretón de los Herreros and Ventura de la Vega, to write for the stage. They soon became the two most important Spanish playwrights in the last ten years of Ferdinand VII's reign. Bretón, Vega, and Grimaldi were close enough to write a political play in collaboration in 1835. It must have been at Grimaldi's suggestion that Ventura de la Vega translated Duval's play into *Shakespeare enamorado* (Shakespeare in Love), a one-act comedy that was staged in the Príncipe theater in 1828.[9]

Keith Gregor has noted that this play "marked the baptism of Shakespeare as a much-loved character on the Spanish stage and that it did so long before the vast majority of Shakespeare's plays had been performed or even heard of."[10] The success of the Spanish translation of Duval's *Shakespeare amoureux* corroborates Péter Dávidházi's thesis that in some European countries Shakespeare the man preceded Shakespeare the body of texts.[11] The only Shakespearean plays performed before Shakespeare the man trod the stages of Madrid, Barcelona, and Seville were four of his tragedies: *Hamlet, Othello, Romeo and Juliet,* and *Macbeth.* One of these, *Othello,* became so well known to Spanish audiences thanks to the performances of Máiquez, that a play about a jealous playwright (Shakespeare) in love with a young actress (Carolina) who—like Shakespeare's Desdemona and Ducis's Edelmira—has a maid and confidante (Enriqueta), could easily prompt Spanish audiences to make a connection between life and œuvre. Besides, Duval and Ventura de la Vega present Shakespeare exactly at the point of his literary career when he is writing *Othello* and this "is presumably sufficient to explain his jealousy."[12] The success of this play containing an iconic representation of Shakespeare as an

Othello turned comedy hero is connected by Gregor, following Par, to a performance of *Hamlet* that may have taken place in Madrid three years earlier (the only one documented since 1772).[13] It seems, though, that this part of the map of Shakespearean reception in Spain requires a new shade: the influence of Grimaldi and contemporary French theatrical life. The source of Grimaldi's interest in having this play performed by the company he directed must be looked for in Talma's success in impersonating Shakespeare at the Comédie-Française and in the fact that it provided an excellent role for Grimaldi's wife Concepción Rodríguez, who, as leading actress in his company, took the role of Carolina, Shakespeare's sweetheart. Performances of *Shakespeare enamorado* were arranged in Barcelona (see appendix 1) precisely when Concepción Rodríguez was on tour there. *Shakespeare enamorado* was performed in Seville in 1830, when Grimaldi took his company there for part of the season and again in 1831, when Grimaldi's company was on a provincial tour.[14] Grimaldi's contribution to making Shakespeare known in Spain was therefore not restricted to Madrid, but extended to Barcelona and Seville.

The importance of *Shakespeare enamorado* stretches beyond the iconic representation of Shakespeare as the man of genius; it also serves to connect *Otelo* with the name of Shakespeare. Par notes that the first recorded performance of *Otelo* in Barcelona was advertised as a "modern" play, and also as a "comedy," with its title erroneously given as "Ofelo."[15] As Isabelle Schwartz-Gastine reminds us, Ducis had his adaptations of Shakespeare's plays "published under his own name—Shakespeare, the original source of his inspiration, was completely omitted from the books or theater bills. So the first theatrical contact with Shakespeare in France was under the name of the adaptor without any reference to Shakespeare."[16] It is not surprising, then, that in 1802 the advertisement of the first performance of *Otelo* in Barcelona assumed it was a translation of a new, contemporary French play.

The popularity of *Othello,* as a play and opera, accounts for the success Ventura de la Vega's translation of Duval's comedy enjoyed in Spain. *Othello* is the play Shakespeare is shown to be in the process of writing when the action of *Shakespeare enamorado* takes place. The year 1828 was exceptional for Shakespeare in Madrid—four plays of Shakespearean interest were performed, and three of them had to do, in one way or another, with *Othello. Otelo, Shakespeare enamorado,* and *El Caliche* (a parody of Ducis's *Othello* presented in the shape of the prototypical Spanish farce or *sainete*) show that Madrid was swept in 1828 by *Othellomania* (see appendix 2 at the end of this essay). Aguilar Piñal has observed that 1828 was also the year in which performances of Ducis's *Otelo* in Lacalle's translation began to alternate in Seville with Rossini's opera.[17]

OTHELLOMANIA

The reception of Shakespeare's tragedies in early nineteenth-century Spain offers a clear pattern of theatrical success and failure. *Othello* and *Romeo and Juliet* did well, whereas *Hamlet* and *Macbeth* failed to engage the attention of Spanish audiences. The fact that the former two tragedies appealed more to contemporary theatrical taste than the latter two can easily account for this diverging fate of Shakespearean tragedy in Romantic Spain. Through the French adaptations used by Spanish translators, early performances of *Othello* and *Romeo and Juliet* in Spain become sentimental and domestic tragedies, as they contain a tragic story with middle-class characters rather than aristocrats, crowned heads, and mythical heroes, and both deal with thwarted love, parental opposition, and social obstacles—features often present in the kind of sentimental drama then fashionable on Spanish stages. In spite of their unhappy endings, both plays also seem to recommend choosing a marriage partner on the basis of love and affection rather than filial obedience or class conventions. Since the political background of *Romeo and Juliet* is overshadowed by its love interest and Iago's role in *Othello* is minimized, these two Shakespearean tragedies could easily be made palatable to audiences with a taste for sentimental drama and dramatic genres such as the *comédie larmoyante,* the *tragédie domestique,* or the *tragédie bourgeoise*.[18]

Hamlet and *Macbeth* did not achieve the popularity *Othello* obtained in the period 1802–33. In 1806, 1808, 1813, 1816, 1819, 1829, 1831, and 1832, *Otelo* was regularly performed in Madrid, Barcelona, and Seville. The success of *Otelo* also reached the provinces. Lucio Izquierdo, who has charted dramatic activity in Valencia between 1800 and 1832, the year in which the theater Botiga de la Balda closed down, shows that *Otelo,* with fourteen performances, appears at the top of the list of plays most often produced in Valencia in this period.[19] *Hamlet,* by contrast, was staged in Madrid, if Par is right, only in 1825 and there is no record of the performance; the assumption that it was performed is based on the nature of the manuscript of the translation by José María Carnerero, one of the men of letters who collaborated with Grimaldi.[20] In the same time span, *Hamlet* is not staged at all in either Barcelona, Seville, or Valencia. *Macbeth,* in Lacalle's translation of Ducis's adaptation, was performed by Máiquez in Madrid in 1803 and 1804 only. A new translation by Dionisio Solís, commissioned by Máiquez and performed in 1812, seems to have been a failure.[21] In Barcelona and Seville, theater audiences could not attend a performance of *Macbeth* until 1830.

When the map of the Spanish reception of Shakespeare is drawn, the unstable political situation of Spain in the early years of the nineteenth century tends to be ignored, but it is, in fact, this political instability that partly accounts for the scant number of Shakespearean plays performed or translated: theatrical activity in Spain during the years between the Napoleonic occupation and the death of the absolutist monarch Ferdinand VII is, at times, uncertain and subject to the effects of war, invasion, revolution, absolutist reaction, and censorship. A complicating factor besides this political instability was the situation of financial and managerial precariousness, which burdened Madrid theaters at the time. Between the resignation of Máiquez (1819) and the arrival of Grimaldi (1823), impresarios in charge of the Príncipe and Cruz often went bankrupt and did not last more than one season in office, partly because of the ruinous demands upon the theaters to meet actors' retirement pensions and payments to several charitable institutions.[22] Given these constraints, it is hardly surprising that Shakespeare's introduction to the Spanish stage was slow, if compared to other European countries, including Russia, and that during the first three decades of the nineteenth century, only four Shakespearean tragedies were known to Spanish audiences. On reflection, it is actually remarkable that, in spite of war, liberal revolutions, reactionary governments, and the difficulties involved in running theaters, one Shakespearean play—*Othello*—was performed year after year in the major Spanish cities. Madrid, Barcelona, and Seville indeed had *Otelo* performed on their stages with considerable frequency between 1802 and 1833 (see appendix 1).[23]

The immediate effect upon theatrical activity of the French occupation of Spain in 1807 was the closure of the theaters.[24] This explains why, although there were performances of *Otelo* in Madrid every year from 1802 to 1806, there are no records of the play being performed in 1807. Theaters were reopened in 1808 and the French authorities tried to encourage performances; *Otelo* was performed again in January and March 1808, before the uprising of Madrid's population on May 2, 1808. There were no performances of *Otelo* in Madrid in the years 1809, 1810, and 1811, while the Napoleonic troops remained in the Spanish capital, perhaps because, as Par points out, "the French occupation wholly disrupted performances until 1812, in spite of the efforts of the invaders to promote them."[25] In 1812, Máiquez performed *Otelo* once, before Wellington and the Spanish generals forced Joseph Bonaparte to leave Madrid twice. Máiquez performed

Otelo again in 1813, three days after the Napoleonic troops and Napoleon's brother had left Madrid for good. Shakespeare had been used as a character to celebrate Napoleon's birthday in Barcelona in 1810; three years later he provided one of the plays performed to celebrate the victory over Napoleon's army.

Par attributes the absence of performances of *Otelo* in the years 1820 and 1821 to the retirement and death of Máiquez, but it may have also been the result of the instability of the revolutionary government during the Constitutional Triennium and the difficulties faced by the impresario who ran the two municipal theaters, the Príncipe and the Cruz.[26] From 1822 to 1833, *Otelo* was performed in Madrid almost yearly, with only three exceptions: the years 1827, 1829, and 1830. Since 1829 and 1830 were the years in which Grimaldi's *La pata de cabra* (The Goat's Leg) became "a smash hit," it is not surprising that *Otelo,* which had been performed by his company at the Príncipe since 1824, had to give way.[27]

Shakespeare and the Circulation of European Cultural Energy

The persistent presence of French culture in early nineteenth-century Spain surely played a crucial role in making Shakespeare known to Spanish audiences and turning *Otelo* into one of the most important repertory plays between 1802 and 1833. This seems to confirm Balz Engler's view that we need to redraw the conventional European map of Shakespearean reception, as France with its love of the rules can no longer be cast in the villain role of preventing Shakespeare's plays from being known, while Germany is no longer the sole champion of Shakespeare as a man of genius.[28] José Lambert has rightly noticed the paradox inherent in the role played by France as mediator in the dissemination of Shakespeare in Europe, a role that clashes with the traditions of French classicism: "It seems paradoxical that, if Germany gives itself a key role in the propagation of Shakespeare's genius, exploiting amongst other things its anti-French policy, France continues to function as mediator for the establishment of a new dramatic paradigm that often seems incompatible with French theatrical tradition."[29]

The recurrent presence of plays of Shakespearean interest on the stages of Madrid, Barcelona, and Seville in the first three decades of the nineteenth century, as shown in appendix 1, confirms French cultural hegemony in the Spanish reception of Shakespeare and highlights the interesting paradox that two French invasions in thirty years, with all the nationalistic and anti-French feelings they gave rise to, could not put an end to French influence on the Spanish stage.

French culture was not, however, the only foreign cultural influence that rendered Shakespeare a popular figure in Spain. The success of *Otelo* and *Romeo y Julieta* in Madrid is partly the result of the success of opera, as Rossini and Bellini helped to make these two Shakespearean tragedies well known in Spain. Even if the popularity of *Othello* partly followed from Máiquez's success as Otelo, and even if its title role became a kind of rite of passage for any Spanish male actor aspiring to fame, the fondness of Spanish audiences for Italian opera no doubt explains why these two Shakespearean plays became so popular in Spain. According to David Gies, Italian operas produced a "furor filarmónico" (philarmonic furore) in Madrid, and the period 1823–33 sees a struggle between drama and opera, with the latter prevailing.[30] Rossini was the favorite composer, but Bellini was also applauded. This perhaps helps to explain why *Othello* and *Romeo and Juliet* were the most successful Shakespeare plays in Romantic Spain. In less than a year, between Easter 1832 and Shrove Tuesday 1833, Rossini's *Otelo* was performed no fewer than five times.[31]

Aguilar Piñal records performances of *Romeo y Julieta o Los bandos de Verona* (Romeo and Juliet, or the Gangs of Verona) in Seville that he suspects may be either performances of Shakespeare's tragedy, adapted by Ducis and translated by Dionisio Solís, or performances of Bellini's opera.[32] Together with the alternation of Ducis's *Othello* and Rossini's opera from 1828, this shows that in Seville, as in Madrid and Barcelona, Shakespeare's works become known through translations of French adaptations as much as of Italian opera. The fact that an English author becomes known in Spain through the influence of the French stage (Talma and Ducis) and Italian opera (Rossini and Bellini) shows that early nineteenth-century Europe shared a common culture and that, at the time, Shakespeare was an integral part of the circulation of cultural energy, in spite of the disintegrating forces of war and emergent national identities and the clash of revolutionary and reactionary forces.

Appendix 1. Shakespearean Performances in Spain, 1802–33.

Year	Madrid	Barcelona	Seville	Valencia
1772	*Hamleto, rey de Dinamarca* (October 4–8)			
1802	*Otelo* (January 1–3, 5–7, 9–10, and 23–24; May 13–16; November 4–7)	*Otelo* (June 29–30; July 1; December 26–27)		
1803	*Otelo* (April 10–12; August 5); *Macbeth* (November 25–27, December 8) *Julia y Romeo* (December 9–13)			
1804	*Macbeth* (January 25) *Otelo* (May 18; December 10)			
1805	*Julieta y Romeo* (opera)			
1806	*Otelo* (November 12)	*Otelo* (August 16, 17, 19; September 11; November 12)	*Otelo* (October 27–29)	
1807			*Otelo* (February 8, November 15)	
1808	*Otelo* (January 23–25; March 27)	*Otelo* (January 7–8)	*Otelo* (February 1)	
1809				
1810		*Shakespeare amoureux* (August 15; September 18; November 8)	*Otelo* (September 20–21)	

(continues)

Appendix 1. Continued.

Year	Madrid	Barcelona	Seville	Valencia
1811		*Othello, ou le maure de Venise* (April 14)	*Otelo* (October 17; November 10)	
1812	*Otelo* (March 29); *Macbé* (May 31)	*Otelo* (November 6–7)		*Otelo* (4 performances)
1813	*Otelo* (May 30–31)	*Otelo* (February 2; May 24; July 5; October 10; December 9)	*Otelo* (April 19; December 27)	*Otelo* (4 performances)
1814	*Otelo* (April 26–29; July 22–24)		*Otelo* (September 1; November 27–28)	*Otelo* (3 performances)
1815		*Otelo* (January 21–22)	*Otelo* (May 25)	
1816	*Otelo* (May 4–6)	*Otelo* (February 16; April 20–21) *Julieta y Romeo* (November 18–20)	*Otelo* (April 20–21; August 11); *Romeo y Julieta* (October 21–22, 30)	
1817		*El Othelo* (July 23–24; December 18) *Julieta y Romeo* (September 29–30)	*Otelo* (May 15; June 4; December 26–27) *Romeo y Julieta* (January 5–6)	
1818	*Otelo* (July 29–31) *Romeo y Julieta* (December 14–16)			
1819	*Otelo* (May 28)	*El Otelo* (May 8)	*Otelo* (August 1)	
1820		*Otelo* (July 1–2) *Julieta y Romeo* (July 22–23)	*Otelo* (May 26–28)	

1821		*Julieta y Romeo* (January 20)	*Otelo* (January 20)	
1822	*Otelo* (January 16, 18, 27, and 31; April 17–19; May 18)	*Otelo* (October 7–8)	*Otelo* (August 8); *Romeo y Julieta* (4–5 February)	
1823	*Otelo* (June 15)	*Otelo* (May 26)		
1824	*Otelo* (Latorre, February 21–23, 27 and 29); *Otelo* (G. Luna, December 17–19)		*Otelo* (September 19; December 12)	
1825	*Otelo* (February 2; May 21–23) ?*Hámlet* (December)		*Otelo* (January 9; April 13; October 8–9, 13 and 20)	
1826	*Otelo* (September 3–5; December 10)	*Otelo* (October 30)		
1827			*Otelo* (August 15)	
1828	*Shakespeare enamorado* (April 18–21; July 7; October 14–17); *Otelo* (June 14–16; November 16) *Romeo y Julieta* (July 21–22); *El Caliche* (November 26–27; December 23)		*Otelo* (May 3; July 29 and 31; August 3, 7 and 10; September 5 and 11; October 12, 16 and 18; November 9 and 30); *Romeo y Julieta* (July 13)	
1829	*Shakespeare enamorado* (January 21; February 19–20)	*Otelo* (September 1; December 11)	*Otelo* (January 15; February 12; October 11; November 15)	

(continues)

Appendix 1. Continued.

Year	Madrid	Barcelona	Seville	Valencia
1830	*El Caliche* (December 27–29)	*El Macbé* (February 5–6); *Caliche de Malacena* (July 5–6) *Julieta y Romeo* (September 20)	*Shakespeare enamorado* (April 19–20; June 13; September 2) *Otelo* (May 2–3; June 29) *Macbet* (December 17 and 19)	
1831	*El Caliche* (January 1 and 3); *Otelo* (September 6–8 and 26)	*Shakespeare enamorado* (June 27–28; October 31) *Otelo* (July 25)	*Otelo* (February 6; September 9) *Shakespeare enamorado* (February 8) *Calichi* (July 7)	
1832	*Otelo* (February 28–29); *El Caliche* (December 7)	*Otelo* (July 21) *Shakespeare enamorado* (October 19)	*Otelo* (January 6)	The theater Botiga de la Balda closes down.
1833	*Otelo* (August 27–28)		*Otelo* (April 18)	

Appendix 2. Plays of Shakespearean Interest in Madrid in 1828.

Month	Days	Play	Leading Actors	Theater
April	18, 19, 20, 21	*Shakespeare enamorado*	Latorre y Rodríguez	Príncipe
June	14, 15, 16	*Otelo*	Latorre y Rodríguez	Príncipe
July	7	*Shakespeare enamorado*	Latorre y Rodríguez	Príncipe
July	21, 22	*Romeo y Julieta*	Latorre y Rodríguez	Príncipe
October	14, 15, 16, 17	*Shakespeare enamorado*	Latorre y Rodríguez	Príncipe
November	16	*Otelo*	Latorre y Rodríguez	Príncipe
November	26, 27	*El Caliche, o la parodia de Otelo*	Cubas, López, Campos, Virg y León	Cruz
December	23	*El Caliche, o la parodia de Otelo*	Cubas, López, Campos, Virg y León	Cruz

Notes

This article is part of the Research Project "La Presencia de Shakespeare en España en el Marco de la Recepción de Shakespeare en la Cultura Europea" (BFF 2002–02019) and FEDER, financed by the Spanish Ministry of Science and Technology.

1. Alberto Colao, *Máiquez, discípulo de Talma* (Cartagena: F. Gómez, 1980).
2. The only study of Shakespeare's iconic presence as a dramatic character in Spanish culture that I know of is Keith Gregor, "Shakespeare as a Character on the Spanish Stage: A Metaphysics of Bardic Presence," in *Four Hundred Years of Shakespeare in Europe,* ed. A. Luis Pujante and Ton Hoenselaars, 43–53 (Newark: University of Delaware Press, 2003). I owe my awareness of the importance of Shakespeare the man in Romantic Spain to this article.
3. Alfonso Par, in *Shakespeare en la literatura española: Juicios de los literatos españoles, con noticias curiosas sobre algunos de ellos y sobre sucesos literarios famosos,* 2 vols. (Madrid / Barcelona: Suárez / Balmes, 1935), 1:159, briefly mentions this performance, adding that it was staged again three months later, on November 8, so it must have had some amount of success. He also speaks disdainfully of it, since it was a one-act play, calling it a mere "paso de comedia," a one-act comedy; see Alfonso Par, *Representaciones shakespearianas en España,* 2 vols. (Madrid / Barcelona: Suárez / Balmes, 1936), 1:74.
4. Par, *Representaciones,* 1:89.
5. Isabelle Schwartz-Gastine, "Shakespeare on the French Stage: A Historical Survey," in *Four Hundred Years,* ed. Pujante and Hoenselaars, 226.
6. Mesoneros Romanos described Juan de Grimaldi as a "theatrical dictator," as David Thatcher Gies points out in *Theatre and Politics in Nineteenth-Century Spain: Juan de Grimaldi as Impresario and Government Agent* (Cambridge: Cambridge University Press, 1988), 1. For Grimaldi's influence on the stage in Romantic Madrid,

see also David Thatcher Gies, "Notas sobre Grimaldi y 'el furor de refundir' en Madrid (1820–1833)," *Cuadernos de Teatro Clásico* 5 (1990): 111–24.

7. David Thatcher Gies, "Juan de Grimaldi y el año teatral madrileño, 1823–24," in *Actas del VIII Congreso de la Asociación Internacional de Hispanistas,* ed. A. David Kossoff et al. (Madrid: Istmo, 1986), 609.

8. Gies, *Theatre and Politics,* 48.

9. Par, in *Representaciones,* 1:74, attributes the idea of translating the play to Ventura de la Vega and the leading actor Carlos Latorre but, in *Theatre and Politics,* Gies presents such a picture of Grimaldi's intellectual and managerial influence on the Madrid stage at the time, and on Vega's literary career, that it seems quite likely that Grimaldi, a French army officer who had recently arrived from France and was endowed with an impresario's mind, must have commissioned the translation of Duval's play, a box-office hit in Paris. On the influence of Grimaldi on Vega, see also David Thatcher Gies, "Grimaldi, Vega y el teatro español (1849)," in *Actas del X Congreso de la Asociación Internacional de Hispanistas,* ed. Antonio Vilanova, 1277–83 (Barcelona: PPU, 1992).

10. Gregor, "Shakespeare as a Character," 45.

11. See Péter Dávidházi, *The Romantic Cult of Shakespeare: Literary Reception in an Anthropological Perspective* (London: Macmillan, 1998).

12. Gregor, "Shakespeare as a Character," 52.

13. Ibid., 45, but see also Par, *Representaciones,* 1:215–16.

14. Gies, *Theatre and Politics,* 58–59.

15. Par, *Representaciones,* 1:84–87.

16. Schwartz-Gastine, "Shakespeare on the French Stage," 225.

17. Francisco Aguilar Piñal, *Cartelera prerromántica sevillana: Años 1800–1836* (Madrid: Consejo Superior de Investigaciones Científicas, 1968), 36.

18. For the use of these terms in eighteenth-century critical literature and their Spanish equivalents, see Guillermo Carnero, *Estudios sobre el teatro español del siglo XVIII* (Zaragoza: Prensas Universitarias de Zaragoza, 1997), as well as María Jesús García Garrosa, "Algunas observaciones sobre la evolución de la comedia sentimental en España," in *El teatro español del siglo XVIII,* ed. Josep Maria Sala Valldaura (Lleida: Universitat de Lleida, 1996), 427–46.

19. See Lucio Izquierdo, "El teatro en Valencia (1800–1832)," *Boletín de la Real Academia Española* 69 (1989): 303. Most of these performances seem to have taken place between 1812 and 1823: four in 1812, four in 1813, and three between 1814 and 1823 (see appendix 1).

20. Par, *Representaciones,* 1:70–71; Pujante and Gregor, in "Conservatism and Liberalism in the Four Spanish Renderings of Ducis's *Hamlet*" (in this volume), cautiously observe that although it looks as if the manuscript had all the prescribed permits required to stage a play, there are no records showing that it was performed.

21. Par, *Representaciones,* 1:52–56.

22. Gies, *Theater and Politics.*

23. The choice of 1802 and 1833 as boundaries for this study is not a random one: 1802 was the year when *Otelo* was first performed in Spain and 1833 saw the death of absolutist monarch Ferdinand VII and marked a crucial change in the Spanish stage. Queen Regent María Cristina appointed moderately liberal ministers who began to dismantle the ancien régime, an amnesty encouraged the return of many exiled men of letters, and Romanticism soon impregnated literary and theatrical activity.

24. Ana Mª Freire, "El definitivo escollo del proyecto neoclásico de reforma del teatro (Panorama teatral de la Guerra de la Independencia)," in *El teatro español del siglo XVIII,* 377–78.

25. la ocupación francesa desorganizó las representaciones teatrales por completo hasta 1812, pese a los esfuerzos alentadores del invasor (*Representaciones*, 1:51; my translation).

26. Par, *Representaciones*, 1:60; Gies, *Theater and Politics*, 12–13.

27. Grimaldi's *comedia de magia* (literally, "comedy of magic") constituted an unprecedented box-office success and an unexpected social phenomenon, with people from the provinces flocking to Madrid just to attend a performance of this play. See Gies, *Theater and Politics*, 63–80, and also his "'Inocente Estupidez': *La pata de cabra* (1829), Grimaldi, and the Regeneration of the Spanish Stage," *Hispanic Review* 54 (1986): 357–96.

28. Balz Engler, "Constructing Shakespeares in Europe," in *Four Hundred Years*, ed. Pujante and Hoenselaars, 32.

29. Le paradoxe est que, si l'Allemagne se donne vite un rôle-clef dans la propagation du génie shakespearien, en l'exploitant d'ailleurs dans sa politique anti-française, la France elle-même va continuer à fonctionner comme médiatrice dans l'établissement d'un nouveau paradigme théâtral qui paraît souvent incompatible avec les traditions françaises. José Lambert, "Shakespeare en France au tournant du XVIIIe siècle: Un dossier européen," in *European Shakespeares: Translating Shakespeare in the Romantic Age*, ed. Dirk Delabastita and Lieven D'hulst, 30 (Amsterdam/Philadelphia: John Benjamins, 1993), my translation.

30. For a study of the "philarmonic furore" that took Madrid by storm between 1823 and 1833, see David Thatcher Gies, "Entre drama y ópera: La lucha por el público teatral en la época de Fernando VII," *Bulletin Hispanique* 91 (1989): 37–60.

31. Ibid., 59.

32. Aguilar Piñal, *Cartelera*, 40. In "Entre drama y ópera," 53, Gies notes that Bellini's *I Capuleti et i Montecchi*, premiered in 1832, was among the most successful operas in Madrid.

The data in appendices 1 and 2 was obtained from José Simón Díaz, *Cartelera teatral madrilena, I: Años 1830–39* (Madrid: Consejo Superior de Investigaciones Científicas, 1961); Izquierdo, "El teatro en Valencia;" Par, *Representaciones*, vol. I; and Piñal, *Cartelera*.

Coriolanus in France from 1933 to 1977: Two Extreme Interpretations
Isabelle Schwartz-Gastine

CONTRARY TO MANY OTHER PLAYS OF THE SHAKESPEAREAN CANON, *Coriolanus* has not been very popular on the French stage. It certainly is a "problem play" in its own Roman kind of way. Coriolanus is a far less well-known hero than Julius Caesar or Brutus, and he lived in a much earlier period, that of the Republic rather than the more glamorous Empire. Nevertheless, all three heroes have one thing in common: Shakespeare borrowed them from the same source, Plutarch's *Lives of the Noble Graecians and Romanes*,[1] in which the author compares the life of Coriolanus with that of Alcibiades, another victorious character who rebelled against his own kin and cynically betrayed his people, and who also attracted the interest of our playwright.

If French productions of the play were few and far between, they were very meaningful, and, as a rule, centered on the eponymous hero. Consider the early rendering by the famous actor François-Joseph Talma in 1806, roughly two centuries after the play had been written. Because he had supported the French Revolution, Talma had been excluded from the Comédie-Française from 1791 to 1799, an exclusion that ironically mirrors the fate of Coriolanus, the Shakespearean hero the actor was to impersonate some years later.[2] As an outcast, Talma spent some time in London, and, following Voltaire's example over sixty years before, he learned the English language (which was still considered to be an act of defiance toward the French authorities as the two countries were archenemies). Being able to enjoy the plays in the original, Talma underwent the influence of John Philip Kemble and his sister Sarah Siddons in terms of their acting style and their interest in antiquity. As a matter of fact, Kemble had played Coriolanus with his sister costarring as Volumnia in a memorable production in 1789, the very year of the French Revolution, a staging that was revived the following seasons due to its great success.[3]

When he rejoined the Comédie-Française once the Revolution was over, Talma played the title role of *Coriolanus* during the reign of Napoleon I, at the emperor's summer residence in Saint-Cloud near Paris, starting in May 1806. The actor wore short wavy hair and a richly draped toga inspired by the classical paintings and sketches of the famous artist Jacques Louis David (1746–1825). Talma's appearance was, of course, very quickly perceived to suggest an impersonation of Napoleon himself. Napoleon wanted to avoid any such direct comparisons with a hero who was a traitor to his country, and he had the play stopped after only four performances, having quickly spotted the threat that it posed to his authority. Indeed, the production did not highlight the qualities of Coriolanus—acclaimed by patricians and plebeians alike—as a victorious soldier, charismatic leader, and defender of his people against foreign invasions (as in the opening of the play). Rather, the portrait that emerged was that of a traitor to his allies and relatives. This interpretation was in fact reinforced by the French version of the text used, an earlier adaptation of the play by Jean-François de La Harpe (1739–1803), which showed a hero who despised all those who dared contradict him.[4] In tune with the spirit of the age, Shakespeare's early Roman soldier had been transformed into a romantic hero garbed as a Napoleon-like figure who suffered from the "melancholy" of being misunderstood not only by the unpredictable plebeians but also by his fellow patricians.

This early staging shows how easily a play like *Coriolanus* could lend itself to politically charged interpretations. In this case, the central character was directly modeled on the current national leader, as a direct, be it somewhat servile, compliment to the victorious emperor of France. Napoleon did not regard this rendering as a compliment on his strong leadership, however, but as a warning that he should not allow any kind of portrayal of himself and his entourage (especially his domineering Corsican mother, matched in the play by Volumnia) that could undermine his image and authority. His decision to forbid further performances of the play was an act of autocracy showing genuine political insight.

As the Talma example suggests, the version of the text used for politically inspired dramatic appropriations of *Coriolanus* needs to be looked into very carefully, since it is through the successive processes of abridgment and adaptation of a text that its potential meanings will emerge. In the case of *Coriolanus,* there is no extant Quarto version, so that the only reference text available is the 1623 Folio. In order to illustrate my point about the political relevance of textual adaptation, I will discuss two versions of *Coriolanus* presented at times of major political upheaval in the twentieth century. The alterations in these texts—ranging from the most trivial (such as adding or omitting single words) to the most general (the conception of the function of theater)—conveyed diametrically opposed messages. The first was a staging at the Comédie-Française in Paris during the 1933–34 season that made the newspaper headlines of the day and was the starting point for very violent political demonstrations. The second, showing the strong influence of Brechtian theories, was premiered at the Avignon Festival in 1976—a long time after the outcry at the Comédie-Française—and revived in the cultural center of a working-class Paris suburb the following year.

I will argue that both of these radically different productions explore some of the dimensions of the original, even though their respective textual bias and one-sidedness prevent them from rendering the subtler nuances that run through Shakespeare's lines. I will further demonstrate that both productions reflect the preoccupations of their age. Rather than being the result of mere chance, or showing an individual effort to present a lesson or a personal compliment to those in power (as in Talma's unsuccessful attempt with Napoleon), they reveal strong trends in the nation's contemporary public opinion as well as the impact of different aesthetic paradigms.

A Riotous Staging at the Comédie-Française in 1933–34

It was the French-speaking Swiss scholar René-Louis Piachaud who wrote the free translation for the 1930s performance at the Comédie-Française. Piachaud was well known for his refined erudition and pure classical style. In the literary world his version had a considerable readership when it first came out with some pictures of the Comédie-Française performance in the color supplement of the famous monthly *L'Illustration,* a Paris-based magazine with a wide distribution throughout the country and even in the French-speaking colonies worldwide.[5] The translation also came out as a separate volume a few months later, with a commentary to justify the translator's policy.[6] More than evoking the English original, Piachaud's dialogues had a vaguely and pleasingly familiar Latinate ring to them, and they would have gratified the most erudite among his readers who could recognize the occasional classical intertextual references. But at least the translator (or was it the publisher?) had the intellectual probity to acknowledge that this rendering—despite being based on Shakespeare and not involving any major alteration of the plot—was a "free translation." Piachaud made it clear that his departures from the original text were meant to be ultimately to Shakespeare's advantage and amounted to a creative writer's tribute to the original.

Piachaud specified in his commentary that the play was "mis au goût du jour" (adapted to suit the taste of the time), a phrase that is far more than just an intellectual nicety. Written as a justification with the benefit of hindsight, the commentary aimed at exonerating the author from the chaos and commotion that had followed the staging of his text. After all, there is no denying that Piachaud seems to have been more concerned with his prospective audience—and their political mind-set—than with Shakespeare and his Elizabethan world. Such a justification may not have been superfluous, as the plays performed at the Comédie-Française could trigger major crises, not only in the literary but also in the political sphere. Indeed, in his memoirs, Émile Fabre, the administrator, recalls a controversy prior to the production of *Coriolanus* concerning a rather trivial two-act curtain-raiser ridiculing a general cheated on by his unfaithful wife. This play was perceived as an insult to the authority of the French army, and had to be withdrawn immediately. In such a sensitive context, the administrator warned the "sociétaires" (full members) and several ministers of state that *Coriolanus* might be the spark that would ignite the already smoldering political dissension. Fabre's warning was brushed aside, and his alarmist predictions were laughed at.[7] In spite of Piachaud's seemingly innocent appeal to the taste of the time, therefore, it seems obvious that, using the authority associated with the play's canonized status, the new version of *Coriolanus* fitted nicely into the newly emerging Fascist ideology, which was only too responsive to this Roman model of authoritarianism. And so Piachaud's Coriolanus is first and foremost the hero who wants to stop the fickle crowds from scheming and fiddling, goaded on as they are by the manipulative tribunes. The translator turns his hero into a haughty patrician, whose loneliness is the price he has to pay for honesty and morality, who scorns mobs and members of his own caste alike, and who has set himself the task of eradicating all malpractice by wielding his natural authority. His ambition having taken on a moral quality, the strong leadership of Coriolanus thus became an obvious "mirror for magistrates," not only Roman or Jacobean ones, but also for the political leaders of France in the 1930s.

The Comédie-Française theater had had a long-standing reputation for impressive scenery and sets that involved static tableaux interrupting the flow of the performance. Contrary to this prevailing practice, the stage designer, André Boll, created simpler sets that remained fixed throughout the performance. This unexpected break with tradition sufficed to provoke a strong audience response. The spirit of historical reconstruction did remain present, but it expressed itself through different means.

The back wall of the stage was simply covered with a painted cloth representing undistinguished bare Roman buildings, in a gradation of soft pink shades, as if the aspect of the stones were changing under the light of the setting sun, and receding toward the outline of a river (probably the Tiber) at the horizon. An imposing row of temples, with their triangular porticoes supported by regular columns, presented their dark fronts to the audience and added to the general verticality of the staging. An atmosphere of dignity and nobility prevailed. The softness of the light colors used gave an impression of quietness but could also signify the end of an era and ominous deeds to come, with the strange abnormality of a setting yet unchanging sun painted on the decor.

A central flight of steps led to acting areas on various levels, allowing for extremely solemn movements that underlined the hierarchical supremacy of the hero over all. At the opening of the play, for instance, after his victory over the Volscians, Caius Marcius, just named Coriolanus, appeared at the top of the stairs. The patricians in their white togas on the various steps, and the plebeians down below on the central stage, all lined up and greeted him with their right arms

Coriolanus (M. Alexandre) acclaimed by the Senators after his victory over the Volscians. Copyright: Collections de la Comédie Française. Photo: Manuel frères.

extended in the Roman salute. The general effect was breathtaking, not only visually, but also acoustically, with the acclaim of all these loud male voices booming in unison (the total number of actors and supernumeraries onstage was over two hundred!). The scene was more than just an evocation of Roman customs (actually pertaining to a much later period) and a tribute to the Shakespearean hero. In France it would also have conveyed a most ominous message about contemporary politics, as the Nazi forces had just adopted precisely such a greeting convention in Germany and they were also known to be very much given to spectacular shows gathering great numbers of disciplined males who expressed their acclaim in loud voices.

Theater critics and other informed members of the audience had no difficulty recognizing the antique city of Rome, yet the scenic representation was sufficiently unspecific to allow for an interpretation of the play in terms of contemporary reality. The two-dimensional set—a novelty as far as the aesthetic traditions of the Comédie-Française were concerned—left more room for the acting area and thus for the movements of the actors. It became possible to have a vast display of people filling the theatrical space and providing highly

A jocund Menenius (Bernard Noël) trying to calm down Coriolanus (M. Alexandre), who vents his contempt for the plebeians. Copyright: Collections de la Comédie Française. Photo: Manuel frères.

spectacular sequences grounded in movement, thus compensating for the lack of the traditional, imposing static sets.

All tickets for the first night were sold out—a surprise for such a reputedly difficult and highly rhetorical tragedy—and the performance was very well received. But the actors were not really acclaimed for their own personal rendering of the characters, although the habit of applauding the star actors individually, occasionally interrupting the course of the performance, was still very much in vogue. Something more sinister was afoot. As the administrator of the Comédie-Française wrote afterward, summing up the events:

> La malchance voulut qu'à ce moment précis un scandale éclatât: l'affaire de l'escroc Stavisky où se trouvaient compromis des députés et des sénateurs et où il apparut même que la police et le parquet n'avaient fait qu'assez mollement leur devoir. Alors le tapage devint plus fort à la Comédie; toutes les phrases qu'on pouvait tourner contre les parlementaires étaient saisies au vol par le public et acclamées.[8]

> [Bad luck would have it that at that very moment a scandal broke out: the case of a crook named Stavisky in which a number of MPs and senators were involved and in which the police and the prosecution had apparently taken a rather soft approach. Then the outcry rose high at the Comédie-Française; all the phrases which could be turned against the MPs were caught up at once by the audience and acclaimed.]

The response from the audience was mostly interpreted as criticism of the financial and political scandals of the time. The spectators thoroughly approved of some of Coriolanus's speeches against the tribunes and they were very quick to apply them to the much-criticized contemporary political leaders:

> *Silencieux au Parlement, les spectateurs se rattrapent à la Maison de Molière où ils applaudissent quand les moeurs parlementaires sont critiquées*
> Comme on le sait, certains passages de *Coriolan* ont suscités des applaudissements de la salle: ceux dans lesquels Shakespeare attaque la vile démagogie. Encore une petite manifestation hier soir.[9]

> [*Spectators make up for their silence in Parliament at the House of Molière, where they applaud criticism of parliamentary morals*
> As we know, some passages from *Coriolanus* have prompted applause from the house: those in which Shakespeare attacks base demagogy. Another small demonstration last night.]

This *Coriolanus* accomplished the rare feat of making the front-page headlines of the national daily newspapers in the months following the premiere. The above extract shows a controlled reaction among the audience still able to respond on an intellectual level to the words of the play. One will notice that the ambiguous phrasing fails to distinguish the spectators of the play from the debating politicians in Parliament, as if they were the same people. The street demonstration that the article goes on to report is also extremely ambiguous: the demonstration was started off outside the Comédie-Française Theater mostly by professional politicians, but members of the audience gradually joined in after the performance. As the days went by, the reactions became more and more riotous within the theater itself, and they were less and less concerned with Shakespeare's play and increasingly with developments in current political affairs.[10]

Five days later, there was so much noise and whistling from all parts of the auditorium that the performance had to be interrupted and the lights switched on.[11] After this night it was impossible to be blind any longer to the connection between developments on the political scene and this staging of *Coriolanus*. Indeed the newspapers continually contrasted the misdoings of the current government with the salutary example of the Roman hero who was outspoken enough to voice his discontent even toward his own kin.

This protest went on as a new government was formed on January 31, 1934, with Édouard Daladier, a radical socialist, as prime minister. The disapproval was general, however, and particularly fierce among the right-wingers. The following day, *Le Figaro* not only criticized all the members of the new government, but also published a front-page article that went so far as to suggest a straightforward correspondence between the eponymous hero of Shakespeare's play and Adolf Hitler, the recently elected chancellor of Germany, and referred to Coriolanus in its argument that Fascism might be the ideal solution to salvage France's democracy, which had fallen into disrepute.[12]

At the Comédie-Française, the administrator, Émile Fabre, had to resign and his post was given to the former head of the police, Mr. Thomé. The following evening's performance turned into a demonstration against this decision. The audience responded strongly to the evocation of the corruption in Rome; some members of the audience stood up and improvised violent speeches against the replacement. Considering that the situation had become too dangerous to continue the performance, Mr. Alexandre, the renowned actor playing Coriolanus, had to use all his authority and charisma to demand full silence.[13] That very evening, around midnight, the new prime minister Édouard Daladier faced an extremely angry crowd under the benevolent eye of the police just outside the theater.[14] The situation soon got out of hand and led to a violent night of fighting and shooting, starting from the Théâtre-Français and spreading all over the nearby Place de la Concorde, where the right-wing and radical right-wing forces had gathered in opposition to the government. The toll was heavy: twelve people killed and hundreds wounded.

In the newspaper reports, the Comédie-Française continued to be on the front page, although the theater remained closed the following days. Émile Fabre was reappointed as administrator on a provisional basis in an effort to stem the crisis. The following day, there was a lot of important national and international political news to be reported: "Défi à la Nation" (the nation challenged), "La situation politique est grave" (the political situation is serious).[15] But, significantly, the reappointment of the administrator was nevertheless given a place on the front page of the same newspaper: "Shakespeare triomphe! ... M. Thomé donne sa démission et M. Fabre reste à son poste" (Shakespeare is triumphant! ... Mr. Thomé steps down and Mr. Fabre keeps his post).[16] Whereupon Mr. Thomé cautiously decided to take *Coriolanus* off the bill to avoid further unrest, and this again was considered to be a newsworthy event, although it only featured in the sixth column of page 4 of *Le Figaro*:

Théâtre Français: Nouvel exil de Coriolan
Coriolan a quitté l'affiche après avoir joué un rôle considérable, non seulement à la scène mais dans la politique. Je ne puis m'empêcher de remarquer combien la destinée de Coriolan est singulière, non pas celle du chef-d'œuvre de Shakespeare, mais du personnage historique lui même. Dès qu'il triomphe, on l'exile. Cela n'a pas manqué. Le Coriolan dramatique ayant obtenu à la Comédie-Française des succès sans précédents et des applaudissements enthousiastes, la crainte des cabales et de bravos séditieux lui fait quitter l'affiche en pleine gloire et le théâtre de son ovation. Y a-t-il chez ces anciens héros, à jamais vivants, une force immortelle qui, de la vie, dite vraie, à la vie de l'art, dite imaginaire, persiste, convainc et autour d'elle, recrée des événements tragiquement civiques? Allons, Coriolan, rentrez dans les livres; dans ce Plutarque ... .[17]

[*Theatre Français: Coriolanus exiled again*
Coriolanus went off the bill after having played a considerable role, not only on stage but also in politics. I cannot help noticing how singular Coriolanus's fate is, not the fate of Shakespeare's masterpiece, but of the historical character himself. As soon as he triumphs, he is exiled. And sure enough, that is what happened. The character of Coriolanus having obtained an unprecedented success on the stage of the Comédie-Française and enthusiastic applause, the fear of riots and seditious cheers is forcing him off the bill in his hour of glory and out of the theater that adored him. Is there in these ever-living ancient heroes an immortal strength which—from the so-called reality of life to the so-called imaginary life of

art—persists, convinces, and recreates around itself tragically civic events? Come on, Coriolanus, return to the books; to this Plutarch . . .]

Coriolanus was replaced by a re-run of the previous year's production of Molière's comedy, *Le Malade imaginaire* (*The Hypochondriac*). Predictably, this change of program was immediately seized upon by commentators who diagnosed the government as a patient in need of a very strong medicine and recommended the cure of a Coriolanus-like politician and a political party modeled on the one that was gaining ground in Germany.

The spirit of the 1933–34 *Coriolanus* was Roman, classical, and scholarly in theory, but the reaction of the audience proved it had been extremely well adapted to suit the moods and political sensibilities of the epoch, and that it was very much in keeping with the growing discontent in the political sphere. The situation that it created was so serious that the production was hardly reviewed in the theater columns of the newspapers but, as I have argued, belonged to current news, having been recuperated ideologically by the political opposition. The times were not favorable to the more customary forms of theater-reviewing. The awkward casting of parts, for example, was not commented upon, as it would have been in less exceptional circumstances.

At this point we should remember that the Comédie-Française still used the old system of privileges among the actors of the company, according to which the most experienced ones could choose their parts first. This system explains why Talma had been the central hero of the production offered to the emperor over a century before, or why, in the 1933–34 production, the famous actor Alexandre could claim the role of Coriolanus despite being much older than the part reasonably required, so that he had to perform with a Volumnia (Colonna Romano, who had had only four days to rehearse the part) belonging to his own generation.[18] Furthermore, the whole production was built around the star actor in order to highlight his (or her) talents. In the present case, this approach not only deprived the character of Coriolanus's mother of some of its importance,[19] but it also drew extra attention to Coriolanus's fiery speeches, which the experienced actor made sure to deliver in the emphatic and vigorous style that had endeared him to his admirers. The conjunction of all these circumstances resulted in a one-sided interpretation that was bound to kindle the emotions of an already very sensitive audience in these troubled times.

For a couple of decades the association of *Coriolanus* with right-wing politics remained so strong that it prevented any real engagement with the play until it was revived in Piachaud's translation at the Comédie-Française in 1956–57, and again in Geneva in 1965.[20] The Comédie-Française performance as such received very limited critical attention, but the translation offered the opportunity and means to emerging Marxist theoreticians such as Bernard Dort to challenge vehemently the current perceptions about Shakespeare's play in France and to offer a completely new and more faithful reading instead.[21] Writing in the same political spirit, Michel Habart wrote in 1957 that in *Coriolanus*, Shakespeare "diagnostique avec une admirable pénétration, les mobiles et le mécanisme de la lutte des classes" (diagnoses the motives and the mechanism of the class-struggle with an admirable penetration).[22] Politically dated as it may sound to us now, this Marxist rhetoric was only natural to the man who was later to translate Bertolt Brecht's adaptation of *Coriolanus* into French.[23]

Avignon and Aubervilliers, 1976–77

Coriolanus was again placed at the center of attention by Gabriel Garran, a theater director who had first launched an amateur theater festival in Aubervilliers, a working-class suburb north of Paris, before becoming the head of the new cultural center erected there (the first of its kind and followed by many others) in accordance with the official cultural policy of the postwar years and early 1960s. Inspired by his left-wing political beliefs, Garran intended to bring some culture to the inhabitants of that district. In this, he favored contemporary plays, although he occasionally turned to classics also, for instance, Shakespeare's *Henry VIII* and *Coriolanus*.

In addition to François-Victor Hugo's translation of Shakespeare's original, Garran consulted some authoritative sources, including Bertolt Brecht's adaptation of *Coriolanus* and the 1957 Brecht-style production at the Piccolo Theater in Milan by Giorgio Strehler. Another source of inspiration was of course Jan Kott's *Shakespeare Our Contemporary*, just published in French in 1964. In the same year, Garran could also turn to the production that was being prepared at the Berliner Ensemble under the joint direction of Manfred Wekwerth and Joachim Tenschert, a production that built on the famous analysis of the first scene and the preparatory work left unfinished by Brecht at his death in 1956.

Clearly, Gabriel Garran's production fits into the "socialist" approach to Shakespeare that developed in the West at the end of the 1950s.[24] This was especially true of his first production of *Coriolanus* in the summer of 1964, when he was the director of the open-air amateur festival of Aubervilliers. Then he commissioned Serge Ganzl to write a clear, straightforward adaptation focusing on the Brechtian theme of the "providential hero," here dressed like and showing the idiosyncrasies of the man who dominated the political scene at the time, General de Gaulle. The second version, of 1976, was also written by Serge Ganzl.[25] Here, too, clarity and straightforwardness prevailed, but, despite the presence of a few slight topical allusions, this time the idea was to avoid obvious analogies with contemporary politics.

In 1964, Garran's aim had been to simplify the text, adapting it to the limited theatrical expertise and experience of both the amateur actors and the working-class audience he was working with, and allowing for action and group movements onstage. In the 1976 production, which was intended for a sophisticated professional cast, the style is still less complex than that of the original play, but the text is much longer than in the 1964 version, and quite a number of speeches have been integrated to convey the different perspectives more subtly. Let us consider just one instance of a minute but meaningful omission in the tribunes' exchange about the anger of the mob in act 2 scene 3: by leaving out the monosyllabic verb "seem" in Sicinius's speech ("and this shall seem, as partly 'tis, their own, which we have goaded onwards," 2.3.260–61), which implies double-dealing, the tribunes' motives are made to appear far more respectable than they are in Shakespeare. But on another occasion, the addition of a short speech makes the text not only un-Shakespearean but also un-Brechtian, inasmuch as it shows a divergence among the representatives of the people as well as their political immaturity. Brutus believes that only Volumnia can go and plead for clemency with Coriolanus:

Sicinius. Brutus, toi aussi, tu vas implorer sa mère?
Brutus. Oui.
(112)

[*Sicinius.* Brutus, you're not going to plead with his mother too, are you?
Brutus. Yes.]

Furthermore, in the 1976 version quite a number of short allusions to the grandeur of war have deliberately been omitted, for example, the discussion between the two servicemen in act 4 who are excited at the idea of going to war ("then we shall have a stirring world again," 4.5.225–32), or, earlier in the play, before they march on to Corioles, Caius Marcius's exhortation to valiant action and the soldiers' eager response (stage direction: "They all shout and wave their swords, take him up in their arms, and cast up their caps," 1.6.66ff.). The Ganzl/Garran version shows a very quiet, pacifist type of citizens who have no connection whatsoever with the patricians, the enemies of the people. Garran's Caius Marcius (Michel Hermon) enters Corioles all alone, not as a charismatic leader, feared and respected, but as a solitary, bloody warrior.

The 1964 amateur staging opposed the Volscians and the Romans in vast groupings over the playing area (Garran had many enthusiastic young people who had to be included in the production somehow, even for mute parts). The 1976 professional production concentrated on the city of Rome to explore another Brechtian theme, "the tragedy of the people which had a hero against it." For Garran the basis of the revolt was now internal and would emerge from the womb of the earth: at the beginning of the performance all the actors playing the plebeians entered the dark stage from a trapdoor situated in the middle of the stage, and then started to write down the reasons for their discontent on a paper wall at the back of the stage, recalling the Chinese *dazibao* or the posters that had covered all the walls in France some years before. After all, the 1968 movement was still fresh in people's memories, a time when there had been a much-praised union

Peace and happiness in Rome after Coriolanus's banishment, from "La fête républicaine" [the republican celebration], a sequence of *Coriolanus*, staging by Gabriel Garran. Théâtre de la Commune d'Aubervilliers (Paris suburbs), 1977. Photo courtesy of Isabelle Schwartz-Gastine.

between the students and the workers. In 1976 there was widespread sympathy and nostalgia for this type of solidarity uniting intellectual and manual laborers against the authorities.

Garran also wanted to make it clear that the tribunes had emerged only recently from the plebs, and as former plebeians, they were both clumsy and naive in their approach to the pragmatics of politics. This made them an easy target for the more experienced patricians, who used to be the sole representatives of authority. Garran cast young actors for these parts.[26] Their youth was an emblem of their new position and an indirect tribute to the leaders of 1968 (young people who had risen to political prominence through sheer talent and charisma), as well as a sign of hope and promise. The more negative aspects of their characters, which Piachaud and the Comédie-Française had amply developed and dramatized in 1933, were here smoothed over or turned to their advantage as the pardonable errors of well-meaning beginners.

For Garran the plebeians were not an anonymous bunch, but a well-defined group of responsible citizens. As he had done with the young amateurs in the 1964 production, after the Brechtian method, he differentiated the various actors, giving each of them a name and an occupation, in order to confer the substance and consistency of real characters to the eleven actors composing the group. There was even a child, called Marcius, who also played young Marcius, Coriolanus's son, and two "musicians" who were actually no other than the composers of the stage music.[27] In the autumn revival at Aubervilliers, Garran had included an actress among the plebeians,[28] an oddity that provided a touch of family homeliness in an otherwise violent setting. Though this concern with the female condition was somewhat anachronistic, it did reflect a common preoccupation at the time of the staging.

Once Coriolanus had been banished from Rome and peace was restored, the plebeians/citizens were seen at work in a touching tableau in a sequence that Garran entitled "La fête républicaine" (the republican celebration). The back stage was organized into little shops (the blacksmith, the potter, the baker, the wine dealer), showing an idyllic glimpse of all the citizens together in complete harmony and going about their everyday lives, at the market and the forum, uniting labor and leisure. This parallel story made up by Garran also enabled the actors-citizens to be more fully present and engage in some meaningful physical activity on the central stage.

The Volscians were not represented, so there were no direct confrontations between the two antagonistic armies, as had been the case in 1964, which had allowed for the massive deployment of actors-citizens across the stage with plenty of shouting and clinking of arms. In 1976, the Roman soldiers spread over the full surface of the stage, turning their backs to the audience, in a massive attack on Corioles, the enemy city. To complete their soldierly outfit, they were all wearing vast cloaks that moved as they ran, taking up all the space and giving a memorable impression of a massive shift. To enhance the metaphor of the "many-headed multitude" (2.3.15), a further device was used: the cloaks were covered with images of helmeted heads, as a visual synecdoche for a full army all moving in unison. But during the assault, the Roman soldiers only faced a mere fortress wall, into which only Caius Marcius dared to penetrate after his truncated exhortation (see above). As the doors shut behind him, the actor disappeared from view and looked more like a prisoner. The Roman soldiers remained on the central stage floor and on the set, now deprived of their leader and engaged in a fight against an invisible enemy, looking ever weaker and more frightened, so that the solitary high deed of Caius Marcius looked even more extraordinary. When Caius Marcius emerged again on the wooden platform above, he looked magnified and in full glory as a kind of lonely superhero.

If Garran's plebeians were portrayed as pacifists or failed soldiers, war really belonged to the patrician ethos. They did enjoy war in terms of its sheer physicality, whether by proxy (cf. Volumnia describing her son's wounds on his coveted body) or as a privileged personal encounter (cf. Coriolanus and Aufidius, his Volscian counterpart). Indeed, the only fight onstage was the single combat between the two champions of the opposed armies, with the Volscian general looking like a double of his Roman opponent. Both were clad in similar, tight, black suits that glittered according to the variations of the light coming from the side wings. These special light effects together with the slow movements of the two actors contributed to the impression of a stylized, emblematic encounter between two exceptional characters whose main aims were the enjoyment of this physical meeting and the achievement of excellence. Not surprisingly, the two ended up on the ground, in a soldierly embrace showing male-to-male exclusive bonding not devoid of homosexual overtones.

Contrary to many interpretations of Shakespeare's play or Plutarch's original story, Coriolanus in this production had no close relationship with his mother. There was no sequence suggesting a special union or proximity between this formidable mother and her valorous son (despite the first citizen's shrewd comment that "he did it to please his mother, and to be partly proud," 1.1.37–38). Garran was keen to avoid any show of sentimentality of the kind that would have prevailed in nineteenth-century renderings, and he may also have wanted to stay clear of any Oedipal double meanings. His was not a psychological but a political message.

Volumnia was portrayed as equally lonely as her son, due to her exceptional nature, as compared to a very fragile and silent Virgilia, for instance. In the sixth sequence entitled "La mère et l'épouse" (the mother and the wife), Volumnia, wearing a most becoming, olive green, fully pleated long dress, acted as a kind of domestic priestess delivering her predictions as she threw some little bundles to kindle a fire in a bowl poised on a metal tripod, placed on a little platform at the front stage. She looked determined and superhuman too, as her figure (magnified as she extended her arms on the sides) was seen through the modulations of the flames. She could be seen as the true representative of patrician values in the changing Roman world.

Both characters were given emblematic sequences of great visual beauty. The special light effects in particular—during Coriolanus's single combat with Aufidius and the open fire in Volumnia's domestic scene—contributed to the overall impression that both mother and son were endowed with magical and superhuman powers. It was impossible to overlook their natural supremacy over all the other characters, including other patricians and also the citizens, who looked rather dull in their uniform, sand-colored costumes of Brechtian inspiration.

Volumnia as a domestic priestess, from "La mère et l'épouse" [the mother and wife], a sequence of *Coriolanus*, staging by Gabriel Garran. Théâtre de la Commune d'Aubervilliers (Paris suburbs), 1977. Photo courtesy of Isabelle Schwartz-Gastine.

Gabriel Garran's sympathetic rendering of the Roman citizens and their newly elected tribunes confirms the Marxist conception underlying the 1976 production of *Coriolanus*. Nevertheless, the characteristics I have just discussed introduce interesting, more complex ambiguities, and so does the fact that he could now use a cast of professional actors, and the circumstance that the staging was premiered at the open-air Avignon Festival, programmed on the official bill and performed for a well-educated audience in a setting of extraordinary beauty: against the ancient stone walls of the old Papal Palace. On top of that, the show featured a talented actor as Coriolanus, Michel Hermon, who could convey both the hero's scorn for the people and the exceptional nature of his character.

Conclusion

It is now widely acknowledged that the staging that prompted the bloody right-wing demonstrations of February 6, 1934, was based on an extremely reductive text that, under the cover of scholarly refinement, emphasized the scorn toward the crowds and the pursuit of personal honor on the part of the hero. The visual effects of the production only reinforced this tendency. This ideological intervention in Shakespeare's original was neither openly acknowledged nor perceived then, but it certainly served the purpose of right-wing radicals at a time of extreme political tension.

Fortunately the 1976–77 production took place in more serene circumstances, and its political resonance remained within the framework of the theater. It seems obvious that a somewhat similar change as in 1933 had been imposed on the text, except that this time the rewriting favored the crowds, excused the dark dealings of the tribunes, and minimized the grandeur of Coriolanus. Also, in this second instance the shifting of political sympathy occurred more openly, namely under the banner of Brechtian theories ("I think we can change Shakespeare if we can change him.")[29] and it was clearly situated in the contemporary spectrum of political and social positions. In this respect, the ambiguity characterizing the 1933–34 version was resolved. But, as I have argued above, other contradictions remain. While Gabriel Garran favored the people and tended to put all the blame on the haughtiness of the patricians, the highly stylized aesthetics prevailing in the sequences involving the two representatives of the patricians contrasted with the sentimental and rather flat rendering of the plebeians, and the special lighting effects, too, looking all the more spectacular against the ancient wall of the Papal Palace of

Avignon, heightened the supremacy of the ruling class, causing the production to waver in its ideological purpose.

Notes

1. Translation by Sir Thomas North, based on the French edition by Jacques Amyot (1587; later editions, with additions in 1595 and 1603). North's translation was Shakespeare's source.

2. But then, the exclusion from revolutionary France may have been a blessing for the actor, who was thus safe from the successive waves of arrests and executions.

3. Victor du Bled, "Les Comédiens Français pendant la Révolution et l'Empire," in *Revue des Deux Mondes* 42 (1894): 573–603.

4. Émile Laugier, *Documents Historiques sur la Comédie Française* (Paris: Firmin Didot, 1853), 105.

5. The translation appeared in *La Petite Illustration* 661 (February 10, 1934): 1–50.

6. René-Louis Piachaud, *La tragédie de Coriolan*, traduite librement de l'anglais de Shakespeare et adaptée à la scène, suivie d'un examen de cette tragédie (Paris: C. Lévy, 1934) [The tragedy of Coriolanus, freely translated from Shakespeare's English and adapted to the stage, followed by an analysis of this tragedy].

7. Émile Fabre, *La Comédie Française* (Paris: Nouvelle Revue Critique, 1942), 117.

8. Ibid.

9. *Le Matin*, December 11, 1933, 1.

10. *Le Figaro*, December 12, 1933, 1.

11. Édouard Champion, *La Comédie-Française, années 1933–34* (Paris: La Comédie Française, 1935), 101.

12. *Le Figaro*, January 1, 1934, 1.

13. Ibid., February 5, 1934, 1.

14. Ibid.

15. Ibid., February 6, 1934, 1.

16. Ibid.

17. Ibid., February 19, 1934, article signed Gérard d'Hourville.

18. Incidentally, the actress was very much criticized in the press for her last-minute casting in Volumnia's role, which she obtained on the strength of the same rule of preeminence and for which she only had four days of rehearsal. See Édouard Champion, *La Comédie-Française*, 174–75, as well as Jacques Copeau, *Les Nouvelles Littéraires*, December 23, 1933 (also quoted by Champion, 175).

19. The French were very well aware of the importance of Volumnia, mainly because of the centrality of the character in Nicolas Poussin's famous oil painting, *Coriolan vaincu par sa mère* from 1642 (Musée Nicolas Poussin, Les Andelys, Eure France). Poussin's renderings of classical scenes were influenced by religious art. Here, Volumnia, clad in a light blue toga and reminding us of a Christian Virgin, leads the group of pleading Roman ladies kneeling in front of Coriolanus.

20. This time with a three-dimensional set, designed by Jean Meyer. See Jean Jacquot, *Shakespeare en France, mises en scène d'hier et d'aujourd'hui* (Paris: Le Temps, 1964), 107; *Journal de Genève*, March 16, 1965.

21. Bernard Dort, "*Coriolan*, pièce fasciste?" *Théâtre Populaire* 29 (March 1958): 7–24.

22. Michel Habart, "Pitié pour Shakespeare," *Les Lettres Françaises* 24 (February 21–28, 1957): 27–46.

23. "*Coriolan*, d'après Shakespeare," in Bertolt Brecht, *Théâtre Complet*, French version by Michel Habert (Paris: L'Arche, 1962), 10:146–245.

24. Dennis Kennedy, "Shakespeare and the Cold War," in *Four Hundred Years of Shakespeare in Europe*, ed. Ángel-Luis Pujante and Ton Hoenselaars, 163–79 (Newark: University of Delaware Press, 2003).

25. Serge Ganzl was a playwright in his own right. Some of his plays (mostly one-act pieces) have been performed at Avignon, even directed by Gabriel Garran, such as *La Bouche* (1972), in which Brigitte Ariel (Virgilia) made her debut.

26. René Loyon as Sicinius and Jacques Pieller as Brutus.

27. He appears as young Marcius in two sequences: a dramatization of Valeria's description of young Marcius's tearing of a butterfly (1.3.53–68), and the fatal pleading of the Roman matrons in which Coriolanus is on the brink of mellowing as he sees his son holding his mother's hand (5.3.23–24); the "musicians" were Joëlle Léandre and Stéphane Grémaud.

28. Michèle Taïeb, who incidentally had been Garran's assistant.

29. Brecht, "Study of the first scene of Shakespeare's *Coriolanus*," *Théâtre Complet,* 10: 255.

Der Merchant von Velence:
The Merchant of Venice in London, Berlin, and Budapest during World War II
Zoltán Márkus

As Dror Abend-David's recent study about translations of *The Merchant of Venice* into German, Hebrew, and Yiddish has shown, Shakespeare's play has often been interpreted, translated, and staged in sharply contrasting ways that could serve even opposing ideological and propagandistic purposes in different (or, occasionally, even identical) geographical, historical, linguistic, or sociopolitical contexts. Abend-David argues that "Shylock, as this character is imagined by many readers and viewers today, is not 'the Jew / that Shakespeare drew,'" as Alexander Pope is said to have put it, and, "similarly, that *The Merchant of Venice*, as it is often presented today is not the same romantic comedy . . . that it may be imagined to have been in London, and in 1594."[1] Although several authors, including Abend-David, urge us that we "return" to the Elizabethan text as a privileged location for understanding what Shakespeare's play may have been, it is in the great multiplicity of its versions, its cultural uses and interpretations, primarily its various editions and productions, that *The Merchant of Venice* exists today. Translation, of course, further complicates this issue. Suspended in the cultural and historical context of their creation, translations of Shakespeare's plays have an "afterlife" significantly detached from the (in Shakespeare's case, imaginary and elusive) original.

By exploring three theatrical appropriations in three different cities in wartime Europe as well as the ways in which they re-imagined *The Merchant of Venice,* this paper aims at outlining the afterlife of Shakespeare's play at a cataclysmic historical moment. Although one of the chief goals of my brief study is to put pressure on the argument that an authentic Shakespearean message was grossly hijacked by these theatrical productions, I do not believe that a Shakespeare play can mean virtually anything. Instead, I attempt to account for a few ways in which cultural, historical, and geographical differences determined the varying meanings, interpretations, and even "identities" of this particular Shakespeare play. On the one hand, my paper explores momentous differences between stage productions of *The Merchant of Venice* and their cultural significance in wartime London, Berlin, and Budapest. On the other, it also considers several continuities that point toward a tentative singularity of Shakespeare's drama and make it possible for us to identify in these varieties the elusive play of *The Merchant of Venice*.

London

In an article published in the *Times* in September 1942, the formidable theater critic James Agate remarks that Donald Wolfit's theater manager informed him that, "at each and every performance" of Shakespeare's plays, "Czechs, Poles, Norwegians, Belgians, and French had accounted for 50 per cent. of the audience and sometimes 75 per cent. The rest have been Jews: had we relied on the Christians, we should have played to empty benches."[2] In an earlier article, published in the *Daily Express,* Agate had reiterated almost verbatim this same observation.[3] Similarly, in a very brief article also appearing in the *Daily Express,* this strange occurrence was further lambasted with a pithy description of the current London theater scene that claimed that the "bulk of audiences" were made up of "foreigners." The reason cited was that they had "learned the plays in their English courses at school."[4] The foreigners' enthusiastic interest in Shakespeare was counterpointed and amplified by the local population's relative indifference to the national Bard. Like others, Agate lamented, "I maintain that with the exception of the Jews, known throughout the civilised world for their magnificent support of the arts, the fashionable play-goers of the West End have no love of Shakespeare, though they may consent to Shakespeare as the price paid for an actor on whom they dote."

The case of *The Merchant of Venice* was different, however, according to Agate. While indifference to Shakespeare was the rule, *The Merchant* was "the exception," "the one Shakespeare play the Christians flock to."[5] *The Merchant,* indeed, was the most frequently produced Shakespeare play in wartime London (along with *Twelfth Night:* seven productions in total) and based on the number of theatrical performances during the war years, only *Hamlet* and *A Midsummer Night's Dream* were performed more often.[6] Agate's observation was a jab at both the extant anti-Jewish prejudice in the city and the local audience's apathy regarding Shakespeare. These evident anxieties about the foreign interest in Shakespeare versus the native disinterest in the national Bard made the relatively frequent staging of *The Merchant of Venice* and its popularity with the British audiences all the more important and revealing.

In *The Observer*, Ivor Brown's scathing remarks about the London audiences' penchant for this particular Shakespeare play echoed Agate's observations and even went further:

> *The Merchant of Venice* appears to be far the most popular of Shakespeare's plays—or, if you prefer it that way, the most difficult to dodge. Mr. Wolfit and Mr. Atkins have played Shylock recently; the Stratford stage is rarely without its gabardine; the "Old Vic." has been C.E.M.A.-touring the Court and the Caskets in large playhouses as in pitman's hall, for over two years. You cannot begin to reason with this play; everybody behaves like a brute or a nit-wit; even Shylock's conduct is inexplicable. The Doge is a duffer, and Portia's cat-and-mouse treatment of Antonio in court is idiotic and insufferable. Bassanio and his boy-friends are cads, go-getters, and bullies, the stuff that Fascists are made of. And yet, heynonny, it is, overwhelmingly, the Shakespeare that the public wants.[7]

Meeting the public demand, Robert Atkins's and Donald Wolfit's theater companies as well as the Old Vic produced *The Merchant* in London during World War II.

I discuss briefly here the Old Vic production in the New Theatre in 1943—partly because this production had the most performances in London (forty-eight altogether: more than Wolfit's five *Merchants* put together), and partly because it offers an odd ironic twist to the reception of Shakespeare's play in wartime London. In this production, staged by Esmé Church, a Continental Jewish émigré played the role of Shylock. As the *Daily Mail* announced, "[t]he Old Vic Company returned to the New Theatre last night with *The Merchant of Venice* and Mr. Frederick Valk, the distinguished Czech actor, as Shylock. This is beyond question a fine performance in a part in which a foreign accent is not a serious handicap."[8]

Although the British press preferred to refer to him as "the distinguished Czech actor," Valk was in fact a German Jew born in Hamburg in 1895; his original name was Fritz Valk. He started acting in his teens in Hamburg and gradually achieved national recognition. In 1933, in the wake of the Nazis' rise to power, he left for Prague, Czechoslovakia, where he became a member of the local German-language New Theater. Just days before the Germans marched into Prague in 1939, Valk moved to London. Since his English was relatively good, he quickly found employment. After a few engagements in London, he joined the Old Vic for a tour of northern England in 1941: he alternated Shylock with Nick the barman in William Saroyan's *The Time of Your Life*. About this *Merchant*, Valk's English wife, Diana Valk (née Quirk), writes, "'Shakespeare at the Coal-face' was one name for these tours and this war-time Shylock was pictured as a farouche, retiring man. He had a touch of the religious fanatic as he stalked black-robed across the narrow stages of miners' halls and community centers."[9] In a chapter devoted to Frederick Valk, tellingly entitled "My Greatest Actor," theater critic Michael Meyer describes the elemental effect Valk's Shylock had on him: "Valk could have been forgiven if he had, at this stage of the war, sentimentalized the Jew, but nothing could have been further from the case. His Shylock was mean, but he was so because of the attitude of everyone around him. It was an age of fine acting in Britain: Olivier, Richardson, Gielgud, Donat, and Redgrave were all at, or approaching, their peak. But now I found myself confronted with a power and—what can I call it?—savagery unlike anything I had experienced."[10] Trained in Germany, Valk's art was a novelty on the London stage. In a postwar interview, he admitted to the uniqueness of his acting style: "I fully recognise . . . that my way of dramatic expression is different from that which is most commonly appreciated in this country."[11]

At the end of the tours of northern England and Scotland, the Old Vic's *Merchant* arrived in London in February 1943. Theater notices of Valk's Shylock remarked that "Mr. Valk seems unwilling to give us anything between a shout and a whisper."[12] The adjectives used most commonly to describe his performances were "powerful" and "passionate." Valk's interpretation of Shylock—according to Agate—was bringing the play back to its true self: "Take Shylock out of the pathetic category and put him into that of the despicable creature who brings about his own doom, and the play again becomes a comedy consistent with itself."[13] With his "fine Old Testament attitudes," and his "power,"[14] Valk conceived of Shylock as a wily character, cognizant of his powers and rejecting sentimental pathos. His self-conscious cunning made it harder to see the noble Jew within.

It seems bizarre today that, in wartime London, to an audience largely consisting of foreigners and Jews, a Jewish foreigner played the part in a way that extended little sympathy to Shylock. There are several reasons for this paradox. Most importantly, perhaps, a nonsympathetic, ogrelike Shylock was precisely the theatrical tradition in which *The Merchant* in Britain was conceived in the 1920s, 1930s, and 1940s.[15] The director of this production of the Old Vic, Esmé Church, explained her dilemma of having to select a lighthearted Shakespearean comedy that would be suitable to entertain the less erudite audiences of the Durham and Northumberland Miners' Association. Church notes: "We thought *Twelfth Night* too sophisticated a play, but they wanted Shakespeare. The *Merchant* was suggested, a good dramatic story, colourful and easy to follow, linked to a charming fairy tale."[16] The description of *The Merchant of Venice* as a play that is "colourful and easy to follow" suggests that Church and the Old Vic interpreted it as a simplistic "fairy tale" about the struggle of good Venetians and the evil ogre-Jew.

Harley Granville-Barker's *Prefaces to Shakespeare* offers a very similar point of view: arguably the most revered theater producer of this period, Granville-Barker also emphasized that the play was a "fairy tale" and "the simplest of plays, so long as we do not bedevil it with sophistries."[17] He contended, "[d]espite the borrowed story, this Shylock is essentially Shakespeare's own. But if he is not a puppet, neither is he a stalking-horse; he is no more a mere means to exemplifying the Semitic problem than is Othello to the raising of the color question."[18] Yet, in arguing against using Shakespeare as an ideologically driven vehicle for expressing topical issues and problems, by insisting that "Shylock" is neither "puppet" nor "stalking-horse," Granville-Barker (advertently or inadvertently) makes an ideologically laden statement. If shorn of his topical relevance and presented as a fairy-tale "ogre," who or what is Shylock in wartime London?

Another explanation for a theatrical interpretation of Shakespeare's play that extended little sympathy to Shylock might have been a general anti-Semitic bias prevalent in the metropolis. In his book investigating the wartime role of the Ministry of Information, Ian McLaine comments on "the widely reported prejudice in the British community against Jews." He points out that, "[f]irst reported in June 1940 — when Jews were supposed to be fleeing from Britain to the United States — and reaching its first peak at the time of the East End Blitz, anti-Semitism became such a regular subject that it was placed in Home Intelligence's 'Constant Topics and Complaints' at the end of each weekly report together with such matters as poor transport and shortage of crockery." The rumors fueling and resulting from anti-Jewish sentiments were that "Jews were said to control the black market, to display ostentatious wealth, to avoid war work and military service, even to force their way to the heads of the queues and to exhibit truculent behavior."[19] Following the very nature of cultural appropriations, the wartime reception of *The Merchant of Venice* in London may have been both indicative and generative of these sentiments.

Berlin

If this play could be used in wartime London as a vehicle for covert or overt anti-Semitism through its interpretation of Shylock, we might expect that it came in handy for National Socialist ideologues and was particularly popular in Germany and its *Reichshauptstadt*, Berlin. But this was not the case at all. *Der Kaufmann von Venedig* was staged only once in Berlin during the Third Reich, and even then in a heavily modified and censored form. Speculating on the possible reasons for *The Merchant*'s lack of popularity in Nazi Germany, Wilhelm Hortmann notes, "[t]he most flattering explanation is that a sense of shame stopped most theatre managements from adding insult to injury," but he offers other—and more pragmatic—explanations as well:

> For rabid anti-Semitic propaganda there was Christopher Marlowe's *The Jew of Malta* to fall back upon. With *The Merchant of Venice* there was a double insecurity, first whether the Jewish subject would be acceptable to the authorities and, more pertinently, how to perform it: as a *Stürmer* caricature, which many directors considered tasteless, or in a pro-Shylock sense, which would have been suicidal. Were Shylock's speeches in act 3 scene i ("Hath not the Jew eyes?") and act 4 scene i ("What judgment shall I dread, doing no wrong? / You have among you many a purchas'd slave") to be given their full weight, or should their impact be cushioned by cuts and deflected by diverting delivery?[20]

These choices, which would allow for a more complex theatrical representation of the play, were, however, simply unavailable to theater producers in the Third Reich: the *Reichsdramaturgie* provided clear directives as to how *Der Kaufmann von Venedig* should be put onstage. The play was only permitted as a two-dimensional morbid burlesque or, as Wilhelm Hortmann puts it, a "*Stürmer* caricature."

In July 1940, *Reichsdramaturg* Rainer Schlösser wrote the following to Goebbels regarding the textual changes making *The Merchant* suitable for Nazi propaganda:

> Responding to an earlier directive, *The Merchant of Venice* in recent years has been removed from the program in Berlin. In the meantime, however, some theaters in the Reich with my agreement have tested a modified version that could be obtained by small corrections. In this version, Jessica is played as not the daughter but only as the foster daughter of the Jew; race-political difficulties, therefore, are cleared out of the way. Since these modifications are not extensive, present no philological offenses to the Shakespearean text as it has come down to us, and as Jessica performed by

German actresses has never been played as a Jewess, I would see no reason why this classic work—which moreover, in a talented performance, can offer support to our anti-Jewish fight—should not be allowed to return to Berlin. The Rose Theater is planning to produce the work in the next season and I ask for a resolution on whether the endeavor can be attempted at this particular venue, which is after all somewhat marginal.[21]

As Schlösser's letter implies, *The Merchant* had been considered potentially subversive and had been virtually banned from Berlin before 1939. Schlösser's adaptation, on the other hand, turned the play into a blatant propagandistic device: in this format, the production of the play was not only permissible but quite desirable.

The stage adaptation at the Rose Theater in Berlin displayed a rabidly anti-Semitic appropriation of Shakespeare's play. Joseph Wulf notes that eyewitnesses to this production related to him that the director Paul Rose had placed a few extras in the auditorium who burst into loud abuse and cursing whenever Shylock entered the stage.[22] The reviewer of the *Völkischer Beobachter* also remarked that the production was conceived in a commedia dell'arte style emphasized by audience participation: "Paul Rose allowed the voice of the people from the gallery to join in with indignant shouts and piercing whistles and an echo from the stalls underlined the climax of the evening."[23]

The production's propagandistic message was not lost on the reviewers of the show. Regarding Shylock, F. A. Dargel of the *Nacht-Express* made the following observations:

> Clearly, the tragic elements are never fully and completely erased, and the present age knows much better and more clearly than all other times about the dreadful seriousness that suddenly emerges from under the Harlequin-leaps and merry disguises! And Shylock will forever remain the symbol of a virtually demonic Jewish hatred.
>
> That is how Georg August Koch represents him here as well. With a yankable reddish beard, with sometimes greedy, sometimes timorous wandering eyes, with hands whose fingers open and close like claws—he is a primeval Golem, who roams the city of the lagoons and lays sinister nocturnal nets so that, with the bait of gold, he can beguile and destroy always new victims.[24]

Dr. Carl Weichardt describes Koch's Shylock in similar terms: "Georg August Koch plays Shylock with a glued on hooked nose, a red and woolly full beard, first almost as a farcical character in the comedy, but in his stubborn hatred he rises to cruelty in order to collapse like a heap of misery in the end."[25] Shylock was represented as a wicked burlesque phenomenon: a caricature rather than a flesh-and-blood character. Conceived as a commedia dell'arte show, the production served populist tastes with comedy, colors, music, dance, and anti-Semitic agitation: it was a popular festival, a "Volksfest." The propagandistic political agendas of the *Reichsdramaturgie* found an ideal and popular outlet in this production.

The privately owned Rose Theater put this anti-Semitic extravaganza on its stage hoping for a decent profit by supplying what was in demand in Berlin in 1942. The timing of this particular production was, however, more than disconcerting: it followed the Wannsee Conference in January of the same year. Mass deportations of Berlin Jews had started in October 1941, but as of July 2, 1942 (less than two months before the Rose Theater's *Merchant* opened), these deportations were reorganized with more people rounded up and sent out to concentration camps. In this context, the burlesque called *Der Kaufmann von Venedig* at the Rose Theater was a harrowing kind of entertainment.

Budapest

The Budapest production of *The Merchant of Venice*, or *A velencei kalmár*, opened in the National Theater on February 13, 1940. By this time Hungarian anti-Semitism was codified: the Hungarian parliament had already passed its First (1938) and Second (1939) Jewish Laws, which drastically reduced the employability of Jewish professionals, among them actors and theater producers. The first included a maximum quota of 20 percent of Jewish membership in the Hungarian Theater Chamber, whereas the second further reduced it to 6 percent. Unemployed Jewish artists founded the Artists' Action of the Országos Magyar Izraelita Közművelődési Egyesület (Hungarian Israelite Cultural Association, or OMIKE), the Hungarian equivalent of the Jüdischer Kulturbund in Berlin.

In this atmosphere of increasing pressure and humiliation of Hungarian Jewry, it might perhaps be expected that *The Merchant* at the National Theater functioned as a piece of anti-Semitic propaganda. That this was not necessarily the case suggests that state control and censorship of theaters were significantly looser in wartime Budapest than in Berlin. The Hungarian Theater Chamber did not have direct power over individual theaters' programs or their policies; the directors were responsible for the activities of their theaters and were answerable to the cultural and interior ministries.

The production at the National was directed by the relatively progressive actor-director Béla Both. Shylock was played by the young actor Tamás Major, who was closely associated with the Communist Party and became the director of the Hungarian National Theater after the war. In a radio interview forty-six years after this production, Major recalls, "putting Shylock on stage was in the air then: those were horrible times, the Jewish laws were already being implemented. Playing Shylock well entailed a political statement."[26] According to Major, the production was banned after the fourth or fifth performance, but Antal Németh, head of the National Theater, was unwilling (and was never forced) to take any disciplinary actions against the actor or any other member of the production.[27] As Major remarked about Németh: "when it became obvious that the Germans would lose the war, his right-wing sympathies also disappeared. What's more, at the end of his directorship, he let us do *everything*. . . . the whole Arrowcross [Hungarian fascist party] press went berserk demanding that Antal Németh should fire us! But he never did."[28] Indeed, a chronicler of the National Theater's wartime history illustrates this relative freedom within the theater community when he reports that at a dinner party, the actor Major (the National Theater's Shylock), apparently fueled by a few drinks, went up to the famous German actor, Heinrich George, who was also present as a guest, gave him a hug, and told him: "Hey, you, superintendent! Look at me! I am a Communist!"[29]

Moreover, responding to the reporter's incredulity in 1986 that a positive image of Shylock was appreciated by an audience in Budapest in 1940, Major went on to explain: "There were no protests in the audience: the whole audience was under the spell of the show, and the reason for its banning was precisely that, when I played Shylock, the show almost could not be continued after Shylock's great soliloquy, 'Hath not a Jew eyes? . . . ,' because they burst into such enthusiastic applause . . ."[30] Contemporary theater reviews, however, do not mention "such enthusiastic applause." What they do mention is that, although the production emphasized the comedic elements of the play, it underlined Shylock's isolation and tragic pathos. Marcell Benedek noted, "[t]he National Theater's production offers a comedy; and although they limit Shylock's dramatic potential, the other characters effectively emphasize Shylock's loneliness with their light and brisk acting. What is drama in *The Merchant of Venice*—the drama of solitude and isolation—is to be forever an alien in a community: this is Hamlet's drama, this is Othello's and Shylock's drama as well. He is the black one among the white ones. And because he cannot destroy the white ones, he destroys himself."[31] Of course, it also depended on the critics' political orientation what they had seen in this production of *The Merchant*. Whereas Benedek perceived a moving tragedy of loneliness and isolation in Major's Shylock, another reviewer praised Major for effectively representing some of the more sinister aspects of the role: "The theater's exceptionally talented and refined actor, Tamás *Major,* strove to emphasize something new in his performance, something different from the characterizations of famous Shylock actors. Even if the direction stressed the comedic elements of the play, the new Shylock represented the miserly and bloodthirsty Jewish merchant by depicting the role's demonic features and its highly dramatized evil and desire for revenge. He frequently played in a stylized way, but he always insisted on psychological credibility. Tamás *Major* achieved a well-deserved success in the part."[32] Although probably less audacious than Major cared to remember forty years after the events, playing a humanized, relatively complex, at times even poignant, Shylock in a milieu of state-sponsored anti-Semitism was nevertheless a commendable theatrical venture.

Der Merchant von Velence

As we have seen, the three productions upon which I have very briefly touched here reveal various ways in which Shylock and, through him, Shakespeare's play were interpreted in these three European cities during the Second World War. The New Theatre's production in London starring Frederick Valk staged what Esmé Church called "a good dramatic story, colourful and easy to follow, linked to a charming fairy tale," which instead of going against the prevailing street-level anti-Semitism, quite fitted into the framework of what Tony Kushner calls the "polite tearoom type anti-Semitism" of wartime London.[33] In contrast to this production, however, we have seen that Nazi censors found the play potentially transgressive and did not permit it to be played without butchering it into a significantly different play. The Hungarian National Theater's production, furthermore, showed that an interpretation that was probably not radically different either aesthetically or even politically from that of the Old Vic came to be seen as a relatively progressive gesture in a political environment of state-sponsored anti-Semitism.

It is noteworthy that in the background of these three different productions, there lurked a rather dubious purist desire to "return to Shakespeare," that is, to gain authentication by an alleged Ur-tradition sanctified by the Bard. National Socialist translator and writer Hermann Kroepelin, for instance, was given the job of tailoring *Der Kaufmann* to Nazi needs in 1936. Having made the necessary changes that *Reichsdramaturg* Rainer Schlösser would report to Goebbels a few years later in a letter that I have quoted earlier, Kroepelin referred to his radical textual alterations of *The Merchant of Venice* as "further thinking in the spirit of Shakespeare" (ein Weiterdenken im Sinne Shakespeares).[34] Kroepelin rationalized his methodology, claiming, "[a]ll of these changes are justified without further ado, because they are made in accordance with Shakespeare's spirit."[35] Kroepelin did not argue that his solution was right and had to be heeded because that was how the play could be adjusted to National Socialist anti-Semitic ideology; instead, he evoked the authority of Shakespeare as the ultimate justification of his view. The ostensible gesture of Kroepelin's appropriation did not, therefore, amount to a modification or interpretation of the play, but to its authentication. With the aid of this gesture, Kroepelin managed to tap into Shakespeare's authority as a highly acclaimed cultural icon, while he simultaneously maintained and reconfirmed Shakespeare's distinct cultural status. In this way, it became possible for him to appreciate Shakespeare's greatness as long as it supported Nazi ideology and vice versa: Nazi ideology was relevant or "true" because it harmonized with "Shakespeare's spirit."

It is important to recognize that the same kind of gesture of authentication can be traced in Harley Granville-Barker's statement that *The Merchant of Venice* was a "fairy tale" and "the simplest of plays, so long as we do not bedevil it with sophistries," since "[d]espite the borrowed story, this Shylock is essentially Shakespeare's own."[36] Obviously, the explanation that an interpretation is valid because it is "Shakespeare's own" is dubious on several accounts. The suggestion that we can find a common denominator between these productions since all three were conceived "in the name of Shakespeare" does not hold: instead of pointing to a homogeneous semantic field of the signifier "Shakespeare," they make the concept even more hazy and blurred.

A major reason for the difficulty in pinning down the significance and possible meanings of the play and its author in the contexts I have discussed here (let alone in a wider context of wartime Europe) is that we have only limited, contradictory, and biased information about these productions available to us. Wartime anti-Semitism and its various manifestations in the British capital are seldom discussed, and are even suppressed by the "Finest Hour" myth. In the case of the Rose Theater production in Berlin, furthermore, it is worth noting that a 1965 monograph on the history of the Rose Theater does not mention the appalling aspects of the production at all. All we can learn from this otherwise extensive study is that the director, Paul Rose, started the show with a "carnival procession," and that the production was "a festive season-opening at the Frankfurter Allee."[37] What this study on the Rose Theater remains troublingly silent about is that the festive carnival atmosphere was amplified by fervent Jew-baiting. In contrast to the post–World War silence surrounding the London and Berlin productions, furthermore, there is a dubious abundance of information on the Budapest *Merchant* dated forty years after the fact: the somewhat self-glorifying accolades of the Hungarian actor who played Shylock are also somewhat suspicious.

Up to this point, I have been arguing that *The Merchant of Venice* was appropriated in three significantly different ways in the three significantly different contexts of wartime London, Berlin, and Budapest. My somewhat bizarre macaronic title, "*Der Merchant von Velence*," is a handy signifier of all the blatant differences that existed between the productions that I have discussed here. On the other hand, its mini-Babel of linguistic confusion notwithstanding, *Der Merchant of Velence* is still recognizable: we know that it refers to *The Merchant of Venice*; we know that it has something German in it; the Hungarian name for Venice is admittedly a little more obscure but is not completely indecipherable either. We are able to fill in the gaps and identify a unity in the discontinuous linguistic fragments.

As the title of this paper anticipates, therefore, I would like to call attention to some general elements identifiable in the radically discontinuous cultural fragments that I have presented above. If my paper has demonstrated so far that *The Merchant of Venice* was an extremely elusive and particularized entity during the Second World War, in closing and in a sort of inductive vein, I would like to fill in the gaps, as it were, and draw a somewhat generalizing brief conclusion about what *The Merchant of Venice* was and did in these three cities. By doing so, I would like to suggest that the play's devious identity rests first and foremost in the history of its interpretations: as a reciprocal object and subject of appropriation, it can be conceived and understood only in and through its historicity. In this sense, the *Merchant of Venice* emerges as a complex play that was perfectly suitable for a stage production conceived in a kind of "tearoom type" anti-Semitism in London, but was quite unsuitable for a racial appropriation according to Nazi ideology (without, at least, decisive alterations) in the Berlin of the Third Reich, and—when unaltered beyond the relatively "faithful" translation—could also be seen as a potentially pro-Jewish play in a political context of state-sponsored anti-Semitism in Budapest.

Notes

1. Dror Abend-David, *"Scorned My Nation": A Comparison of Translations of* The Merchant of Venice *into German, Hebrew, and Yiddish*, Comparative Cultures and Literatures, vol. 16 (New York: Peter Lang, 2003), 2.

2. James Agate, "The West End and Shakespeare," *Times,* September 6, 1942.

3. James Agate, "Henceforth—I shall be a Russian," *Daily Express,* January 31, 1942. This very same statement is also quoted in Ronald Harwood, *Sir Donald Wolfit C.B.E.: His Life and Work in the Unfashionable Theatre* (New York: St. Martin's Press, 1971), 172.

4. "As They Like It," *Daily Express,* August 4, 1942.

5. James Agate, "The West End and Shakespeare" (1942).

6. According to J. P. Wearing's *The London Stage, 1940–1949* (London: Scarecrow Press, 1991), in wartime London there were 213 performances of *Hamlet* (6 productions), 170 performances of *A Midsummer Night's Dream* (5 productions), and 131 performances of *The Merchant* (7 productions).

7. Ivor Brown, "Theatre and Life," *Observer,* February 21, 1943.

8. "Czech Actor as Shylock," *Daily Mail,* February 17, 1943.

9. Diana Valk, *Shylock for a Summer: The Story of One Year (1954–5) in the Life of Frederick Valk* (London: Cassell, 1958), 35–36.

10. Michael Meyer, *Words Through a Windowpane: A Life in London's Literary and Theatrical Scenes* (New York: Grove Weidenfeld, 1989), 237. Meyer closes this chapter on Valk with the following lines: "Twenty years later [after Valk's death in 1956], as we were lunching at the Savile, Ralph Richardson asked me: 'Whom do you think the greatest actor you have seen?' I hesitated out of politeness to him. He said: 'Valk?' I nodded, and so did he" (247).

11. Edgar Ralph, "Acting at Home and Abroad: Frederick Valk Talks on Two 'Schools'," *Stage,* July 4, 1946.

12. "Czech Actor as Shylock," *Daily Mail,* February 17, 1943.

13. James Agate, "Which Shylock?" *Times,* February 21, 1943.

14. Ibid.

15. See Charles Edelman, *The Merchant of Venice,* Shakespeare in Production (Cambridge: Cambridge University Press, 2002).

16. *Report on Recent Activities of the Old Vic and Sadler's Wells Companies* (Burnley: Old Vic and Sadler's Wells, 1941), 9.

17. Harley Granville-Barker, *Prefaces to Shakespeare* (Princeton: Princeton University Press, 1946), 4:88–89.

18. Ibid., 4:106.

19. Ian McLaine, *Ministry of Morale: Home Front Morale and the Ministry of Information in World War II* (London: George Allen and Unwin, 1979), 167.

20. Wilhelm Hortmann, *Shakespeare on the German Stage: The Twentieth Century* (Cambridge: Cambridge University Press, 1998), 135.

21. Früherer Weisung entsprechend, ist der *Kaufmann von Venedig* in Berlin in den letzten Jahren vom Spielplan zurückgesetzt worden. Inzwischen haben aber einige Bühnen im Reich mit meiner Zustimmung eine mit kleinen Korrekturen zu erreichende abgeänderte Fassung ausprobiert, bei der Jessica nicht als die Tochter, sondern nur als die Pflegetochter des Juden erscheint und somit rassenpolitische Schwierigkeiten aus dem Weg geräumt werden. Da diese Änderungen nicht umfangreich sind, bei der Textüberlieferung der Shakespeare-Stücke auch keine philologische Sünde darstellen und Jessica von den deutschen Schauspielerinnen nie als Jüdin gespielt wurde, sähe ich keine Bedenken, das klassische Werk, das überdies bei geschickter Darstellung eine Unterstützung unseres antijüdischen Kampfes bedeuten kann, auch in Berlin wieder zuzulassen. Das Rose-Theater hat den Plan, das Werk in der nächsten Spielzeit herauszubringen, und ich bitte um Entscheidung, ob man an dieser, immerhin am Rande gelegenen Stelle den Versuch machen könnte. Documents of the Reichsministerium für Volksaufklärung und Propaganda, Bundesarchiv Berlin-Lichterfelde, R55/20218/285. See Thomas Eicher, Barbara Panse, and Henning

Rischbieter, *Theater im "Dritten Reich": Theaterpolitik, Spielplanstruktur, NS-Dramatik* (Seelze-Velber: Kallmeyer, 2000), 308. See also Thomas Eicher, *Theater im "Dritten Reich": Eine Spielplananalyse der deutschen Schauspieltheater, 1929–1944,* PhD dissertation, Institut für Theaterwissenschaft (Berlin: Freie Universität, 1992), 55–56.

22. Joseph Wulf, *Theater und Film im Dritten Reich: Eine Dokumentation* (Gütersloh: Mohn, 1964), 258.

23. Paul Rose ließ von der Empore die Volksstimme mit empörten Rufen und gellenden Pfiffen einfallen, und hier unterstrich auch ein Echo aus dem Parkett den Höhepunkt des Abends. Wilhelm Grundschöttel, "Shylock im Fasching—Paul Rose inszeniert den *Kaufmann von Venedig*," *Völkischer Beobachter,* September 2, 1942. See Joseph Wulf, *Theater und Film im Dritten Reich* (1964), 258.

24. Völlig freilich werden die tragischen Elemente niemals zu löschen sein, und die Gegenwart weiß ja besser und klarer als alle andere Zeiten um den furchtbaren Ernst, der hier unter Harlekinsprüngen und fröhlichen Vermummungen sich jäh offenbart! Und Shylock wird für immer das Symbol eines geradezu dämonischen jüdischen Hasses bleiben. . . . So zeigt ihn auch hier Georg August Koch. Mit zausigem rötlichen Bart, mit bald gierig, bald furchtsam irrenden Augen, mit Händen, deren Finger wie Krallen sich öffnen und schließen—ein urwelthafter Golem, der durch die Stadt der Lagunen streift und unheimliche nächtliche Netze legt, um mit dem Köder des Goldes immer neue Opfer zu betören und zu vernichten. F. A. Dargel, "Großer Beifall im Rose-Theater: *Der Kaufmann von Venedig*," *Nacht-Expreß,* September 1, 1942.

25. Georg August Koch ist der Shylock, mit geklebter Hakennase, rotem Voll- und Wollbart, zuerst im Lustspielstil fast eine Possenfigur, doch in seinem hartnäckigen Haß sich zur Grausigkeit steigernd, um schließlich wie ein Haufen Elend zusammenzubrechen. Dr. Carl Weichardt, "Der Jude von Venedig: Spielbeginn im Rose-Theater mit Shakespeares *Kaufmann von Venedig*," *Berliner Morgenpost,* September 2, 1942.

26. Shylock eljátszása benne volt a levegőben. Nagyon rossz idők jártak, már készülődtek a zsidótörvények. Shylockot eljátszani egyet jelentett politikai kiállással . . . Hungarian Theater Institute, Budapest: Folder "*The Merchant of Venice*"; typed manuscript; "Gondolat-jel," Radio Kossuth, Budapest, March 30, 1986: Ilona Mélykuti's interview with Tamás Major.

27. It seems to me that Major's statement about the banning of this production "after the 4th or 5th performance" has to be taken with a pinch of salt. Although the statistical data in the 1941 *Yearbook of the Hungarian National Theatre* concur with Major's claim that the production survived only five evening performances in spring 1940, they also indicate that the same production was put on three additional times as a matinee and once as a special performance for workers. In addition, this *Merchant* production was further performed a few times in autumn 1940 as well. *Nemzeti Színház, 1941* (Budapest: Directorate of the National Theatre, 1942), 102, 114–15, and 333.

28. Amikor kiderült, hogy a németek elvesztik a háborút, akkor az ő jobboldalisága is teljesen megszűnt. Sőt, az igazgatása vége felé *mindent* engedett nekünk. . . . az egész nyilas sajtó őrjöngött, és követelte a Németh Antaltól, hogy rúgjon ki bennünket! És ő nem tette ezt meg. Ilona Mélykuti's interview with Tamás Major (1986).

29. Du, Intendant! Schau mich an! Ich bin ein Kommunist! Bálint Magyar, *A Nemzeti Színház története a két világháború között (1917–1944)* (Budapest: Szépirodalmi, 1977), 407.

30. Egy pillanatig sem volt nem-tetszés: az egész közönség a hatása alá került, és a

betiltás oka éppen az volt, hogy mikor én játszottam a Shylockot, akkor óriási nagymonológja—a: "Nincs a zsidónak szíve, keze? Keze, lába, gondolatai... ," azután majdnem nem lehetett folytatni az előadást, olyan viharos ünneplésben törtek ki.... Ilona Mélykuti's interview with Tamás Major (1986).

31. A Nemzeti Színház előadása vígjátékot ad és bár mérsékli Shylock drámai lehetőségét, a többi szereplő könnyű és fürge játékával hatásosan emeli ki Shylock magányát. Az, ami a A velencei kalmárban drama—a magány és az elszigeteltség drámája—örökre idegennek lenni a közösségben: ez Hamlet drámája, ez Othello és Shylock drámája is. Ő a fekete a fehérek között. S mert nem pusztíthatja el a fehéreket, önmagát pusztítja el. Marcell Benedek, "Két Shakespeare-felújítás: Shylock," February 25, 1940. Hungarian Theater Institute, Budapest: Folder *"The Merchant of Venice."*

32. A színház rendkívül tehetséges és kulturált fiatal színésze, *Major* Tamás igyekezett a nagynevű Shylock szereplők alakításától eltérően valami újat kidomborítani játékában. Ha a rendezés a vígjátéki elemekre fektette is a fősúlyt, az új Shylock, a szerep démonikus tulajdonságainak és a drámai magasságokba fokozott bosszúvágynak és gonoszságnak rajzával vetítette ki, sokszor stilizálva, de mindig a lélekábrázolás őszinteségéhez ragaszkodva, a zsugori, vérszomjas zsidó kalmár jellemét. *Major* Tamás megérdemelt sikert aratott alakításával. "A Velencei Kalmár—fiatalokkal," *Függetlenség,* February 15, 1940.

33. *Report on Recent Activities of the Old Vic and Sadler's Wells Companies* (Burnley: Old Vic and Sadler's Wells, 1941), 9; Tony Kushner, *The Persistence of Prejudice: Antisemitism in British Society during the Second World War* (Manchester: Manchester University Press, 1989), 2.

34. Documents of the Reichsministerium für Volksaufklärung und Propaganda, Bundesarchiv Berlin-Lichterfelde, R55/20218/93. Eicher, *Theater im "Dritten Reich",* 50.

35. Alle Änderungen lassen sich ohne weiteres verantworten, weil sie so auch schon im Sinne Shakespeares sind. Und den Zusatz am Schluß kann uns auch das übelwollendste Ausland nicht zum Vorwurf machen: wir haben in keiner Weise am Werk des Dichters gerührt, wir haben es nur an einer wichtigen Stelle weitergedacht und gestaltet. Documents of the Reichsministerium für Volksaufklärung und Propaganda, Bundesarchiv Berlin-Lichterfelde, R55/20218/93. Eicher, *Theater im "Dritten Reich,"* 50.

36. Harley Granville-Barker, *Prefaces to Shakespeare,* 4:88–89.

37. Heinz-Dieter Heinrichs, *Das Rose-Theater: Ein volkstümliches Familientheater in Berlin von 1906 bis 1944,* Theater und Drama, vol. 29 (Berlin: Colloquium, 1965), 82–83.

Measuring the "Most Cheerful Barrack": Shakespeare's *Measure for Measure* in Hungary under the Kádár Regime (1964–85)

Veronika Schandl

THE YEAR 1985 SAW TWO PRODUCTIONS OF *MEASURE FOR MEASURE* IN Hungary. One in the renowned middle-class theater of the capital, Madách, the other in a small town in the countryside, in Veszprém. The first was directed by Ádám Szirtes, a director wanting to return to nonpolitical "pure" Shakespeare, the second by István Paál, a producer coming from the amateur theater movement and famous for his political, sometimes even scandalous, shows.

The production in Budapest was performed against a background of cream-colored curtains with Viennese pictures on them, the actors wearing yellow costumes, with the exception of Angelo, who was dressed in black, all aiming to make a favorable impression. The play was put on as a fairy tale, in a comic more than a serious vein, with the Duke and Isabella falling in love with each other, and Angelo becoming a pocket-Tartuffe. As the director argued in a radio interview, the only way to present a successful interpretation of the play after so many failures is to refrain from putting one's own ideas before those of Shakespeare and not to draw any "parallels between current political and social situations" and the plot of the play.[1]

István Paál came to quite different conclusions, openly wanting to hold a mirror up to contemporary Hungary, where smiles had faded, and "only terrible things occurred, where jokes were out of tune, and puns almost hurt."[2] As the curtain rose in Veszprém, a threatening, massive cage—for wild animals or for hardened criminals?—was seen in the middle of the stage, and in one of its corners a dirty man squatted in ragged clothes. Farther up, at the top of a staircase, a spooky figure wrapped in bandages like a modern mummy was waiting for him with a huge axe in his hand. Cold beams of light patrolled above the scenery, and an unpleasant scratching sound was heard. Suddenly all lights went out, and where previously the executioner had stood, now Vincentio presided over his people. The basic tone of the production was thus set: all the world's a cage, Vienna is a prison.

Critics reacted *unisono,* rejecting the Budapest production, calling it "a boring, button-down, commercial comedy" and preferring the darkness of the Veszprém performance to its shades of beige.[3] A jovial Vincentio, a neat Isabella, and a ridiculous Angelo were seen as misinterpretations; a comic, even sexy *Measure for Measure* was taken to be alien to Hungarian traditions. By 1985 the claim that productions of this play would tell us not only about Shakespeare but at least as much "about our own stormy, controversial age, so rich in social struggles,"[4] advanced by the famous reviewer Judit Szántó back in 1976, no longer seemed far-fetched at all, for, as we will see, in the previous decade a series of productions had begun to underline the topicality and relevance of *Measure for Measure* for contemporary Hungary, giving renewed legitimacy to a play generally forgotten in Hungarian theaters.

The 1960s: The Crisis of Humanism and the Shadow of Tyranny

None of this was in the cards in the 1960s, however, when the play started its career on Hungarian stages. Official scholarship, best exemplified by a monograph on Shakespearean comedies published in 1964 by László Kéry, described the "problem plays" as responses to the changed sociopolitical system of Shakespeare's England, when the horrors of early capitalism shook the Bard's humanistic worldview manifest in earlier romantic comedies.[5] Using the two terms most often associated with the Shakespearean oeuvre in Socialist criticism—realism and humanism—Kéry further argued that *Troilus and Cressida, All's Well That Ends Well,* and *Measure for Measure* reflected the antagonisms of the age they had been written in, but also attempted to overcome them, pointing to the virtue of humanism as a way out. He states, however, that in the case of *Measure for Measure* this experiment went astray, for though the concept of the play was that of a lucid and flawless comedy, the play's subject matter resisted such an approach, the end result thus being disharmonious and unconvincing.[6] Other Hungarian critics in the 1960s also classified this drama among Shakespeare's weaker plays, drawing attention to its many psychological and logical inconsistencies.[7]

Theaters, however, were beginning to take to the play. Performed only once before the sixties (in 1927), between 1964 and 1985, *Measure for Measure* was put onstage in no fewer than eight different productions. The Universitas Ensemble, led by a young director József Ruszt, the first to rediscover the play in 1964, did not yet claim any correlation between the worlds on and off the stage. The performance was generally reviewed as a "rustic, full-blooded folk play, a tale which is not to be taken seriously."[8] Géza Fodor, however, a critic writing for the university paper (*Egyetemi Lapok*), disagreed with this reading of the play and argued that it is really about much more than "juvenile gaiety through which the sunbeam of comedy" radiates.[9] But it seems that none of the "serious, unresolved problems" nor the "mental loops of despair" he saw in the text were to be found in the performance.[10]

The first director to choose the play for its topicality was Vilmos Dobai, in Pécs, in 1966. As he explained in an interview later published in the program, "[t]o talk about the abuse of power right now, in the stable period after the Stalinist regime is extremely relevant."[11] The production focused on the question of rule and government, and it strove to illustrate through Angelo's example how political power ends up corrupting everybody. The actor György Bánffy—playing Angelo—summed up the argument as follows: "We cannot occupy a position which lies far beyond our own limits."[12] From contemporary reviews, however, it seems that the production itself failed to match the claims that had been made about it. The production still emphasized the "gaudy tale" in the drama, while, by then, critics—including Péter Molnár Gál, the renowned journalist of the party paper, *Népszabadság*—already wished to see its more somber, disillusioned aspect as well.[13]

The 1970s: The Great Manipulator

The first who reportedly "succeeded in bringing the problems of the comedy close to present times" was Tamás Major.[14] Some even declared his direction of the performance to have been "an exact political position paper, as if taken from a news report."[15] Having been in the theater business since the 1930s, Major had a good nose for potentially intriguing plays, so it may not be a coincidence that he was among the first to try his hand at this bitter comedy. He first staged *Measure for Measure* in 1973, in the National Theater, then again almost exactly ten years later in Miskolc. As he himself stated, he aimed at creating what he called "dangerous theater," which "always has to feel the tensions of the age, and constantly react to them by the means of art," thus "holding up a mirror to society. For theater is not an illusion, but an assignment: to reveal, to revolt, and to reject stupidities."[16] He tried to combine this message with Brechtian theater techniques, such as the use of an almost barren stage and of alienation effects, and the overall concept of understanding dramatic conflicts as social conflicts. Last but not least, as opposed to the primarily literary orientation of the traditional theater, he imagined a true spectacle, using circuslike elements such as clowns and brass bands, as well as mixing various styles and tones.

Talking about Major, we should always bear in mind that he held the highly controversial position of a modern-time court jester, an official critic of the regime. Be that as it may, by putting his hands on Shakespeare from the 1960s, he paved the way for others, using his own authority to legitimize possible critical approaches. The success of his *Measure for Measure*—his *Romeo and Juliet* two years earlier had been a flop—showed that this time Major's concept did match the public feeling and was able to transform the general political condition into a theatrical metaphor. To understand, however, how Vincentio's Vienna could possibly have been similar to Kádár's Budapest, we need a short digression to describe the political situation in Hungary after 1956.

With the 1956 revolution defeated, it quickly became clear that no democratic changes were possible in the foreseeable future, so people tried to live within the boundaries of the Socialist state, and János Kádár, the new party leader who came in with the Russian tanks, made it easier for them. After the "necessary" purges, executions, and imprisonments, Kádár knew that another fake consensus like that of 1947, when the Communists came to power by manipulating the election results and imposing their rule on the people under the mighty shadow of the glorious Soviet forces, would lead to another revolution. Therefore he seemingly removed politics from the private lives of people, and provided a relative degree of material wealth for the masses. Whereas in the previous Stalinist Rákosi regime the state wished to control the private sphere as well—telling you what to think and monitoring your life in Big Brother fashion—the new dogma was that, unless you rebelled openly against the state, you could say or think whatever you wished within the walls of your home. Thus political debates moved from the streets and instead of entering Parliament invaded the pubs, the living rooms, and even the state-financed cultural forums, such as the theaters.

The general directive of "those who are not against us are with us" was extended to cultural matters as well, and this enabled the theater and the arts in general to function as safety valves through which society could release pent-up pressure, creating overtly political productions where criticism of the regime was much more evident than ever in previous performances. The establishment of this so-called "Goulash Communism" with its far more lenient state directive made Hungary the "most cheerful barrack" of the Eastern bloc, and led to the fact that by the 1970s most people had come to accept the status quo. This was the time in Hungarian history when the Kádár regime gained increasing international legitimacy and Kádár openly rejected his Stalinist forerunners; the economy also started to boom thanks to the so-called "New Mechanism," so it seemed that the country was making excellent progress. Still, this "brave new world" was built on the ruins of a hopeful revolution labeled as a counterrevolution at that time, and was thus living with a lie about its past.[17] The question naturally arose: who is to blame?

Major's version of *Measure for Measure*—this play full of "false situations and pseudo-judgments, petty faults dimming real crimes and dark retortions"—shifted the blame to the Duke, making him the protagonist of this production.[18] Ferenc Kállay gave an outstanding performance as Duke Vincentio, displaying his magnificent authority and making it clear that he was the chief force in Vienna. He was not a congenial figure, but a "really dangerous, smiling manipulator" who left his throne because he was unable to face the consequences of his strict laws.[19] What is more, he was unwilling to lose the popularity that was so dear to him. Despite his claims that he did not "relish well" the "loud applause and *Aves* vehement" of his people (1.1.69–70),[20] he set all the machinations into operation to make sure he did receive them in the end. He knew Angelo and was sure that his rule would result in tyranny; the audience was not surprised at this either, István Iglódi's Angelo being young and weak, not a hardened criminal but the perfect puppet for the dirty job, extremely easy to break.[21] Though Vincentio often stressed how much he believed in him, it became clear very soon that, cloaked in benignity, he was just waiting for the right moment to prove his guilt and "by cold gradation, and well balanc'd form" proceed with him (4.3.99–100). His Janus-faced nature was very aptly shown in the way his people misunderstood and disliked him—most clearly the provost and Claudio—and how they rejected his moral ideas expounded in lengthy speeches. It is not the Angelos who count, Major suggested, but the Dukes, "who can remain Dukes just because they always find their Angelos at the right moment" and thus can keep up the spotless picture of themselves as being justice personified.[22]

Kállay/Vincentio clearly sensed and was disgusted by the filthy and immoral state of his Vienna, but he did not do anything to alter it, thus becoming even baser than those he ruled. For, whereas his subjects at least did not fancy themselves righteous, his power "did not only show its infamy, but boasted in 'selling' this ignominy as moral eminence."[23] He finally left the real sinners unpunished, and let the immoral conditions stagnate, making himself—with his self-created anarchy in the background—nothing more than "the fanciless denunciator of base practices."[24] Even though he returned to his court as the righteous disguised king of Hungarian folktales—generously forgiving everybody, expecting them in return to rejoice wholeheartedly in the happy reunion—this play could not end on a happy note. Creating a last scene, which was hailed by critics as "one of the great theatrical moments,"[25] Major showed that absolute harmony could only be achieved in tales, or onstage, but never in reality. After the Duke gave his hand to a truly shocked and humiliated Isabella, the quick, circuslike pace of the performance slowed down, like a gramophone winding down. Ironically, the trumpet of the previous acts was replaced by a sweet cello tune, to which actors started moving in slow motion.[26] They fluttered with their hands, as happy angels on cloud nine, and put masks on their faces; "Angelo flew around as an innocent boy, while Isabella, forgetting her celibacy vow turned to the Santa-Claus-like Duke with the daemonic smile of a lipstick model."[27] Major gives us a happy ending of a kind, but leaves us with the final conclusion that, although "Vincentio's manipulated kingdom provides more acceptable living conditions than those of Angelo's 'chaste order' . . . , the Duke's Vienna is also corrupt and rotten at its core."[28]

Major's influence was long-lasting, for after 1973, three productions followed suit, all centering on the figure of the Duke, questioning *his* role in the events, and stressing the final disappointment of the "happy ending." The first of these was János Sándor's direction in Debrecen, in 1975. The "young, energetic, strong-willed, and cynical" Vincentio,[29] György Cserhalmi, was simply bored with ruling, so he left the throne, looking for something more thrilling to do among his people. After he withdrew from the throne, the vivid colors of his Vienna were replaced by Angelo's eye-hurting purple uniforms, also worn by Lucio, who adopted the spirit and the morals of his new lord well, with Angelo taking over his role, though remaining "ungainly, austere, dark, and awkward,"[30] also when wanton. Relying far more strongly on the circus scenario, with gongs at the end of each scene, and with the Romanian guest designer Frentin Sever's satiric costumes on a "surprisingly barren, empty and bleak set," the main argument of the show was that "in a state lacking ideals one cannot bring forth changes, either with new measures, or with reforms."[31] Though in the end the tall clown hats fell off Angelo's and Lucio's heads, at least their heads stayed on their necks.

By the end of the 1970s *Measure for Measure* productions had turned darker. Starting with László Babarczy's show in Kaposvár in 1978—directed with the avowed intention to "amplify all the traits which make the play topical today"—they stressed the fears of a generation that the system would prevail forever, that they would be unable to generate changes, and that the well-trained masses would accept any yoke.[32] By this time the Kádár regime had consolidated itself, and with the standard of living rising considerably, the majority of the society accepted the status quo. By concentrating on *how* they lived, they seemed to forget *where* they lived, adopting the axiom of the writer István Örkény according to which in the twentieth century there was a stark choice between staying morally intact and staying alive.[33] In state politics, and especially in the cultural field, a strange dichotomy seemed to prevail, for while the range of things that could be said out loud had widened and taboos were now less in number, the state never stopped introducing new measures against somebody or something,[34] as if guarding itself against visible signs of ever stronger resistance, one form of which was still the theater.

Babarczy's Kaposvár *Measure for Measure,* played in hippie costumes among neon lights, became "a social satire in *cinéma vérité* style, guffawing into the face of contemporary society."[35] The key figure of the play, Vincentio, played by Vilmos Kun, was sanctimonious and jovial at first sight, but as soon as he hid behind a pseudonym and a disguise, it turned out that he had not set out on his journey for the sole purpose of social observation.[36] Leaving the throne to Angelo, the "deputy head of the department," he tortured Claudio "first with unconcealed sadism, then cuddled him with suspicious intimacy, while confusing matters to suit his fancy."[37] Still in control over everything through his secret police—men in bowler hats carrying briefcases strolling up and down the stage—he let the naive Angelo walk into his trap, so that in the end he could come back to humiliate everybody and to create a forced happy ending, no matter whether the others liked it or not. The last scene showed that the price to be paid for this was "man's dignity," for "behind the triumphant prince his rifled victims stood apathetic, emerging from the manipulations of Vincentio as marionettes, broken, mocked, ravished, but ready for the next happy ending."[38] Or, as Tamás Mészáros saw Vincentio: "the riding master with a rakish moustache stood before his well-trained animals, left with helpless disgust in their eyes."[39]

The 1980s: The Prison Door Closes

Still bearing in mind that "the text does not make an effect for its own sake, but it exists in a certain social situation and aims at creating real social bonds when uttered by the characters,"[40] and not forgetting that ten years had gone by, Major's return to the play in 1983, in Miskolc, a large industrial town in eastern Hungary, bore more sober undertones as well. The clowns disappeared, and the Duke—the "absolute protagonist," as in Major's first production—had changed as well.[41] Sitting alone at the top of a dazzlingly white staircase, in a white armchair, he looked more somber and sinister. Never letting anybody get a full insight into his plans, he left his throne precipitously, and though it seemed to be an old plan of his to get rid of Angelo, he still acted on the spur of the moment, suddenly letting the reins of power slip from his hands. Having let the genie out of the bottle, he quickly lost control over the whole scheme, and thus needed the remainder of the play to set things more or less right again. As the hidden stage manager of the plot, the Duke knew that to make his performance a success he first of all needed the right cast. Thus using honest but weak Angelo, and "maintaining an overall uncertainty in the final outcome, he achieved that everybody took the position he offered them in the end."[42]

The only character who seemed to be able to see through Vincentio's manipulations was Lucio, not the nonchalant vagabond of the 1973 production, but a humanist clown, a Chaplin-like figure, who conarrated the play. Though sometimes naive and grotesque, he had an eye for worldly affairs, thus almost forcing the audience to trust his comments on the Duke's real nature. This sentiment was also emphasized by the fact that there was no trace in this performance of the sin and decay among the people of Vienna, so often referred to in Shakespeare's text.

In the final act of amnesty everybody seemed to rejoice, not looking for justice, but primarily for forgiveness. Still the Duke's motives for all his machinations remained enigmatic and dubious; even critics could not agree on them. Some viewed his actions as acts of benevolence, others claimed that he only wanted to test how far he could go, while Tamás Koltay even suspected a hidden political conspiracy between Vincentio and the provost.[43] They all agreed, however, that the Duke learned nothing during his descent among his people, never coming to an understanding of how they thought or why they accepted him as a ruler at all. Major once again emphasized the final discord resulting from these facts in the last scene. The newly formed couples put on broadly smiling masks and, accompanied by nuptial music, they danced off the stage. The Duke himself was so joyful that he did not realize his bride had left him on their way out, for Isabella remained onstage alone, taking off her mask with a renouncing, desperate gesture, as if she had understood her role in Vincentio's ugly game.[44] She also gestured toward the audience, indicating that, in this foolish world of theirs, happy endings can only be appreciated with widely grinning masks on.

We can now see why in 1985 the public as well as the professional critics appreciated the darker tones and the prison of the Veszprém production, and were disappointed by the show in the capital. Only twenty years had passed since 1964, but thanks to the theater productions that had opened new horizons by the end of the 1980s, *Measure for Measure* had become a "masterpiece," one among "the five or six best plays written by Shakespeare."[45] István Paál's political concept, throwing into prominence the parallel between Vincentio's Vienna and his Hungary, was based on that new axiom introduced into Hungarian Shakespeare criticism in the 1970s, which revaluated *Measure for Measure* not as the drama "of Angelo and Isabella, not a play on character and private life, but as one mainly concerned with public life, government and public morals, with the Duke, or if you like the Duke and the people of Vienna at its core."[46]

Paál, the director, the rebel of the amateur theater movement who first brought Jarry, Albee, and Mrožek onto Hungarian stages, had always openly sympathized with the mission of a socially sensitive theater. For him theater was not an aim in itself, but a tool, a social forum where he could express his views about the world and himself.[47] In *Measure for Measure* he was looking for answers to questions such as "social and ethical problems, the relationship of the individual and society, the ethical conflicts arising from this relation, the connections of the private and the social self, as well as the conflicts and failures of bigger and smaller social groups."[48] His keywords in this were manipulation, justice, ethics, and law; his key character the disguised Duke, the only figure who could leave the prison cell of Vienna. But he could only do so as someone else, for as a ruler he was a prisoner, too, as lonely and scared as everybody else. To become the friar he did not need a disguise, since nobody recognized him when he was outside, as those within the bars did not even discover that he was not sharing their captivity any longer.[49] As a voyeur, seeing everything, and being present in each scene, he took sadistic pleasure in watching others in pain, being totally indifferent toward human misery; thus "we could not believe for a second that anything would have happened against his will."[50] His constant helpers were Escalus, the eager-beaver *chinovnik* (clerk of the Russian civil service) and constable Elbow, more frightening than simple, "who froze the smiles on our faces whenever he lifted his eyes upon us."[51]

Throughout the play the Duke was depicted as conducting "strange experiments, some being so cruel that they would make any animal-rights activist protest in disgust if they had been performed on mice or rabbits,"[52] as one reviewer wrote. This sadistic mechanism slowly buried Angelo, in this production a typical everyman acting against his will,[53] as well as Isabella, the perplexed, defenseless nun, who even lost her white gown in the end, and thus went naked and defeated into the Duke's bed. In this Vienna no one's hands stayed clean, only those of Lucio, the mouthpiece of common thoughts. The reward for his honesty was death in the end, the hangman waiting for him, repeating the first scene, while the repeated metallic noise became "unendurably loud—as if introducing some destructive irrational force to come and invade the future."[54]

As it happened, the future of Hungary presented a different reality, one that showed a closer match with the Budapest production from 1985, and the theater, instead of keeping up the mirror to contemporary politics, became the medium of entertainment again. This era is, however, beyond the scope of this essay.

Notes

1. Radio Kossuth, November 24, 1985, 6:00 PM, in the *Jó reggelt!* [Good Morning!] program. Transcripts at the Hungarian Theatrical Institute. Unless indicated otherwise all translations are mine.
2. László Zappe, "Mit akarunk a színháztól?" *Népszabadság,* December 31, 1985, 16.
3. Júlia Szekrényessy, "Hát élet ez?" *Élet és Irodalom,* December 6, 1985, 21.
4. Judit Szántó, "Két kalap a földön," *Színház* 9.7 (1976): 24.
5. László Kéry, *Shakespeare vígjátékai* (Budapest: Gondolat Kiadó, 1964), 290.
6. Ibid., 258.
7. Tibor Lutter, "*Szeget szeggel,*" in *Shakespeare Összes Drámái—Színművek* (Budapest: Európa Könyvkiadó, 1961), 906; Éva Róna, "*Szeget szeggel,* vagy szemet szemért?" in *Shakespeare-tanulmányok,* ed. László Kéry, László Országh, and Miklós Szenczi, 318 (Budapest: Akadémiai Kiadó, 1965).
8. Unsigned review, "Bemutató!" *Egyetemi Lapok,* March 14, 1964, 15.
9. Review signed "f.f.," "Fiatalos derű," *Esti Hírlap,* March 26, 1964, 14.
10. Géza Fodor, "*Szeget szeggel,* avagy egy kritika kritikája," *Egyetemi Lapok,* April 24, 1964, 9.
11. Program, *Szeget szeggel* (Pécs: National Theater of Pécs, 1966), 2.
12. Árpád Thiery, "Angelo—Bánffy György," *Dunántúli Napló,* October 9, 1966, 10.
13. Péter Molnár Gál, "*Szeget szeggel,*" *Népszabadság,* October 6, 1966, 15.
14. Béla Mátrai-Betegh, "*Szeget szeggel,*" *Magyar Nemzet,* January 14, 1973, 12.
15. György Csapó, "Egy érdekes Shakespeare-bemutatóról," *Ország Világ,* February 7, 1973, 24.
16. L. Mihály Kocsis, *Van itt valaki* (Budapest: Minerva, 1987), 81 and 34.
17. See Tibor Valuch, "A gulyáskommunizmus," in *Mítoszok, legendák, tévhitek a 20. századi magyar történelemről,* ed. Ignác Romsics (Budapest: Osiris, 2002); Miklós Szabó, "A Kádár-rendszer," *Rubicon* 9.1 (1998): 29.
18. Iván Sándor, "*Szeget szeggel,*" *Film Színház Muzsika* 9.2 (1973): 14.
19. Tamás Koltai, "*Szeget szeggel,*" *Népszabadság,* January 10, 1973, 15.

20. J. W. Lever, ed., *William Shakespeare, Measure for Measure*, the Arden Shakespeare, 2nd series (New York: Routledge, 1996 [1965]).
21. Erika Szántó, "Hitványságbörze—a *Szeget szeggel* a Nemzetiben," *Színház* 9.4 (1973): 23.
22. Ibid.
23. Unsigned review, "Szeget szeggel," *Néző* 19.2 (1973): 3.
24. Sándor, "Szeget szeggel," 14.
25. Antal Papp, "*Szeget szeggel*—felfedezés értékű bemutató a Nemzeti Színházban," *Népszava*, January 8, 1973, 15.
26. Ibid.
27. Vera Létay, "Szemet szemért?" *Élet és Irodalom*, January 27, 1973, 19.
28. Gábor Mihályi, "Hogyan ját(sz)szunk Shakespeare-t," typescript in the Hungarian Theatrical Institute.
29. Ibolya Cs. Nagy, "Shakespeare—*Szeget szeggel*," *Bihari Napló*, January 26, 1976, 10.
30. Szántó, "Hitványságbörze," 24.
31. Ibid.
32. Kaposvár was a hidden countryside town to which the intellectuals flocked in pilgrimages to watch revolutionary productions. Judit Nagy, "Kaposvár—*Szeget szeggel*," *Film Színház Muzsika*, November 11, 1978, 24.
33. Ignác Romsics, *Magyarország története a 20. században* (Budapest: Osiris, 2002), 497.
34. Ibid., 499.
35. Review signed "k," "A szó a tárgyhoz alkalmazkodik—A kaposváriak Shakespeare-jéről," *Dunaújvárosi Hírlap*, April 10, 1979, 10.
36. Tamás Koltai, "Így sújt le a félisten, a Hatóság . . . ," *Színház* 12.3 (1979): 25.
37. Tamás Mészáros, "Szeget szeggel," *Új Tükör*, February 11, 1979, 18; László Leskó, "A bécsi bácsi," *Somogyi Néplap*, November 19, 1978, 11.
38. Koltai, 25.
39. Tamás Mészáros, "*Szeget szeggel*—Kaposvári Csiky Gergely Színház," *Új Tükör*, February 11, 1979, 23.
40. Program, *Szeget szeggel* (Miskolc: National Theater of Miskolc, 1983), 3.
41. Gábor Antal, "Szeget szeggel," *Magyar Nemzet*, January 25, 1983, 10; Tamás Mészáros, "Fo a szereposztás," *Magyar Hírlap*, January 22, 1983, 17.
42. Mészáros, "Fő a szereposztás," 17.
43. Tamás Szabados, "Major Tamás újra Miskolcon rendez," *Déli Hírlap*, December 16, 1982, 8; Júlia Szekrényessy, "Minemű érték?" *Élet és Irodalom*, January 28, 1983, 24; Tamás Koltai, "Működik a törvény—A *Szeget szeggel* Miskolcon," *Új Tükör*, February 13, 1983, 17.
44. Gábor Mihályi, "Bordélyház és kolostor—A *Szeget szeggel* Miskolcon," *Színház* 16.4 (1983): 16.
45. László Cs. Szabó, "Szeget szeggel," typescript in the Hungarian Theatrical Institute.
46. Szántó, "Hitványságbörze," 24.
47. Program, *Szeget szeggel* (Veszprém: Petőfi Sándor Theatre Veszprém, 1985), 2.
48. Unsigned review, "Shakespeare: *Szeget szeggel*," *Napló*, November 26, 1985, 7.
49. Judit Szántó, "Shakespeare – *Szeget szeggel*," *Kritika* 18.4 (1986): 19.
50. Sándor Köröspataki Kiss, "Felkél a jog," *Új Tükör*, December 15, 1985, 14.
51. Ibid.
52. Júlia Szekrényessy, "Hát élet ez?" *Élet és Irodalom*, December 6, 1985, 21.
53. Zappe, "Mit akarunk a színháztól?" 16.
54. Mária Novák, "Vienna börtön," *Színház* 19.2 (1986): 24.

Feminist Movement and the Balance of Power in John Cranko's Ballet *The Taming of the Shrew* (Stuttgart, 1969)

Nancy Isenberg

IN THE LATE 1960S, EDUCATED MIDDLE-CLASS WOMEN THROUGHOUT Western Europe and the United States began organizing—intensely, aggressively, and separately from male-dominated leftist structures—in the "second wave" women's movement. In those same years and in the same parts of the world, classical ballet was enjoying one of its most glorious moments of the century.[1] What could be more diametrically opposed than the female identities being proposed in those very different contexts, or the connotations of "movement" for the women inhabiting those different spheres?

DISTINCTLY DIFFERENT FEMALE IDENTITIES

In the world at large, women strove toward liberation not only by rebelling against their place of subordination in a patriarchal society, but also by rejecting the "cosmetic" abuses they had until then voluntarily imposed upon their bodies in the name of femininity. Simultaneously, ballerinas continued to strive, as the tradition of their art dictated, for their own form of liberation—from the natural laws of gravity—that gave them seeming weightlessness in their elevations and effortless balance in their poses. Razors, tweezers, hair curlers, high heels, tight belts, and braziers wound up materially or metaphorically in "freedom trash cans" wherever feminists gathered. And ballerinas continued to tend to their blistered toes and aching limbs, adjust their tutus, lacquer their hair into tight buns, and leap into men's arms, getting bruised in the ribs and grabbed in the crotch as they did.

Our memory of those years is, in part, a composite of Margot Fonteyn mesmerizing viewers in the great opera houses of Europe in her sublime performances with Rudolf Nureyev, and young feminists marching angrily out of leftist political rallies and throwing tomatoes (Frankfurt, September 1968, 23rd SDS Congress of Delegates) at the men they had once considered their comrades. And so, at the same time that the works of Kate Millet, Betty Friedan, and Germaine Greer crossed the Atlantic Ocean, providing the kindling that would turn the feminist flame on the Old Continent into an indomitable wildfire,[2] the internationally renowned choreographer John Cranko decided to create a ballet version of *Taming of the Shrew* for the Stuttgart Ballet. Given the political context, one can only presume he was aware his Kate would stand challengingly at the crossroad between those two very distinct female identities, the feminist's and the ballerina's.

As we know, those were challenging times for *The Taming of the Shrew* in Shakespearean performance and criticism. The whip-cracking Petruchio and the submissive Kate of the final scene clashed harshly with the call outside for a new sexual politics. Robert Heilman's 1966 survey of criticism on *Taming*, closely contemporary to Cranko's ballet, reflects the new critical consciousness developing in those years about what goes on onstage. Heilman indicated the mid-twentieth century as a turning point in interpretations of the "taming" theme and the roles of Petruchio and Kate: "after three centuries of relative stability ... Petruchio has developed rather quickly, first from an animal tamer to a gentleman-lover who simply brings out the best in Kate, and then at last to a laughable victim of the superior spouse who dupes him." As for Kate, Heilman noted that it was Nevill Coghill in 1950 who launched her in her career as a modern woman who "triumphs over" both her family and her husband, but lets her spouse play the dominating role in public. A year later, Harold Goddard offered a psychological rationale for Kate's shrewishness, which he saw resulting from her father's partiality toward Bianca (she is the "cross child who is starved for love"). In 1956, Margaret Webster added a sociological excuse for Kate's "negative" character: in her view, Kate was "shut up in a society where women were supposed only to look decorative." By 1961, Peter Alexander could acknowledge Kate's power as a woman who "stoops to conquer," and five years later, Heilman could proclaim that Kate had developed into a "fighting young feminist."[3]

As the legend goes, Cranko was drawn to Shakespeare's play primarily by the role of Petruchio. He had been looking for a very strong part for an exceptionally vibrant and acrobatic dancer in his company, Richard Cragun. Stuttgart Ballet by the mid-1960s had already made its mark on the map as "the miracle ballet company." Under Cranko's direction, it had risen from provincial mediocrity to become a world-class company, and it numbered many unusually talented dancers. For the purposes of the present volume, which focuses on European culture, it is worth pointing out that neither Cranko nor his company framed themselves within any particular national context. The choreographer, who was South African by birth, had developed professionally in various parts of the European continent,[4] and his company counted eighty-five members representing no fewer than twenty different nationalities. Stuttgart Ballet considered itself polyglot both in speech and in the language of dance.[5]

Besides wanting a suitable role for Cragun, Cranko was also seeking a challenge for his fiery Brazilian ballerina, Marcia Haydee. He found it, of course, in Kate. Furthermore, *Taming* offered an unusual number of strong supporting male roles, even after the inevitable simplification of plot that ballet required.[6] Thus *Taming* gave Cranko further creative space to exploit many of the wonderful male talents of his company. Perhaps Cranko's homosexuality had something to do with his being attracted to a play with numerous strong male roles. And it may also have made him more sensitive to the politics of gender stirring up so much trouble in the world outside his dance studio.[7]

Dancing the Domestic and Liberating Carnival

In those years, according to choreographer-turned-filmmaker Yvonne Rainer, "if you walked as a dancer, you walked as though you were a queen, an aristocrat, a character—someone who was *more* than ordinary, more than human."[8] Cranko's Kate, however, is very human. Far from the virginal Odettes and Giselles, seductive Odiles and Sylphs, and fairy-tale Cinderellas and Sleeping Beauties with whom we associate women in ballet narrative, she brings the ordinary, everyday, and domestic into ballet—perhaps for the first time. Her performance space is devoid of the enchantments and magic, evil villains, and charming princes one expects in ballet. And she certainly challenges Rainer's 1960s ballerina as she stomps across the stage hard on her heels, chin out, arms pumping aggressively. She mocks the codified gestures of femininity in ballet when she lifts her leg with bent knee and flexed foot, when she reels and teeters with anger, and when she extends her arm with a thrust and a punch. Cranko's fist-clenching Kate brought into ballet the 1960s avant-garde aesthetic trend. But as ballet is arguably the performing art with the strongest conservative tendencies, Cranko's choreography was an unusually daring and bold challenging of the boundaries between art and everyday life.[9]

Cranko's *Taming*, following so closely after Zeffirelli's highly popular film with Elizabeth Taylor and Richard Burton (1966), obviously invites a comparison. Although the scope of this paper is not a comparative analysis of the two adaptations, it is useful, in order to bring out certain characteristics of the ballet, occasionally to pit Cranko's work against Zeffirelli's.

Graham Holderness, in his discussion of Zeffirelli's work, acknowledges that "the sexual politics of the film can only ... be interpreted and evaluated in terms of its own cultural context and historical moment," and in this light he considers Zeffirelli's film "not so much anti-feminist as a-feminist."[10] I think it is more correct to say that Zeffirelli used the strength of feminist politics to his advantage, to inflame and excite the antagonism between his Kate and Petruchio, while safely enjoying the sure appeal of his Taylor and Burton, and the blurring of their turbulent private and stage roles.[11] Cranko, I hope to show, had a different agenda.

There is one coincidence of particular importance in Zeffirelli's and Cranko's works regarding script adaptation for which Cranko may have drawn inspiration from Zeffirelli, although his use of the adaptation is entirely different. It has to do with incorporating a weakness for alcohol into the character of Petruchio. The seed for this attribute is already in Shakespeare, in the wedding scene, but in Burton's Petruchio this is usually seen as a case of "the character embodying the actor" (Burton's problems with alcoholism were known to all). Much more than a character trait in Cranko, this attribute serves a fundamental narrative function. He introduces it in his choreography immediately following 1.1, in which Kate dumps the contents of a chamber pot from her balcony onto Bianca's suitors, thus establishing her half of the problem that the main plot will deal with. In 1.2, Petruchio makes his stage entrance in a tavern. Succumbing there to the flattering attention of three prostitutes, he drinks himself into a stupor and wakes a changed man: stripped by the women of his clothes and purse, he is unable to command the respect he is accustomed to, or to pay his bill at the tavern. At this point Bianca's suitors enter and offer to bail him out if he agrees to marry Kate.

The tavern scene thus introduces Petruchio's narrative function while it weaves together the main plot and the subplot. And in its analogies with Shakespeare's induction, which is not present in Cranko's choreography, this scene takes on some of its functions. In both, we find a drunkard who falls asleep in a tavern and does not have the means to pay his bill; a trick is played on him by men or women of a different rank from his; the clothes that "made the man" are taken away leading to a reversal of social power; a wife comes into the picture who wasn't there before. Today we see the induction as a device that distances and deflects the taming plot from the theater audience. Since the taming plot is performed for the onstage Sly, who at that moment is acting the part of the lord, the induction invites us to look at a high-ranking man who underneath his patriarchal assuredness is merely an unpleasant and unattractive fool, no more appealing than a shrew. This same description works for Cranko's Petruchio in the tavern scene.[12]

A foolish, drunk gentleman being duped by prostitutes lends an air of carnival to Cranko's *Taming* as it portrays a brief moment of anarchy or liberation from established hierarchy.[13] And carnival in its connotations of "anarchy" and "liberation" playfully calls to mind the political atmosphere in the streets outside the theater. The carnival theme is further politicized and engendered in Cranko's choreography where he introduces a "disguise to trick" not in Shakespeare: in the place of reported news of Hortensio's marriage to a widow, Cranko stages the duping of Gremio and Hortensio by Lucentio into marrying two prostitutes disguised as Bianca. The prostitute is obviously a more colorful female role than that of the widow, and two prostitutes onstage certainly make more of a point than one widow offstage. Together, in Shakespeare's time, widows and prostitutes—not married and not virgins—had comprised a category of women that resisted patriarchal control. Cranko substituted one component for the other.

Returning once again to Zeffirelli, and to Holderness's study, we can find another useful springboard for discussing a point about Cranko's choreography. Holderness offers a Bakhtinian reading of the film, in which "the function of carnival is to promote social integration" and the purpose of carnival's disorder "to endorse the stability of the order that can afford to permit its own temporary abolition."[14] Such definitions are entirely appropriate in a discussion of Zeffirelli's film. Cranko's carnival, however, although equally readable in Bakhtinian terms, does not support this view about endorsing the stability of the existing order. For his carnival focuses rather on ways in which new modes of interrelationship can be worked out between individuals. For one thing, in the social integration that Cranko's carnival promotes, women who can dodge male authority (prostitutes) have a powerful role, both in the public and private spheres. Compared to his Shakespearean source, Cranko gives considerable space to that category of women, and by making his prostitutes wives as well, Cranko introduces their "liberated" status into the domestic sphere. For another, the three pas de deux danced by Kate and Petruchio, which make up the mainstay of Cranko's choreography, clearly indicate a point of contact—literally, between two dancing bodies—for negotiating a way through hierarchical barriers and for the establishing of more balanced relations.

Negotiating Difference

The three pas de deux map the evolution of Kate's and Petruchio's characters and their relationship. In the first of these, in the wooing scene (1.3), the two are on a reactive par ("equal but different"). When Petruchio blocks Kate's movement in midexecution and gets her into a tight hold, she knows how to get herself free. When she tricks him into losing his balance, he knows how to trip her back. Their movements are violent and acrobatic, almost grotesque. They are rarely aligned, and they use each other's bodies to build up their own counteractive energy. Kate, dropped from a lift she has been fighting her way out of and tumbled to the floor, trips Petruchio and pulls him down. They roll and push at each other before separating and retreating back into their separate choreographic spaces.

The next pas (2.2) is at Petruchio's house, after the long journey, the uneaten supper and the night in the cold. The choreography here has progressed from reactive to interactive ("integration"). As Petruchio lifts Kate, she assists him with a plié and a leap. His extended hand serves to guide the transition of her weight from one pose to another. They travel through their separate spaces mirroring each other's movements, creating distance and then eliminating it as if they were preparing to weave those separate spaces into a greater whole.

Their final pas de deux is at Bianca's wedding (2.6), Petruchio's and Kate's first public appearance as a married couple. This is a harmonious duet, more in line with the traditional lyricism of classical ballet ("partnership"). Their two bodies move as one compounded unit, creating patterns as they replicate each other's movements, as each appears to be an extension of the other, while at the same time they assert those very different gender codes that are at the heart of every aspect of ballet.[15] As we reflect on the message of cooperation and mutual respect this duet embodies, we should remember the threatening determination of Kate, who, when annoyed, was capable of emptying a chamber pot from her balcony onto the heads of Bianca's suitors (1.1), and we should remember the fallibility of Petruchio, who could be duped into drunkenness and out of his clothes and purse by a bevy of prostitutes (1.2). Theirs is a contract in which potential threats keep power in balance.

When Kate dances out the submission speech, it falls into place as the last of a series of staged performances the audience has witnessed, from those of Bianca's impersonating suitors, to Petruchio's foolery at his wedding ceremony, and his servants' mock madness in the mentally or physically deficient roles Petruchio assigned them in preparation for Kate's arrival at his country home.[16] Kate, in her final gesture toward the other women present, to bow their heads and kiss their husbands' hands, appropriates the wink Mary Pickford introduced into *Taming* performance history in her 1929 film with Douglas Fairbanks. That wink had already become very popular in 1950s performances, as the tendency spread in film and onstage to depict women as smarter than their husbands, but willing to pamper them into believing they were the ones in command. All the winking Kates make use of a ploy—that of deliberately assuming a female role—that converts subordination into affirmation and by so doing thwarts it. A decade after Cranko's ballet, the French feminist critic Luce Irigaray would give this liberating subterfuge—"mimesis," as she named it—the dignity of theoretical attention. From then on, what artists from Pickford to Cranko had previously intuited became a clearly recognizable feminist strategy to "make 'visible', by an effect of playful repetition, what was supposed to remain invisible . . . to 'unveil' the fact that, if women are such good mimics, it is because they are not simply resorbed to this function. They *also remain elsewhere.*"[17]

The order reestablished at the end of Cranko's ballet has been in the making since the wooing scene. In fact, Kate already reveals there a hint of interest in Petruchio, and shows concern for wanting to hide this from him, as her power lies in concealing it from him. We might want to read the three pas de deux as embodying Germaine Greer's interpretation of the relationship between Kate and Petruchio, as she presented it in *Female Eunuch:* "Kate . . . has the uncommon good fortune to find Petruchio who is man enough to know what he wants and how to get it. He wants her spirit and her energy because he wants a wife worth keeping . . . only Kates make good wives, and then only to Petruchios."[18] It is worth pointing out here that, as with Irigaray's study, Cranko's choreography also precedes Greer's comment, in this case by a year.

Cooperative Interaction in *Taming* and Beyond

Cranko's *Taming* embodies the highly gendered political crisis of the moment—the tension of feminism pitted against male patriarchy—and negotiates it through the diversely but equally intensely gendered conventions of ballet, the one a site of contestation, the other of conservation. Cranko's language lies in the bodies of male and female dancers. His discourse is patterned on their cooperative interaction. Without it, there would be no ballet. Perhaps it is the essential corporeality of narrative in dance, its primary location in the bodies of the dancers who work together as a corps, that made it possible for Cranko to elaborate relational strategies that only later would be expounded verbally, and appear in the writing of a distinguished feminist. Those strategies would go on to influence not just performative situations, but also those in the real world between men and women. At the same time, Cranko's work provoked some of the gender-bound conventions of his art, by letting in a little light from the world outside.

Cranko's *Taming of the Shrew* has entered the repertoires of ballet companies around the globe where Kate is the preferred role for many ballerinas. They love the strongly marked choreography and more so the strength of the character that unfolds through Kate's dancing in opposition to and then in cooperation with Petruchio. They love to dance the role of a woman who—for once—manages to escape from her position of submission without having to die for it.

Notes

1. The long, narrative ballet—which forty years earlier, in the days of Isadora Duncan and Martha Graham, seemed on its way to extinction—was once again thriving in theaters around the globe. New York City alone offered eleven long ballets in the 1969 season. A full picture of this fortunate period was captured in the reviews of three major dance journals in print in the 1960s: *Ballet Review, Dance Magazine,* and *Dancing Times.*

2. See, for example, Gisela Bock, *Women in European History,* trans. Allison Brown (Oxford: Blackwell, 2001); Gisela Kaplan, *Contemporary Western European Feminism* (New York: New York University Press, 1992).

3. Robert Heilman, "The *Taming* Untamed, or, The Return of the Shrew," in *The Taming of the Shrew: Critical Essays,* ed. Dana Aspinall, 46–48 (London: Routledge, 2002). See also, Barbara Hodgdon, "Katherina Bound, or Play(K)ating the Strictures of Everyday Life," in Aspinall, ed., 351–87; introduction in William Shakespeare, *The Taming of the Shrew,* ed. Stephen Orgel (New York: Penguin, 2000), xxxii–xl; Margaret Loftus Ranald, "The Performance of Feminism in *The Taming of the Shrew,*" in Aspinall, ed., 318–30; introduction in William Shakespeare, *The Taming of the Shrew,* ed. Ann Thompson (Cambridge: Cambridge University Press, 2003).

4. See John Percival, *Theatre in My Blood: A Biography of John Cranko* (New York: F. Watts, 1983), the only full-length biographical study of Cranko. Further biographical information on Cranko is scattered in reviews and articles in a range of dance magazines (see the online catalog of the Dance Collection, New York Public Library, www.nypl.org).

5. Jack Anderson, "Mr. Cranko and his Castle," *Dance Magazine,* June 1969, 46.

See also, Suzanne McCarthy, "What to look for in John Cranko," *Ballet Magazine,* February 2002, www.ballet.co.uk.

6. The roles of Lucentio, Hortensio, Gremio, and Baptista are preserved in the choreography. Those of Vincentio, Tranio, Biondello, Grumio, and the Pedant are not.

7. See, for example, Rob Burns, ed., *German Cultural Studies: An Introduction* (Oxford: Oxford University Press, 1995); Ute Gerhard, "The Women's Movement in Germany," in *Thinking Differently: A Reader in European Women's Studies,* ed. Gabriele Griffin and Rosi Braidotti, 321–31 (London and New York: Zed Books, 2002).

8. Sally Banes, "Gulliver's Hamburger: Defamiliarization and the Ordinary in the 1960s Avant-Garde," in *Reinventing Dance in the 1960s: Everything Was Possible,* ed. Sally Banes (Madison: University of Wisconsin Press, 2003), 3.

9. There is no commercial video of Cranko's choreography of *Taming of the Shrew.* My discussion of the ballet is based on a performance at the Rome Opera House in 1997 and an in-house video of a performance at Boston Ballet in 1995. I am grateful to Janet Howes, stage manager of Boston Ballet, for allowing me to have access to that invaluable resource.

10. Graham Holderness, *Shakespeare in Performance: The Taming of the Shrew* (Manchester and New York: University of Manchester Press, 1989), 71. Michael Dobson, in discussing adaptations from earlier times, remarks on the "seemingly minor changes in the text" that can "mute . . . the outright feudal masculinism of *The Taming of the Shrew* in favour of guardedly egalitarian, and specifically private, contemporary versions of sympathy and domestic virtue." *Making of the National Poet: Shakespeare, Adaptation and Authorship, 1660–1769* (Oxford: Clarendon, 1992), 190.

11. Diana Henderson observes that the Taylor-Burton performance (along with the Pickford-Fairbanks one in Sam Taylor's 1929 United Artists film), marks the exception to the norm in modern video versions of *Shrew,* which offer a viewing of the story "in a euphemized and relatively untroubled way from Petruchio's perspective." She underlines the coincidence that in both exceptions, the principal actors are "Hollywood's most famous couples for their respective generations." "A Shrew for All Times, Revisited," in *Shakespeare, the Movie II,* ed. Richard Burt and Lynda E. Boose (New York: Routledge, 2003), 120.

12. The blurring of the roles of Sly and Petruchio exists also in performances of Shakespeare's play where directors often cast the same actor in both roles. See, for example, the Royal Shakespeare Company performance, Stratford-upon-Avon, 1995, directed by Gale Edwards.

13. The scope of this paper unfortunately does not allow space to discuss the role of the music in Cranko's ballet. One brief comment here will have to suffice. Scarlatti's sonatas, which are the backbone of the score, are mostly constructed of hierarchical pair patterns, one pair of sounds building into another more dominant pair. The effect is that of rondeau with a strong chase rhythm. This lends a farcical tone to much of the action, thus reinforcing the carnival atmosphere, and helping to soften the reactive nature of the protagonists' relationship (see, e.g., John Sankey, "The Sonatas of Domenico Scarlatti," www.midiworld.com/Scarlatti/htm).

14. Holderness, *Shakespeare in Performance,* 59.

15. See Judith Lynne Hanna, *Dance, Sex and Gender: Signs of Identity, Dominance, Defiance, and Desire* (Chicago: University of Chicago Press, 1988). See also Ann Daly, "Classical Ballet: A Discourse of Difference," in *Meaning in Motion: New Cultural Studies of Dance,* ed. Jane C. Desmond (Durham, NC: Duke University Press, 1997), 111–20; Jane Desmond, "Embodying Difference: Issues in Dance and

Cultural Studies," in *The Routledge Dance Studies Reader,* ed. Alexandra Carter (London: Routledge, 1998), 154–62; Nancy Isenberg, "Dalla farsa misogina alla commedia allegra: Shakespeare e Cranko a confronto su *La bisbetica domata,*" in *La bisbetica domata* (Roma: Teatro dell'Opera, 1997), 25–32; Randy Martin, *Critical Moves: Dance Studies in Theory and Politics* (Durham, NC: Duke University Press, 1998); Ted Polhemus, "Dance, Gender and Culture," in Carter, *Routledge Dance Studies Reader,* 171–79.

16. This is Cranko's performed substitution for Petruchio's reported ill-treatment of his servants. Cranko's solution, which is much more theatrical, maintains the original function of making Kate feel ill at ease.

17. Luce Irigaray, *This Sex Which Is Not One,* trans. Catherine Porter (Ithaca: Cornell, 1985), 76 [*Ce sexe qui n'en est pas un* (Paris: Les Éditions de Minuit, 1977)].

18. Germaine Greer, *Female Eunuch* (New York: Farrar, Straus and Giroux, 2002 [1970]), 234.

Rewriting Shakespeare: Bertolt Brecht, Heiner Müller, and the Politics of Performance

Lawrence Guntner

BERTOLT BRECHT AND HEINER MÜLLER LAVISHED MORE TIME AND energy on Shakespeare than on any other author. There are references to nineteen dramas by Shakespeare in Brecht's writings, and at the time of Brecht's death, there was supposedly a copy of Shakespeare's sonnets in the translation by Karl Krauss and Schiller's adaptation of *Macbeth* on the table in his workroom. As for Müller, he translated, adapted, and reworked four of Shakespeare's plays: *As You Like It, Titus Andronicus, Macbeth,* and *Hamlet*.[1] Brecht and Müller both approached Shakespeare as a practicing dramatist/director with an eye to a contemporary audience; both tried to liberate Shakespeare from the pantheon of German classics and a bourgeois performance tradition that had smothered any relevance to present-day politics under pomp and circumstance; both plundered Shakespeare for *Materialwert* (raw material) to historicize and thus distance the hero in order to discourage empathy (*Einfühlung*); both stood for a theater that was in contradiction to the official East German *Kulturpolitik*; and both had difficulties in having their reworkings of Shakespeare performed in a socialist state, which they supported as a better vision for humanity. But here the similarities end.

For Müller, Brecht's reduction of Shakespeare's fable to a political formula was a gross simplification. His "antidote" was to attack the authority of the Shakespearean text, ripping it apart if necessary, deleting, adding, and rearranging scenes and characters, or even the author himself. Müller relocates the fable, the story, in and on the player who creates the accidents central to epic theater in performance. In a letter to the Bulgarian director Dimiter Gotscheff, Müller remarks, "Helene Weigel thought [my play] *Philoktet* ... to be unperformable. For her it lacked the accidental, 'the gravel' ('Kies'). She did not see, and as an actress into the tradition of Brecht, could not see, that ... only the actor can introduce the accidental in the performance, his body is 'the gravel,' in which the text inscribes itself and loses itself in the same gesture, a substitute for other bodies."[2] The results are interruptions and disruptions (*Brüche*) in Shakespeare's dramaturgy as well as his blank verse that force his audience to interpret for themselves each and every evening anew what the plays might mean to them. Whereas Brecht did not live to see any productions of his renderings of Shakespeare, Müller was able to see all of his adaptations performed and even directed three of them himself: *Macbeth, Hamlet,* and *Hamletmaschine*.[3] In a sense Müller became the executor of Brecht's literary testament of Shakespeare rewritings. I will focus on *Macbeth* and *Hamlet*, since these are the plays to which both Brecht and Müller repeatedly returned.

Brecht

Throughout his life Brecht's main target would be the "plaster monument grandeur" characteristic of too much of German stage performance in the late nineteenth and the first half of the twentieth centuries. Brecht launched his first attack on this tradition with his adaptation of Christopher Marlowe's *Edward II*, entitled *Leben Eduard des Zweiten von England* (Life of Edward the Second of England), which he wrote in collaboration with Leon Feuchtwanger and directed himself at the Munich Chamber Theater (March 18, 1924). Looking back at this production, Brecht remarked, "We wanted to make a performance possible that would break with the Shakespeare tradition of the German stage, that plaster of Paris, monumental style so dear to the hearts of the petit bourgeois."[4] It established a cut-and-paste pattern of borrowing (or was it sacking?), amputating, and inserting, which Brecht would repeat throughout his life.

The plot was abbreviated (80 percent of Marlowe's play was omitted) and reassembled to emphasize the parable (*Episierung der Handlung*) and the number of characters was reduced to highlight the conflicts in the play (in this case, Edward versus the Peers). Parallel scenes from *Macbeth* were inserted, and parallel motifs from *Richard II, Richard III*, and even *Measure for Measure* were added as well. For example, the wife who spurs her husband on to murder, the banquet scene with a ghost, economic forces at work, and characters similar to Lady Anne and Richard Gloucester.[5] His purpose was to "distance" both action and characters to prevent any *Einfühlung* (emotional empathy) on the part of the audience. The spectators were to perceive, in Brecht's words, "the events behind the events as man-made events."[6] In the words of Herbert Ihering, Brecht "requested that events be accounted for. He demanded simple gestures. He forced actors to speak clearly, coolly. Emotionalism was not permitted. This resulted in the objective, the 'epic style.' "[7] This distancing of the hero would influence the manner in which later directors would approach Shakespeare, especially the history plays, and would provide a new form for dealing with classic drama that took into account the time and place of the performance. Although Brecht does not begin to formulate his attitudes toward classic drama in writing until 1926 with *Wie soll man heute Klassiker spielen* (How to Perform Classic Drama Today), the seeds of his ideas on an "epic theater" sprouted, as Bernhard Reich has pointed out, already in *Eduard II*.[8]

On October 14, 1927, the Berliner Rundfunk radio station broadcast Shakespeare's *Macbeth* in an adaptation by Brecht, directed by Alfred Braun, with music by Edmund Meisel, the musical director in Piscator's theater. It was one of the very first radio broadcasts of a Shakespearean play in Germany. Unfortunately, the original manuscript has been lost, except for two and a half typescript pages that contain the opening dialogue between Macbeth and Banquo. The witches have been cut and replaced by an "Echo." The witches' lines have been placed in the mouths of Banquo and Macbeth. To make sense of the "Echo," Banquo concocts a witch's brew in his helmet in which Macbeth reads the witches' prophecies that he will become Thane of Cawdor and later king, but that Banquo's progeny will ascend the throne thereafter. Brecht later wrote an extra scene set in the porter's house (2.3) featuring the porter, his wife, a beggar, and housemaids of Lady Macbeth, who have come to pick up a Chinese god of good fortune that Lady Macbeth had ordered for her birthday but that was damaged when the porter let it drop. In a plot reminiscent of *The Second Shepherd's Play*, the porter and his wife attempt to cover up the dilemma by blaming the beggar. The scene was not included in the radio broadcast.[9]

In the "Prologue to *Macbeth*" he wrote especially for the broadcast, Brecht sardonically claims that Shakespeare's play would not stand the test of contemporary theater criticism.[10] Nor would contemporary theater be able to cope with the plot, which consists of a series of illogical events that are continually interrupted. Brecht observes: "It is exactly through those epic elements contained in Shakespeare's drama, which make the theatrical rendering of them so difficult today, that Shakespeare was able to capture this truth."[11] Thus to stage Shakespeare as if all were clear and coherent was to rob the plays of their philosophical core (*den philosophischen Gehalt*), because it is precisely in the disjointedness of their plot that the audience recognizes the disjointedness and incoherence of life.[12] It follows that Brecht should view Shakespeare's plays as quarries of pure material or "stuff" (*Materialwert*), to be mined for a new dramaturgy, an epic theater, that would make the plays relevant to the present-day world in which we live.

Strangely enough, most commentators have missed the point of Brecht's sarcasm. It is not directed at Shakespeare at all but at the manner in which Brecht's contemporaries had staged him and at the theater critics who continued to support this kind of performance. Brecht was attacking a naturalistic dramaturgy based on the notion of an illusionist and cathartic mimesis that strove to explain the causality of every detail of the dramatic action to its audiences.[13]

On January 31, 1931, the Berliner Rundfunk broadcast Brecht's rendition of *Hamlet,* again directed by Alfred Braun, with Fritz Körtner as Hamlet and Oskar Homolka as Claudius. All that has been preserved of this adaptation are the introductory text spoken by the radio announcer, the final report on Hamlet's demise, and an intermediary, or parallel, scene dealing with Hamlet's departure for England. Again, the play was "epicized," that is, reduced to individual scenes connected by intermediary commentary. As if to foreshadow Orson Welles's notorious broadcast of *War of the Worlds* on October 30, 1938, a voice announced, "We now interrupt this tragedy for a special broadcast with Hamlet at the cemetery where Queen Gertrude will give us an extraordinary report on the death of Ophelia."[14] Not only did Brecht drastically cut the plot and link the scenes with a narrator's voice from offstage, but he also reassembled (re-pasted) the scenes in a new order. Ophelia's death (scene 4.7) and the gravedigger scene (5.1) were moved up to follow the closet scene (3.4), and the final five scenes (4.5 to 5.2) were cut completely, since Brecht disapproved of the blood-and-guts finale. The intermediary, or parallel, scene that Brecht wrote, was to have been added after Hamlet's soliloquy "How all occasions do inform against me . . ." (4.4). Whether this scene was actually inserted in the broadcast or only intended for rehearsal, as was claimed later, is not completely clear.

Hamlet had long been the darling of the German psyche and the Shakespearean figure with which many German intellectuals "self-fashioned" their own anxieties and insecurities. This posturing had become iconicized in a German performance tradition that romanticized and heroicized the protagonist. Brecht's solution was to "distance" the audience from the hero by "historicizing" his situation and him as a character. To do so, he claimed that Shakespeare was, in fact, rewriting an earlier play by Thomas Kyd, dated ca. 1589. Brecht saw Hamlet's plight as that of a youngster who had been given the Herculean task of cleaning up the mess at Elsinore. However, Burbage, the star of the Globe, was no longer a youngster but corpulent and short of breath (*breit und kurzatmig*) and thus lacking the physical stamina required for the acrobatics of Kydian revenge tragedy.[15] Brecht also claimed that Shakespeare had deliberately added moments of delay to Kyd's *Ur-Hamlet,* the basis for Brecht's new version of the Hamlet story. These "epic elements" added psychological complexity and dramaturgical depth to the play while providing interruptions (*Brüche*) that granted Burbage an opportunity to relax and recuperate from grunting and sweating under a weary life of playing Hamlet.

Brecht attributed Hamlet's delay to bourgeois reasoning (*bürgerliches Denken*). For Brecht—and later Heiner Müller—Hamlet is positioned, or entrapped, between two worlds: the modern world of bourgeois humanistic ideals and the feudal world of blood revenge, between the world of Wittenberg and the world of Elsinore. Since Goethe's distinction between art and politics, German productions of the play had portrayed Hamlet as a highly sensitive young man unable to cope with the dirty dealings of mundane politics. Freud's suggestion that Hamlet's behavior might have something to do with oedipal urges delivered a psychological source for his delay.[16] Whatever the reason, Hamlet's arbitrary slaughter in act 5 was viewed as a strong, manly solution to the problem. Brecht vehemently disagreed. He argued that Hamlet's delay was actually the correct behavior given the situation and that his relapse into the primitive behavior patterns of a feudal warlord cannot be convincingly motivated by his chance encounter with Fortinbras in scene 4.4.[17] Brecht's conviction was reinforced by the fact that German directors had often omitted this scene that was so crucial for him. This was another justification for the parallel scene that Brecht invented for rehearsal purposes to train the actors in the *gestus* of the production.

The parallel scene, mentioned at various places in his writings, is roughly as follows: on his way to the boat bound for England, Hamlet questions the ferryman about a nearby castle that had been built to guard the Danish coast. He is told that it is now being used for salting fish to be exported to Norway. Asked about the present state of the hostilities between Denmark and Norway, the ferryman replies that they have since been resolved by a trade agreement between the feuding countries. When Hamlet's companion asks, "But what about honor?" Hamlet himself answers, "Honestly, I don't see any wounded honor. It's the new method, friend. You find it everywhere today. Blood no longer smells good. A change in taste."[18] In Brecht's reading of *Hamlet,* exporting fish has replaced war, the Danish diplomat has to swallow insults, Claudius is admired for his economic policies, and last but not least, Hamlet will be honored for not killing King Claudius, who has brought the country economic prosperity.

But then, Hamlet chances to meet Fortinbras on his way to Poland, and following his example, hastens back to Elsinore to kill Claudius and Laertes, losing his own life in the process. For Brecht, Hamlet's relapse into feudal barbarity embodied the dilemma of the bourgeoisie, its manner of reasoning and behavior, in the seventeenth century as well as the twentieth. It was unable to solve Hamlet's dilemma and it had been powerless to prevent Fascism and World War II.[19] The purpose of this extra scene for rehearsal was to help the audience to bridge the gap between Hamlet's past and the audience's present, if not in the dramaturgical fable, then at least in the performative *gestus* of the actors.

The question for Brecht was always how to make Shakespeare current, but there was a hitch to this. As Heiner Müller pointed out to the annual meeting of the German Shakespeare Society in Weimar in 1988, "[t]he play itself is an attempt to describe an experience that has no reality in the time of its description. . . . Shakespeare is a mirror through the ages, our hope a world he doesn't reflect anymore."[20] Therefore, the task for the director striving to develop a politically relevant performance tradition is to find a way of connecting Shakespeare's past to the audience's present, without narrowing and simplifying Shakespeare's variety in the process.[21] Although his readings and rewritings may be viewed today with a jaundiced eye, they were Brecht's attempt to make Shakespeare politically relevant at a time when Fascism was on the march and reducing European "civilization" to a heap of rubble in the process. Margot Heinemann has asked us to remember the historical situation, excuse possible simplifications, and honor "[t]he heroic determination that made him go on studying and working on Shakespeare as well as his own plays, even at a time when he had no theatre to stage them and didn't know if he ever would have one again, [which] also made him focus his interest in terms of the immediate struggle, recognising that in some ways this narrows it."[22]

Müller: *Macbeth*

Brecht died in 1956 when the German Democratic Republic (GDR) was only seven years old, still hoping that state socialism was a vision of a future world that would be friendlier, more just, and more humane than the world he had experienced in his lifetime. Müller, who passed away in 1996, outlived the GDR brand of *realexistierender Sozialismus* (real-life socialism) by six years. Even if the GDR remained the "better" Germany for him, Müller's experience taught him that the way of the world under state socialism matched neither the official version of the present nor the projected version of the future. His own plays were viewed as being critical of contemporary East German history and life. Prevented from having them performed on East German stages, Müller turned to reworking dramatic classics, including Shakespeare, to transform the stage into an ersatz for a critical public forum.

Heiner Müller described his relationship to Shakespeare, especially to *Hamlet,* as a personal "obsession" dating back to his childhood.[23] Müller saw several parallels between himself and Shakespeare: both lived in transitional periods between two epochs, had an interest in history and history as drama, were forced to flatter those in power while at the same time exposing their psychology, and were in the habit of basing their work on earlier sources.[24] Müller also had obvious affinities with Brecht. His attire and the cigar, his cultivation of the interview as an art form, and his habit of answering questions with references to or anecdotes about Brecht suggested a deep artistic identification with him. Oddly enough, however, Müller's personal relationship to Brecht was only superficial. In fact, his application to become a *Meisterschüler* under Brecht at the Berliner Ensemble was turned down, which he later realized was a blessing in disguise.[25] For Müller, Shakespeare provided "an antidote to Brecht, to the simplification in Brecht."[26] A case in point is his rejection of Brecht's *Coriolan* on the grounds that it reduced the complexity of Shakespeare's play to a single problem: the hero cult surrounding Stalin. As such, Müller argued, Brecht had trivialized Shakespeare.[27] Only by tearing the texts apart, by peeling away the surface layers, did Müller feel that he could arrive at the original sources and the truth underlying them. This was his way to strip away bourgeois assumptions about the classics and to make Shakespeare relevant again for today's audience.

Macbeth (nach Shakespeare), Müller's adaptation from 1971, can be described as a dialogue between Müller and Shakespeare. The subtitle *nach Shakespeare* can be translated as "according to Shakespeare" or as "after, later than, Shakespeare." Line by line, Müller cut away the bright surface of Shakespeare's blank verse, translating, altering, deleting, and finally rendering it into a "flat and mundane idiom" in search of a dramatic language bereft of any pretensions of nobility, endearment, or politeness.[28] Similarly, *Shakespeare Factory* is an especially mundane title for his collected adaptations of Shakespeare; it suggests that Shakespearean plays are not inspirations of genius, but result from hard labor by the sweat of the author's brow. Appropriately, on the title page of the first volume there is a picture of a dead moose being dressed out by a butcher, the butchered animal a metaphor for what Müller does to Shakespeare's text. In *Macbeth (nach Shakespeare)* Müller presents us with a world void of human dignity, in which arbitrary savagery and torture are the daily fare, in which the peasants have no stake—except a stake on which they can be abused, for, like the moose, they can be, and are, butchered at will in this production.

Like Brecht, Müller formally abandons the act/scene structure (there are twenty-three scenes in his *Macbeth*), adds his own intermediary scenes, and inserts lines not from Shakespeare.[29] However, Müller goes beyond Brecht in trying to connect Macbeth's past with our present. With excessive images of violence to bodies, with arbitrarily brutalized peasants and tortured nobles, Müller challenges our senses and our sensibilities. As we shall see, by altering the function of the witches, he denies even the possibility of human tragedy. Unlike Brecht, Müller's version of *Macbeth* suggests that the processes of history are not changeable, but a self-perpetuating cycle of violence and brutality. His rendition of Macbeth's speech, "Is this a dagger which I see before me?" (scene 2.1) is "The way of the world leads to the knacker / With daggers in the dagger is its course."[30] In his play killing and torture are just another form of "work," a sinister satire of the trivialization of the Marxist notion of work in official GDR jargon: slitting Duncan's throat is "work," commissioning Banquo's and Fleance's murders is "work," nailing the porter to the door and slicing off his tongue is "work." Müller reminds us that the language we use is crucial to the kind of culture we live in. If we are callous in our use of the idiom, we should not be surprised if our culture is callous as well.

If Müller's 1971 adaptation was a dialogue between the translator and Shakespeare, the 1982 production of the play directed by Müller and his then-wife Ginka Tscholakowa at the Volksbühne in East Berlin became a dialogue between the translator and his own translation. The one-dimensionality of the action and the characters in Müller's 1971 text was replaced in performance by a many-faceted network of associations and dissociations, assonances and dissonances. Müller's production relocated Macbeth's Dunsinane in the courtyard of a run-down East Berlin tenement, a metaphor for the current state of the world, including East Germany. The performance insisted upon the cyclical nature of the story, showed dramatic character as role playing, and exaggerated the violence. According to Hans-Thies Lehmann, this is a surrealistic "montage dramaturgy . . . in which the reality-level of characters and events vacillates hazily between life and dream and the stage becomes a hotbed of spirits and quotes outside

[of] any homogenous notion of time and space."³¹ The result was a theater of cruelty that laid bare the cruelty of politics.³²

When the audience entered the auditorium, they saw Malcolm (Susanne Düllmann) sitting in an old armchair of the kind frequently found in German living rooms in the 1930s and 1940s. It would later serve as the royal throne. The name "Malcolm" was written in large white letters on the back of her coat. In front of Malcolm in the orchestra pit was the "underworld" in silver and black. Behind "Malcolm" was a wall consisting of twenty-seven large mirrors in which the audience could see itself reflected. The gap between stage and auditorium, actor and audience was closed. The action onstage began not with the witches but with Duncan announcing the approach of the bloodied soldier; in Müller's rendition: "What's that coming covered in blood?" (*Was kommt in Blut?*). Müller's *Macbeth* text opens with a reference to "blood," and in the course of the performance, blood would become an extended metaphor for the relentless repetition of slaughter. In Müller's rewriting of the Macbeth story, there is no progress, thus no history, and no future.

In scene 3, the witches, divas with bald heads painted silver and blue and wearing long elegant gowns, climbed out of the "underworld" (the orchestra pit) to waltz with the three Macbeths to the tune of Johan Strauss's "Wiener Blut" played from an old 78 rpm record. By placing their entrance *after* Duncan has advanced Macbeth to Thane of Cawdor, the supernatural element in the play was removed, and the "tragedy" of Macbeth's fate was negated. In this performance there was no "flaw" in Macbeth. It suggested that things have always been this way and always will be. All of the characters were simply "roles," the players arbitrary, in the recurring puppet show we call history. The program notes contained excerpts from Roland Barthes's comments on the three "scripts" of Japanese Bunraku theater: the puppeteer, the actor, the voice.³³ This trifurcation of the performative sign was approximated in the performance. The signs/roles/masks that the characters assumed were ambiguous and variable: Macbeth was also Macduff as well as the English doctor; Banquo was also Seyton and a tortured lord; the antagonist was in reality the protagonist; the hangman was a healer; and the victim, the murderer.

For Brecht "doubling"—actor/role, costume/role—is an integral principle of all theater signs.³⁴ However, Müller and Tscholakowa went beyond Brecht by multiplying the many masks of evil/power a person may assume simultaneously in his or her relationship to himself, to each other, and to society. Ten actresses played thirty-four roles, and five actors played thirteen roles. For example, Ursula Karusseit played a bloodied soldier, a baldheaded witch, the porter, and one of the murderers; Heide Kipp played Duncan, a witch, a murderer, a lord, Lady Macduff, a soldier, and a servant. The costumes were also dissonant to the characters who wore them. As the porter, Karusseit wore a lady's jacket over her long witch's gown; on her right foot a high-laced, high-heeled shoe, on her left foot a flat, on her head old-fashioned racing goggles and a lady's hat, over her right shoulder a purse, and in her right hand a brandy flask. Her left arm had been amputated. Often the names of the characters were painted on the costumes—"Macduff," "Malcolm," "Courtesan"—or they changed their costumes onstage to remind the audience of the artificiality of what they were seeing. For example, Karusseit peeled off a leather army overcoat and helmet to become a baldheaded witch in a floor-length gown.

This bi- and trifurcation of actor and role, role and costume, body and voice characteristic of Bunraku was continued in the actors' delivery, which was characterized by halts and starts in order to disrupt any sense of a regular linguistic rhythm—let alone meter—or melody in the language. This was essential for the portrayal of Macbeth. Played by three different actors, they represented at least three different sides of Shakespeare's character of the same name: Dieter Montag played Macbeth 1, the pragmatic butcher full of pathos for his victims; Hermann Beyer played Macbeth 2, the public ideologue; and Michael Gwisdek played Macbeth 3, the wire-pulling politician and private person. Frequently all three were onstage at the same time: one body acted, another spoke or commented on the action, while a third looked on. Macbeth 1 and Lady Macbeth planned Duncan's murder, while Macbeth 2 sat in the electric chair in the rear reciting a text on the behavior of mallard ducks during mating season, and Macbeth 3 looked on from a window. In this performance identity and appearance, voice and body, actor and role were in a constant state of displacement.

The displacement and doubling of actor and role was also central to the dramaturgy of the performance. Inserted scenes that showed soldiers brutalizing peasants were doubled by scenes with peasant soldiers brutalizing a lord while Macbeth 1, from the electric chair mentioned above, recited Ovid's description of how Apollo flayed the musician (and farmer) Marsyas alive. In the end the audience was cheated out of catharsis. Macbeth died not through the hand of Macduff, who was likewise Macbeth 2, but rather, stagehands entered, cleared the stage, and then surrounded Macbeth 1. Macduff (Macbeth 2) approached and Macbeth dropped dead. Macduff brought Macbeth's head to Malcolm and said, "The head belongs to the crown." Malcolm replied, "You thought / you could play with the little boy

Malcolm. / There is space for your head on my spear, too." Malcolm wept and wished he were back in England. The three Macbeths entered from behind and placed the crown on Malcolm's head.[35] Now the bloody cycle could begin again, a da capo revision of Shakespeare's ending that had become popular in the West since the publication of Jan Kott's *Shakespeare Our Contemporary* in English and in German in 1964, as well as Roman Polanski's film adaptation of the play in 1972. Both were officially disdained in the East, however, for their pessimistic and cynical views of history.

MÜLLER: *HAMLET*

After *Macbeth (nach Shakespeare)*, Müller went on to rid not only *Hamlet*, but also himself as author, of "flesh and surface." In 1977 Benno Besson, the most influential and gifted of Brecht's pupils, was staging *Hamlet* at the Volksbühne. He commissioned Müller together with Matthias Langhoff to prepare a new translation of the play. One product of their efforts was a derivative "reworking" of a translation by Adolf Dresen and Maik Hamburger, which itself had stirred up considerable controversy; the other was *Die Hamletmaschine*, a fragment, a "shrunken head *Hamlet*," that dismantles not only Shakespeare's dramaturgy, characters, and blank verse text, but the whole "taxonomy of dramatic literature," including the author who is disposed of before the eyes of the audience when a photograph of Müller is torn up onstage.[36] In Müller's own words: "*Hamletmaschine* is not a drama. Actually it marks the end of drama. The machine has stopped running. The oil is leaking out, and the gears no longer work."[37] Correspondences to Shakespeare are evident (e.g., five acts, figures named "Hamlet" and "Ophelia"), but there is only a faint similarity to Shakespeare's play. Müller's dream of having his *Hamletmaschine* performed together with *Hamlet* was not to be realized until 1990. It is a text that forces actors to abandon the familiar safety they associate with Shakespeare, such as characters that are an integral part of a structured action or the blank verse rhythm. "The actor playing Hamlet" says, "I'm not Hamlet. I don't take part anymore. My words have nothing to tell me anymore. My thoughts suck the blood out of the images. My drama doesn't happen anymore. Behind me the set is put up. By people who aren't interested in my drama, for people to whom it means nothing. I'm not interested in it anymore either. I won't play along anymore."[38] In 1988 Müller proposed to the Deutsches Theater that he direct a production of his own translation of *Hamlet* together with *Hamletmaschine*. It was to be the first time that his play would be performed on an East German stage. The rehearsals began in September 1989 just as demonstrations were bringing the reigning geriatric oligarchy to their knees. The opening performance on March 24, 1990 occurred one week after an East German electorate had voted in a conservative, Christian Democratic government, whose chief accomplishment was to dissolve the GDR and unite it with the Federal Republic.

The time of historical changeover in which Hamlet is entrapped—or "encased" in this performance—was now being acted out in front of the theater, in the streets of Leipzig, Berlin, and elsewhere, with the audience having swapped places with the players and now performing history themselves. In the face of such epochal developments, the director was unable to position his production against a specific political backdrop. A political parable was impossible. Only the rehearsal provided an impression of structured continuity in the daily lives of the ensemble, "somehow like a clock that kept ticking slower," commented Margarete Broich, who played Ophelia.[39]

In Müller's staging, Hamlet, and by implication the theater, is incapable of active and willful resistance to the power politics surrounding him. In "Note 409" Müller himself wrote, "'I am an actor, not the people,' says Hamlet."[40] It was as if his text for Hamlet Actor in *Hamletmaschine* had become a self-fulfilling prophecy: "I am not Hamlet. I perform no roles anymore. . . . My play no longer takes place." Hamlet, played by Ulrich Mühe, repeatedly uttered Müller's lines from *Hamletmaschine,* which, as Brecht had suggested earlier, were a necessary injection after scene 4.4: "I was Hamlet. I stood on the coast talking to the breakers, blabla, behind me the ruins of Europe."[41] This was not an optimistic, or even critical, vision of a better future in a united Germany, but a ritual wake for a country—and a civilization—whose cultural dogma viewed Shakespeare's *Hamlet* as the epitome of human culture.

The confession, or prayer scene, played on a huge double bed downstage center, became an intimate (step)father-to-(step)son talk between Claudius and Hamlet, in which Claudius recited Shakespeare's lines and Hamlet nodded like an obedient son. Claudius even went so far as to give Hamlet a lollipop and drag him kicking onto his lap. A surprise to all in the audience, it mirrored the situation of many intellectuals and artists in the GDR. The state (Claudius) "confessed" its shortcomings to the artist and intellectuals in opposition (Hamlet), and received, in turn, a reprieve from punishment. This scene revealed to the audience how even private lives could become a political issue in the GDR.

The idea of time running out—on the East German state, on history, on civilization, on the world—is central to Müller's work, and central to this production of *Hamlet*. The tempo of the performance decelerated and the climax became ritualized slow-motion slapstick in the final duel with Laertes, as if two mechanical puppets were slowly winding down. By the end of the play, the protagonists as well as the audience seemed to be relieved that it was finally time to die, and Jörg Gudzuhn as Claudius eagerly grabbed the chalice and greedily gulped the poison down.

The audience was overwhelmed by the monumental scenery (the most expensive set in GDR history), the monumental length of the performance (up to eight hours), and the complete lack of any kind of dialogic interaction between the performers and the spectators.[42] But this was Müller's intent. Elsewhere he says that theater can only rediscover its memory for reality if it forgets its audience. The contribution of the actor to the emancipation of the spectator is his emancipation from the spectator.[43] Müller's Hamlet simply waits too long and time runs out on him as it does on Claudius and Gertrude and any hope for a socialist future.

Shakespeare—Brecht—Müller

Shakespeare–Brecht–Müller, Müller–Brecht–Shakespeare: What do they share? Where are the differences? And how would Shakespeare have rewritten Brecht had he chanced to discover the latter's *Coriolan* fragment, or what would he have done to Müller's *Macbeth*? We will never know, of course. Yet in their everyday work of writing plays, there are affinities. Like Brecht and Müller, Shakespeare was an avid recycler of existing interesting material (*Materialwert*), borrowing and stealing wherever he could, but also elevating that material poetically. If John Dover Wilson was right about him having rewritten an *Ur-Hamlet* by Kyd,[44] then Shakespeare was not above playing the magpie himself. And, as Robert Weimann has shown, Shakespeare, like Brecht, distanced his heroes by building in a "complementary perspective" on their actions, often from below. And like his German successors, Shakespeare lived during a changeover period in history, a time of absolutist monarchs, which furnished him with a seemingly inexhaustible supply of dramatic material for the stage—that which Brecht called "stuff." Asked why he never left the GDR, Müller gave the example of Brecht who, he claimed, was first and foremost an artist and not a politician: "For a playwright, a dictatorship is, of course, more colorful than a democracy. Shakespeare is unthinkable in a democracy."[45] Shakespeare created a vision of history as performance that could be staged, a vision that Brecht and Müller, and many a politician have since appropriated for their own purposes.

For all of Brecht's brilliant insights into how to highlight Shakespeare's present meaning for a contemporary audience through various forms of alienation, I would argue that Müller's judgment on Brecht's adaptations of Shakespeare is justified. Reducing the fable to a basic concept is a simplification that limits the complexity of Shakespeare's drama as well as the potential responses of the audience. Whether Müller's technique of stripping the dramatic flesh from Shakespeare's text to get at the bone marrow of his source material is more effective in bridging the gap between Shakespeare's dramatic past and today, or whether it makes his reworkings of Shakespeare's plays more pleasurable for an audience is another matter. Nonetheless, Müller's rewritings of Shakespeare, which would transfer the *gestus* of Shakespeare performance onto today's actors, have opened a new chapter in Shakespeare's stage history. They continually challenge the actors, keeping them perpetually off balance and alienating them from all the routine they have learned. As a result, the actor must become, as in Shakespeare's day, a player whose total *gestus* transports the story, always fresh, with each performance.

Notes

1. Heiner Müller's Shakespearean rewritings are collected in his *Shakespeare Factory*, 2 vols. (Berlin: Rotbuch, 1985 and 1989).
2. Heiner Müller, *Herzstück* (Berlin: Rotbuch, 1983), 103; my translation. Unless otherwise indicated, all translations are mine.
3. Brecht's relationship to Shakespeare has frequently been the subject of examination, and Roland Petersohn has investigated the links between Shakespeare and Müller, but no one to my knowledge has tackled the links between Shakespeare, Brecht, and Müller in any detail, or attempted to point out their differences.
4. Wir wollten eine Aufführung ermöglichen, die mit der Shakespeare-Tradition der deutschen Bühne brechen sollte, jenem gipsigen monumentalen Stil, der den Spießbürgern so teuer ist. Bertolt Brecht, "Bei der Durchsicht meiner ersten Stücke" (November 1954), included in his *Schriften zum Theater*, ed. Werner Hecht, 7 vols. (Frankfurt am Main: Suhrkamp, 1964), 6:398.
5. See Rodney Symington, *Brecht and Shakespeare* (Bonn: Bouvier Verlag, 1970), 57–68.
6. Die Vorgänge hinter den Vorgängen, als Vorgänge unter Menschen. See "Über eine nichtaristotelische Dramatik," in Brecht, *Schriften zum Theater*, 3:44.
7. From Ihering's *Reinhardt, Jessner, Piscator oder Klassikertod?* (1929), quoted in Wilhelm Hortmann, *Shakespeare on the German Stage: The Twentieth Century* (Cambridge: Cambridge University Press, 1998), 81.
8. Bernard Reich, "Erinnerungen an Brecht," *Theater der Zeit* 14 (1966): 6.
9. *Bertolt Brecht Werke,* ed. Werner Hecht, Jan Knopf, Werner Mittenzwei, and

Klaus-Detlef Müller, 32 vols. (Berlin/Weimar: Aufbau-Verlag and Frankfurt am Main: Suhrkamp, 1997), 10.1:550–53.

10. Ibid., 546–49.

11. Ibid., 548.

12. In der Zusammenhangslosigkeit seiner Akte erkennt man wieder die Zusammenhangslosigkeit eines menschlichen Schicksals. Ibid., 549.

13. We should not, however, be misled to believe that Brecht's was a voice crying in the wilderness. John Fuegi provides an interesting assessment of Brecht in comparison with his contemporaries Jessner and Piscator: "However much Brecht may have liked to imagine himself later to be the Einstein of the new stage form, in fact we can see Brecht as having been, in many ways, among the more conservative of the avant-garde directors of the 1920s. He preserved the classical theater but did so in a mode well suited to the modern age. He refused to be drawn into the trap of trying to represent 'the real world' on the stage. He knew that this could not work, that it was massively expensive, and that it was pedagogically and artistically unsatisfying to try." See John Fuegi, *Bertolt Brecht: Chaos According to Plan* (Cambridge: Cambridge University Press, 1987), 43.

14. *Bertolt Brecht Werke*, 10.1:351.

15. Brecht, "Das Theater des Shakespeares," in *Schriften zum Theater*, 5:123.

16. Originally a footnote in Freud's *Traumdeutung* (1900), it was expanded into an article by Ernest Jones entitled "The Oedipus Complex as an Explanation of Hamlet's Mystery," first published in *The American Journal of Psychology* (January 1910) and one year later in German as "Das Problem des Hamlet und der Oedipus-Komplex." A revised version was published in English as a book in 1949 under the title *"Hamlet" and Oedipus* (New York: W. W. Norton).

17. "Zwischenszenen," in *Schriften zum Theater,* 5:198–200.

18. Ibid., 199.

19. An attitude shared by Jan Kott, *Shakespeare Our Contemporary* (London: Methuen, 1964), 56.

20. "Shakespeare eine Differenz," trans. Carl Weber, in *Performing Arts Journal* 35/36 (1990): 31–32.

21. Robert Weimann, "Shakespeare on the Modern Stage: Past Significance and Present Meaning," *Shakespeare Survey* 20 (1967): 113–20.

22. Margot Heinemann, "How Brecht Read Shakespeare," in *Political Shakespeare,* ed. Jonathan Dollimore and Alan Sinfield, 227 (Manchester: Manchester University Press, 1985).

23. Heiner Müller, *Krieg ohne Schlacht: Leben in zwei Diktaturen* (Cologne: Kiepenheuer & Witsch, 1992), 265.

24. See his *Gesammelte Irrtümer 1* (Frankfurt am Main: Verlag der Autoren, 1986), 148, and *Gesammelte Irrtümer 2* (Frankfurt am Main: Verlag der Autoren, 1990), 135.

25. *Krieg ohne Schlacht,* 82.

26. Shakespeare war für mich auch ein Gegengift gegen Brecht, gegen die Vereinfachung bei Brecht, gegen die Simplifizierung. Ibid., 265.

27. Ibid., 125, 204–6.

28. Jonathan Kalb, *Theater of Heiner Müller* (Cambridge: Cambridge University Press, 1998), 90.

29. See Bernhard Greiner, "Explosion einer Erinnerung in einer abgestorbenen dramatischen Struktur: Heiner Müller's *Shakespeare Factory,*" *Shakespeare Jahrbuch (West)* (1989): 91–92.

30. Die Welt hat keinen anderen Ausgang als zum Schinder. / Mit Messern in das

Messer ist die Laufbahn. Heiner Müller, *Macbeth (nach Shakespeare),* in *Shakespeare Factory 1* (Berlin: Rotbuch Verlag, 1989), 197–98.

31. "Heiner Müller's Spectres," in *Heiner Müller: ConTEXTS and HISTORY,* ed. Gerhard Fischer (Tübingen: Stauffenburg, 1995), 90.

32. Indispensible for an analysis of the performance is the complete documentation compiled by Lily Leder and Angela Kuberski, *MACBETH von Heiner Müller nach Shakespeare,* Theaterarbeit in der DDR (Berlin: Verband der Theaterschaffenden der DDR, 1982). See also Roland Petersohn, *Heiner Müller's Shakespeare-Rezeption: Texte und Kontexte* (Frankfurt am Main: Peter Lang, 1993). For a description of the performance in German as well as Müller's comments on it, see *Berliner Theater: 100 Aufführungen aus drei Jahrzehnten,* ed. Dieter Kranz (Berlin: Henschel Verlag, 1990), 358–63. For a detailed account in English, see Lawrence Guntner, "'Working at the Difference': The Politics of Deconstruction in *MACBETH von Heiner Müller nach Shakespeare* (Volksbühne Berlin, 1982)," in *Against the Grain / Gegen den Strich gelesen: Studies in English and American Theory and Literature: Festschrift für Wolfgang Wicht,* ed. Peter Drexler and Rainer Schnoor, 147–60 (Berlin: Trafo Verlag, 2004), into which some of the material on Müller's *Macbeth* has been incorporated.

33. Leder and Kuberski, *MACBETH von Heiner Müller nach Shakespeare,* 20–22.

34. See Manfred Wekwerth, "Der Zeichencharakter des Theaters: Ein Experiment," in *Schriften: Arbeit mit Brecht,* 2nd ed. (Berlin: Henschel Verlag, 1975), 463.

35. Müller's text and stage directions in *Shakespeare Factory 1,* 239; the Volksbühne text in Leder and Kuberski, 204.

36. Müller and Matthias Langhoff, his collaborator on the original version, were accused of plagiarism. Asked for an expert evaluation of the Volksbühne version, Anselm Schlösser, the nestor of East German Shakespeare studies, defined the provenance of the text as follows: 80 percent Hamburger/Dresen, 10 percent Müller, 10 percent Schlegel-Tieck. A hearing took place at the Copyright Court in Leipzig in 1977, but the case was never settled. See Kalb, *Theater of Heiner Müller,* 210–11n23 and 108. In an age of intertextuality, this case raises a variety of intriguing questions as to what legally constitutes an author as a creator of a unique text, and in what sense and to what extent any text can ever be original or intellectual property. See also Maik Hamburger, "Translating and Copyright," in *Shakespeare and the Language of Translation,* the Arden Shakespeare, ed. Ton Hoenselaars, 148–66 (London: Thomson, 2004). On the relationship between Shakespeare's *Hamlet* and Müller's *Hamletmaschine,* see Petersohn, *Heiner Müllers Shakespeare-Rezeption,* 81–82, as well as Bernhard Greiner, "Explosion einer Erinnerung in einer abgestorbenen dramatischen Struktur: Heiner Müllers *Shakespeare Factory,*" *Shakespeare Jahrbuch (West)* (1989): 99–100. For an excellent discussion of *Hamletmaschine* in English, see Kalb, *Theater of Heiner Müller,* 104–26.

37. Quoted in Jan-Christoph Hauschild, *Heiner Müller oder das Prinzip Zweifel: Eine Biographie* (Berlin: Aufbau-Verlag, 2001), 347.

38. Ich bin nicht Hamlet. Ich spiele keine Rolle mehr. Meine Worte haben mir nichts mehr zu sagen. Meine Gedanken saugen den Bildern das Blut aus. Mein Drama findet nicht mehr statt. Hinter mir wird die Dekoration aufgebaut. Von Leuten, die mein Drama nicht interessiert, für Leute, die es nichts angeht. Mich interessiert es auch nicht mehr. Ich spiele nicht mehr mit. See Frank Hörnigk, *Heiner Müller Material* (Leipzig: Reclam, 1989), 45. English translation by Carl Weber, *"Hamletmachine" and Other Texts for the Stage,* ed. and trans. Carl Weber (New York: Performing Arts Journal Publications, 1984), 56.

39. Martin Linzer and Peter Ullrich, eds., *Regie: Heiner Müller* (Berlin: Zentrum für Theaterdokumentation und -information, 1993), 94.

40. ICH BIN SCHAUSPIELER, KEIN VOLK, sagt Hamlet, "Notiz 409," in *Hamlet/Machine: Tokyo Material,* ed. Azisa Haas (Berlin: Alexander Verlag, 1996), 214.

41. Ich war Hamlet. Ich stand an der Küste und redete mit der Brandung BLABLA, im Rücken die Ruinen von Europa. Hörnigk, *Heiner Müller Material,* 41; translation Weber, *"Hamletmachine" and Other Texts,* 53.

42. For discussions of the production in English, see Maik Hamburger, "Theater under Socialism," in Wilhelm Hortmann, *Shakespeare on the German Stage* (Cambridge: Cambridge University Press, 1998), 428–34; Andreas Höfele, "A Theater of Exhaustion? 'Posthistoire' in Recent German Shakespeare Productions," *Shakespeare Quarterly* 43:1 (1992): 84–85; Lawrence Guntner, "Brecht and Beyond: Shakespeare on the East German Stage," in *Foreign Shakespeare: Contemporary Performance,* ed. Dennis Kennedy, 130–34 (Cambridge: Cambridge University Press, 1993), and "In Search of a Socialist Shakespeare: *Hamlet* on East German Stages," in *Shakespeare in the Worlds of Communism,* ed. Irena Makaryk and Joseph Price, 192–97 (Toronto: University of Toronto Press, 2006).

43. "Das Theater kann sein Gedächtnis für die Wirklichkeit nur wiederfinden, wenn es sein Publikum vergißt. Der Beitrag des Schauspielers zur Emanzipation des Zuschauers ist seine Emanzipation vom Zuschauer," from back cover of Haas, *Hamlet/Machine: Tokyo Material.*

44. See John Dover Wilson, ed., *Hamlet* (Cambridge: Cambridge University Press, 1967), xvi–xxi.

45. Natürlich ist eine Diktatur für Dramatiker farbiger als eine Demokratie, Shakespeare ist in einer Demokratie undenkbar, *Krieg ohne Schlacht,* 112.

Hybridization: A New Trend in German Shakespeare Productions

Wilhelm Hortmann

IN 1952, THE LEGENDARY GUSTAF GRÜNDGENS—THE MOST BRILLIANT actor of Nazi Berlin, the Mephisto of Klaus Mann's novel and of Ariane Mnouchkine's play, a daring political tightrope walker, a dazzling and ambivalent figure—convened the leading figures of the postwar German theatrical profession in order to make them swear an oath of allegiance, allegiance not only to Goethe and Schiller but also to the third "German" classic, Shakespeare. The meeting resulted in the "Düsseldorfer Manifest gegen Regiewillkür" (the Düsseldorf Manifesto Against Directorial License). Gründgens insisted on a "theater of great form" showing the qualities of "human truth, spiritual discipline, noblesse, and elegant acting."[1] Such conservatism was not for all tastes, not even in 1952. However, protests had to remain muted. City fathers who were spending fabulous sums on the reconstruction of theater buildings wanted to invest in an ideologically safe and socially harmonizing medium. The theater was expected to confirm ethical norms, not to question them. It was supposed to establish aesthetic standards, not to disturb the public peace with unsettling innovations. A successful Christian Democrat election slogan of the time (1957) demanded "Keine Experimente!" (no experiments!).

This peaceful postwar consensus was ultimately broken up by "1968 and all that," in politics as well as on the stage. Gründgens still believed in the "imperishable" work of art and hoped to make his colleagues pledge service to the "unique and unalterable" work of genius: "Werktreue." By the time of his death in 1963, his program of textual fidelity was fast losing support, and now, forty years later, alteration is rampant, directors have turned authors, or auteurs, who are busy rewriting, reshaping, reshuffling, or even "dismembering" the once-sacrosanct creation of genius in order to try out new combinations and marry it to strange bedfellows, in other words: they are hybridizing with gusto.

Hybridization is one of the buzzwords of cultural theorists and a useful catchall phrase. It denotes, according to some, a new cultural paradigm, and they promise a millennium of global hybrid culture to supplant exhausted postmodernism. According to others, it is merely an umbrella term to cover a daunting variety of diverse and complex developments. The hybridity discourse is a swelling theme: it has entered politics (where it is to be found in debates about ethnic identity, migration, or postcolonialism); it is well established in sociology (where hybridity is mentioned in practically all research into demographic changes, gender attitudes, and new ethnic, sexual, or social minorities); the hybridity discourse is markedly present in social psychology (e.g. in discussions of phenomena such as multiple identities, provisory biographies, and crumbling role models); and, above all, hybridity relates to the media, where all these factual changes are presented and debated and turned into TV features. Which means that actual reality—once it is processed in the media—is often dehistoricized and decontextualized and becomes an item in such hybrids as "infotainment" or "edutainment" for consumption in the global village. The media are the greatest hybridizers of all.[2]

Of course, hybridization is nothing new. Botanists and animal breeders have employed it for thousands of years. Grafting new shoots on ancient stocks, cross-fertilizing plants and crossbreeding animals were and are recognized crafts and have produced stunning results. So has the fertile imagination of poets, painters and sculptors. Of poets, for instance in the case of the metaphysicals with their witty conceits and far-fetched imagery in which "the most heterogeneous ideas are by violence yoked together" (Dr. Johnson in *Life of Cowley*); of painters (Arcimboldo and Hieronymus Bosch are obvious examples); of sculptors (think of the countless stonemasons who created chimeras, griffins, centaurs, mermaids, monsters for the parks and waterworks of aristocratic employers). All in all, in looking back, one sees a long line of most ingenious and prolific artistic hybridizers.

The horrific inventions of Hieronymus Bosch also indicate the negative side of hybridization: its proximity to what is monstrous, unnatural, degenerate. There seems to be an unbridgeable opposition between the ideal and the debased, between, on the one side, purebred or thoroughbred form (with a capital F), and, on the other, the mongrel or bastard "deviation" (with a capital D), an enmity of long standing that can be studied in many fields. Traditionalists yearn for homogeneity and unmixed purity. This seems harmless enough, but it is a desire that may inspire racial intolerance and lead to ethnic cleansings; it is at the bottom of religious fundamentalisms; and, on a less existential level, it pops up whenever the Académie Française denounces the "Franglais" of the media and warns against the danger of creolizing the pure French mother tongue.

The hybridity discourse can be recognized by the frequent use of four characteristic prefixes, namely "inter," "trans," "pluri," or "multi." It is a discourse that rejects all monistic, essentialist, and fundamentalist notions as gross simplifications. The exponents of hybridity regard binary oppositions as limiting mental constructs, incapable of explaining a world of increasing plurality and heterogeneity. Male *or* female, believer *or* unbeliever, self *or* other, indigenous *or* alien, such essentialist dichotomies are no longer viable in view of a world gone hybrid, a world where formerly insurmountable boundaries are transgressed with ease and without compunction. Nowadays we are no longer confronted with a stern "either-or" but invited to partake of the options of "as well as." Hybridity is all around us: we enjoy *info*tainment or seek *edu*tainment, we watch *docu*dramas, or we dress *cross*-sexually for dinner in *multi*cultural company enjoying *inter*national cuisine listening to bands offering a *blend* of high and low, U and non-U, while we glance at the TV screen showing the Bacardi commercial with its breathless *super*impositions of *fragmented* shots. Or, if one looks at the cover of the 2001 *Shakespeare Jahrbuch,* one can watch the Chandos Shakespeare *morphing* into a shapeless squiggle and back again.

Purists will deplore all this as cultural decline; advocates of hybridity will celebrate the transgression of boundaries as a means to create synergies, new webs, networks, and interfaces, and they will point to Peter Greenaway's *Prospero's Books* as a prime example. The upholders of a homogeneous, pure, and unmixed culture are definitely on the defensive. Avant-garde cultural theory puts a premium on whatever is provisory, processual, dynamic, and even fragmentary: all of these are likely to be preferred to whatever is complete, finished, static.

Hybridity, Theater, and Shakespeare

It might be argued that ever since theater separated from ritual it started becoming a hybrid medium, and that theater history from then on can be read as a succession of hybridizations: with ever wilder mixtures of high and low, language and music, acrobatics and dance. At the same time that French court theater presented heroic emotions in noble language and stylized attitudes, that is, strove for classical purity, the Italian operas of the period produced high-class hybrids with magnificent fireworks, conflagrations, and sea battles, a composite form in which Italian engineers excelled. A frequently mentioned example is *Il pomo d'oro,* which Ottavio Burnacini (architect, scenographer, theater engineer) produced at the court of Leopold I in Vienna in 1668.

Less spectacular but equally stunning hybridizations are to be found when classical texts are burlesqued or parodied. The ubiquity and proliferation of parodistic versions and the close temporal proximity between the appearance of the grand text and its parodistic offshoots support Mikhail Bakhtin's theory of the existence of a counterculture from below that subverts official ideologies and value systems. Shakespeare integrates both high and counterculture in the same play when the Bakhtinian Falstaff is allowed to undermine the heroic ethos of his superiors with his seductive sybarite's plea for indulgence of the senses. Shakespeare's philosophical fools, by contrast, question the prevailing order on intellectual grounds without attempting to supplant it. Neither of these can claim the status of hybridizations, however. These occur when the parodistic intention uses alien forms to break up the complex cohesion of the Shakespearean cosmos in order to create something different and new, as is the case in burlesques and travesties, which began to appear at the same time as the first adaptations: "The first full-scale travesty is Thomas Duffett's *The Mock-Tempest, or The Enchanted Castle,* of 1674, in which Prospero's island becomes a brothel. Vigorous, amusing, and obscene, it burlesques a current production of Thomas Shadwell's operatic version of the Dryden-Davenant adaptation."[3] The genre reached its peak popularity in the nineteenth century, often parodying current theatrical events and famous performers as much as the plays themselves.

This concomitance of "high" and "low" indicates an interesting coexistence of what seem to be mutually exclusive attitudes to Shakespeare's texts. On the one hand, following the deification of the National Poet, one registers the progressive sacralization of the text; on the other, there is a vigorous impulse to put the "sacred" text to profane uses. Bardolatry and genius-worship together, the latter supported by the heavy artillery of Carlyle, Ruskin, and Browning, were responsible for giving the work of genius the aura of an inviolable utterance. Their cult of genius apparently answered a general need. Thomas Carlyle ("in such a time as ours it requires a Prophet or Poet to teach us"), Robert Browning (Genius perceives "the seeds of creation lying burningly on the Divine hand"), and John Ruskin ("Let it be understood once for all that imagination [Genius] never deigns to touch anything but Truth") raised the genius from the sphere of art to the sphere of ethics.[4] The Victorians, outwardly self-certain, but inwardly troubled by anxieties and needing spiritual comfort, were certainly reassured by this message from the philosophical triumvirate: Creative Genius, in touch with the Divine Spirit speaking Truth. It goes without saying that the emanations from such creative, inspired, and truthful sources must be treated as sacrosanct and utterly above mundane uses, in other words, as classics!

Strangely enough, this hero worship of Genius took root in Germany even more profoundly than in England. Shakespeare's supreme influence on the liberation of German literature from French models in the eighteenth century and his afterlife in Germany's intellectual history gave his works a unique status. The Schlegel-Tieck translations were felt to be (at least) equal to the English originals, "der deutsche Shakespeare." Karl Kraus (1874–1936), the Viennese pamphleteer, playwright, and propagandist for verbal precision, declared "Ein Schlegel'scher Irrtum im *Hamlet* ist wertvoller und dem Original gemässer als die tadelloseste Übersetzung, in der er beseitigt erscheint" (one Schlegel mistake in *Hamlet* is more valuable and true to the original than the most immaculate translation in which it has been corrected).[5] In such an atmosphere, which persisted well into the twentieth century, textual manipulations concerning an author whom the nation's poets and literati had taken such trouble to appropriate were regarded as near-blasphemous.

Apparently, as amply documented in Stanley Wells's five-volume edition of *Nineteenth-Century Shakespeare Burlesques* (1977), British writers were less solemnly devoted to the Bard. Their multiform adaptations show a healthy irreverence and an impish glee altogether alien to the serious-minded German dedication to Shakespeare as an overwhelming cultural heritage. But for all the mental agility, formal versatility, and outrageous humor that feed the hybridizations displayed in these burlesques, their basic impulse was not directed against Shakespeare as such, nor meant to supplant the unique character and form of the original. Shakespeare's plays and their travestied offshoots, it must be remembered, were not competing in the same arena. The cultural icon remained untarnished by being exposed to the topical allusions, the mix of genres, and the general topsy-turvydom of its burlesques. Their study, therefore, under the aspect of hybridization, is of little advantage when trying to find out how far the term can aid the understanding of the highly unusual phenomena in the national and international theater world of today. First a quick look at the international scene.

Shakespeare Internationalized and Hybridized

Shakespeare, as Ben Jonson claimed, "is not for an age, but for all time." Today he would have to add that he is also "for all nations."

The first foreign national appropriations of Shakespeare *as literature,* beginning in the mid-eighteenth century in Germany and from there sweeping through East European and Scandinavian countries, all aimed at reconstructing the original: reconstructing the original in translations as true to the master's word—and, later on, in productions as true to the master's spirit—as possible. Nobody in these countries dreamed of amalgamating Shakespeare with indigenous cultural forms, and even in the far-flung Empire on which the sun never set, Shakespeare was taught and played as in the mother country. Traveling companies from England or groups made up of expatriate residents helped to establish and reinforce the tradition. It was only when these countries achieved independence and had to combine their indigenous with their colonial cultural heritage that Shakespeare *the one* became Shakespeare *the many.* He found himself dressed in outlandish garbs, had to dance to wild and throbbing rhythms, accept alien bedfellows, and learn to discover in himself new meanings. In short, he "suffer[ed] a sea-change / Into something rich and strange." By the 1970s, the Empire was not only writing, but also adapting and performing back with a vengeance! And producing a wonderful array of hybrids in the process.

This fascinating subject has been studied by many renowned scholars. *New Sites for Shakespeare* is the title of John Russell Brown's 1999 study of Shakespeare in Asia. Other scholars have visited surprising sites for the Bard in Africa, South America, or the Caribbean. Conversely, Shakespeare's work itself is one of the sites on which the cultural, political, and emancipatory aspirations of many groups in Third World countries are inscribed. The resulting adaptations represent a rich body of material for studying processes of intercultural assimilation and appropriation. Among the scholars who have dealt with these phenomena, either in theory or in field studies, are Erika Fischer-Lichte, Richard Schechner, Rustom Bharucha, Martin Banham, Marvin Carlson, John Drakakis, together with many others who can be found, for example, in *The Intercultural Performance Reader* (1996) edited by Patrice Pavis, or in *Post-Colonial Shakespeares* (1998) edited by Ania Loomba and Martin Orkin. Japanese Shakespeare adaptations are in a class by themselves. Some of them, under avant-garde directors, have made their way to the West, like Yukio Ninagawa's *Tempest* at the Edinburgh Festival in 1993, or *The Tale of Lear* at the Barbican in 1994, in which Tadashi Suzuki larded his adaptation of Shakespeare's play with references to European drama from Euripides to Beckett.

Japanese endeavors to present Shakespeare in the context of a theater culture so diverse as to include Noh, Kabuki, and Bunraku necessarily produce hybrids. This hybridity is increased when productions are designed for export. The global circuit of touring events demands—as Dennis Kennedy has taught us—a consumable product. The uninitiated spectator can only relish its fantastic exoticism; he remains outside, on the surface. Yet he may, on occasions, be lucky and experience truly epiphanous moments that arise when the conjunction of heterogeneous elements actually fits and deepens understanding. One such moment occurred in 2000, in the joint production of *The Tempest* by the Bremer Shakespeare Company and the Indian Kathakali Dance Group under Annette Leday (and with this we turn at last to concrete examples of hybrid Shakespeare productions on the German stage).

Hybrid Shakespeare in Germany

What shape should Ariel assume? Should he be a flat-chested girl in powdered wig and white frock? A lissome ballet dancer in tutu with wings on her back? A lanky androgynous youth in nondescript garb, or should he even be Board President Prospero's personal assistant, in business suit with cell phone and palm-held? All of these have worked well enough. But one problem always remained, and that is Prospero's dominance which instrumentalizes everything and everybody. The Prospero in the Bremen production was no exception, every inch a king and ruler. But the spirits who served him came from a different world, spoke in foreign tongues, were in command of quite unusual forms of physical expression in gesture, movement, and mime, and they made strange music. Ariel, a delicately limbed actor dressed like an Indian prince and his four spirit helpers, trained Kathakali dancers all, obeyed Prospero's demands in accordance with the text. But the way in which they transformed their master's requests into dance made it clear they were beings of a separate order. Prospero remained master and magician, but Ariel and his dancers were in command of the magic, for which they had nothing but their bodies to put it in action. Spectators were confronted with an expressive body language in a highly developed but totally foreign idiom whose vocabulary, or rather signs, they had to learn to read. Prospero fared no better. When Ariel demanded his freedom—verbal communication being impossible—Prospero first had to translate the latter's physical display into words before he could grasp its meaning. In this way spectators experienced both simultaneously: the expressive body and the verbally abstract meaning.

The storm at sea and the shipwreck of the first scene were truly *embodied,* not just mimed but presented in a novel physical medium, by the dancers. They took loving, though wordless, care of Ferdinand, and they twisted their bodies into incredible shapes to lead the other stranded voyagers astray. According to the text the group is driven to distraction; here one could watch *how*. The dancing spirits made rollicking fun of Stefano, Trinculo, and Caliban. As Juno, Iris, and Ceres they presented a divine wedding entertainment, and Ariel performed a splendid pantomime to convey in what evil-smelling calamities he had left Caliban and the clowns. The magic transfusing the island—in other productions of *The Tempest* taxing the theater's machine park to its limits—here gained living shape and physical immediacy. That is why even the customary imbalance between dominant, overbearing Prospero and the cowed rest of the cast was here (at least partially) suspended. The princely Ariel, in his way also a lord and a ruler over serviceable spirits, captivated proud Prospero by the strangeness of his art and moved him toward greater clemency and to giving up thoughts of revenge.

The end brought a sense of separation: Prospero, renouncing his magic, leaves Ariel and his servants, Miranda renounces the well-meant but stifling domination by her father, and Caliban rejects the false God. No general reconciliation but freedom for all whom a strange power had brought together on the utopian isle for a short spell. Magic here was not a bag of tricks but the visible and palpable, yet unbridgeably alien Other. As such it was granted the same weight as Caliban with his anticolonialist demands. Pit Holzwarth, the director, avoided the ideological mistakes of many German *Tempest* productions of the preceding decade (listless or ill-tempered Prosperos, nymphomaniac Mirandas, and, of course, angry, aggressive Calibans with whom directors salved their bad neocolonial consciences). Instead, Holzwarth relied on the effect of conjoining incommensurable worlds. Its symbol, as it were, was the Kalam, a ritual design of wavy lines and figures that an Indian artist, imperturbably squatting front right during the whole performance, created on the stage floor with differently colored powders. An admired work of art that—as apparently is the custom in India—was destroyed immediately after its completion. But not, as in India, by the artist himself; here it was destroyed by Prospero when he renounced his magic. To the unwitting spectator this came as a shock; it was also a visible demonstration of the loss of beauty that the renunciation entails. The whole performance was a truly spellbinding *interpenetration* of two differently articulated cultures.

Such congenial and mutually enhancing conjunctions are rare. Other directors employ masses of extremely heterogeneous pictorial and textual allusions to disrupt traditional reception modes. The set of Jürgen Kruse's *Tempest* (Bochum, 1999) placed Prospero's isle anywhere between Greece, Africa, and the Pacific Ocean. Shrunken heads sprouted decoratively on wires next to Easter Island stone sculptures, Greek statues flanked the stage portal, and Africa was brought in by a troupe of pickaninnies in ballet dress with colorful umbrellas who circled the wrecked ship and sang out their names: "Sunday, Monday, Tuesday, Wednesday, Thursday," and so on. Obviously, Goodman Friday and perhaps Robinson Crusoe himself had been there ten years before and peopled the isle, even if not with Calibans. There were other supernumeraries. Ariel, played by a girl, had a mute elflike follower, a young man in pink evening gown who appeared off and on and was apparently besotted enough with Ariel to stuff himself with "Ariel" washing powder from a household-size packet. The director took the various references to the isle being filled with strange sounds and music as an invitation to drown the stage in his favorite pop tunes and bands, from the Beach Boys and Harry Belafonte to the Rolling Stones and Status Quo. Shakespeare's text was severely cut, parts of it spoken in English or even Italian, and it was interspersed with fragments from other sources, the odd Shakespeare sonnet or even Friedrich Hölderlin's "Hälfte des Lebens," a beautiful poem, deep, plaintive, distant, and harrowing by the common knowledge of the poor poet having gone mad the year before he wrote it in 1804—but in no way linkable to *The Tempest.*

Spectators in Bochum also wondered why, before being allowed to restore their numbed spirits in the interval, they were made to listen to a seated actor who stumblingly read one of Richard II's soliloquies from a book. It was, as transpired weeks later, intended as therapy for the poor man's drug addiction. Perhaps none of this would have mattered if the director had managed to establish credible relationships between the figures, but not knowing what to do with the figure of Prospero and preoccupied with his obsession to reshape the play by means of inserts and superimpositions, he (and Prospero) left the actors to fend for themselves. Some of them managed gloriously, such as Ariel on her high stilts with her birdlike shrieks and daring gymnastics, and Caliban hanging like an ape in the spider web-like net covering the front of the stage, grinning fiendishly and baring his fangs. Most of his speech was indistinct, but for the argument with Prospero about possession of the isle, he removed the hampering false teeth, which made his accusation ring clear and cold.

Jürgen Kruse's mix of heterogeneous elements is neither rule nor exception. There are a number of other directors who are in the habit of taking similar liberties. Most of them would reject the suggestion that they are "distorting" or "dismembering" Shakespeare for ideological reasons. This, they will argue, was done by their predecessors from the midsixties to the early eighties, when theater people still had a cause. The theatrical hybridizers of today enjoy the freedom of a double heritage. First, they no longer feel bound to take up a political position. The second freedom they enjoy is that they no longer feel bound to use the opportunities of free choice opened up by postmodernism according to a consistent artistic plan. Free choice, that is, from the world's cultural storehouse of images, melodies, or reference: older postmodernists saw this as a challenge to create a new, somehow *concordant whole* from the limitless variables. The young generation of directors are freewheeling experimenters exploring with relish the most *incongruous and arbitrary combinations.* The results are so personal and subjective that they cannot be categorized—because there is no discernible pattern. There is, for example, although both are thoroughly hybrid, not an inch of common ground between Karin Beier's multilingual *Midsummer Night's Dream* of 1995 (fourteen actors, nine languages) and Christoph Schlingensief's Zürich *Hamlet* of 2001 (which brought on groups of young neo-Nazis willing to opt out and, after September 11, put Claudius and Gertrude in Taliban garb and the neo-Nazis in GI battle dress).

By contrast, the older generation of hybridizing directors, for example, Andrea Breth in *Twelfth Night* at Bochum in 1989, worked along recognizable aesthetic lines to create a novel, but *persuasive,* whole. Andrea Breth created a texture of pictorial reference in order to show that all the characters of the play led double, triple, quadruple existences. They lived not only in illusions (which is what all lovers in Shakespeare's comedies do) but each character in this production was shown to live in several self-imagined worlds, in fictions and fantasies, in stylizations and adopted stances, in a network of temporary and largely imagined selves from which there was no escape. This subtle multiplicity was presented by pictorial allusions either in the costumes, props, set, lighting, or projections, to religion, mythology, painting, literature, and films, an intriguing network of cultural reference.

Most of the recent hybridizations are less sophisticated. Their directors neither have Andrea Breth's philosophical depth nor do they aim, like her, at a unifying artistic vision. On the contrary, they reject any curtailment of the newly won possibilities of free choice and instead zestfully explore the limitless options contained in random eclecticism. While Breth, as it were, established the play's characters and involved the spectators in a wondrous moving picture, her young colleagues are channel-hoppers. Nor do they have her unshakable respect for Shakespeare's text. Frank Castorf and Christoph Schlingensief regard Shakespeare's text as "Material" to be treated at will. The term "Material" is hallowed through its use by Bertolt Brecht and Heiner Müller. Brecht applied it to the reworkable substance of a play; for Heiner Müller "Material" meant the gritty, primal substance of history. Castorf, instead, took the term quite literally: dramatic works of the past were "Material" and nothing more, just so much junk from the scrap-yard of literary history. "I've tried to take the stuff apart, derust and oil the pieces and remount them in a new manner," Castorf proclaimed in the program to his rendering of *Hamlet* (Cologne, 1988/89).

Many recent productions resulting from such unchecked power over the text on the one hand and from having (in electronic form) unlimited visual and auditory references at their disposal on the other, show that the diverse materials and allusions apparently need no longer be part of a recognizable artistic concept. It is sufficient if they make a fleeting point or illustrate a passing idea in what basically has become a game with changing rules. The options that were open to serious-minded postmodernists like Andrea Breth have multiplied, and so have the possibilities of the game. The medium has become the message; subjective haphazardry rules; a production need no longer be a whole, but can remain piecework. It is sufficient unto itself, and exists only in its present performance before audiences who no longer expect to see a *literary* text brought to life and visualized. Traditional theatergoers increasingly tend to avoid such performances; the young generation seek them out for the sake of experiencing a colorful and zestful "event" without, like their grandparents, worrying about whether "this is the Shakespeare we knew."

In hybrid productions, both performers and audiences enter into a new kind of freedom. They are no longer slavishly fettered to the text, nor are they required to build an aesthetically consistent structure in a complex search for meaning, but they can now enjoy limitless combinations. Under the sign of hybridization directors need have no fear of taking on the grand old plays again because these no longer represent an *existential* challenge to wrestle with. On the contrary, directors can now adapt with impunity and assimilate these plays to their own essentially modern subjectivity, which means, in many cases, to subject and reshape them to fit mental frames formed by the mass media. Conservative critics abhor the resultant promiscuity of the genres and accuse the hybridizing directors of selling the classical substance for laughs, for a succession of kicks, and of trading the deep glow and fire for evanescent sparks.

Their defenders, however, plead for an aesthetic of openness and indeterminacy that allows directors to try out multiperspective and associative approaches. They uphold the director's right to experiment with a decentered or plurifocused dramaturgy, and they see new aesthetic possibilities in nonlinearity or even diffuseness. Authenticity, they will argue, has become folklore. Identity, they say, has become a simulated ownness we project for others. Our culture already *is* mixed, our societies already *are* multicultural. Progressive critics wholeheartedly support Salman Rushdie's plea for hybridity as an answer to his question "How does newness come into the world?" and hope for new theories of transculturality to solve the dilemma.

In practical theatrical terms, the dilemma is far from being resolved. As far as the situation in Germany is concerned, "auteurism rampant" is the obvious diagnosis. How it works and whether it comes off could be studied in Klaus Weise's *Othello* of 1994 and *Hamlet* of 1998. For the acts on Cyprus, the stage for *Othello* had been turned into a fancy oasis with palm trees, giraffes, a local company of belly dancers (Weise had obviously profited from his training under Peter Zadek, the most flamboyant iconoclast on the postwar German stage), a fire-eater, and a rhinoceros traversing the scene on and off, besides two slapstick additions invented by the director. Bianca, in grass skirt and flower garland, picked a lover from the first row, a wispy and most unlikely elderly gentleman, whom she returned to his seat several scenes later visibly the worse for wear: to the great amusement of the audience. The second concerned Roderigo. In the fourth act he suddenly "opted out": he tore off his costume, officially gave notice, and fulminated against his idiotic part, the play, the set, the Oberhausen theater in general, before he could be persuaded to get back to work for the sake of an audience wild with laughter.

In *Hamlet* (1998) there was considerably more divergent material. Instead of waiting for Claudius to explain the history of his accession to the throne in the court scene, Gertrude crooned "Needless to say I'm sorry" into the microphone, thus opening the way for a musical potpourri containing among others a Monteverdi madrigal, Alfred Schnittke's "Concerto grosso," "Greensleeves," a tarantella, and a pop song praising the "Schöne Isabella von Kastilien." The director obviously saw no need to follow a unified concept or to tell a story relevant for the present, as was done in the ideological theater battles of the 1970s and early 1980s. Weise simply used the Hamlet story as an imaginative frame to create moments of pathos, surprise, or comic relief from the heterogeneous material. How intelligently this was done can be seen from two examples. For the "To be or not to be" soliloquy Hamlet wore a black T-shirt with "Sein" in big letters on the chest. When he turned around to greet Ophelia, the audience saw the "Nichtsein" printed on the back; there was a shocked laugh, which stopped when he pulled the T-shirt over both their bodies and one realized that this was how he linked their fates. Another indicative instance concerned Ophelia in her madness. In Oberhausen she not only appeared with flowers for King, Queen, and Laertes but, dressed and florally decorated like a bride, in the company of a serious, beautifully built naked young man, St. Valentine in person (obviously to the shrieking delight of the teenage girls in the audience for whom this was more to the point than the customary St. Valentine's song).

The pièce de résistance was an entr'acte given over to Rosencrantz and Guildenstern. The two suddenly found themselves alone in front of the curtain and an expectant audience whom they had to entertain at all costs. Guildenstern did clowned gymnastics, even managed a somersault; Rosencrantz worked his way through a long joke in Hamburg accent about Hamlet buying a coffin for his father and successively beating down the price for consecutively lesser quality and fewer frills. Furthermore, in word, song, or gesture the two entertainers brought in quotations from and allusions to current hits in the media: *Star Wars, Titanic, Gangster Rapper, Emergency Room, Frankenstein.*

It remains to be seen whether such furious hybridizing is only a fleeting fashion or will turn into a new paradigm. It clearly appeals to younger audiences and responds to the long-neglected need for entertainment in the German theater. Hybridization allows enormous freedom in the combination of disparate material. It also speeds up and multiplies the individual references and impressions, comparable to the fast-paced cuts in commercials, yet it takes a truly creative imagination and a great deal of self-discipline to handle with success.

But what is "success" in an art form that by definition defies rules? Each hybrid is something new and unique, even in its way "original," and therefore difficult to compare since comparisons as such fail to do justice to the uniqueness of the particular combination of its ingredients. Critics who register the hybrid's distance from Shakespeare's text have not grasped that they are being confronted with a new aesthetic paradigm. That is why they invariably go astray. They complain that the iconoclasm of the 1970s had at least a recognizable (if unwelcome) political purpose behind it that made the then-aesthetic disruptions understandable. By comparison, the hybrid productions of today appear to them as an arbitrary mélange devoid of ulterior aims. On the other hand, critics who praise hybrid theater events rarely provide ultimate insight either. Hybrid productions, it must be admitted, by their very nature are notoriously difficult to critique. A surprise and an obvious delight to (young) audiences, a minefield to critics, the freedoms they offer are a godsend to the director.

Apparently the temptation issuing from the "license to hybridize" is not restricted to German director's theater alone. The 1998 Andalusian theater festival in Cadiz, for example, showed a Cuban version of *The Tempest* in which Shylock, Hamlet, Othello, and Macbeth also put in an appearance. According to the German critic Renate Klett, this was a "confrontation of European and African culture" of great power and immediacy, "Shakespeare as a carnival of bodies, cries, light and drums—it is a sensual delight to let yourself be swamped by it, it would be torture to try and understand it."[6]

Hybridization, so botanists and zoologists tell us, can do either—ennoble or degrade, improve or impoverish. The vitalists among us are tempted to believe that hybridization, as the bastard Edmund Gloucester claims in *King Lear*, will

> ... in the lusty stealth of nature, take
> More composition and fierce quality
> Than doth, within a dull, stale, tired bed,
> Go to th' creating of a whole tribe of fops,
> Got 'tween asleep and wake.
>
> (1.2.11–15)

It may be so, and it may not. Bastard Edmund, the vitalist, sounds right, but in the end he proves wrong. Bastard Edmund prides himself on what botanists call heterosis, or hybrid vigor. Heterosis, botanists say, is responsible for high increases in the yields of field crops such as maize, sorghum, and sunflower. The production of hybrid seeds is agricultural Big Business, and there is no end in sight to the combinations that are being tried out. Or, in scientific language: "Major yield gains have come from the discovery of well-balanced heterotic combinations of superior new germplasm families."[7] Finding well-balanced heterotic combinations keeps the seed-production industry in business. Why? Because scientists have not solved the problem of the hybrid's spasmodic infertility. In the early days of seed hybridization, African farmers harvested most bountiful crops from hybrid seed corn sent by the United Nations, but only in the first year. In the second, their fields remained barren. Hybridization: a bad omen for the theater? Who can tell? Genetic manipulation—one step further from hybridization—is at present opening up a world of possibilities in what is perhaps the final step in our conquest of Nature. On the other hand, genetic manipulation or GM for short, may—as the Welsh biologist Andrew Lord suggests—be "the last and most arrogant nail in our coffin, overbrained crawlers on the bosom of the earth, that we are, trying to outwit 20 million years of evolution in a few decades. And, in the process, in order to achieve what we hope is final knowledge, we are ready to face utter annihilation by tampering with the inner seeds of creation" (personal communication). Shakespeare calls these inner seeds "Nature's germens," and "the treasure of nature's germen" is his phrase for the world's gene pool. Macbeth is prepared to brave the world's final genetic confusion to learn his fate,

> . . . though *the treasure*
> *Of nature's germen* tumble all together,
> Even till destruction sicken, answer me
> To what I ask you
>
> (*Macbeth*, 4.1.58–61)

and King Lear also—in one of the most terrible curses in literature—is willing to pay the ultimate price of confounding the genes (a hair-raising thought!), if only he, Lear, can have his will:

> Smite flat the thick rotundity o'the world!
> Crack nature's moulds, *all germens spill at once*
> That make ingrateful man!
>
> (*King Lear*, 3.2.7–9)

Rose-growers know of a "hybrid perpetual," a rose that blooms throughout the season. This is unknown in the theater. In the theater there is no telling until after the event whether the hybrid is an abysmal flop, or whether it entitles the director to proclaim, like Edmund, "I grow, I prosper; / Now, gods, stand up for bastards!" (*King Lear*, 1.2.21–22).

Notes

1. Günther Rühle (in *Theater in unserer Zeit* [Frankfurt: Suhrkamp Verlag, 1976], 270), summing up Gründgens's postwar achievement and the tenor of his many addresses collected in *Wirklichkeit des Theaters* (Frankfurt: Suhrkamp Verlag, 1953), 177.

2. For a general survey of hybridity in modern culture, see the collection of essays, *Hybridkultur: Medien, Netze, Künste*, ed. Irmela Schneider and Christian W. Thomsen (Cologne: Wienand Verlag, 1997).

3. Stanley Wells, in *The Oxford Companion to Shakespeare* (Oxford: Oxford University Press, 2001), 58.

4. "The Hero as Divinity," in *On Heroes, Hero-Worship and the Heroic in His-

tory, quoted in *The Victorian Age,* ed. J. W. Bowyer and J. L. Brooks (New York: F. S. Crofts, 1941), 185; *Browning's Essay on Shelley* [1851], ed. Richard Garnett (London: Alexander Moring, 1903), 38; *The Works of John Ruskin,* ed. E. T. Cook and Alexander Wedderburn, Library Edition, 39 vols. (London: George Allen, 1903–12), 4:247.

5. Quoted in *Shakespeare Handbuch,* ed. Ina Schabert (Stuttgart: Alfred Kröner, 1972), 908.

6. *Frankfurter Allgemeine Zeitung,* September 18, 1998.

7. Donald N. Duvick, "Heterosis: Feeding People and Protecting Natural Resources," in *The Genetics and Exploitation of Heterosis in Crops,* ed. J. G. Coors and S. Pandey, 19–29 (Madison, WI: American Society of Agronomy, 2001), 19.

III
The Politics of Criticism

Introduction
Manfred Pfister

CRITICISM IN GENERAL, AND SHAKESPEAREAN CRITICISM IN PARTICular, always has a range of agendas that go beyond merely philological, literary, or aesthetic understanding and appreciation. It always has ulterior axes to grind, and frequently these axes are political. This is true both of critical writings that address overtly political texts as, in Shakespeare's case, his history plays, and of criticism dealing with apparently unpolitical texts, his comedies, for instance.

We can see this already in the earliest Shakespeare criticism, that of his contemporaries. When Thomas Nashe in his *Pierce Penilesse* (1592) praises the Talbot scenes of *1 Henry VI*, he praises them not only in terms of their spectacular theatricality but also for their power to stir the patriotic spirits of their audience against the enemy across the Channel: "How would it have joyed brave *Talbot* (the terror of the French) to thinke that after he had lyne two hundred yeares in his Tombe, hee should triumphe againe on the Stage, and have his bones newe embalmed with the teares of ten thousand spectators at least (at severall times), who, in the Tragedian that represents his person, imagine they behold him fresh bleeding."[1] The heightened tone of this revenant fantasy of a pristine English valor and male heroism returning onto the English stage reflects a crisis in Anglo-French relations and national self-confidence, and this reminds us that the words "criticism" and "crisis," both referring to crucial distinctions or decisive turning points, are etymologically closely related. No less political is what Francis Meres has to say about Shakespeare in his *Palladis Tamia* (1598), although Meres at first sight does not address himself to political concerns at all. All he seems to do is compare Shakespeare and some of his English contemporaries with the great canonical authors of Greek and Latin classical literature:

> As the Greeke tongue is made famous and eloquent by *Homer, Hesiod* ... and *Aristophanes;* and the Latine tongue by *Virgill, Ovid* ... and *Claudianus:* so the English tongue is mightily enriched, and gorgeouslie invested in rare ornaments and resplendent abiliments by Sir *Philip Sidney, Spen-*

cer, *Daniel, Drayton, Warner, Shakespeare, Marlow* and *Chapman*. . . . As *Plautus* and *Seneca* are accounted the best for Comedy and Tragedy among the Latines: so *Shakespeare* among ye English is the most excellent in both kinds for the stage. . . .[2]

In these comparisons there is, however, more at stake than just literary appreciation: what they claim is that the contemporary English language, literature and culture are on a par with the Greek and Roman models. By constructing a tradition that links contemporary English literature with the classical canon, Meres elevates English literature, so long at the receiving end of French, Italian, Spanish, or Dutch culture and aware of its own marginal status, to European canonical heights. Moreover, what could be a more forcefully patriotic gesture here than the eloquent silence with which Meres dismisses the rest of Europe from his roll call of national cultural achievement! And Ben Jonson, of course, in his dedicatory poem to the First Folio (1623) will spell out this new sense of national self-confidence and superiority over the cultures of the European rivals across the Channel with particular patriotic ardor:

> Triúmph, my *Britaine,* thou hast one to showe,
> To whom all Scenes of *Europe* homage owe.[3]

This is not the place to rehearse once again a history of Shakespearean criticism as a history of political criticism. Suffice it to say here that an awareness of the close, if frequently implicit, nexus between politics and Shakespearean criticism had been growing inside the theoretical debates in Shakespeare studies in the course of the last century before it led to large-scale rewritings of the history of Shakespeare criticism in terms of its more or less hidden political agendas. The project of tracing the history of the politics of Shakespeare criticism was first launched in the middle of the 1980s, a time when Europe was approaching a critical sea change in its political constitution. It began on a nationally contained scale with British cultural materialism staging its war against Thatcherite England as a war against the ways in which the scholastic, academic, and cultural establishment had processed Shakespeare into a national figurehead and conservative icon.[4] Soon, however, this concern with the current English politics of Shakespeare criticism fanned out into wider domains: historically into the past, as with Jonathan Bate's *Shakespearean Constitutions* (1989), or geographically into an international, even global scope, as with Gary Taylor's *Reinventing Shakespeare* (1989).[5] This was also the context that triggered the informal network of Shakespeare scholars from all over Europe who, under the acronym SHINE (Shakespeare in the New Europe), first assembled in Sofia in 1991 to study and compare the political uses of Shakespeare and of Shakespearean performance and criticism in their various countries,[6] and this network in turn engendered the Utrecht conference of 2003 documented in this volume and in particular its metacritical section on "The Politics of Criticism," based on a seminar that drew scholars from more than a dozen countries.

The selected contributions presented here all qualify as metacriticism: their immediate object is not Shakespeare but the criticism of Shakespeare, and their objective is to reveal and interrogate the political agendas inscribed in Shakespearean criticism either in blatant rhetoric or as a latent subtext. They are, whether their authors have attended the Frankfurt School or not, exercises in *Ideologiekritik,* exercises in *Hinterfragen,* that is, in questioning insistently and deeply the imbrications of Shakespearean criticism in political constructions of gender, class, or national identity.[7] The greater challenge is posed by critical texts that claim to have no "further business" beyond an exclusive concern with the aesthetic structures of Shakespearean drama, such as, for instance, readings of Shakespeare aligned with an allegedly unpolitical or politically disinterested "New Criticism." The greater the challenge, however, the more incisive are the insights to be gained here. And, of course, the difficulty increases the closer we get to the present, or to ourselves: it may be fairly easy to discover the political bias in earlier criticism, but what political agendas underlie our own metacriticism? What we would need here is a new "New Historicism" applied to the circulation of political energies in our own criticism, or a hermeneutics whose circular loops would not stop short at our own critical metadiscourses.

The contribution that covers the widest ground is Bettina Boecker's essay on "Groundlings, Gallants, Grocers: Shakespeare's Elizabethan Audience and the Political Agendas of Shakespeare Criticism." It deals with what might appear to be a mere question of theater history to be resolved by a careful scrutiny of the extant plays and documents. What her survey of shifting positions—from the eighteenth century, and Romantic and Victorian criticism, to Harbage, Weimann, and Anne Jennalie Cook—persuasively demonstrates, however, is how the changing views of Shakespeare's audience reflect the critics' politically grounded preconceptions of class relations. Whether they consider the Elizabethan audience as an asset or a liability for Shakespeare's dramatic and theatrical art, as dominated by the "groundlings," to whose low tastes the great genius unfortunately had to make concessions, or as a cross-section of Elizabethan society, which stimulated the wide spectrum of ideological positions in his public theater, proves therefore to be less a matter of historical scholarship than of the critics' class alignments, their cultural elitism or populism, their aristocratic or democratic identifications. In this sense, they all "invent" an audience to suit their own ideological needs, and by writing about Shakespeare's audience, they ventilate their dismay, anxiety, or enthusiasm about the increasingly "mass" audiences of their own times.

The contributions by Janet Clare—"*Hamlet* and Modernism: T. S. Eliot and G. Wilson Knight"—and Antonella Piazza—"'What dost thou think 'tis worth?': *Timon of Athens* and Politics as a Nonreligious Religion"—are closely related to each other, although they discuss critical reactions to two different plays and come to fairly divergent conclusions. Where they converge is the Nietzschean legacy of modernist New Criticism in England, and this legacy, transmitted through Knight to Eliot, is of a highly volatile political charge. According to Clare, Eliot's early *Hamlet* essay of 1920 already foreshadows his later political convictions, his desire for order, clarity, and control, which makes him subvert Nietzsche's celebration of *Hamlet* as imaging a Dionysian moment of truth; G. Wilson Knight, in a complex relationship of similarity and contrast to Eliot, responds to the Nietzschean gospel of the Übermensch with a vision of national leadership that dreams of a Claudius-like "true leader" to heal the spiritual atrophy and stop the death drift of a Hamlet-like England between the two great wars. In Clare's reading, Knight's belief in the mystical charisma of monarchical leadership gets uncomfortably close to "a fascist view of existence."

Piazza, by contrast, emphasizes in her reading of Knight's reading of *Timon of Athens* his humanist interpretation of Nietzsche's aristocratic ideal of "the good," which he sees misappropriated by the contemporary German Fascists. Her Knight is engaged in a passionate struggle against both Fascist and Communist totalitarianism, holding up Timon's flow of warm magnanimity in the first two acts against Marx's reading of the play in *Das Kapital,* where it provides the one extensive Shakespeare quotation and illustrates the reifying and alienating power of money, which destroys all real values, as well as against Fascist ideologies of "the good" based on blood and race. What Piazza sees foreshadowed in Knight's reading of *Timon* is a "new political sense of community" based on a "nonreligious bond (re-ligio)," which only Derridean critics like Ken Jackson have fully captured.

The last contribution to this section—Andreas Höfele's "Reeducating Germany: BBC Shakespeare 1945"—shows politics at work in, and through, Shakespeare criticism in a much more direct and practical sense. Höfele's fascinating case study is not concerned with subtle critical interventions but with propaganda—with the British effort to bring the Germans back into the fold of civilized nations after the barbarism of their Third Reich and the material and moral devastations of the war. To invoke in this the help of the British Bard and what he has been made to stand for—a pastoral England, British common sense, a universally shared humanity, the Christian message of forgiveness—is as revealing of the cultural politics of England and its international voice, the BBC, as of the German audience at which the *Shakespeare Feature* was targeted in June 1945. After all, even Nazi Germany had paid lip service to Shakespeare as, next to Goethe and Schiller, the greatest German classic, so that the voice of the reeducator spoke in an already familiar idiom of isles sceptered or full of noises, of being or not being, of Jews having eyes, or the quality of mercy not being strained. This may not have been subtle criticism, but as propaganda it was subtle and effective enough and demonstrates once again to what powerful political uses Shakespeare and Shakespeare criticism can be put.

Notes

1. Quoted from Stephen Greenblatt et al., eds., *The Norton Shakespeare* (New York: Norton, 1997), 3322.

2. Ibid., 3324–25.

3. Ibid., 3352. For the politics of the European canonization of Shakespeare, see my essay "'In states unborn and accents yet unknown': Shakespeare and the European Canon," in *Shifting the Scene: Shakespeare in European Culture*, ed. Ladina Bezzola Lambert and Balz Engler, 41–63 (Newark: University of Delaware Press, 2004).

4. Two mideighties collections of critical essays proved seminal here: Jonathan Dollimore and Alan Sinfield, eds., *Political Shakespeare: New Essays in Cultural Materialism* (Manchester: Manchester University Press, 1985), and John Drakakis, ed., *Alternative Shakespeares* (London: Methuen, 1985). See also the highly influential metacritical writings of Terence Hawkes, in particular *That Shakespeherian Rag: Essays on a Critical Process* (London: Methuen, 1986).

5. Jonathan Bate, *Shakespearean Constitutions: Politics, Theatre, Criticism, 1730–1830* (Oxford: Clarendon Press, 1989); for the politics of "modernist" attitudes to Shakespeare, see Hugh Grady, *The Modernist Shakespeare: Critical Texts in a Material World* (Oxford: Clarendon Press, 1991); Gary Taylor, *Reinventing Shakespeare: A Cultural History from the Restoration to the Present* (New York: Weidenfeld & Nicolson, 1989).

6. The contributions are collected in Michael Hattaway, Boika Sokolova, and Derek Roper, eds., *Shakespeare in the New Europe* (Sheffield: Sheffield Academic Press, 1994).

7. On *Ideologiekritik*, see Christopher Butler, *Interpretation, Deconstruction, and Ideology: An Introduction to Some Current Issues in Literary Theory* (Oxford: Clarendon Press, 1984; 2nd ed. 1998), and Terry Eagleton, *The Ideology of the Aesthetic* (Oxford: Blackwell, 1990; 2nd ed. 1995).

Groundlings, Gallants, Grocers: Shakespeare's Elizabethan Audience and the Political Agendas of Shakespeare Criticism

Bettina Boecker

THEATERGOERS IN RENAISSANCE LONDON HAVE BEEN SUBJECT TO much debate. The sheer amount of writing on Shakespeare's original audience and the assurance with which critics have used Elizabethan spectators to bolster their theories about Shakespeare and his plays can easily obscure the fact that very little is actually known about those who frequented the theaters during the Bard's lifetime. What evidence we have is often marred by a high degree of subjectivity, sometimes amounting to outright partisanship. Contemporary commentaries on the theaters and their patrons frequently reflect the religious and political agendas of Puritan authors, and, on the other end of the spectrum, the dramatists themselves hardly qualify as disinterested observers of those on whose approval they depended for a livelihood.

In view of this rather unreliable source material, it is perhaps not wholly surprising that the divergence and partiality of contemporary descriptions of Shakespeare's audience has translated into similarly biased and conflicting views of the audience in Shakespeare criticism throughout the centuries. As a recent study of the Elizabethan theater public puts it: "[M]odern accounts of the audience suffer from the bias of the writer fully as much as did the contemporary accounts. . . . As often as not, an interpretation reveals more about the interpreter's mind than it does about the mysteries of the past."[1]

More or less explicit acknowledgments of the fact that images of Shakespeare's original audience have as much to do with a critic's "mind"—and how that mind envisages Shakespeare—as with what used to be called the historical facts are by no means scarce. As early as 1849, G. H. Lewes summarized the role of the audience in eighteenth-century Shakespeare criticism as follows: "If [Shakespeare] wrote trash sometimes, it was to please the groundlings. . . . Thus

Pope, in his celebrated Preface, attributes the bombast and triviality to be found in Shakespeare, wholly to the necessity of addressing a vulgar audience. And with this judgment Warburton agrees."[2] What Lewes (understandably) fails to notice is that the Shakespearean critics of his own day were also "inventing" an audience to suit their own needs: at least in the eyes of posterity, nineteenth-century conceptions of Shakespeare's original audience seem "begotten of an honest though ill-considered attempt to reconcile the Victorian conception of Shakespeare with certain facts which the Victorians overlooked or found it convenient to ignore."[3] In reproaching the preceding generation of critics for an insufficiently objective stance toward Renaissance theatergoers, both commentators make an important point about the role of the early modern theater public in Shakespeare criticism—the Elizabethan audience plays a significant part in aligning Shakespeare with the norms and values of later ages.

Blame Not the Bard: Groundlings

As Lewes and Wilson observe quite rightly, one of the main functions of the Elizabethan audience has been to excuse the Bard's perceived faults and shortcomings. It is already in the very early stages of Shakespeare criticism that this tradition is established: the representatives of an age perceived as uncivilized and rude, Renaissance theatergoers personify the allegedly detrimental influence of Shakespeare's historical situation on his work. The "faults" that eighteenth-century criticism perceived in the plays are, in the view of many critics, directly related to the demands that a semibarbarous audience made on the dramatist. Shakespeare's "beauties," on the other hand, are construed as manifestations of his timeless literary genius.

If blaming the audience for "corrupting" Shakespeare seems, at first glance, to be nothing more than a less-abstract version of blaming the age, it is important to note that several eighteenth-century critics implicitly or explicitly characterize Shakespeare's original audience as lower class. Taylor portrays Renaissance theatergoers as "illiterate, low-liv'd mechanics," while Pope ascribes Shakespeare's faults to the necessity of pleasing "the populace," "the meaner sort of people."[4] This nexus between Shakespeare's "un-Shakespearean" bits and the lower social orders remains undisturbed by the Romantics' reevaluation of the concept of the people. Wordsworth—like many eighteenth-century critics before him—proposes that certain passages were "foisted in by the Players, for the gratification of the many."[5] Coleridge calls the audience at the Globe a "mob" and credits only a few elite spectators with the capability of truly appreciating the Bard. Nevertheless, he views the Renaissance as a whole in a positive light, as does Hazlitt, who emphatically rejects the eighteenth-century notion that Shakespeare's genius is quintessentially ahistorical:

> We affect to wonder at Shakespear, and one or two more of that period, as solitary instances upon record; whereas it is our own dearth of information that makes the waste; for there is no time more populous of intellect, or more prolific of intellectual wealth, than the one we are speaking of. Shakespear did not look upon himself in this light, as a sort of monster of poetical genius, or on his contemporaries as "less than smallest dwarfs," when he speaks with true, not false modesty, of himself and them, and of his wayward thoughts, "desiring this man's art and that man's scope." . . . He indeed overlooks and commands the admiration of posterity, but he does it from the *tableland* of the age in which he lived. . . . He was not something sacred and aloof from the vulgar herd of men, but shook hands with nature and the circumstances of the time, and is distinguished from his immediate contemporaries, not in kind, but in degree and greater variety of excellence. He did not form a class or species by himself, but belonged to a class or species.[7]

Hazlitt's revaluation of the Renaissance goes hand in hand with a reconceptualization of the relationship between the great dramatist and the "vulgar herd of men." Both he and Coleridge reject the historical apology devised by eighteenth-century criticism, but for Hazlitt this includes a repudiation of the sociological argument that had frequently formed an integral part of it. Coleridge, on the other hand, despite a generally positive view of the early modern age, perpetuates the notion that, in contrast to the cultivated elite, the "mob" in the theaters was largely incapable of appreciating Shakespeare's works. The lower orders of the Renaissance are thus excluded from any participation in, or understanding of, the Bard's extraordinary literary achievement.

This narrowing down of the historical apology into a sociological one has been extremely influential. From the nineteenth century onward, it is increasingly the notorious groundlings, and not Renaissance spectators in their entirety, who have to take the blame for passages difficult to reconcile with Shakespeare's status as a cultural icon. While the term "groundlings" is first used by Hamlet in his admonition to the players at Elsinore, it does not gain widespread currency until the Victorian age. Nineteenth-century critics ascribe a fairly specific set of elements in Shakespeare's plays to the tastes of this subsection of the Elizabethan audience. The view put forward by A. C. Bradley is representative:

> [T]he mass of the audience in both kinds of theatre [public and private] ... must have liked excitement, the open exhibition of violent and bloody deeds, and the intermixture of seriousness and mirth. What distinguished the more popular section in it, was a higher degree of this indifference and this liking, and in addition a special fondness for certain sources of inartistic joy. The most prominent of these, perhaps, were noise; rant; mere bawdry; "shews"; irrelevant songs, ballads, jokes, dances, and clownage in general; and, lastly, target-fighting and battles. . . . The audience liked tragedy to be relieved by rough mirth, and it got the Grave-diggers in *Hamlet* and the old countryman in *Antony and Cleopatra*. It liked a "drum and trumpet" history, and it got *Henry V*. It liked clowns and fools, and it got Feste and the Fool in *King Lear*.[8]

The spectators in the yard—"the more popular section" of the audience—have to take the blame for those passages where Shakespeare comes too close for comfort to the "sensationalism" of nineteenth-century melodrama.[9] Unmotivated turns of the plot or irrational behavior on the part of the characters, like the jealousy of Othello or Leontes, as well as spectacular visual or aural effects, such as supernatural apparitions (e.g., the ghost in *Hamlet*), stage fights, or "drums and trumpets" apparently reminded critics of a genre they were unwilling to associate with the Bard. But above all, the groundlings are made to account for those (all too frequent) passages where Shakespeare violates Victorian moral sensibilities, such as the porter scene in *Macbeth* or the gravediggers in *Hamlet*. While Bradley is fairly moderate on this point, others were incited to what can only be described as moral outrage. Poet laureate Robert Bridges warns:

> Shakespeare should not be put into the hands of the young without the warning that the foolish things in his plays were written to please the foolish, the filthy for the filthy, and the brutal for the brutal; and that, if out of veneration for his genius we are led to admire or even tolerate such things, we may be thereby not conforming ourselves to him, but only degrading ourselves to the level of his audience, and learning contamination from those wretched beings who can never be forgiven their share in preventing the greatest poet and dramatist of the world from being the best artist.[10]

The salient feature of groundling tastes and groundling morals as envisioned by nineteenth-century criticism is that they show a close resemblance to the way the Victorian lower classes were perceived by their social superiors. The alleged depravity of the common people features prominently in studies such as Henry Mayhew's *London Labour and the London Poor* (1851–61). Again and again it is (unfavorably) contrasted with the standards of decency advocated by the middle and upper reaches of society. Victorian morality functioned as a means of social differentiation, and to a certain degree this also holds true for the theater: not least because of its supposedly immoral tendencies, the melodrama was considered a domain of the lower classes.[11] In asserting that the "melodramatic" elements in Shakespeare were a concession to the lower-class spectators of his own day, critics were policing the boundary between what was considered a mindless and even morally corrupting form of stage entertainment, and the "serious" theater of the middle and upper classes, which increasingly defined Shakespearean drama as educative and even edifying.

If groundling tastes, clearly, are lower-class tastes, the emergence of this "class myth" can be traced back to a conflict between an inclusive national culture and an exclusive high culture—both of which claimed Shakespeare as their own.[12] The appropriation of Shakespeare as a symbol of Englishness and of national unity made it increasingly inconvenient to condemn Renaissance audiences in their entirety: after all, the Age of Elizabeth had been established as one of the great eras of the English nation. However, a complete revaluation of a public that was traditionally associated with the lower classes would have presented serious difficulties to those who increasingly and very effectively were turning Shakespeare into a high-culture icon. Blaming the groundlings for his shortcomings fulfilled the double purpose of keeping the Bard well within the confines of what had been defined as high culture, while keeping the groundlings, and, more importantly, their modern-day counterparts, well out of it.

A Bard of Their Own: Gallants

The tendency to exclude certain sectors of the Renaissance public from the "real" Shakespeare becomes even more pronounced once the Bard has been established as one of the main raisons d'être of English as a university discipline. The trained specialists in literature who replace Victorian "gentlemen critics" from the early twentieth century onward require a text that is demanding enough to reward their professional efforts. Whether it is because ostentatiously complex literary texts by authors like Eliot, Pound, or Joyce influence perspectives on the Bard, or because the new caste of academics wishes to exercise its professional skills on the most prestigious author around,[13] from the early twentieth century onward, critics increasingly focus on the multiple layers of meaning, linguistic complexity, and intellectual exactingness of Shakespeare's plays. This, however, requires at least a partial reconfiguration of the situation in the theaters of the English Renaissance: an audience of "illiterate, low-liv'd mechanics" would arguably have missed most, if not all, of the complexity and subtlety attributed to Shakespeare by his modern critics.

Just as Victorian Shakespeare criticism had presented the groundlings as those responsible for offensive passages in the plays, critics now pick out a target group for their intricate patterns of thought and language. Instead of simply attributing the intellectual capability to understand Shakespeare to everyone in the audience apart from the groundlings, they isolate yet another subsection, in this case one that is especially receptive to Shakespeare's demands on the intellect: the "gallants." Although the term designates a social rather than an intellectual elite, critics often conflate the two categories: "We have not, I think, allowed sufficiently for the presence of [cultured men of high rank] in Shakespeare's audience," states Dover Wilson in 1929—a neglect that critics such as W. W. Greg, Q. D. Leavis, or H. S. Bennett are quick to make up for.[14]

Greg—to give but one example—relies heavily on the superior intellect (if not necessarily the superior social standing) of the "judicious few" to lend credibility to his interpretation of *Hamlet.* In Greg's view, Hamlet is familiar with the play within the play, *The Murder of Gonzago,* long before he has it performed at the Danish court. If the particular method of poisoning, which his father's ghost describes exactly, resembles the one in *The Murder of Gonzago,* it is because the ghost is a hallucination of the prince's mind for which the play, as it were, provides the details.[15] This immensely complex version of what "really" happens in *Hamlet,* Greg admits, is hard to comprehend for an audience viewing the play for the first time. He insists, however, that there must have been Elizabethan spectators who took a more scholarly approach to the drama:

> How far the subtler meaning can ever have been appreciated on the stage even by the "judicious" is a point difficult to determine. It may be that no unprepared spectator, witnessing the play for the first time, would be able to grasp it. But need we suppose that plays were never discussed in the taverns among the finer wits, that the latter never thought over a performance they had seen and stumbled upon points whose significance had passed unnoticed at the time or remembered difficulties that had given but a moment's pause in the excitement of representation, and that they never returned and sat through a second performance with a view to getting a clearer conception of the author's meaning?[16]

As the addressees of Shakespeare's multilayered intellectual subtlety, these "finer wits" assume paramount importance, and not just for

Greg. However, the attempt to align Shakespeare's reception during his own lifetime with early twentieth-century conceptions of the Bard is not without its pitfalls. Shakespeare's proven popularity with early modern audiences makes the assumption that only a small elite had the intellectual capability to appreciate his work somewhat unconvincing. Obviously, many Renaissance theatergoers were far from dissatisfied or bored with his "exacting" plays. Why, one wonders, did the unsophisticated Many go to the theaters at all if only the privileged Few were capable of enjoying the plays?

Critics try to overcome this difficulty by using two different strategies. Some describe the meaning of the plays as "concentric," that is, as revealing itself in different degrees of completeness to different sections of the audience. Others, drawing on a central concept of modernist aesthetics, read them as ironic.[17] In this version, Shakespeare's satire eludes the broad majority of playgoers. While they take the plays at their face value, it is only the "judicious few" who are able to discern Shakespeare's real intentions. The theater experience of the elite is thus more or less unrelated to that of the majority. This, however, puts a considerable strain on the relation between the critical minority and the undiscerning masses—even if, like Q. D. Leavis, one assumes a "concentric" meaning and thus a more or less "common" culture:

> [T]o object that most of the [Elizabethan] audience could not possibly understand the play and only went to the theatre because the alternative to *Hamlet* was the bear-pit is beside the point for the purposes of the student of cultural history; the importance of this for him is that the masses were receiving their amusement from above (instead of being specially catered for by journalists, film-directors and popular novelists, as they are now). They had to take the same amusements as their betters, and if *Hamlet* was only a glorious melodrama to the groundlings, they were none the less living for the time being in Shakespeare's blank verse . . . ; to argue that they would have preferred Tom Mix or *Tarzan of the Apes* is idle. Happily they had no choice, and education of ear and mind is none the less valuable for being acquired unconsciously.[18]

Since a common culture apparently depends on the lower orders not having a choice, it is not surprising that Leavis approvingly quotes Edmund Gosse's prediction that a spread of "the democratic sentiment" would lead to a decline of literary standards: "If literature is to be judged by a plebiscite and if the plebs recognizes its power, it will certainly by degrees cease to support reputations which give it no pleasure and which it cannot comprehend."[19] Perhaps even more significantly, the "plebs" will also cease to support those who consider themselves the guardians of literary standards and reputations: the "cultured minority."

As an icon of high culture, Shakespeare commands a certain exclusivity. In order to qualify as an embodiment of the—literary as well as nonliterary—norms of society as a whole, he does, however, need a degree of general acceptance, a more or less broad consensus that his plays are indeed not only valuable as literary artifacts but also, however vaguely, relevant to the concerns of the community at large. Conceptions of Shakespeare's Elizabethan audience reflect this tension: in a democratic society, a Shakespeare who is made to embody the exclusive standards of the elites—who in their turn are under constant pressure to justify their existence in such a society—risks losing his status as an accepted site of cultural meaning. This threat can only partially (if at all) be deflected by presenting the "authentic" Bard as a dramatist who addressed himself to the elites of his own lifetime. To secure his position as a cultural icon in the twentieth century, Shakespeare needs some popular credentials.

Make Him Our Bard: Grocers

In 1941, Alfred Harbage published a study that marks a decisive turning point in the discourse on Elizabethan theatergoers. Unlike almost all his predecessors, Harbage attributes the special quality of Shakespeare's plays to the special quality of his audience—all of his audience, not just a small part of it:

> Shakespeare's audience was socially, economically, educationally heterogeneous. It was motley, and for this we must be thankful. An audience so mixed compelled the most discerning of all authors to address himself to men and not to their badges, to men's intelligence and not to its levels. The influence upon the individual exerted by class, whether high or low, is a cramping influence, narrowing the horizon, warping the sympathies, prejudicing the mind. But where all classes are there is no class; there is that common humanity which subtends all. To the kind of audience for which he wrote . . . we owe Shakespeare's universality.[20]

Whereas eighteenth-century Shakespeare criticism had pictured the Elizabethan audience as "the people" in the sense of "the lower classes," Harbage's quintessentially American vision presents Renaissance theatergoers as a miniature model of "the people" in a far more comprehensive sense. The grocer, his wife, and their young apprentice at whom Beaumont directs his satire in *The Knight of the Burning Pestle* become Harbage's representative spectators; they personify the broad middle section of a community based on compromise and a balance of power that is presented as the enabling condition, the sine qua non, of Shakespeare's greatness. In doing so, Harbage indeed raises Elizabethan spectators "from Victorian contemptibility to working class respectability," "pitt[ing] the proletarian moral soundness that gave birth to Shakespeare against the decadence of elitist tastes."[21] His contribution to the continuing iconicity of Shakespeare in Western societies is not to be underrated: a "democratic institution in an intensely undemocratic age" in which "the rights of privilege and class melted before the magical process of dropping pennies in a box,"[22] Harbage's Renaissance theater is modeled on an idealized version of the United States in the 1940s. The democratic optimism that informs his view of the Elizabethan audience—and, by extension, his view of Shakespeare himself—agrees extremely well with the official version of what it is like to live in the free West.

Harbage's view remained the standard one for several decades and still has canonical status, probably not least because of the liberating effects it attributes to capitalism. While eighteenth- and nineteenth-century critics implicitly and explicitly draw a connection between perceived blemishes in Shakespeare's works and the fact that the Globe was a profit-oriented enterprise (it is only as paying customers that the "rabble" can exercise an undue influence over the Bard), Harbage emphasizes the potentially egalitarian aspects of the theaters' orientation toward the market (it was money, and not the more exclusive criterion of rank, that granted Elizabethans access to Shakespeare's outstanding drama).

Harbage's endorsement of equality and democracy, however, is not entirely unequivocal. When he states, "Craftsmen . . . with their families, journeymen, and apprentices, must have composed the vast majority of 'groundlings.' Many were skilled, performing functions now allotted to the chemist, architect and engineer," he clearly elevates what he repeatedly refers to as an audience of "workmen" into the ranks of the (upper) middle class, to which "chemist[s], architect[s] and engineer[s]" would have belonged in the 1940s (and still do).[23] The "wretched beings" whom Robert Bridges had blamed for Shakespeare's perceived moral lapses, the "populace" to whose influence Pope had attributed the Bard's faults, remain excluded from "Shakespeare's Globe."

Nevertheless, the Globe continues to represent the dream of a unified cultural sphere. At the same time, the revaluation of Elizabethan audiences and especially of the groundlings has been taken even further in the second half of the twentieth century. These tendencies are not mutually exclusive: Robert Weimann's seminal *Shakespeare und die Tradition des Volkstheaters* (translated as *Shakespeare and the Popular Tradition in the Theater*),[24] like many studies by avowedly leftist critics, does not—as one might expect—present Elizabethan theatergoers as a kind of proletariat avant la lettre, but rather as a miniature version of society as a whole, the embodiment of "the people" in the most comprehensive sense: "Shakespeare writes for a popular, yet professional Renaissance theater which, during its national phase, attracts an audience from many classes and social strata."[25] However, even if the theaters attracted visitors from all sectors of society, Weimann insists that the lower classes played a decisive role in Shakespeare's extraordinary dramatic achievements:

> At the doors of the famous theaters . . . , courtier and artisan, apprentice and student, nobleman and plebeian met. All were more or less equally interested in a drama the versatility of which managed to bridge existing differences in taste without discarding the conventions of earlier folk traditions. This would hardly have been possible in the first place, let alone necessary: the plebeians in the yard, the most numerous as well as the most vociferous section of the audience, were quite open to artistic experiments! In the later years [of the Elizabethan age], dramatists may have looked down on these "groundlings" with studious contempt; but even if—like Beaumont in *The Knight of the Burning Pestle*—they brought them on the stage only to ridicule them, they had to pay tribute to their astonishing qualities. *The Spanish Tragedy, Doctor Faustus, Henry IV* and *Hamlet* were favorites of the despised multitude! In reality, both the acting conventions and the dramatic art of the Elizabethan theater were unthinkable without these "groundlings," the standing multitude in the yard which surrounded the Shakespearean platform stage from three sides.[26]

Weimann's argumentative strategies resemble those used by Harbage. Both state that Elizabethan audiences are representative of society as a whole, but then go on to claim that a specific social group played a decisive role in the development of English Renaissance drama. Both identify the groundlings as the seminal group in question, but they differ in the exact social position they assign them. What is decisive, in any case, is that both critics argue for a sort of collective claim to Shakespeare as a cultural icon. If certain groups are more important to the development of his supreme dramatic art than others, this is meant to prove their special relevance for society as a whole, not their exclusive "right" to the Bard.

It is in this respect that, from the 1980s onward, one can detect a shift toward greater polarization. Critics like David Margolies have used the notion of a largely proletarian Elizabethan audience to bolster their claims to "correctness" in the interpretation of Shakespeare's plays—and to ascribe a generally "subversive" political stance to the Bard.[27] There have also been theater productions explicitly setting out to "give Shakespeare back to the groundlings,"[28] implying that this is where he rightfully belongs. Somewhat ironically, these attempts to claim (or reclaim?) Shakespeare for a popular counterculture seem to be extremely marketable: groundlings play an important role in the image of Renaissance theater projected by the New Globe—not only on tours of the site itself, but also in its shop, where "groundling" T-shirts are available as souvenirs.

However, there have also been revaluations of Shakespeare's original audience that run directly counter to these attempts to "popularize" the Bard. Ann Jennalie Cook's *The Privileged Playgoers of Shakespeare's London,* arguably the most controversial contribution to the discourse on Renaissance theatergoers in the last twenty-five years, altogether denies that the lower classes could have attended the Renaissance theaters in significant numbers, since, according to Cook, they would have had neither the money nor the leisure to do so.[29] This position has come under vehement attack,[30] not only because of alleged weaknesses in Cook's method, but also because of her implied claim that the excellence of Shakespearean drama is in some way linked to the fact that it was written for a socially elevated audience. In the meantime, Cook has partially modified her position.[31]

Whose Shakespeare?

The political issues raised by the way we envision Shakespeare's original spectators and his relation to them are obviously far from settled. In view of the nature of these issues, this is hardly surprising. Conflicting conceptions of the Bard's Renaissance public point directly to questions of cultural "ownership" and "entitlement." If Shakespeare wrote for an uneducated, predominantly lower-class audience, it becomes harder for later ages to appropriate him for an upper middle-class high culture. If, on the other hand, he wrote for a small elite of cultured "gallants," the Bard's claim to universal significance for *all* sections of later societies is called into question. There are good reasons why Harbage's model has gone unchallenged for so long: his conception of Shakespeare's audience as an egalitarian enclave in a nonegalitarian age is the one most suited to promoting the Bard's prestige in societies that consider themselves democratic. If Harbage's idea of a community free from internal divisions as the basis for Shakespeare's outstanding drama has been disputed from more than one side in the last two or three decades, this points toward the fact that this ideal of a society largely without conflict has become problematical or even suspect. However, it can also be seen as reflecting the development of Shakespeare criticism itself. A discipline that likes to think of the object of its endeavors as a "site of cultural struggle and change,"[32] and that does not believe in disinterested interpretation any longer will obviously sympathize most with an Elizabethan audience that is also forced to take sides.

Notes

1. Ann Jennalie Cook, *The Privileged Playgoers of Shakespeare's London, 1576–1642* (Princeton: Princeton University Press, 1981), 3.
2. George Henry Lewes, "Shakespeare's Critics: English and Foreign," *Edinburgh Review* 90 (1849): 46–47.
3. John Dover Wilson, *The Elizabethan Shakespeare: Annual Shakespeare Lecture of the British Academy* (London: Humphrey Milford, 1929), 20–21.
4. Edward Taylor, "Cursory Remarks on Tragedy, on Shakespeare, and on Certain French and Italian Poets, Principally Tragedians," in *Shakespeare: The Critical Heritage,* vol. 6, 1774–1801, ed. Brian Vickers (London: Routledge & Kegan Paul, 1981), 129; Alexander Pope, "The Preface of the Editor to *The Works of Shakespear,*" in *The Prose Works of Alexander Pope,* vol. 2, *The Major Works, 1725–1744,* ed. Rosemary Cowler (Oxford: Blackwell, 1986), 15.
5. William Wordsworth, "Essay, Supplementary to the Preface to *The Excursion,*" in *Wordsworth's Literary Criticism,* ed. W. J. B. Owen (London: Routledge & Kegan Paul, 1974), 198.
6. Samuel Taylor Coleridge, *Lectures, 1808–1819: On Literature,* vol. 5 of *The Collected Works of Samuel Taylor Coleridge,* 2 vols., ed. Reginald A. Foakes (London: Routledge & Kegan Paul, 1987), 1:353.
7. William Hazlitt, *Lectures on the English Comic Writers and Lectures on the Age of Elizabeth,* vol. 6 of *The Complete Works of William Hazlitt,* ed. P. P. Howe (London and Toronto: J. M. Dent, 1931), 180.
8. A. C. Bradley, "Shakespeare's Theatre and Audience," in Bradley, *Oxford Lectures on Poetry* (London: Macmillan, 1934), 364–65.
9. Bradley explicitly mentions the melodrama some pages later: "Four times in *Macbeth,* when the Witches appear, thunder is heard. It thunders and lightens at intervals through the storm-scenes in *King Lear.* Casca and Cassius, dark thoughts within them, walk the streets of Rome in a terrific thunderstorm. That loud insistent knocking which appalled Macbeth is repeated thrice at intervals while Lady Macbeth in vain endeavours to calm him, and five times while the porter fumbles for his keys. The gate has hardly been opened and murder discovered when the castle-bell begins its hideous alarum. The alarm-bell is used for the same purpose of intensifying excitement in the brawl that ruins Cassio, and its effect is manifest in Othello's immediate order, 'Silence that dreadful bell.' I will add but one instance more. In the days of my youth, before the melodrama audience dreamed of seeing chariot-races, railway accidents, or the infernal regions, on the stage, it loved few things better than the explosion of fire-arms; and its favourite weapon was the pistol. The Elizabethans had the same fancy for fire-arms, only they preferred cannon" (371).

10. Robert Bridges, *The Influence of the Audience on Shakespeare's Drama*, vol. 1 of *Collected Essays Papers & c. of Robert Bridges* (London: Oxford University Press, 1927), 28–29. I have normalized Bridges's spelling.
11. Michael R. Booth, *Theatre in the Victorian Age* (Cambridge: Cambridge University Press, 1991), 162–63.
12. Simon Shepherd and Peter Womack, *English Drama: A Cultural History* (Oxford: Blackwell, 1996), 112.
13. On the rise of professionalism in Shakespeare criticism, see Hugh Grady, *The Modernist Shakespeare: Critical Texts in a Material World* (Oxford: Clarendon Press, 1991).
14. W. W. Greg, "Hamlet's Hallucination," *Modern Language Review* 12 (1917): 393–421, and W. W. Greg, "Re-Enter Ghost: A Reply to Mr. J. Dover Wilson," *Modern Language Review* 14 (1919): 353–69; Q. D. Leavis, *Fiction and the Reading Public* (1932; reissue, London: Chatto & Windus, 1965); all subsequent references are to the 1965 edition; H. S. Bennett, *Shakespeare's Audience: Annual Shakespeare Lecture of the British Academy* (London: Humphrey Milford, 1944), 6–7.
15. Greg, "Hamlet's Hallucination," 415–19.
16. Greg, "Re-Enter Ghost," 354–55.
17. As Richard Halpern puts it, "[irony] is modernism's protective amulet in the cultural wasteland—and it [is] draped not only around Eliot's neck, but, increasingly, around Shakespeare's as well." Richard Halpern, *Shakespeare Among the Moderns* (Ithaca: Cornell University Press, 1997), 95.
18. Leavis, *Fiction and the Reading Public*, 85.
19. Sir Edmund Gosse, *Questions at Issue* (London: Heinemann, 1893), quoted in Leavis, 190.
20. Alfred Harbage, *Shakespeare's Audience* (1941; repr., New York: Columbia University Press, 1961), 162; all subsequent references are to the 1961 edition.
21. Ann Jennalie Cook, "Audiences: Investigation, Interpretation, Invention," in *A New History of Early English Drama*, ed. John D. Cox and David Scott Kastan, 316 (New York: Columbia University Press, 1997).
22. Harbage, *Shakespeare's Audience*, 11–12.
23. Ibid., 60. This is pointed out by Ann Jennalie Cook in "The Audience of Shakespeare's Plays: A Reconsideration," *Shakespeare Studies* 7 (1974): 284.
24. Robert Weimann, *Shakespeare and the Popular Tradition in the Theater: Studies in the Social Dimension of Dramatic Form and Function*, ed. Robert Schwartz (Baltimore: Johns Hopkins University Press, 1978).
25. Shakespeare schreibt für ein volkstümliches, doch professionelles Renaissance-Theater, das in seinem nationalen Stadium ein Publikum aus vielen Klassen und Schichten anzieht. Robert Weimann, *Shakespeare und die Tradition des Volkstheaters: Soziologie-Dramaturgie-Gestaltung*, 2nd ed. (Berlin: Henschelverlag, 1975), 17; my translation (the passage is from Weimann's methodological preface to the German edition, which was not included in the English translation).
26. Vor den Toren der berühmten Theater, vor dem *Globe* und dem *Swan*, trafen sich Hofmann und Handwerker, Lehrling und Student, Edelmann und Plebejer. Mehr oder weniger folgten sie mit gleichem Interesse einem Schauspiel, dessen Vielseitigkeit die vorhandenen Geschmacksdivergenzen überbrückte, ohne dabei die Konventionen des älteren Volksschauspiels zu verleugnen. Dies war auch kaum möglich oder gar nötig: Das in Menge und Lautstärke dominierende plebejische Publikum im Parterre war künstlerisch durchaus aufgeschlossen! Der Dramatiker der späteren Jahre mochte mit geflissentlicher Geringschätzung auf diese "Gründlinge" herabsehen; aber selbst wenn er sie—wie Beaumont in *The Knight of the Burning*

Pestle—auf die Bühne brachte, nur um sie zu verspotten, musste er ihren erstaunlichen Qualitäten Rechnung tragen. *The Spanish Tragedy, Doctor Faustus, Henry IV* und *Hamlet* waren Lieblingsstücke der verachteten Menge! In Wirklichkeit waren Spielweise und Kunstübung des elisabethanischen Theaters undenkbar ohne diese "Gründlinge"—eben die stehende Menge im Parterre, von der die Shakespearesche Plattformbühne dreiseitig umlagert wurde. Weimann, *Shakespeare und die Tradition* 295–96; my translation (again, this section was not included in the English edition).

27. David Margolies, "Teaching the Handsaw to Fly: Shakespeare as a Hegemonic Instrument," in *The Shakespeare Myth*, ed. Graham Holderness (Manchester: Manchester University Press, 1988), 42–53.

28. Shepherd and Womack, *English Drama*, 110.

29. Cook, *Privileged Playgoers*, 224–30.

30. See Margolies, "Teaching the Handsaw to Fly," 53. See also Martin Butler, *Theatre and Crisis, 1632–1642* (Cambridge: Cambridge University Press, 1984), 294; Walter Cohen, *Drama of a Nation: Public Theater in Renaissance England and Spain* (Ithaca: Cornell University Press, 1985), 168; and Andrew Gurr, *Playgoing in Shakespeare's London* (Cambridge: Cambridge University Press, 1987), 4.

31. In her contribution to the *New History of Early English Drama* by Cox and Kastan, Cook admits: "The evidence presently gives no definitive answers to many pressing questions, especially those related to frequency of attendance, the sizes of audiences, the economics of playgoing, or the social composition of spectators at the large open air houses. . . . Too much evidence supports the presence of ordinary folk at the large public playhouses to suggest that they seldom attended." Cook, "Audiences: Investigation, Interpretation, Invention," 306, 317.

32. Alan Sinfield, "Introduction: Reproductions, Interventions," in *Political Shakespeare: New Essays in Cultural Materialism*, ed. Jonathan Dollimore and Alan Sinfield, 131 (Manchester: Manchester University Press, 1985).

Hamlet and Modernism: T. S. Eliot and G. Wilson Knight

Janet Clare

IN THIS ESSAY I WANT TO EXAMINE THE RESPONSES TO *HAMLET* BY two modernist critics, T. S. Eliot and G. Wilson Knight. Both began writing in the interwar years, and their early work on *Hamlet* was published in that period. The connection between the two is not arbitrary. Wilson Knight's Shakespearean criticism has been seen as an extension of the modernist spatial aesthetic of Joyce, Eliot, and Woolf into the realm of interpretative practice.[1] Conversely, Eliot had written an introduction to Wilson Knight's *The Wheel of Fire* (1930), in which Knight's "Embassy of Death: An Essay on *Hamlet*" first appeared, and had endorsed Knight's advocacy of interpretation over criticism and his elucidation of the patterns of poetic drama.

In subsequent decades Eliot and Knight were variously to declare specific allegiances. Eliot famously pronounced his belief in classicism in art, monarchical government, and the Catholic Church. G. Wilson Knight's work consistently returned to and reiterated a sense of British imperial destiny and the mystique of kingship that he saw embedded in the plays of Shakespeare. He reiterated emphatically a view that saw literature as a living record that was more vital than history. In an article published in the *Times Literary Supplement* in 1941, for example, he elaborated his belief that through an inspection of "great writers who speak for imperial Britain we may explore the soul-force from which her power and influence have grown."[2] Consistently, his writing, reading, and recital of Shakespearean drama—which he saw as the national drama—in the years immediate to and of the Second World War were imbricated in "the search for solutions to our own national problems."[3] The ideological convictions of Knight and Eliot, deepened by the catastrophes of two world wars, are not self-evident in their early criticism of *Hamlet*. Nonetheless, by considering the trajectory of their later work, we can see the larger implications of thought submerged in the early writing.

Eliot, "Hamlet and His Problems," J. M. Robertson, *The Problem of Hamlet,* and Nietzsche, *The Birth of Tragedy*

T. S. Eliot's "Hamlet and His Problems" appeared in *The Sacred Wood* (1920), and the essay has a curious intertextuality exemplifying Eliot's own dictum that influence hardly matters: "to be influenced by a writer is to have a chance inspiration from him; or to take what one wants."[4] Seen from this perspective, "Hamlet and His Problems" is a composite of the positivist approach to the Shakespearean canon represented by the modernizer J. M. Robertson and Nietzsche's antipositivist *Birth of Tragedy.* It could be said that Eliot takes what he wants from the former and has received chance inspiration from the latter.

Eliot's criticism of *Hamlet* owes more to the work of Victorian textual "disintegrators," particularly that of J. M. Robertson, than it does to later modernist critiques of Shakespeare.[5] Robertson's *The Problem of Hamlet,* published a year before Eliot's essay, was a groundbreaking proto-bibliographical study in which he argued that Shakespeare, working as an adaptor and reconstructor, had taken up an old play and transmuted it. Thus, any attempt to shape the play to aesthetic consistency was bound to end in failure. Only a few years later, proponents of modernism, with unshakable faith in the autonomy of the text, were to reject implicitly such questions about origins and sources asked by Robertson and adopted by Eliot. Eliot approvingly alludes to Robertson's approach for its focus on the stratification of the text, representing "the efforts of a series of men, each making what he could out of the work of his predecessors."[6] Robertson had argued that the text of *Hamlet* was determined by a pre-Shakespearean play accounting for the interpretative conundrums that had for a century misled critics, particularly in England and Germany.

Robertson held no academic post and he was not therefore party to the crusade of the post–First World War years to define the study of English literature as part of a cultural heritage free from the "alien yoke of Teutonic philology."[7] Nonetheless his approach is fueled by current national hostilities, which are particularly evident in his survey of *Hamlet* and Germanic scholarship. An anti-German bias is typically exemplified in his comments on mid- to late nineteenth-century pronouncements on the play's problems, which he dismisses as "a protracted process of thesis making."[8] Against the "Goethean formula of temperamental incompetence," Robertson traces a line of German criticism that emphasized objective hindrances. In brief, J. L. Klein had argued that Hamlet had been barred from action by the manner and nature of the crime; Hamlet's knowledge of it could not be offered as evidence to justify an assassination of the guilty king. Karl Werder, in his Berlin Shakespeare lectures published in the *Preussische Jahrbücher* (1873–74), had propounded a similar thesis and thus, according to Robertson, had contributed to the endless and misguided discussion of the aesthetic problem. Werder's lectures, Robertson declared, are marked by "the tactic of driving the thesis anyhow through or over the facts which is so characteristic of German publicism—and politics."[9] Robertson's reaction is here, as elsewhere, transparent in its antipathies: Werder's dogmatic insistence on a theory without regard to all the evidence that Robertson thinks goes against it is generalized as a German characteristic and found again in German politics.

Robertson's response to such positivism was to concentrate on the disintegration of the text, which precluded the reduction of the play to formal consistency. Despite his sustained denigration of what he refers to as the "Germanic ethic of Werder," Robertson's own work, interestingly, is closer to the philological tradition than the antipositivist, chauvinist literary appreciation then current within the English profession. At Cambridge, for example, Sir Arthur Quiller-Couch, the Shakespeare scholar and later general editor of the New Cambridge Shakespeare, argued in a series of lectures, "Patriotism in English Literature," published in 1918, that German scholarship was unfit to approach "the lovely and living art" of English literature. To German scholars it "must be for ever, a dead science—a *hortus siccus;* to be tabulated, not to be planted or watered."[10] Quiller-Couch has been seen as highly influential in freeing Cambridge from an overemphasis on the philological aspects of literature, but there has been a lack of emphasis on this development as a strange fruit of anti-German feeling.

It is a curious fact of cultural criticism that, shorn of anti-Germanic impulse, Robertson's theory of the disintegration of the text infiltrates Eliot's short—arguably classic—essay. Eliot's objections are reserved for those studies of *Hamlet,* epitomized in the pronouncements of Goethe and Coleridge, that instead of addressing the play's artistic problems focused on a subjective response to Hamlet. He ends the essay with a forensic summing-up of the play's defects, beginning with the gambit "We must simply admit that here Shakespeare tackled a problem which proved too much for him." Why Shakespeare tried to write the play is an "insoluble puzzle." What made him do it "we cannot ever know"; "we need a great many facts in his biography." Yet the latter, even if they were available, could hardly illuminate the unfathomed depths, as the closing sentences recognize: "We should have, finally, to know something which is by hypothesis unknowable ... We should have to understand things which Shakespeare did not understand himself."[11] In his closing argument Eliot has clearly departed from Robertson in eliding stratification of the text with a failure of artistic intent. As a work of art *Hamlet* fails because it is inexpressive of organic totality.

Eliot was clearly uneasy in the face of a play whose direction is elusive and indeterminable. What we see in Eliot's commentary is a deeply conservative temperament resisting subversive impulses and this bears directly on his familiar proposition that the only way of expressing emotion in the form of art is by finding an "objective correlative," with the corollary that Shakespeare found none in *Hamlet*: "[He] is up against the difficulty that his disgust is occasioned by his mother, but that his mother is not an adequate equivalent for it; his disgust envelops and exceeds her. It is thus a feeling which he cannot understand; he cannot objectify it, and it therefore remains to poison life and obstruct action."[12]

In response to Eliot's objections it could be said that it is not Hamlet who is up against this difficulty: it is Eliot. Hamlet does not need to "objectify" his disgust. He is not an artist; he does not feel a disgust for which he then seeks an adequate equivalent. His disgust is there when he thinks of his mother or sees her, and from there it taints his world. Gertrude is the object, and though we may or may not feel that his outrage is excessive, Hamlet certainly does not. Eliot's aesthetics and his later to be declared politics are a perfect match. In both there is a demand for order, clarity, and control, and a dislike for anything dark, disruptive, and subversive.

As an expatriate writing during the interwar years, Eliot's criticism is free of the religiose Englishness that then predominated. Eliot reached back, in poetry and criticism, to a European scope as a check to the chauvinist voice emanating from the universities and to the anti-Teutonic element evident in Robertson's commentary on studies of *Hamlet*. While at Oxford and Cambridge there were campaigns to denigrate any German cultural influence, Eliot was to write, "It is the final perfection, the consummation of an American to become, not an Englishman, but a European—something which no born European, no person of any European nationality, can become."[13] As Chris Baldick has commented in his account of the Arnoldian tradition in English criticism, "Eliot, at the right time, attempted to see European culture steadily and to see it whole."[14] It is perhaps not surprising then that the germ of Eliot's thinking on *Hamlet* is foreshadowed in Friedrich Nietzsche's *The Birth of Tragedy,* published in Hausmann's translation in 1909.[15] Nietzsche's comments on the enigmas of both Euripidean tragedy and *Hamlet* lie behind Eliot's comments, although Eliot puts them to quite a different use. Some fifty years before the publication of Eliot's essay, Nietzsche in *The Birth of Tragedy* had imagined that Euripides had seen in Aeschylus an "enigmatic" depth not dissimilar to Eliot's encounter with Hamlet. Euripides, Nietzsche posits, "had discovered what anyone initiated into the deep secrets of Aeschylean tragedy might have expected: in every feature, in every line, he found something incommensurable, a certain deceptive precision and at the same time an enigmatic depth, an infinite background."[16] When Nietzsche imagines Euripides being baffled in this way by Aeschylus, we think of Eliot puzzling over *Hamlet* and writing it off in the end as an artistic failure. Not only does Nietzsche anticipate Eliot when he talks of plays where "the myth does not at all find its adequate objectification in the spoken word," but he adduces *Hamlet* as an exemplary case. He finds clearly, with a "deeper wisdom than the poet can put into words and concepts," a lesson only discernible through "a more profound contemplation and survey of the whole." Eliot says, "When we search for this feeling, we find it, as in the sonnets, very difficult to localize. You cannot point to it in the speeches . . . We find Shakespeare's *Hamlet* not in the action, not in any quotation that we might select, so much as in an unmistakable tone."[17] There is a shift from Nietzsche's sense of the whole being deeper than its parts to Eliot's allusion to the play's "unmistakable tone"; otherwise the correspondence is close.

For all the arresting convergences of critical vocabulary, however, Eliot is far from agreeing with Nietzsche. In *The Birth of Tragedy* Nietzsche expressed no doubts about *Hamlet* or its artistic coherence; he is sure of both play and character. Hamlet is his exemplary tragic hero whose deepest insight moves toward the Dionysian moment of truth when the veil of illusion is torn and the futility of individual existence is glimpsed between ecstasy and nausea. Despite the negative-sounding inflections of the myth not finding adequate objectification, Nietzsche is evidently not faulting Greek tragedy or *Hamlet.* "Art," Nietzsche claims, "is able to transform these nauseating reflections on the awfulness or absurdity of existence into representations wherewith it is possible to live." When Nietzsche talks of the transfiguring power of art, which must include the structure of the play as a whole, he has in mind the "Apollonian" moment, the play of formative energy in the elements of drama that lifts us above "the awfulness or absurdity of existence."[18] Like Euripides, who in the

Nietzschean scheme of things inaugurates the death of Attic tragedy, Eliot recoils from "intense feeling, ecstatic or terrible, without an object or exceeding its object." But he inverts Nietzsche's case, insisting on the stuff of the play being "intelligible, self-complete, in the sunlight." Here, Apollo is in charge and Dionysus subdued, if not banished altogether. The implicit rejection of Nietzsche's Dionysiac allegiances points toward another possible inversion, for Nietzsche had already presented a powerful counterargument nearly fifty years before Eliot's essay was published. Although the genealogy of *Hamlet* could hardly have interested Nietzsche as it did Eliot, his sense of the interplay of surface and depth, Apollo and Dionysus, is nevertheless a flexible and suggestive paradigm to counter the twentieth-century obsession with textual indeterminacy and the play's structural and temporal problems.

The Nationalist Agenda of G. Wilson Knight

The cultural complex of Nietzsche and T. S. Eliot can be profitably extended to G. Wilson Knight, whose work on Shakespeare is infused with Nietzschean allusions. Whereas Eliot's debt to *The Birth of Tragedy* can be seen as an inversion of Nietzsche, Knight noted retrospectively that aspects of his reading of *Hamlet* coincided with that of Nietzsche. In a footnote to a 1949 reprint of "An Essay on *Hamlet*" in *The Wheel of Fire*, Knight added that his reading of *Hamlet* could be usefully compared to that of Nietzsche in *The Birth of Tragedy*. In *The Sovereign Flower* (1958) he equated his "spatial poetics," the term that he had coined for the interpretation of Shakespearean drama, with Nietzsche's Dionysian element; both, he suggested, are dynamic, the resolving elements of the drama existing not on the surface, but below. It is, according to Knight, following Nietzsche, the "Dionysian otherness" that is the true source of dramatic power.[19]

Christ and Nietzsche was published in 1948, although Knight records that his book was in progress in 1940.[20] The study, as much about Shakespeare and Nietzsche as about Christ and Nietzsche, now seems for all its vast historical perspectives a product of wartime Britain. But in this—albeit limited—reading of Nietzsche's work (based on *The Birth of Tragedy* and *Thus Spake Zarathustra*), Knight went further than to figure comparable aesthetic values between Shakespeare and Nietzsche. Shakespeare's fusion of Christian values with the concept of secular power produces a message "on a national scale analogous to Nietzsche's psychological and individualistic gospel."[21]

As in the final chapter, the notion of national identity and character is deeply embedded, and repeatedly England and Germany are treated as though they are individuals. Their respective literature and philosophy are entirely characteristic of country. Presumably alluding to Nietzsche, Knight declares that "in German philosophy there is a clearer understanding of the dynamic within all drama than English thinkers have mastered."[22] In the study aesthetics and nationality become bound together and Nietzsche becomes a stimulant for a dulled national tradition that can be recovered through Shakespeare.

Notably, here, as elsewhere in his writing, *Hamlet* is the play most readily appropriated for Knight's diagnosis of the national condition and international relations. There is an implicit cultural materialism in Knight's explication of current meaning and social relevance in the play: "You need not think the problems confronting Hamlet out of date: put international for personal action and we find ourselves similarly at a loss, equally inexpert in, yet dominated by, the laws of blood and force. In an age of civic calm such works are often best understood in reference to national issues; while conversely national problems may often best be resolved by inspection [of] dramas of that human personality [that] runs central through our various and manifold perplexities."[23]

Hence Hamlet can be made to stand for England: "Like us, like England . . . he suffers from inferiority and self-criticism." Germany, on the other hand, "thirsting for the one burning positive, plunges through an almost comic extravagance of ambition to what has proved a tragic self-immolation." Again, there is an antagonistic confraternity as German philosophy, "appallingly aware," is something the English critic would do well to turn to "if only to learn what the poetry on which he claims to pronounce judgement is about." Repeatedly, here and elsewhere, Knight interpreted *Hamlet* as a national paradigm, with Hamlet representing and speaking for prewar and wartime Britain. He typified Hamlet's self-doubt and bitter ironies as part of the national consciousness of 1939. The two longest soliloquies ("O what a rogue and peasant slave" and "How all occasions") "serve to reflect the soul of England during the last twenty years suffering inward division and tortured by depth of insight and maturity of experience leading to what appears a relaxation of militancy, while younger, and seemingly more virile nations, Italy and Germany, get down to business with the thoughtless energies of a Laertes or a Fortinbras."[24] The play becomes a parable of England's supposed abhorrence of warfare; realization of its absurdity has put the nation at a disadvantage beside less responsible and more thoughtless nations. Similarly, Hamlet is at a disadvantage beside Laertes and Fortinbras, ardent young men for whom his problems do not exist.

Reading such responses to the play, we can only judge them as historically relative: national appropriations of *Hamlet*, born of their moment. There is no such extension of the alleged malaise of dramatic protagonist to nation in the 1930 essay "The Embassy of Death." Nevertheless, in the designation in the latter essay of Claudius as a "true leader," there is a trace not only of Knight's profound and unshakable belief in royalism and the mystical power of the crown but also perhaps of his belief in national leadership congenial to a Fascist view of existence.

It was in *The Wheel of Fire*—last reprinted in 2002—that Wilson Knight proposed his truly radical principles of interpretation, arguing for an approach to the Shakespearean text that recognizes "spatial" as well as "temporal" necessity:

> Since in Shakespeare there is this close fusion of the temporal, that is, the plot-chain of event following event, with the spatial, that is, the omnipresent and mysterious reality brooding motionless over and within the play's movement, it is evident that my two principles thus firmly divided in analysis are no more than provisional abstractions from the whole. However, since to make the first abstraction with especial crudity, that is, to analyse the sequences of events, the "causes" linking dramatic motive to action and action to result in time, is a blunder instinctive to the human intellect, I make no apology for restoring balance by insistence on the other.[25]

As Hugh Grady has persuasively argued in his study of Shakespeare and modernism, Knight's critical paradigm was a brilliantly devised strategy to accomplish goals of modern aesthetics. Shakespeare's plays could now be interpreted as modernist artworks. According to Grady, Knight was instrumental in transforming Shakespeare from a monument of nineteenth-century culture to a modernist icon.[26] The central epistemological categories of time and space had been reordered and the autonomy of the text had been restated. Based on the Romantic notion of the organic nature of the text, the approach pioneered by Knight has been widely adopted in teaching and remains a respectable practice in academic literary criticism.

The result of applying such critical aesthetics to *Hamlet* produced in "The Embassy of Death," a curious, idiosyncratic, if not downright perverse essay. In emphasizing the fusion of the temporal and the spatial, Wilson Knight dismisses "causality" as an interpretative key: "we must think less on causality and more in terms of imaginative impact." Knight focuses on Hamlet's state of being, his spiritual atrophy, which he deems beyond causality and which has to be related to the supernatural, to the Ghost. It is the malignancy of the Ghost and its injunction that wreak havoc in Elsinore. Of the two things that the Ghost commands Hamlet—revenge and remembrance—it is the latter that is branded most deeply in Hamlet's mind; but remembering only the Ghost's command to remember he is paralyzed.[27] Hamlet, Knight observed, would have done well to forget the Ghost. The pervasive imagery is of death and decay, and the horror of death and decay has disintegrated Hamlet's mind.

This diagnosis of Hamlet's state of mind appears to lead to the strange moral reversal of protagonist and antagonist: Hamlet is "an ambassador of death spreading destruction wherever he goes" while Claudius is "a man kindly, confident," and "shows every sign of being an excellent diplomatist and king." Thus Hamlet is first perceived and set in relief against the "gay glitter of the court" with all its "brilliance, robustness, health and happiness." Knight's essay, as Philip Edwards has demonstrated in his Cambridge introduction to the play, "swiftly and silently infused itself into the consciousness of literary criticism."[28] In the equally influential *The Imperial Theme,* published the following year, Knight rehearsed the same view of the king: Claudius, although a criminal, is "finely drawn as a politic, wise and gentle king"; Hamlet is opposed not only to certain forms of life, but to life itself.[29] Here again Knight reiterates what he sees as central to Shakespeare, the power and centrality of kingship and order opposed by violence; in so doing he must gloss over the irregularities of Claudius's accession. Knight admits that Claudius cannot be allowed perfected kingliness and love, but nonetheless "he lives up well through the greater part of the play to the kingly ideal in spite of his previous crime." In what seems to amount to a reworking of the medieval and Renaissance theory of the king's two bodies, Knight affirms that the ideal of the king is as independent of Claudius's crime "as the Priest's sacred office when celebrating Mass [is] independent of his private life."[30]

G. Wilson Knight: Aesthetics and Ideology

Knight's modernist critical aesthetics have very little to do with determining such a radical interpretation of Claudius. Rather, his idiosyncratic representation of Claudius in "The Embassy of Death" can best be understood in the context of several disquisitions on kingship in criticism of this period. Here we can recognize a link—if subterranean—between seemingly critical aesthetics and an implicit political agenda. Claudius signifies the crown of Denmark that undoubtedly seems fused in Knight's understanding with the British crown. The latter, he eulogized in his unpublished work *A Royal Propaganda,* is "a dream, a myth, a work of poetic creation, a mighty symbol; the central hope of Christian mankind." It is Knight's implicit faith in the sacrosanctity of kingship and the divine right of the office that produces his skewed reading of the play. Claudius may compromise this ideal of kingship, but nevertheless he is the only living approximation of it in *Hamlet.*

Knight's nostalgic, spiritual, and symbolic view of kingship as a source of ideological stimulus and moral edification is explicit in work published during and after the Second World War. In international conflict the Crown acquires great potency symbolic of the nation's imperial destiny. Knight states categorically that the message that Shakespeare's plays must communicate to Britain is not "the choice between power and the absence of power, but between royalty in the Shakespeare sense and tyranny."[31] Seen in this light, it is fairly clear why G. Wilson Knight allows the weak moral foundations of Claudius's kingship to stand. The king has a symbolic function: he is expressive of the general will, and he must be defended at all costs. As his "mighty opposite," Hamlet, who seems little preoccupied with divine majesty, is represented as a hostile force. The more overtly politicized writings of the war period are indeed anticipated in the comments on Claudius and Hamlet in *The Imperial Theme* and *The Wheel of Fire.*

Such political readings of *Hamlet* and Knight's nonanalytical view of kingship now seem anachronistic, and even—as his unpublished work declared—royal propaganda. Views of Shakespeare's plays "as enclosed and firmly clasped by a national or patriotic framework" are not of course in fashion, even if they are not untenable.[32] His aesthetic paradigm, on the contrary, has been resilient to encroachments from more theoretically informed readings of the play. For all his manifold idiosyncrasies and eccentricities, undoubtedly Knight initiated a radical new approach to the interpretation of the Shakespeare text. Contemporary studies of *Hamlet,* which have included the cultural and historicist work of Michael Neill and Stephen Greenblatt, and the generic approach of John Kerrigan, have responded to the play's poetics, stressing the pervasiveness of death, loss, and memory, and the inherent tensions between remembrance and revenge.[33] Commenting on the Ghost's command "Remember me," Greenblatt observes, "What is at stake in the shift of emphasis from vengeance to remembrance is nothing less than the whole play."[34] Similarly adopting Wilson Knight's premise, John Kerrigan argues that revenge in the body of the play, as in the first encounter with the Ghost, is far less important to Hamlet than the impulse to remember. Hamlet, he asserts, "never promises to revenge only to remember."[35] As a revenge tragedy, Michael Neill sees *Hamlet* as extending the genre to expose the "terrible power of memory." That none of these authors refers to Wilson Knight, while evidently echoing ideas expressed in "The Embassy of Death," indicates how thoroughly assimilated into critical consciousness the paradigm of spatial poetics has become.

In the evolving paradigm of modernist Shakespeare, Eliot and Knight clearly have a centrality. Both, as the Nietzschean influence suggests, resisted the parochial and chauvinist crosscurrents in the professionalization of English studies of their time. If, however, we are to compare the critical aesthetics of the early Eliot with the early Knight, it is the latter who has proved more resilient. Eliot's positivist reading of *Hamlet* now seems more dated and largely of historical interest. Again, despite a shared preoccupation with royalist ideology and a sympathetic engagement with the ideas of the other, their respective critical legacies have been markedly different. Eliot's royalism, bound up with the assumptions of the seventeenth century, appears antiquated and prescriptive, whereas Knight's less-historicized ideals could be seen to pave the way for "presentist" readings of Shakespeare. Somewhat ironically, the premise of Knight's belief that solutions to national problems can be found in the mirror of our own national drama is not far distant from the cultural materialist assertion that we can only read a Shakespeare play from our own ideological vantage point. While it is not rationalized as such, G. Wilson Knight's reading of *Hamlet* anticipates the premise of Terence Hawkes when he states "the critic's own situatedness constitutes the only means by which it is possible to see the past and perhaps comprehend it."[36] It is perhaps an indication of the independence and originality of Knight's criticism that his methodology and his critical aesthetics have been espoused by latter-day critics of quite different ideological persuasions.

Notes

I am grateful to Raymond Hargreaves, formerly of the German department, University of Leeds, for advice and comment.

1. See Hugh Grady, *The Modernist Shakespeare: Critical Texts in a Material World* (Oxford: Clarendon Press, 1991), 98–102.

2. *Times Literary Supplement,* April 5, 1941, 266–72.

3. G. Wilson Knight, *The Olive and the Sword: A Study of England's Shakespeare* (London: Oxford University Press, 1944), 43.

4. T. S. Eliot, *The Sacred Wood: Essays on Poetry and Criticism* (London: Methuen, 1920), 95–103; "In Memory of Henry James," *Egoist* 5 (1918): 1.

5. J. M. Robertson, *The Problem of Hamlet* (London: George Allen and Unwin, 1919); see Grady, *The Modernist Shakespeare,* 47–51, 74–75.

6. Eliot, "Hamlet and His Problems," 82.
7. Basil Willey, *Cambridge and Other Memories* (1964), 23–24. Quoted by Chris Baldick, in *The Social Mission of English Criticism, 1848–1932* (Oxford: Clarendon Press, 1987; first printed 1983), 87.
8. J. M. Robertson, *The Problem of Hamlet*, 78.
9. Ibid., 20.
10. Quoted in Baldick, *The Social Mission of English Criticism*, 88.
11. "Hamlet and His Problems," 87.
12. Ibid., 86.
13. *Egoist* 5 (1918): 1.
14. *The Social Mission of English Criticism*, 111.
15. In 1953 Wilson Knight added a note to "The Embassy of Death: An Essay on *Hamlet*": "My reading of *Hamlet* may be profitably compared with that outlined by Nietzsche in *The Birth of Tragedy*, VII," and in "*Hamlet* Reconsidered," he refers to the Nietzschean sense of "being" in the context of Hamlet's "To be, or not to be" soliloquy (*The Wheel of Fire*, 308).
16. Friedrich Nietzsche, *The Birth of Tragedy*, in *The Complete Works of Friedrich Nietzsche*, trans. W. A. Hausmann, ed. Oscar Levy (London: T. N. Foulis, 1909–13), 1:58.
17. "Hamlet and His Problems," 85.
18. See *The Birth of Tragedy*, 61–62.
19. G. Wilson Knight, *The Sovereign Flower* (London: Methuen, 1958), 254–55.
20. See *A Royal Propaganda* (Unpublished: British Library).
21. *Christ and Nietzsche: An Essay in Poetic Wisdom* (London and New York: Staples Press, 1948), 221.
22. Ibid., 39.
23. Ibid., 27–28.
24. *The Olive and the Sword*, 42.
25. *The Wheel of Fire*, 5.
26. *The Modernist Shakespeare*, 98.
27. *The Wheel of Fire*, 44.
28. *Hamlet*, ed. Philip Edwards (Cambridge: Cambridge University Press, 1985), 38.
29. *The Imperial Theme: Further Interpretations of Shakespeare's Tragedies Including the Roman Plays* (London: Oxford University Press, 1931), 102.
30. Ibid., 114.
31. *A Royal Propaganda*, 57.
32. Ibid., 70.
33. See Stephen Greenblatt, *Hamlet in Purgatory* (Princeton: Princeton University Press, 2001); Michael Neill, *Issues of Death: Mortality and Identity in English Renaissance Tragedy* (Oxford: Clarendon Press, 1997); John Kerrigan, *Revenge Tragedy: Aeschylus to Armageddon* (Oxford: Clarendon Press, 1996).
34. *Hamlet in Purgatory*, 208.
35. *Revenge Tragedy*, 182.
36. Terence Hawkes, *Shakespeare in the Present* (London: Routledge, 2002), 3.

"What dost thou think 'tis worth?"
Timon of Athens and Politics as a Nonreligious Religion

Antonella Piazza

IN HIS ARTICLE "'IN STATES UNBORN AND ACCENTS YET UNKNOWN': Shakespeare and the European Canon," Manfred Pfister painstakingly searches for the causes of Shakespeare's uninterrupted European canonization.[1] Slightly correcting Gadamer's hermeneutics of questions and answers, Pfister maintains that Shakespeare's text can still help the contemporary reader/interpreter to formulate questions, both crucial and deeply felt by contemporaneity, rather than provide answers. He also agrees with contemporary cultural historians who regard Shakespeare's early modern age as the genetic ground of our early global Europe. Pfister's idea of Shakespearean *performability*, brought about by a textual structural opening, is in many respects close to John Joughin's idea of Shakespeare's adaptation/adaptability.[2] According to Joughin, the Shakespearean text makes "the work of following and the following work" possible through a continuous "adjustment." This word refers less to the interpretative act of doing "justice" to the text than to its creative translation into an ethical/political process, a process toward what is "just," an "ad-justment." This makes Shakespearean hermeneutics a responsible political action.

A Radical Tragedy

If Othello is a character "perplex'd in the extreme," *Timon of Athens,* indeed, perplexes in the extreme. Apemantus, the Cynic philosopher of Shakespeare's Athens, suitably introduces Timon: "The middle of humanity thou never knewest, but the *extremity of both ends*" (4.3.301–2). Because it pushes extremes to the limit, *Timon* is a paradigmatically excessive and liminal play. Timon's abrupt and radical metamorphosis from a model of philanthropy into a figure of misanthropy actually makes the reading of the play a radical cultural experience.

The Athens of Shakespeare's Timon is governed by a weak and corrupt oligarchy, a Senate whose irrational rigor almost provokes a civil war: thievery and prostitution proliferate and the State is unable to keep Athenian bellicosity at bay. Indiscriminately open to everybody, Timon's house seems to be the only place in Athens where friendship, sympathy, and companionship are possible, and where positive social energies may circulate. But when the sociopolitical values of generosity and hospitality are overthrown and denied (indeed, in his moment of need Timon's friends all prove to be hard-hearted and ungrateful), Timon turns from a paragon of philanthropy into a monster of misanthropy. Paradoxically, however, Timon's self-inflicted exile (he leaves the polis, dies in the woods, and is found buried on the shore) makes peace and social coexistence possible again, allowing for a different economy to take over.

At some point, an amoral economy seems to get the better of Timon's search for an ideal sociopolitical model of disinterested companionship. The victory of revengeful Alcibiades' economic individualism, with its circular economy of exchange, is apparently designed to counter Timon's ideal of a religious community. But Alcibiades' triumph is not the end of the story. Further questions arise: What keeps the polis, a political community, together? Who creates social space? Is there any space for ethics and economics to share, for politics and the market? Such problematizing raises political issues with which Western culture has been very familiar since Karl Marx.

When Timon goes to the woods and digs the earth, hungry for both literal and metaphorical roots, he finds gold. It is then that Timon, including Mother Nature in his vengeful wrath, voices an extremely puritanical attack against gold:

> Gold? Yellow, glittering, precious gold?
> No, gods, I am no idle votarist.
> Roots, you clear heavens! Thus much of this will make
> Black, white; foul, fair, wrong, right;
> Base, noble; old, young; coward, valiant.
> Ha, you gods! Why this? What this, you gods? . . .
> . . . Come, damn'd earth,
> Thou common whore of mankind, that puts odds
> Among the rout of nations.
>
> (4.3.26–43)

These are the lines that Karl Marx quotes in *Capital* when, by appropriating and "ad-justing" Timon's attack, he formulates one of his main propositions against the omnipotence of gold and its power to reify human relations: "By possessing the property of buying everything, by possessing the property of appropriating all objects, money is thus the object of eminent possession. The universality of its property is the *omnipotence* of its being. It is therefore regarded as *omnipotent* . . . Money is the procurer between man's need and the object, between his life and his means of life. But that which mediates my life for me, also mediates the existence of other people for me. For me it is the other person."[3] Thus Marx accurately describes the kind of relational value—founded on the use and the exchange of gold and objects—which *Timon* radically opposes in both its parts. Opposition and negation are textual strategies with which the drama keeps formulating its most radical and extreme question: "What dost thou think 'tis worth?" (1.1.211).

If omnipotence and magic are attributes Marx associates with money, Timon's "magic of bounty" is, as we shall see, related to a kind of economics that tries to do without money as a universal mediator.

Wilson Knight's Political *Timon*

Timon's critical reception has been as extreme as its textual performance. The play has been either rejected or extolled, and Timon's generosity has been considered either as an attribute of a demented mind or as the measure of excellency. According to Hugh Grady, the play is the site where the shift of Shakespearean critical paradigms—from the Victorian to the modernist up to the postmodernist—becomes fully visible: "We can take up the narrative of evolution from within the Modernist critical paradigms . . . if we turn to a different play, one whose anomalies and problematics have made it virtually a 'blank screen' on which could be projected the disparate critical methodologies of the history of Shakespeare criticism: *Timon of Athens*."[4] Because of his ability to achieve what Grady calls a "spatialization" of the text, George Wilson Knight is taken to be one of the main modernist Shakespearean critics. Influenced by the aesthetic paradigm of modernism, which substituted space for the emphasis on time proper to the previous realist and positivist cultural paradigm, Wilson Knight saw organic unity—that is, a network of coherent figures—as the main criterion for critical interpretation and aesthetic judgment.

During its critical history, *Timon of Athens* has been considered an extremely irregular text: it had never been acted during the playwright's life, there was just the edition included in the Folio in an awkward position between *Romeo and Juliet* and *Julius Caesar,* its date of composition was uncertain (now 1607–8 is widely accepted as the most probable date), the authorship was also debatable, and for a long time *Timon* had been considered the play of at least two authors, and for this reason it was thought of as uneven and also unfinished. So Wilson Knight's identification of an organic unity in the text was evidence not just for its aesthetic value, but also for single authorship, which was declared undeniably Shakespearean. Wilson Knight is consequently rightly held responsible by Grady for rescuing *Timon* from the Victorian "disintegrators" and for its final canonization as a Shakespearean tragedy. But in focusing on the provocative modernist declaration of art as an autonomous sphere, Grady leaves out the political implications of Wilson Knight's Nietzschean reading of *Timon of Athens.*

Wilson Knight was virtually haunted by that play: after consecrating *Timon* as *the* exemplary Shakespearean tragic paradigm in *The Wheel of Fire,* he kept writing about it throughout his life until he eventually came to a Buddhist reading.[5] The political and cultural implications of some critical points he made in the 1930s and '40s are particularly relevant to our argument. In the following excerpts from *The Wheel of Fire,* both the unitary cluster of aesthetic and thematic values and the idealization of Timon's metamorphosis are thrown into full light. A universal and natural lover, Timon is taken to embody the utopia of an earthly paradise, which, on the other hand, Athens is blamed for having slaughtered: "Timon is a universal lover, not by principle but by nature.... If this [Timon's] transcendent love can be bodied into shapes and forms which are finite; if the world of actuality and sense does not play Timon false, an earthly paradise is no deceiving dream.... The crime of Athens is this: they have preferred the gold of coins to the gold of love. They have slaughtered love. Timon is dead."[6]

Timon's "heart of gold" stands out clearly as the organic center that holds Shakespeare's text together and, more importantly, as the governing principle that qualifies Wilson Knight's interpretation both from a political and ideological point of view. Though certainly concerned with underscoring the formal/structural unity of the text, Wilson Knight is far more committed to strenuously defending the "value" of Timon himself, seen as a paradigm of moral and intellectual aristocracy, the embodiment of sensual and spiritual generosity, according to Nietzsche's definitions of good and evil.[7] From this vantage point acts 1 and 2 are blessed by Timon's flow of warm magnanimity, which make his home "an idealized perfected civilization."[8] Timon's rebutting of Ventidius's offer to reciprocate his gift:

> . . . O by no means,
> Honest Ventidius. You mistake my love;
> I gave it freely ever, and there's none
> Can truly say he gives, if he receives
>
> (1.2.8–11)

is seen to encapsulate the formula of an ideal humanist socioeconomic bond: "His generosity lacks wisdom, but is itself noble; his riches reflect the inborn aristocracy of his heart."[9] The superiority of this Nietzschean Timon is not founded on blood and/or on racial and racist grounds, as indeed was the case with the Nietzsche appropriated by the Nazis. On the contrary, through his humanist interpretation of Nietzsche's aristocratic "good," Wilson Knight endows his modernist reading of *Timon* with political cogency, turning the play into a bulwark against Europe's emerging totalitarianism. In *The Genealogy of Morals,* Nietzsche had argued:

> [T]he judgment "good" did *not* originate with those to whom "goodness" was shown! Rather it was "the good" themselves, that is to say, the noble, powerful, high-stationed and high-minded, who felt and established themselves and their actions as good, that is, of the first rank, in contradistinction to all the low, low-minded, common and plebeian. . . . what had they to do with utility! . . . The pathos of nobility and distance, as aforesaid, the protracted and domineering fundamental total feeling on the part of a higher ruling order in relation to a lower order, to a "below"—*that* is the origin of the antithesis "good" and "bad."[10]

When as late as 1940 Wilson Knight wondered: "Why should a play so poignantly relevant to present conflicts as Shakespeare's *Timon of Athens* have been consistently neglected?,"[11] he was passionately fighting against *Timon*'s possible appropriations both by Fascists and Communists, as the following extended quotation fully demonstrates:

> Contemporary Fascism scores a point, especially if it chooses to quote from Spengler's *Decline of the West:* "A power can be overthrown only by another power, not by a principle, and no power that can confront money is left but this one. Money is overthrown and abolished only by blood."
> "Blood," here meaning racial instinct, is however a dangerously ambiguous word . . . and when [Timon] hopes Alcibiades and Athens will plague each other to exhaustion, the modern communist might, in his turn, nod a generous approval, and he could, indeed, urge that the action proves the inherent unwisdom of private ownership, disastrous alike in a Timon's expenditure and his friends' selfishness.

But, though including these suggestions, the play as a whole transcends such partialities ... Once money, wealth, mechanical inventions, learning, or any other good ceases to function as a sacrament of the heart's gold it becomes suicidal. This is *Timon of Athens* with no less authority and much of the tone of Hebraic prophecy; and our neglect hitherto measures perhaps our unwillingness to dig out its riches in ourselves.

Wilson Knight's rereading of *Timon* through the lens of totalitarian threats shows the ways modernist Shakespeare could be put to profitable political use in contemporary Europe. And, in spite of its occasional outdated flavor, it still remains influential even nowadays, especially insofar as it pinpoints the problematic relation between economic and moral values: "Now *Timon* perhaps alone in dramatic history has powerfully fused these two realms, imposing on the crude fact of monetary greed the mighty periods of great poetry."[12]

Timon and Postmodernity

Two more recent examples taken from postmodern Shakespearean criticism will help to articulate the reading of the relation between politics and ethics and economics and religion at the core of the play. In Coppélia Kahn's feminist, Kleinian, and New Historicist reading, Timon the character is overtly downsized.[13] Kahn actually reads Timon's phil/misanthropy as a case of pre-oedipal fixation: he either totally identifies with the mother's body when gifts and love and favor flow from him, or totally dis-identifies from the mother and the cosmos, thus cutting off all relation with the other. Timon's pathological narcissism is therefore seen to mirror James I's similar psychic compulsion with its presumably ensuing patronage system. In exploring the violence underlying the entanglement of gender, power, and identity, Kahn reads Timon's generosity as an aggression against the other.

Kahn's interpretation is radically reoriented by Ken Jackson's Derridean reading. In spite of his deconstructive stance, Jackson acknowledges his indebtedness to Wilson Knight's liberal humanism, which he extols as the initiation of an ethically and politically responsible critical tradition: "In that Knight takes into account the extraordinary quality of his giving in understanding Timon's nature, his argument has much explanatory power."[14] But Jackson also pinpoints Wilson Knight's critical shortcomings when he complains about his neglecting "to explain why giving would be the chosen vehicle to express this nature."[15] As his starting point, Jackson takes Derrida's philosophical interpretation of the gift as impossible, as it always presupposes a quid pro quo, whether it is another gift, obligation, or gratitude, now or in the future. A gift, therefore, is always a matter of exchange, never a true gift, the sole exception being gifts bestowed by God. In this light, Jackson rereads Timon's crucial question "What dost thou think 'tis worth?," postulating that the "worth" is a gift which, however, is shown to be impossible since its value should not be trapped in the circular economy of exchange: "Derrida's work prompts us to focus on Timon's giving rather than on the character's essence. His work illuminates not Timon but his extraordinary and complicated giving. Timon seeks to give; that he remains trapped in a world of exchange condemns the world not his efforts."[16] In Jackson's Derridean interpretation of *Timon*, what really matters, is, in fact, not the character, but the nature of generosity itself: "No character pushes down through Christianity to its desire for the 'other and . . . utterly other' in the way Timon does, forcing us to consider where that response and responsibility to 'give' comes from. Shakespeare's drama suggests a direction . . . The obligation to give, the obligation to the other, does not come from anywhere: the obligation precedes everything else."[17] While focusing on *Timon*'s Derridean insistence on the uneconomic character of faith (citing John Caputo's saying that "faith is always a matter of the gift and giving"),[18] Jackson moves away from Knight's reading, which he eventually develops into an entirely different critical approach whose political resonance becomes crucial for contemporary Europe. In contrast with Knight, and in the aftermath of Derrida, Jackson does in fact see as positive Timon's endless searching "for the possibility of the impossible," his "sketching out impossible responses to the seemingly all-encompassing economy of exchange."[19] Timon's faith does not fade away in the misanthropic second half of the play. On the contrary, Timon's religious misanthropy is shown to reverberate throughout the first half and to disclose, along with the religious nature of his philanthropy, a sort of unethical hate and distancing wholly unexpected in religion (nonreligious religion), but traditionally associated with an Abrahamic attitude.

In the woods, exiled from Athens, metamorphosed from a "phoenix" to "a naked gull," Timon rejects all his previous guests: artists, senators, thieves, prostitutes, nature itself, and whatever his prophetic eye sees as entrapped within the circular, sacrificial economy of exchange. But, as Jackson perceptively notes, there is one moment when the gift is delivered from that enchaining prison. This is when Timon recognizes his steward Flavius as "one honest man," nobly loving and giving like himself:

> My most honoured lord,
> For any benefit that points to me,
> Either in hope or present, I'd exchange
> For this one wish: that you had power and wealth
> To requite me by making rich yourself.
>
> (4.3.522–26)

Timon's encounter with Flavius is read by Jackson as the paradigmatic foundation of an ideal nonreligious bond (cf. Latin *re-ligio*), foundational of human communities:

> In the space of the gift, the impossible, appears a passionate "wish" for and toward the other individual ... and the sense of the wholly other ... both the "other and the utterly other," as I said at the outset. Timon, who has been seeking the wholly other all along, finds it here in the figure of Flavius's "impossible" gesture. He discovers, at least as much as is possible, a pure obligation or ethics toward the other, one not grounded in any economy of exchange but grounded on itself alone: a religion without religion. This obligation to the other precedes everything else. Timon had suggested something of the primacy of this obligation early on, again perhaps without fully understanding it: "We are born to do benefits" (1.2.101).[20]

Removed from the circular economy of exchange, the bond may be seen, through Timon's eyes, as a frail but viable political "root" capable of mediating between market and ethics.

Addressed to Flavius, Timon's final remark about his coming death: "Nothing will bring me everything" (5.1.187) should therefore be taken both as an utterly misanthropic statement and as a typically generous opening to the utterly other. Timon's awareness of death and loss stands out as the necessary condition for reparation, the ethical move that is needed for the foundation of a new political sense of community.

Notes

1. The quote in the chapter title is from William Shakespeare, *Timon of Athens*, ed. H. J. Oliver, the Arden Shakespeare (Walton-on-Thames: Nelson, 1997), 1.1.211. All subsequent references will be to this edition. Pfister's article "'In states unborn and accents yet unknown': Shakespeare and the European Canon" appeared in Ladina Bezzola Lambert and Balz Engler, eds., *Shifting the Scene: Shakespeare in European Culture*, 41–63 (Newark: University of Delaware Press, 2004): repr. as "'In states unborn and accents yet unknown': Shakespeare e il canone europeo," in *Shakespeare in Europa*, ed. Antonella Piazza (Naples: Cuen, 2004).

2. John J. Joughin, "Shakespeare's Genius: *Hamlet,* Adaptation and the Work of

Following," in *The New Aestheticism,* ed. John J. Joughin and S. Malpas (Manchester and New York: Manchester University Press, 2003), 131–50.

3. Karl Marx, *Capital,* 3 vols. (1867, 1885, 1894; London: Lawrence & Wishart, 1961–71), 1:41; emphasis added.

4. Hugh Grady, *The Modernist Shakespeare: Critical Texts in a Material World* (Oxford: Clarendon Press, 1991), 197.

5. G. Wilson Knight, *The Wheel of Fire* (1930; New York: Routledge, 1989) and "*Timon of Athens* and Buddhism," *Essays in Criticism* 30.2 (1980): 105–23.

6. Wilson Knight, *Wheel of Fire,* 241 and 269, respectively.

7. Friedrich Nietzsche, *On the Genealogy of Morals* (1887), trans. Walter Kaufmann and R. J. Hollingdale, in *On the Genealogy of Morals and Ecce Homo* (New York: Random House, 1967).

8. Wilson Knight, *Wheel of Fire,* 239.

9. Ibid.

10. Nietzsche, *Genealogy,* 59.

11. G. Wilson Knight, *Shakespearean Dimensions* (Boston: Barnes and Noble, 1984), 67.

12. Ibid., 70.

13. Coppélia Kahn, "'Magic of bounty': *Timon of Athens,* Jacobean Patronage, and Maternal Power," *Shakespeare Quarterly* 38.1 (1987): 34–57.

14. Ken Jackson, "'One Wish' or the Possibility of the Impossible: Derrida, the Gift, and God in *Timon of Athens,*" *Shakespeare Quarterly* 52.1 (2001): 51.

15. Ibid.

16. Ibid.

17. Ibid., 37.

18. Ibid., 45.

19. Ibid., 60.

20. Ibid., 65.

Reeducating Germany: BBC Shakespeare 1945
Andreas Höfele

Goebbels in Reverse?

IN SEPTEMBER 1939, THE LEFT-WING LABOUR POLITICIAN STAFFORD Cripps expressed a view shared by many people in Britain at the time: "Our enemy is Hitler and the Nazi system and not the German people."[1] But such distinction between a relatively small number of political gangsters and a more or less innocent majority of "good Germans" became rapidly obsolete when German bombs began to hit British cities in 1940. The distinction was totally swept away when the horrors of the concentration camps were disclosed by the advancing Allied armies in early 1945.[2] Even the *Economist*—hardly among the more hawkish voices of the British press—was then moved to declare that "there must be a deep-seated moral sickness in a people that could find enough members to do such dirty work, in a people that, dictatorship or no, could tolerate such things, in a people whose senses were so indelicate that they could now profess ignorance of what for twelve years has been stinking to high heaven in their midst." The conclusion of the article conjures up, without actually citing it, a familiar image from Shakespeare's *Macbeth:* "the German people will have to spend many years on their knees before the stains are scrubbed out."[3]

The association of Germany with *Macbeth* was not new. It had first been postulated by the playwright Henry Arthur Jones in response to a preface by Gerhart Hauptmann in the 1915 yearbook of the German Shakespeare Society.[4] Far from being introspective Hamlets, Jones wrote at the height of the First World War, the Germans were really much more like bloody Macbeths.[5] As the Second World War was drawing to a close and the issue was no longer how to defeat the Germans but what to do with them afterward, the focus of attention shifted from "bloody Macbeth" to the dilemma personified by his lady. In act 5 of Shakespeare's play, no amount of scrubbing will do to remove the stains from her bloody hands. The message of the *Economist* article is thus fraught with ambiguity. Along with the need for atonement, its Shakespearean overtones convey a sense that this may quite possibly prove futile.

From the start, similar doubts haunted the discussions about how to reeducate the Germans once the war was over. "What a fantastic idea it is," said the MP for Marylebone in a parliamentary debate in 1943, "to attempt to educate a whole race to be peaceful, a race that for centuries has had an instinct for war deep down in its nature. I believe it would be much easier to educate 80 million baboons."[6]

Such rhetorical vehemence attests to the, by then, wide currency of a concept whose precise origin historians have yet to establish. According to one British source, "the term 're-education' was first used by Vansittart or one of his votaries in 1941."[7] Lord Robert Vansittart, permanent undersecretary of state in the Foreign Office from 1930 to 1938 and a staunch opponent of appeasement, is chiefly remembered today for his extreme views on the German national character. In *Black Record,* a book published in 1941 that was also broadcast by the BBC, he argued that the present rule of Nazi terror, far from being a singular occurrence in German history, was only the latest outburst of a murderous aggressiveness deeply ingrained in the psyche of the "Hun." Its precedents, he claimed, stretched as far back as the battle of Adrianople in the year AD 378, in which Latin civilization had succumbed to German barbarism, with dire consequences for the subsequent course of European history.[8]

The officials in charge of planning a postwar future for Germany never subscribed to the more maniacal aspects of Vansittart's creed. But they went along with him in believing that in order to secure a lasting peace with Germany, more would be required than just the elimination of Hitler and the Nazi party. Nothing would do but a fundamental "change of heart" in a population whose mentality had been shaped by the authoritarian tradition of Prussian militarism and more than a decade of indoctrination by Goebbels's ministry of propaganda.[9] "We were Goebbels in reverse," as a former US reeducation officer alleged in retrospect.[10] But this was precisely what the planners of reeducation on both sides of the Atlantic strove to avoid at all cost. If, as a British Foreign Office paper stated in 1943, "[t]he long-term aim [was] to integrate Germany into a peaceful and prosperous European order [then] no attempt should be made, as had been the German way, to ram the victor's culture down the vanquished's throat."[11] In theory this was clear enough. In practice it turned out to be somewhat difficult to convince the Germans that reeducation did not mean just that: ramming democracy down their throats. As a US theater officer complained, the Germans were "abnormally quick to suspect any statement addressed to them of containing [propaganda]."[12] And a British official noted in 1948, "We are all agreed that re-education is one of the chief objects of our Occupation. It must be remembered, however, that there is no word the Germans, even the most friendly Germans, detest so much and none which is liable to call forth such powerful reactions, as the word 're-education.'"[13]

Projecting Britain

When the fighting ceased and the Allied powers took over, the sheer chaos prevailing in the devastated country dictated priorities other than cultural. The British zone, an "utterly arbitrary geographical area" lacking the agricultural resources to provide adequate food supplies, turned out to be "close to ungovernable."[14] The most daunting task facing the British military administration was to keep the people of the *Ruhrgebiet,* Germany's industrial heartland, from starving. Driven to desperation, it was feared, these people might do anything—even turn Communist and go over to the Russians. Wartime planning and the exigencies of grim postwar reality proved hard to reconcile.[15] The principle of "indirect control," adopted both from financial necessity and a belief that "imposing liberalism by authority" could not work,[16] often served as a euphemism for muddling through. Several major objectives of British occupation policy were not achieved. Most notoriously, the process of denazification—though the British never envisaged it to be as radical as the Americans did—remained "unfinished business" (which was to surface again during the student protests of the late sixties).[17] Attempts to introduce more democratic structures into the conservative university and school system were defeated by stubborn German resistance.[18] Not implausibly, the British effort to place Germany on the road to democracy has been told as a story of missed chances.[19] A lack of direction—and of clear directives—has been considered responsible for this. The Americans, it is argued, achieved more because they were less hesitant to use direct control and—under the command of a military governor with proconsular power—more efficiently organized to enforce it.[20] The pervasive US influence on the Federal Republic would seem to confirm this, although the so-called "Americanization" of West Germany can hardly be put down to the effectiveness of US reorientation policy alone.[21]

The British approach, on the other hand, also has its defenders. Michael Balfour, Chief of Information Services in Germany from 1945–47, suggests that while "[n]obody knew precisely what [reeducation] meant or how it was to be carried out . . . its ambiguity was a considerable advantage,"[22] covering a variety of procedures and political agendas. Other observers go even further. Invoking "the British genius for improvisation under stress,"[23] they turn imperfection into a blessing, a hallmark of pragmatism triumphant. Precisely because it was unhampered by a systematic master plan, they claim, "the day-to-day handling of British occupation principles very quickly acquired . . . a more pragmatic and constructive approach, thereby becoming 'more British' in character."[24] The method (or lack of it) can thus be construed as the perfect medium for what it was meant to convey: "the Projection of Britain." It is with this term that British reeducators most consistently defined the goal of their cultural policy, the purpose to be served by disseminating English books, newspapers, plays, music, films, and radio broadcasts to the German people.

However, the term "the Projection of Britain" was directly derived from prewar cultural propaganda.[25] The catchphrase for promoting democratic ideas in postwar Germany first appeared in 1932 as the title of a pamphlet by Sir Stephen Tallents, Secretary of the Empire Marketing Board, the organization responsible for the first "Buy British" campaign. The title of the pamphlet quickly caught on as the favorite euphemism for what in Foreign Office circles was still perceived as somehow distasteful, even "un-British," that is, propaganda.[26] In the heyday of the Empire there had obviously been no need for self-advertisement. The need for it in the 1930s could, however, no longer be in doubt. Britain's status as a major force in world politics was seen to be declining. Her overseas markets were threatened by increasing foreign competition, particularly by the aggressively anti-British Axis powers.[27] In view of such adversities it was imperative to make it clear to the world, as one official put it in 1931, that "Britain is still a virile [*sic*!], cultured nation with immense manufacturing resources and technical ability, and is still in the forefront of scientific research and material progress."[28]

In 1945, the emergent superpower conflict created an even greater need to compensate for the loss of actual power by resorting to a policy of vigorous self-promotion. "The Projection of Britain" thus served the double purpose of spreading democracy and of laying the foundations for long-term British influence in central Europe. It also became part of an anti-Soviet containment strategy. By the end of the war, it was unmistakable that the ensuing "battle of the mind" was going to be fought not on one, but on two fronts, against both an old enemy, Nazism, and a new one, Communism, which conveniently also happened to be the old archenemy of Nazi-Germany and of Germany's conservative bourgeoisie prior to 1933. "[I]f Germany is won this may well decide the fate of liberalism throughout the world."[29] This statement from a Foreign Office memorandum dated July 11, 1945 illustrates the cold war "logic of a divided Germany,"[30] long before this division was ratified by the founding of the two German states in 1949.

Theater Among the Ruins

In the competition for the minds of the German people, the Soviets were quickest off the mark. Their cultural offensive throughout Europe was seen to be so threateningly effective as to call for a US counteroffensive.[31] By comparison, "the Projection of Britain" was slow in getting under way. In Berlin, for example, where the four occupying forces were vying for cultural preeminence, the British operation was the least visible of all in the period from 1945–47.[32] The first major undertaking seems to have been the 1948 "Elizabethan Festival," which offered a lecture series, poetry readings, concerts by the Madrigal Society, a film program, and stagings of Webster and Shakespeare by the Marlowe Society.[33] Although the Bard did feature in this—the largest public event organized by any of the occupying powers during the Berlin blockade[34]—on the whole he did not play as prominent a part in the "Projection of Britain" as might be expected. Modern authors such as Priestley, Maugham, and T. S. Eliot—not to mention American and French authors such as Hemingway, Thornton Wilder, Sartre, and Anouilh—were and are perceived to have been much more central to reeducation. Understandably, there was a keen interest among German readers and theatergoers to catch up on all the international modern literature that had been unavailable to them for the past twelve years. Shakespeare, on the other hand, did not have to be introduced to the Germans; he was already very much with them, a central figure of their literary culture since the eighteenth century.[35] His special status is clear from the fact that he alone of all so-called "enemy dramatists" was staged in the Third Reich right up to the official closing of the theaters, by Goebbels's decree, in September 1944.[36] He was among the very first dramatists to be performed again when theaters reopened and—hardly to be expected after the end of a total war—a veritable "theater frenzy" broke out amid the rubble of the bombed-out cities.[37] Shakespeare, the supreme representative of "world literature," was ideally suited to mark both a new beginning and a survival, the continuation of a stage tradition that prided itself on having preserved its integrity through the "dark years of barbarism" by a firm commitment to apolitical "Klassikerpflege."

"Pflege," comprising the meanings of "cultivation," "nursing," "maintenance," and "upkeep," describes an approach that treats the plays of Shakespeare much like the National Trust treats historic buildings. Protecting and preserving the classics by defending their timeless universality against the ugly realities of the present and against ideological appropriation of any kind, this was a project to be carried over into the era of newly regained humanism, whether Christian, liberal, or a combination of the two. The doctrine of "Werktreue" (aptly paraphrased by Wilhelm Hortmann as "the devoted service to the interests of the poet") set the norm by which this kind of conservatism defined its aesthetic ideal.[38] It was programmatically proclaimed by Gustaf Gründgens, head of the Prussian State Theater from 1935–45, in the so-called Düsseldorf "Manifesto Against Directorial License" of 1952.[39] The political advantages of the doctrine are not difficult to see. Whereas everything had changed politically, hardly anything needed to be changed in one's approach to the classics. Indeed, the more one continued as before, the more this proved that the right thing had actually been done all along. What this story of continuity tacitly elides is the enforced discontinuation of the avant-garde theater of the 1920s, the modernism of a Brecht, Piscator, or Leopold Jessner (Gründgens's predecessor at the Preussisches Staatsschauspiel),[40] which had made Berlin the international theater capital before the takeover of the Nazis. The rejection of directorial license, which remained the theatrical norm well into the sixties, drew at least some of its urgency from a desire to give credence to a story that provided a "usable past."

Radio Shakespeare: A British Bard

What, then, were British reeducators to do with an English author—*the* English author—who had become Germany's "third classic" and whom Germans of all kinds and persuasions—including Nazi ideologists—had claimed as a kindred spirit? The answer was to re-Anglicize him. This was the approach chosen by the BBC's German Language Service (GLS) in a radio broadcast on June 7, 1945, barely a month after Germany's capitulation. It is the first of six Shakespeare features broadcast by that service over the course of the first twelve months after V-E Day.[41] It is also one of the very earliest documents of reeducation in practice coming from any of the four occupation powers. Its purpose within the overall political agenda of the BBC GLS is clearly expressed in a policy statement drawn up at Bush House, some five months later (November 24, 1945): "The reeducation of the German people is the direct concern of the B.B.C. German Service. The projection of Britain, in the widest sense of the term, must be one of the main tasks of any B.B.C. service to Europe and will contribute directly to the end of reeducation."[42]

Its wartime broadcasts had earned the BBC immense prestige among its clandestine German listeners. To them, these broadcasts—typically opening with the announcement "Hier ist England"—very much represented the voice of Britain itself.[43] Anything on Shakespeare issuing from this source would thus carry considerable authority.

The typescript of the forty-five-minute program is simply entitled *Shakespeare Feature,* but it was actually broadcast as "England—die unbekannte Insel" (England—the Unknown Island).[44] Its author was the German Service's productions director, the well-known Shakespearean and West End actor Marius Goring (1912–98), whose postwar screen appearances included so many Nazi villains "that he claimed to have played every rank in the German Army from private to field marshal."[45] In 1939 he had given a highly convincing performance as the voice of Adolf Hitler in an anti-Nazi radio serial, *The Shadow of the Swastika.* Of Anglo-Scots parentage, Goring was fluent enough in both French and German to perform in either language to native-speaker audiences.[46] To his German listeners he chose to be Charles Richardson—presumably because his real second name was distinguished by a mere umlaut from that of Hitler's *Reichsmarschall.*[47]

Goring's *Shakespeare Feature* program begins with a fade-up of Elgar's "Enigma," the announcement of the title, "England—die unbekannte Insel," and—in a deft piece of island-swapping between the North Sea and the Mediterranean—a recitation of Caliban's "The isle is full of noises" speech (*Tempest,* 3.2) in both English and German. This is followed by Goring/Richardson's opening monologue, which, similar to Gloucester's in *Richard III,* hinges on the transition from war to peace. Unlike Richard, however, Richardson is not determined to prove a villain—nor stern taskmaster, prosecutor, judge, or preacher—but a friend, and a rather close one at that: one who has been his audience's trustworthy companion during the harrowing experience of war. "For six years," Richardson says, "you have been listening to our voices on the air—we spoke about war and politics." Now for the first time, he says, "it will be my great pleasure to speak to you about something that has nothing to do with war or politics—a theme that leads me back to my true [*eigentliche*] profession as an actor, to my work prior to the year '39, to a time when I had not yet plunged into the fight which in one way or another has now taken possession of all of us." (1)[48]

Considering the date of the broadcast, the tone of the passage is remarkable. At a time when a strict antifraternization rule was in force in the British zone, when the Americans made unwilling Germans watch newsreel footage of death camp victims in a none too successful campaign of "guilt mobilization," the BBC is offering its listeners a break, a little touch of Shakespeare for the night. Had Goring wanted to provide a textbook example of how to win over a German audience, he could not have done better. Only four weeks after the end of the war, his text smoothly turns deadly antagonism into common experience, which "in one way or another" *we* have all been through. Building on and reconfirming the very special relationship between the BBC and its German listeners, Goring's opening remarks follow the procedural principles outlined by the planners of reeducation to a T.[49] His painstakingly tactful approach to his theme could not contrast more sharply with the aggressively proprietary claim to Shakespeare made by Henry Arthur Jones in 1916. Instead of denigrating the German Shakespeare tradition, Richardson begins by paying respect to it. Shakespeare is universal, he says, and this "is one of the reasons why the German Shakespeare translations—especially those of Schlegel and Tieck—are so good" (1).

Translation and universality, nevertheless, have to take second place to the mother tongue and national identity. "Each poet, after all, has his own language and nationality, just as he has his own body" (2). At this point the text is suddenly inundated with Englishness. Shakespeare wrote about "man as such," but man as he knew him was "der englische Mensch": "His sky was an English sky, his landscape was an English landscape, and the feelings of his characters were nearly always the feelings of the Englishman" (2). Lest this flare-up of patriotic zeal be mistaken for something like "Goebbels in reverse," Richardson hastens to qualify it:

> Do not, for God's sake, get me wrong; by no means do I want to claim that all that is good in the world has to be English. I do not believe that, and Shakespeare certainly did not believe it either. In my opinion, no one ought to think in terms of race—and the greater the man, the greater is his desire to understand every aspect of humanity in the whole world. . . . I believe that Shakespeare's greatness was founded on the fact that he lived and died an Englishman, an Englishman who, at the same time, understood and loved the whole world. He had an English mind,[50] but a worldwide imagination; in his imagination he roamed through Italy, through France, through Greece, and then he transplanted the foreign flowers into the English language, into the world of English thought, he took the best

the world had to give and transformed it into a part of the English heritage. (2)

Heavy-handed though the abrupt shift from English sky and English landscape to an appeal against racism may be, its very awkwardness reveals something of the extremity of the political and existential situation in which this feature was produced and broadcast in early June 1945. It is a situation that Goring seeks at once to address and to efface with his conciliatory offer of an acoustic "clear area" of studied normality in which it is possible to talk about Shakespeare even after Auschwitz.

While the notion of Shakespeare's acquisitive imagination picking the best from everywhere seems to be modeled on imperial Britannia and her dealings with the colonies, the end of the quoted passage again, if somewhat more obliquely, hints at the issue of racism. The final word of the quoted passage, *Erbgut* in the original German, combines the meaning of "heritage" with that of "genetic makeup." *Erbgut* figures prominently in Nazi race theory. The use of this term here may just be a slip of the pen, but it all too clearly attests to the continuing presence of what had been, up until four weeks earlier, the dominant jargon. The contrast between the racist purism of the Nazis and the nonpurist integrative liberalism of the English is spelled out when Richardson exemplifies Shakespeare's Englishness, along with English open-mindedness, by taking his listeners to Belmont. Lorenzo and Jessica deliver excerpts from their lovers' duet "in such a night" before being found asleep by the returning Portia (*The Merchant of Venice*, 5.1). "The characters," Richardson comments after the dialogue, "have foreign names and foreign costumes, but they speak to us in our English mother tongue—and suddenly they are for us: Lorenzo, a charming young Englishman, Jessica, a charming young English Jewess, and Portia, an English girl with a good heart and common sense [mit Herz und Verstand]" (3).

The choice of this passage is highly charged. Up until not quite a month before the date of this broadcast, the relationship between Lorenzo and Jessica would have constituted miscegenation in Germany (*Rassenschande*), an offense punishable by death. In Third Reich productions of the *Merchant*,[51] therefore, Jessica had to become a gentile, Shylock's daughter by adoption, not by birth. In contrast to this, Richardson's Shakespeare generously extends English citizenship to the Jewish Jessica, who is just as charming and just as English as Lorenzo—and perhaps only a touch less so than Portia herself, whose good heart and common sense raise her to the Englishness level of one's favorite Jane Austen heroine.

Portia will reappear later in the program, but first another theme is taken up: Shakespeare as the poet of the English countryside. This theme is introduced with a song from *Love's Labour's Lost*, "When Daisies Pied." It does not matter, Richardson tells his listeners, if you do not understand the English lyrics: they are only about cowslips and violets and girls washing their summer dresses. All that matters is the feeling of spring that this simple song conveys; of English spring, to be sure, because only if you know and have suffered English weather will you be able to appreciate the brief joy of English spring that the song celebrates. "I am," Richardson says, "a true admirer of Schubert and Mendelssohn; their Shakespeare compositions are superb. Schubert and Mendelssohn have given us something new which is perhaps equally good—but it is different from the original. It is not English" (4).

To prove this, he slots in a recording of Schubert's "Silvia" and of the Scherzo from Mendelssohn's *Midsummer Night's Dream*. This serves to make the point again: great music, certainly, "the music of a genius"—but not Shakespeare. The fairies it conjures up are "Mendelssohn fairies, not Shakespeare fairies" (6), because Shakespeare's are much more down-to-earth, much more like ordinary human beings. Their nature is therefore captured far better by a song that is "not artistically perfect like Mendelssohn's fairy music," but that is "quite a simple tune in the middle of which a dog is barking and whose ending sounds like the crowing of a cockerel" (6). It is Ariel's song, "Come Unto These Yellow Sands" (*The Tempest*, 1.2).

The escapist appeal that such a pastoral Shakespeare would have had in 1945, a Shakespeare deeply rooted in the sentimentalized simplicity of rural England, is not difficult to see. But the nostalgic ruralism of the BBC Shakespeare was entirely typical of "the Projection of Britain," and had been ever since the United Kingdom staged its belated entry into the arena of cultural propaganda under this motto in the early thirties. While the idea was to prove to the world that Britain was still "in the forefront of scientific research and material progress,"[52] the list of items to be projected as typically British that the initiator of the campaign, Sir Stephen Tallents, drew up creates an interestingly different image. It includes "the monarchy, parliamentary institutions, the Royal Navy, the English Bible and the works of Dickens and Shakespeare . . . the Derby and the Grand National; Henley and the Boat Race; Test Matches; the Trooping of the Colour; . . . Bond Street; Big Ben; Oxford and Edinburgh; . . . *The Times*, *Punch* and the *Manchester Guardian;* English countryside and villages; foxhunting; English servants; English bloodstock and pedigree stock; the arts of gardening and tailoring."[53] "In short," comments the historian Philip Taylor, "this was the England of a ... man who would have been more suited to the role of an eighteenth-century country squire than that of a senior civil servant."[54] But the point is that this traditionalist vision of England was very much the rule among twentieth-century British elites. And it was again mobilized as the image of Englishness to be communicated to Germany during the postwar reeducation campaign. As the American historian Martin J. Wiener points out: "It is a historic irony that the nation that gave birth to the industrial revolution and exported it to the world, should have ... adopt[ed] a conception of Englishness that virtually excluded industrialism."[55] It is true that the policy of projecting a quaintly pastoral Britain to the Germans had its critics among British reeducation officials. One of them demanded, for instance, that "Cotswolds cottages should be shown only as a contrast to a modern housing estate," but it can be safely assumed that in terms of actual exposure the Cotswolds cottage and all it stood for easily eclipsed its modern counterparts.[56] The Shakespeare to go with the cottage is the Shakespeare of the heritage industry; the Shakespeare who was and still is—in the words of Gary Taylor—the "cash-cow" of that industry.[57] In 1945 just such a Shakespeare was a natural first choice as an antidote to the nightmares of a century that had seen progress culminate in the industrialization of murder.[58]

Hamlet, Shylock, and the Holocaust

Richardson's forty-five-minute tour of Shakespeare takes in three more ports of call: Hamlet, Shylock, and Prospero. From the rustic harmony conjured up in the name of Shakespeare, the poet-magician for whom "all things in nature are one" (6), some twenty lines plunge the listener into the existential dilemma of Hamlet. "If we are all one," the narrator continues, "we should live in peace; but instead one nation fights against another, one individual against another ... What can the poet do in his desperation? In the end he longs for death, for only in death will he be able to find complete peace and harmony. But is this longing for death a good thing? That is the question ... 'Seyn oder Nichtseyn, das ist hier die Frage.' "[59]

Hamlet's famous monologue, which the BBC *Shakespeare Feature* recites in full, constitutes something like the innermost sanctum of Germany's Shakespeare adoration, the site where the English bard and the German *Geist* consummate their mystical union. Quoting the passage is therefore just as inevitable as it is fraught with potentially undesirable associations, associations with a peculiarly Teutonic tradition of speculative philosophizing, a tradition that not only proved incapable of stemming the tide of Germany's recent disastrous history but was perhaps actually conducive to it. A. O. Lovejoy claimed such a pernicious philosophical continuity in an article published in his own *Journal for the History of Ideas* in 1941, which drew a vehement reply from Leo Spitzer.[60] But the most damning case in point was no less a luminary than the author of *Being and Time*, Martin Heidegger, who became the first rector of Freiburg University under the Nazis in 1933 and in that capacity not only paid homage to the Führer but also brought his university vigorously into line with the new regime. In June 1945, the German philosophical tradition—deeply compromised by the implication in Hitler's tyranny of its latest and most sophisticated branch—did not have much to recommend it ideologically.[61]

Goring nimbly extricates Hamlet from this tradition with a sideswipe of no more than four words. Both Shakespeare and Hamlet, he declares, answer the temptation of suicide with a clear no—"anders als Goethes Werther" (unlike Goethe's Werther) (7). In highly suggestive historical shorthand, the name of Werther, Goethe's sensitive ersatz-Hamlet, thus comes to stand both for a persistent German misreading of Shakespeare's true English message and for the wrong turn the history of a whole nation had taken. But to a German radio audience on June 7, 1945, the mention of Werther's suicide would have resonated with much more recent memories. It could hardly fail to call up the suicides of Hitler and Goebbels, less than six weeks earlier, and that of Heinrich Himmler, leader of the SS, who killed himself just over a fortnight before the *Shakespeare Feature* went on the air.[62]

The extremes of German culture and German barbarism thus blend into one another, as if to confirm Walter Benjamin's dictum that every cultural monument conceals, within itself, a document of barbarism—a dictum visibly perpetuated to this day by the close proximity of Weimar and the site of the Buchenwald concentration camp.[63] Rejecting the drive toward self-destruction, the 1945 BBC Hamlet finally makes up his mind that life, "in spite of everything, must be lived to its natural conclusion" (7). It is this message that Richardson extracts (with a bit of arm-twisting) from the prince's dying words to Horatio: "Absent thee from felicity awhile." Again Hamlet and Shakespeare become one and the same person. The poet, we learn, must live on "to tell his story," and the purpose of his living on is "to castigate injustice wherever he finds it" (7).

The Shakespearean code word for the most horrendous injustice, the one most painfully relevant to Goring's German audience is, of course, Shylock, whose speech—"Has not a Jew eyes"—the program renders in full. Goring's presentation of that speech is highly instructive. He could have used it as a devastating indictment of German collective guilt, collective moral failure. He could, in other words, have adopted the stance of the *Economist* article quoted above, and impressed on his listeners the gravity of their failing. The speech itself, one may of course argue, says it all. But the commentary before and after it is clearly designed to soften, not to increase the speech's shock potential. Rather than seeking to confront the German listeners with their shame, it cushions them from that shame. In his lead-in, Goring again uses the conciliatory "we" very effectively, and he heightens the effect by embedding it in a rhetorical question that creates a rapport between speaker and addressee by assuming agreement: "Can there be a more uncompromising condemnation of that race prejudice which *we* all know so well than these sentences from *The Merchant of Venice?*" (7). The comment after Shylock's speech is even more remarkable. Shakespeare demands justice, the text says, but justice is not all. "Justice must not be cruel: cruelty must be overcome by mercy" (8). Shylock is put in his place, his demand for justice overruled by Portia's "The quality of mercy is not strained," which is also quoted in full.

A radio broadcast cannot be stopped and repeated by the listener at will. The implication of Goring's argument—the glib transition from a Jew demanding equal rights to a Christian extolling mercy—may thus have escaped the program's first audience. Within a matter of seconds, the program puts Jews back where, in Germany, they had been for the last twelve years: that is, in the dock. But what could not have failed to communicate itself—and no doubt constituted the program's intended "official" message—was the comforting promise of forgiveness: forgiveness instead of retaliation, a sense of being let off the hook, and of having, like the narrowly escaped Antonio, Portia-England on one's side. The encouraging rather than punitive tenor of the passage, and of the *Shakespeare Feature* as a whole, is fully in keeping with the programmatics of reeducation.[64] And so is the Projection of Britain, which dominates the next passage. In extolling mercy and justice, Richardson says, Shakespeare celebrates the two essential norms of English civilization. This, rather predictably, leads up to Gaunt's "sceptred isle" speech from *Richard II*, which is, however, accompanied by the democratic caveat that blind patriotism is wrong.

The Englishness the BBC *Shakespeare Feature* projects is a compound of pragmatism and nostalgia. It reflects both an enduringly dominant strand in the discourse of English national identity and the intellectual climate of a particular historical moment. The former, *longue durée* ingredient of the mixture is the empiricist tradition, which the late Anthony Easthope identified as the discursive mold in which a characteristically English intellectual and rhetorical habitus has been shaped from Hobbes to present-day "middle-brow" literary journalism.[65]

It is this discourse that informs the *Shakespeare Feature*'s consistent praise of simplicity and common sense over complexity and speculation: Shakespeare's simple English song over the symphonic intricacy of German Romanticism; Shakespeare's "artless," down-to-earth fairies over the artificial creatures of Mendelssohn's magnificent but un-English *Midsummer Night's Dream;* a Hamlet whose dying words endorse an ethics of robust pragmatism over a Werther-like procrastinator whose metaphysical speculation can only lead to suicide. Shakespeare emerges as an eminently reasonable author endowed with, and advocating, the typically British quality of common sense: just the right kind of genius, in other words, for a reeducation policy whose "pragmatic and constructive approach" was to prove, time and again, "the British genius for improvisation under stress."[66]

The historically more specific 1940s' coloring that this celebration of pragmatism adopts in Goring's *Shakespeare Feature* is a marked nostalgia for a better, that is, rural past; for an England of English sky and English countryside; an England where dogs are barking, cockerels are crowing, and forests teem with English fairies. There is not a word about cities, not a word of the rifts and fissures of Shakespeare's age that appear everywhere in his plays. The Shakespeare Goring presents to the Germans in order to direct them toward a democratic future is, like Tillyard's Shakespeare, the prophet of a golden past, where all conflict was ultimately resolved and sublated in the "'organic' [harmony] of a unitary culture."[67] Goring's feature shows an equally close affinity to the vision of a preindustrial England that informs the cultural critique of F. R. Leavis. It is as though the task of guiding the Germans back into the fold of civilization provided Goring with an opportunity to give vent to what David Gervais, speaking of F. R. Leavis, has called an "anxiety to recover an untarnished, life-enhancing England"[68]—remarkably, an England as far removed from postwar Britain as it was from Germany.

Prospero, or, Forgiveness and Mercy

Having started with *The Tempest,* the BBC *Shakespeare Feature* finally returns to it and, leading up to Prospero's "We are such stuff as dreams are made on," has this to say: "In a cruel and unjust world he [Shakespeare] had found his peace in the certain knowledge that, in this life, there is only one weapon against injustice: justice and mercy; and that after this life everything—his own country as well as other countries, human cruelty and kindness, fame and vanity, love, hate, human beings themselves and all things in nature pass into the unalterable will of God and dissolve into peaceful forgetting. Thus speaks Prospero, the great magician, the great poet, Shakespeare in his own person" (9).

It is easy to dismiss this—and much else in the forty-five-minute program—as piously platitudinous. The point is, however, that it is also very revealing. Quickstepping from Shylock's demand for justice to Portia's decree of mercy to Prospero's peaceful forgetting, the program manages, as it were, to face and efface the Holocaust, or, more precisely, to not *quite* face and not *quite* efface it. In doing so, it offers its German listeners the terms of a contract: a toning down of the all-too-insistent voice of memory for a willingness to cooperate. It offers Germans a not-too-uncomfortable starting point for a new future on condition that this future be governed by an acceptance of the rules of Western democracy. Much of the reeducation effort, it seems to me, hinged on such a contract.[69]

In Goring's version of the contract the Christian element, pulled out of the hat just before reaching the telos of peaceful forgetting, adds a note of cosmic quietism reminiscent of Thornton Wilder, whose plays were among the most popular with postwar German audiences.[70] Human agency, which the program had earlier enlisted for the good fight against injustice, is ultimately rendered futile by "the unalterable will of God." There is comfort in this too, though. If the Almighty is responsible, politics becomes fate and Hitler something like a natural disaster beyond human control. Goring does not spell this out, but his text indicates the kind of premise from which such exoneration became possible, and indeed widespread, in German writing of the time. One cannot but marvel at the degree of psychological intuition that allowed him to register and cater to the sensibilities of his audience with such precision. Setting out to demonstrate the Englishness of Shakespeare, Goring makes him a composite portrait of topical German issues;[71] and in retrospect, the treatment of these issues looks like a blueprint of the attitudes and mentalities that were to become typical of the Adenauer era. *Forgiveness and Mercy in Shakespeare* (*Vergebung und Gnade bei Shakespeare*), the title of one of the few German Shakespeare monographs of the early postwar period, may serve to illustrate this point. Published in 1952, the book established its author, the Göttingen professor of English Ernst Theodor Sehrt, as one of the country's leading Shakespeareans. "Forgiveness," Sehrt sums up his findings, "is the point in Shakespeare, which opens the passage from the tragic to the Christian." Of all his Elizabethan contemporaries, "the poet of England . . . has most clearly shown the access to a spiritual world where human weakness finds its answer in forgiving love."[72] This German Shakespeare could easily pass for a twin brother of Goring's English one. "Influence," however, would hardly be the right term to describe the complex processes of reception and resistance on which this family likeness is founded. Neither would "reeducation," if we mean by this just a one-way flow of political instruction.

What appears to me a more pertinent characterization of these processes is to be found in a phrase taken from Salman Rushdie's *The Satanic Verses:* "How does newness come into the world? . . . Of what fusions, translations, conjoinings is it made?" asks the narrator.[73] The BBC *Shakespeare Feature* of June 1945 may be described as one small contribution to the "fusions, translations and conjoinings" that shaped the course of postwar German history.[74]

Notes

1. *Tribune*, September 15, 1939, quoted in Lothar Kettenacker, *Krieg zur Friedenssicherung: Die Deutschlandplanung der britischen Regierung während des zweiten Weltkrieges* (Göttingen: Vandenhoeck & Ruprecht, 1989), 32.

2. See Anthony J. Nicholls, "The German 'National Character' in British Perspective," *Conditions of Surrender: Britons and Germans Witness the End of the War*, ed. Ulrike Jordan (London and New York: Tauris, 1997), 26–39.

3. "Notes of the Week," *Economist*, April 21, 1945, 506.

4. Gerhart Hauptmann, "Deutschland und Shakespeare," *Shakespeare Jahrbuch* 51 (1915): vii–xii.

5. Cf. Henry Arthur Jones, *Shakespeare and Germany* (London: Chiswick Press, 1916), 22: "not the Prince of Denmark, but the murderer of Duncan and of Macduff's children is the true and dreadful image of themselves." For a discussion of this Anglo-German "war of pamphlets" over the ownership of Shakespeare, see Werner Habicht, "Shakespeare Celebrations in Times of War," *Shakespeare Quarterly* 52 (2001): 441–55, especially 451–55.

6. Captain Cunningham-Reid in an adjournment debate, May 27, 1943, quoted in Michael Balfour, "In Retrospect: Britain's Policy of 'Re-education'," in *The Political Re-education of Germany and Her Allies after World War II*, ed. Nicholas Pronay and Keith Wilson, 140 (Totowa, NJ: Barnes & Noble, 1985).

7. Balfour, "In Retrospect," 140. Another possible inventor of the term is the US journalist Leopold Schwarzschild, who claims to have used it in an article published as early as summer 1939. Vice President Henry Wallace, so Schwarzschild maintains, promptly took up the term, thus ensuring its wide circulation. Cf. Leopold Schwarzschild, *Primer of the Coming World* (London: Hamilton, 1944), 165-66.

8. Robert Vansittart, *Black Record: Germans Past and Present* (London: Hamish/Hamilton, 1941), 21. "In the thirteenth century a great part of Europe was overrun

by Mongols known as the Golden Horde, who committed the most appalling atrocities. Germans in the plural are the Brazen Horde. At least the Golden Horde was not brazen enough to pretend that they were anything but barbarians. Other people grew up and settled down. The Germans never did. The Brazen Horde remained savages at heart. That is far the greatest tragedy in the world. . . . Wherever they went, the invaders submerged all culture; . . . the word 'vandalism' was coined to describe gratuitous German savagery" (20–21). In view of such inveterate belligerence, it seems somewhat incongruous to have called for reeducation. If the Germans were as inherently evil as Vansittart claimed they were, was it not futile to hope their barbarous nature would be amenable to any measures of civilizing nurture? Indeed, might one not just as well attempt to educate 80 million baboons?

9. An article entitled "Can We Re-educate Germany?" in the *British Zone Review*, the official review of the Control Commission for Germany (British Element), of December 8, 1945 puts it thus: "to effect a radical and lasting change of heart in the hard-working, efficient, inflammable, ruthless and war-loving German people . . . would . . . be the greatest and most durable guarantee of the peace of Europe that we could hope to attain." Quoted in Kurt Jürgensen, "The Concept and Practice of 'Reeducation' in Germany 1945–50," Pronay and Wilson, eds., *The Political Re-education,* 88. Also see Churchill, in a speech on September 21, 1943: "Nazi tyranny *and* Prussian militarism are the two main elements in German life which must be absolutely destroyed." Charles Eade, ed., *The War Speeches of the Rt. Hon. Winston S. Churchill* (London: Cassell, 1962), 3:478.

10. Robert Wolfe, quoted by Hansjörg Gehring, *Amerikanische Kulturpolitik in Deutschland, 1945–1953* (Stuttgart: Deutsche Verlagsanstalt, 1976), 29.

11. Con O'Neill, in a secret paper entitled "Lines for Emergency Plan, Propaganda to Germany after her Defeat," July 6, 1943. O'Neill was chairman of the German Sub-Committee of the Joint Political Warfare Executive (PWE) / Ministry of Information (MOI) / BBC Re-Occupation Committee; quoted in Kurt Koszyk, "The Press in the British Zone of Germany," Pronay and Wilson, eds., *The Political Re-education,* 108.

12. Eugene H. Bahn, RG 260 OMGUS 5/291–3/8. The reference is to the microfiche collection of selected Office of Military Government (US) (OMGUS) records at the Munich Institut für Zeitgeschichte.

13. PRO/FO 371/70713. In response to the negative reactions to the word "re-education," it was officially abandoned by the US military government and replaced by the more agreeable term "cultural re-orientation" (Joint Chiefs of Staff Directive 1779, July 11, 1947), but by then it was too late to disperse the negative associations. Heinz Koeppler, the founder and *spiritus rector* of the Wilton Park project, whose study courses for POWs and later for German exchange students were among the most successful of all reeducation programs, expressly banned the word "re-education" entirely, characterizing it as "arrogance caused by ignorance." Cf. David Welch, "Citizenship and Politics: The Legacy of Wilton Park for Post-War Reconstruction," in *The Cultural Legacy of the British Occupation in Germany,* ed. Alan Bance (Stuttgart: H.-D. Heinz, 1997), 225.

14. John E. Farquharson, "The British Occupation of Germany, 1945–6: A Badly Managed Disaster Area?" *German History* 11.3 (1993): 326, and Alan Bance, introduction to *The Cultural Legacy ,* ed. Bance, 10.

15. Cf. Lothar Kettenacker, "British Post-War Planning for Germany: Haunted by the Past," Jordan, ed., *Conditions of Surrender,* 13–25.

16. Bance, introduction to *The Cultural Legacy,* 14.

17. Ian Turner, "Denazification in the British Zone," in *Reconstruction in Post-*

War Germany: British Occupation Policy and the Western Zones, 1945–55, ed. Ian Turner (New York: Berg, 1989), 239–67; Tom Bower, Blind Eye to Murder: Britain, America and the Purging of Nazi Germany. A Pledge Betrayed, 2nd ed. (London: Warner Books, 1997).

18. Jürgensen, "The Concept and Practice," 92 ("University Officers had a particularly difficult task because of the rigid and authoritarian academic structure and the academic pride of the professors").

19. Cf. Günter Pakschies, *Umerziehung in der britischen Zone, 1945–1949*, 2nd ed. (Cologne and Vienna: Böhlau, 1984), 16–17.

20. It is one of the ironies of the British occupation that the policy of indirect control, intended to keep expenditure down, ultimately required an enormous amount of personnel. While only 1,500 civil servants had been sufficient to run the colonial administration of prewar India with its 300 million inhabitants, the apparatus catering for a mere 23 million Germans finally comprised 26,000 employees. See Jochen Thies, "What is going on in Germany? Britische Militärverwaltung in Deutschland 1945/46," in *Die Deutschlandpolitik Großbritanniens und die britische Zone, 1945–1949*, ed. Claus Scharf and Hans-Jürgen Schröder (Wiesbaden: Franz Steiner Verlag, 1979), 40–41.

21. To what extent West Germany was shaped by "Americanization" has been a controversial issue ever since Arnold Bergsträsser raised it in his 1962 address to the German Society for American Studies; see Arnold Bergsträsser, "Zum Problem der sogenannten Amerikanisierung Deutschlands," *Jahrbuch für Amerikastudien* 8 (1963): 13–23. The decade from 1990 to 2000 alone saw some 120 publications on the subject; see Ursula Lehmkuhl, Stefanie Schneider, and Frank Schumacher, eds., *Kulturtransfer und Kalter Krieg: Westeuropa als Bühne und Akteur im Amerikanisierungsprozess* (Erfurt: Universität Erfurt, 2001). For a survey of the debate, see Berndt Ostendorf, "'Die sogenannte Amerikanisierung Deutschlands': Eine Bilanz nach 40 Jahren," in *Amerikanisierung als Herausforderung / The Challenge of Americanization*, ed. Winfried Herget (Trier: WVT, 2004), 1–23; Berndt Ostendorf, "Americanization and Anti-Americanization in the Age of Globalization," in *The Norte-Americanización of Latin America?* ed. Stefan Rinke and H.-J. König (Stuttgart: Heinz, 2004), 19–45.

22. Balfour, "In Retrospect," 140–41.

23. Donald C. Watt, *Britain Looks to Germany: British Opinion and Policy towards Germany since 1945* (London: Wolff, 1965), 70.

24. Frank S. V. Donnison, *Civil Affairs and Military Government: North-West Europe, 1944–1946* (London: Her Majesty's Stationery Office, 1961), 205.

25. For an in-depth account of the continuity between prewar British cultural propaganda and the cultural policy pursued in the British zone of Germany from 1945 to 1949, see Gabriele Clemens, *Britische Kulturpolitik in Deutschland, 1945–1949* (Stuttgart: Franz Steiner, 1997).

26. The most enduring legacy of the "Projection of Britain" campaign is the British Council, which was founded in 1934. However, the British Council was not involved in the reeducation of Germany during the crucial years of 1945–49. Some British Council activities in Germany commenced in 1950, but it was not until 1959, when the Council took over the British information centers known as *Die Brücke*, that its operation in Germany became fully institutionalized. Cf. Frances Donaldson, *The British Council: The First Fifty Years* (London: Jonathan Cape, 1984). On the Brücken, see Clemens, *Britische Kulturpolitik*, 204–9.

27. Philip M. Taylor, *The Projection of Britain: British Overseas Publicity and Propaganda, 1919–1939* (Cambridge: Cambridge University Press, 1981), 87.

28. The memorandum by an unidentified Department of Overseas Trade official, dated March 30, 1931, is quoted by Taylor, *The Projection of Britain*, 106.
29. Sir Orme Sargent, "Stock Taking after VE day," Rohan Butler and M. E. Pelly, eds., *Documents on British Policy Overseas*, 1st ser., vol. 1 (London: HMSO, 1984), 181.
30. Anne Deighton, *The Impossible Peace: Britain, the Division of Germany and the Origins of the Cold War* (Oxford: Clarendon, 1990), 20.
31. This led, among other things, to the founding of the CIA-sponsored Congress for Cultural Freedom and its clandestine long-term financing of leading intellectual journals in Germany, France, Britain, and Italy. These journals were *Der Monat, Encounter* (edited by the poet Stephen Spender), *Preuves* (edited by François Bondy), and *Tempo Presente*. See Frances S. Saunders, *Who Paid the Piper? The CIA and the Cultural Cold War* (London: Granta Books, 1999).
32. British films, for example, signally failed to impress the German viewers in comparison with the American and French competition. The only one that caused something of a stir was David Lean's *Oliver Twist*, because its portrayal of Fagin was criticized as anti-Semitic. See Cyril Buffet, "'Ganz Berlin ist eine Bühne': Die kulturpolitischen Vorstellungen des Vereinigten Königreichs," in *Die vier Besatzungsmächte und die Kultur in Berlin, 1945–1949*, ed. Hans-Martin Hinz, Cyril Buffet, Bernard Genton, Pierre Jardin, and Angéla DeGroot, 206–7 (Leipzig: Universitätsverlag, 1999).
33. Buffet, "Ganz Berlin," 204.
34. Ibid.
35. The story of his "nostrification" (*Nostrifizierung*)—a neologism coined in the 1850s and adopted by the founders of the German Shakespeare Society in 1864—has often been told. The most recent, and comprehensive, account is Roger Paulin, *The Critical Reception of Shakespeare in Germany, 1682–1914: Native Literature and Foreign Genius* (Hildesheim: Olms, 2003). Cf. also Werner Habicht, "Shakespeare in Nineteenth-Century Germany: The Making of a Myth," in *Nineteenth-Century Germany: A Symposium*, ed. Modris Eksteins and Hildegard Hammerschmidt, 141–57 (Tübingen: Narr, 1983); Werner Habicht, *Shakespeare and the German Imagination* (Hertford: International Shakespeare Association, 1994), 11–15; Wilhelm Hortmann, *Shakespeare on the German Stage: The Twentieth Century* (Cambridge: Cambridge University Press, 1998), 1–7; Ruth Freifrau von Ledebur, *Der Mythos vom deutschen Shakespeare: Die deutsche Shakespeare-Gesellschaft zwischen Politik und Wissenschaft, 1918–1945* (Köln: Böhlau, 2002); Manfred Pfister, "Germany is Hamlet: The History of a Political Interpretation," *New Comparison* 2 (Autumn 1986): 106–26; Simon Williams, *Shakespeare on the German Stage, 1586–1914* (Cambridge: Cambridge University Press, 1990); Heiner O. Zimmermann, "Is Hamlet Germany? On the Political Reception of *Hamlet*," in *New Essays on "Hamlet*," ed. Mark Thornton Burnett and John Manning, 293–318 (New York: AMS Press, 1994).
36. Another exception was George Bernard Shaw, an Irishman and an outspoken critic of "British plutocracy." This seemed to put him on Germany's side. But while his plays were performed in the Reich even during the war, he did not receive royalties for them. Boguslaw Drewniak, *Das Theater im NS-Staat* (Düsseldorf: Droste, 1983), 255–59. See also Jutta Wardetzky, *Theaterpolitik im faschistischen Deutschland* (Berlin: Henschel, 1983), 81.
37. Hermann Glaser, *Kulturgeschichte der Bundesrepublik Deutschland, 1945–1989* (München: Hanser, 1991), 106. Cf. Andreas Höfele, "From Reeducation to Alternative Theater: German-American Theater Relations," in *The United States and Germany in the Era of the Cold War*, vol. 1, 1945–1968, ed. Detlef Junker (Cambridge: Cambridge University Press, 2004), 464–71.

38. Hortmann, *Shakespeare on the German Stage*, 185.

39. By this time Gründgens, having undergone denazification, was director of the Düsseldorf Schauspielhaus (1947–55). Gründgens's role during the Third Reich has been much debated. It seems clear now that the image of the unscrupulous opportunist projected by Klaus Mann's roman à clef *Mephisto* (first published in Amsterdam 1936) is a distortion.

40. See Andreas Höfele, "Leopold Jessner's Shakespeare Productions 1920–1930," *Theatre History Studies* 12 (1992): 139–55.

41. The others were radio adaptations of *Macbeth* (October 6, 1945) and of *Much Ado About Nothing* (February 19–20, 1946); a presentation of Olivier's film of *Henry V* (June 20–21 and August 7, 1945; author: J. Pereszlenyi, alias Martin Esslin); a feature on *Shakespeare's England* (April 15–16, 1946); and one on Shakespeare's life (*Shakespeare's Birthday, 1946;* April 22, 1946). The typed scripts of these programs (of which no recordings survive) are in the BBC Written Archives Centre, Caversham Park, Reading. They were brought to my attention by Martina Kögl, who discusses these and other BBC GLS materials in her unpublished Heidelberg MA thesis *Hörspiel und Re-education: Zum Hörspielprogramm des German Language Service der BBC im ersten Nachkriegsjahr* (2000). My thanks go to Ms. Kögl for giving me access to the material and to the BBC for permission to quote from it.

42. "Respective Functions of B.B.C. German Service and N.W.D.R. Statement of Policy." BBC WAE E1/757 German Service/Policy. In contrast to the BBC GLS, which "speaks with a British voice," the NWDR, whose function was to be that of a "Home Service" for the British zone of Germany, "must not be too obviously concerned with the reeducation of the audience or even with the raising of its cultural standards" (ibid.). The NWDR, which went on air in 1945, became the prototype of postwar German public radio. The BBC GLS continued to operate until 1999. What has been said about the sluggish beginnings and general haphazardness of British reeducation has to be qualified with regard to radio. With the BBC GLS already established, Britain clearly had the edge over the other occupying powers and in the years to follow played a decisive part in shaping the West German broadcasting system. For a personal account, see Sir Hugh Carleton Greene, *The Third Floor Front: A View of Broadcasting in the Sixties* (London: Bodley Head, 1969). Greene, brother of the novelist Graham Greene, served as head of the BBC GLS from 1940 to 1958 and was highly influential in the restructuring of German radio after the war.

43. While the wartime broadcasts of the BBC GLS are well documented, little has been published about its activities during the early postwar phase. For a general survey, see British Broadcasting Corporation, ed., *"Hier ist England"—"Live aus London": Das deutsche Programm der British Broadcasting Cooperation, 1938–1988* (London: BBC External Services, 1988). Some aspects of the early postwar years are dealt with in Charmian Brinson and Richard Dove, eds., *"Stimme der Wahrheit": German-Language Broadcasting by the BBC* (Amsterdam and New York: Rodopi, 2003).

44. BBC WAC German Service Scripts/Features/June 1945–February 1946.

45. *New York Times*, October 6, 1998, obituary by Ralph Blumenthal.

46. According to the *Daily Telegraph* obituary (October 10, 1998), he "briefly attended the universities of Frankfurt, Vienna, Paris and Munich before studying at the Old Vic dramatic school from 1929 to 1932." These periods must have been brief indeed—spanning, all in all, no more than a year; and Goring, aged sixteen, must have been at least two, if not three years younger than the youngest of his continental fellow students. After playing Romeo to Peggy Ashcroft's Juliet at the Old Vic in 1932, he toured France and the Low Countries with Jacques Copeau's *Compagnie*

des Quinze, playing Hamlet and other roles in French. After the war he and his wife, Lucie Mannheim, toured the British zone of Germany, performing in German. Mannheim, a former principal actress of the Berlin Theater who had escaped from the Nazis and continued her career in Britain, heads the cast list of the BBC *Shakespeare Feature.*

47. Werner Habicht, one of the BBC German Service's regular listeners at the time, recalled to the author that at some point after the war Richardson dropped his alias and revealed his true name.

48. All translations from Goring's script, which is in German, are my own.

49. The most "scientific" exposition of these principles was proffered by the American psychiatrist Richard M. Brickner. In a book entitled *Is Germany Incurable?* (Philadelphia: Lippincott, 1943), to which Margaret Mead contributed a preface, Brickner diagnosed Germany's problem as one of collective paranoia, "as grim an ill as mind is heir to" (30). Just as with an individual paranoia patient, he argued, therapy had to be directed at those "clear areas" that the disease had left unaffected. Goring treats his German radio audience as precisely such a "clear area," although his approach was probably informed by the more traditional, diplomatic thinking of the British Foreign Office. For the contributions of Brickner, Mead, Talcott Parsons, and other prominent social scientists to the planning of the US reeducation program, see Uta Gerhardt, "A Hidden Agenda of Recovery: The Psychiatric Conceptualization of Re-education for Germany in the United States during World War II," *German History* 14 (1996): 297–324.

50. Or "spirit," or "soul"; the notoriously multifaceted German word here is *Geist.*

51. Of which there were actually—contrary to a popular misconception—very few. See Drewniak, *Das Theater im NS-Staat,* 250–51; Hortmann, *Shakespeare on the German Stage,* 134–36.

52. See above, note 30.

53. P. Taylor, *The Projection of Britain,* 119–20.

54. Ibid.

55. Martin J. Wiener, *English Culture and the Decline of the Industrial Spirit, 1850–1980* (Cambridge: Cambridge University Press, 1981), 5.

56. Public Records Office, Foreign Office 898/413, Political Warfare Executive: "The Projection of Britain," August 17, 1942. It is a telling coincidence that the magazine *Der Monat,* in an article by Hilde Spiel (12 [1949]: 87), should make so much of the fact that the dramatist Christopher Fry, who is characterized as "typically English," resides in an old cottage in the Cotswolds. In the late forties, Fry was sometimes hailed as a new Shakespeare.

57. Gary Taylor, "The Heaven of Invention" (review of Michael Wood's BBC documentary *In Search of Shakespeare*), *Independent,* July 12, 2003.

58. The logic of this process is the subject of Max Horkheimer and Theodor W. Adorno, *Dialectic of Enlightenment,* trans. John Cumming (orig. 1944; New York: Continuum, 1976).

59. The famous monologue is cited here in nineteenth-century spelling. In modern spelling, it is "Sein oder Nichtsein."

60. A. O. Lovejoy, "The Meaning of Romanticism for the Historian of Ideas," *Journal for the History of Ideas* 2 (1941): 257–78; Leo Spitzer, "Geistesgeschichte vs. History of Ideas as Applied to Hitlerism," *JHI* 5 (1944): 191–203.

61. The debate over Heidegger's complicity with Nazism, and the extent to which this was not just a question of personal opportunism, but also compromises his philosophy, was reignited by the publication of Victor Farias's *Heidegger et le nazisme*

(Lagrasse: Verdier, 1987). By then the acknowledged forerunner of French poststructuralism, Heidegger was defended by, among others, Jacques Derrida and Jean-François Lyotard, *Heidegger et "les juifs"* (Paris: Galilée, 1988), and, most vehemently, Philippe Lacoue-Labarthe, *La fiction du politique* (Paris: Bourgeois, 1988). For a survey of the debate, see Richard Wolin, ed., *The Heidegger Controversy: A Critical Reader* (Cambridge: MIT Press, 1993).

62. Captured by British troops near Lüneburg on May 23, 1945, he poisoned himself when his identity was discovered.

63. This was pointed out by Geoffrey Hartman in his 1993 keynote address to the German Shakespeare Society in Weimar: "Poesie und Einfühlungskraft: Shakespeare und die ethische Frage," *Shakespeare Jahrbuch* (1994): 23.

64. See, for example, PRO/FO 1056/7, the minutes of a meeting of the Select Book Committee held on January 17, 1946. "Guilt mobilization," which the Americans attempted for a short while, was never part of the British reeducation agenda. On the contrary, anything confronting the Germans with their moral failings was considered detrimental to the cause of winning them over to democracy.

65. Antony Easthope, *Englishness and National Culture* (London: Routledge, 1999). As a German of the postwar generation and thus a beneficiary of the Allied reeducation effort, I find it hard to agree with Easthope's sweeping condemnation of a tradition that did, after all, lay the foundation for a democratic civil society in my country.

66. Cf. notes 23 and 24 above.

67. E. M. W. Tillyard's *The Elizabethan World Picture* appeared in 1943 (London: Chatto & Windus), his *Shakespeare's History Plays* (London: Chatto & Windus) in 1944; Hugh Grady, "Instituting Shakespeare: Hegemony and Tillyard's Historical Criticism," in *Assays: Critical Approaches to Medieval and Renaissance Texts,* ed. Peggy A. Knapp (Pittsburgh: University of Pittsburgh Press, 1989), 5:51.

68. David Gervais, *Literary Englands: Versions of "Englishness" in Modern Writing* (Cambridge: Cambridge University Press, 1994), 141.

69. The contract, it should be understood, was not offered out of disinterested sympathy but under the threat—part real, part illusory—of Soviet expansionism. So-called "postrevisionist" historians have tended to substantiate the reality of that threat against the view that it was nothing but a figment of McCarthyite paranoia. For an assessment of recent scholarship, see John Lewis Gaddis, *We Now Know: Rethinking Cold War History* (Oxford: Oxford University Press, 1997). Cf. also Anne Deighton, *The Impossible Peace.*

70. Paul Fussell ("Thornton Wilder and the German Psyche," *Nation,* 1958) castigated the (West) "German canonization of Wilder" as an aberration of the "German psyche . . . which, after wallowing from 1933 until 1945 in brute political realities, now hankers as violently after the spiritual, the disembodied, and the ideal" (395). The point Fussell's critique misses is that the craze for Wilder is much more symptomatic of continuity than of a radical break with the past. Withdrawal into a supposedly apolitical realm of idealist spirituality was precisely the escape route taken by many intellectuals between 1933 and 1945—a strategy that became known as *Innere Emigration* (inner emigration). For a contemporary rejoinder to Fussell, see Horst Frenz, "American Playwrights and the German Psyche," *Die Neueren Sprachen* (1961): 170–78.

71. Goring himself cites the reactions to the program in the introduction to his second Shakespeare feature, a radio adaptation of *Macbeth* broadcast on October 6, 1945. English listeners, he reports, complained that he had not emphasized Shakespeare's Englishness ("das rein englische [!] an Shakespeare") enough, while German

listeners said he had overemphasized it. This interesting passage—like most of the first page of the script—is crossed out, so presumably it was not actually used in the broadcast.

72. Ernst Theodor Sehrt, *Vergebung und Gnade bei Shakespeare* (Stuttgart: K. F. Koehler, 1952), 256. Sehrt's brand of *Geistesgeschichte,* though typical of the intellectual climate of the 1950s, did not become the leading paradigm of German Shakespeare studies. That role fell to the kind of New Critical close reading exemplified by Wolfgang Clemen's *The Development of Shakespeare's Imagery* (London: Methuen, 1951). Clemen's study received high praise in what could be described as the "handbook" of the New Criticism, Wellek and Warren's *Theory of Literature* (New York: Harcourt & Brace, 1949), 217, which was widely read and taught in Germany.

73. Salman Rushdie, *The Satanic Verses* (Dover, DE: Consortium, 1992), 8.

74. I would like to thank Werner Habicht, Ruth von Ledebur, and Mr. Jeff Walden of the BBC Written Archives Centre, Reading, for their advice, and, once again, Martina Kögl, for drawing my attention to the unpublished material discussed in this essay.

IV
Translating Politics, Politicizing Translation

Introduction
Rui Carvalho Homem

THE FAVOR CURRENTLY ENJOYED BY TRANSLATION CAN HARDLY BE dissociated from the politics of critical inquiry that have prevailed in the humanities in recent years. Indeed, translation's multivalent status as a textual practice that has become an object of study in its own right, as much as a master metaphor for a range of relational processes, has made it ever more central to a context informed by poststructuralist modes of reading. Further, its traditional representation as secondary writing, and hence its conventional demotion to the periphery of literary creation, have made it attractive, as an enlightening analogy, to the discourses on the oppressed and the subaltern fostered by gender studies and postcolonial criticism. Translation has been claimed by cultural theorists as a model for all intercultural relations, its scope described as coterminous with the "in-between" space said to define culture itself. The discipline (or rather, "interdiscipline") of translation studies has been one of the immediate beneficiaries of the exploding of the self-contained study of national literatures, a task undertaken and largely effected by comparative literature. Likewise, it has derived considerable critical capital from the erosion of the literary canon, especially in view of its querying of a sense of the "original" and of clear-cut distinctions between the "creative" and the "derivative."[1]

Current critical mores and their ensuing politics have thus promoted translation to the center of a context of inquiry that itself has proved overwhelmingly concerned with politics, with issues of power. This is in fact aptly suggested by the title of this section: "translating politics" can certainly be glossed as "the politics of translation," but it can equally mean the process of producing a discourse on politics that will render its dynamics and workings clearer to all those intent on "reading" politics; and "politicizing translation" can be both an acknowledgment of translation's proneness to being politicized and a vindication of its power to highlight the political implications of texts as much as their circumstances.

For reasons that one feels tempted to construe as neatly symmetrical to the rising favor of translation, as delineated above, Shakespeare has become a fundamental proving ground for critical strategies intent on tackling the "center of the canon" (Harold Bloom, ipse dixit) in order to activate previously suppressed significations.[2] By relating Shakespeare to a range of other texts (verbal or otherwise), such strategies highlight the relations and "circulations" that make up the dynamics of change in early modern culture.[3] This certainly includes reading Shakespeare from a variety of standpoints defined by an attention to gender, ethnicity, and geography; retrieving otherwise forgotten texts onto a platform of sharp critical attention; and giving salience to the ways in which the Shakespearean text itself thrives on appropriation, rewriting, and translation of its vast array of sources. It likewise involves giving unparalleled attention to the many contexts, forms, and media in which Shakespeare has been received and appropriated in his already long and disseminated afterlife. The considerable number of publications and initiatives of recent years that pluralize the name of the bard (*"Shakespeares"*) in their title is indeed one of the most immediate manifestations of the favor currently enjoyed by the study of his complex lineage, the multifarious ascent and descent of his texts.

The articles included in this section certainly belong within this critical context, variously addressing the panorama of the relations—textual, historical, political, semiotic—that are prompted or enabled by Shakespeare's texts. Dirk Delabastita's article on "Anthologies, Translations, and European Identities" indeed offers an overall characterization of that panorama, in the variety of geographic and cultural spaces it covers. This variety is visually expounded through the article's accompanying diagram, which helps readers better recognize the disparate domains into which Shakespeare's afterlife can be analyzed. But this is not underscored by a totalizing design: in fact, Delabastita's apparent search for a "uniform pattern" that could be a basis for a "common European Shakespeare" is ultimately a rhetorical gesture that allows him to argue the elusiveness of such a pattern. This is followed and confirmed by Delabastita's critique of the possibility, sometimes postulated rather than proved, of defining a common Europeanness on the basis of a transnational canon of "luminaries"—a literary pantheon of figures such as "Aristotle, Dante, Cervantes or indeed Shakespeare." The point of view from which Delabastita launches his inquiry, based on close consideration of the implications to be derived from the present volume's title, is indeed broader than the literary, concerning rather "the identity-building and nation-building that takes place specifically on the European scale." But his study is especially alert to "the correlation between the rise of nationalisms in Europe and the development of Europe's various national literary canons," as much as between the rise of nationalism and the rise of philology.

This is an important connection with Michael Cronin's contribution on "Shakespeare, Translation, and Identity," focusing as it does on the connection between language and power in the early modern period. Cronin highlights the cultural and political resonance of the Renaissance belief in eloquence and in the transformative power wielded by the word as regards the world, as well as the affinities between this and the general "effervescence" of literature, philology and translation in sixteenth- and seventeenth-century England. This is then articulated with the role played by language in the expansionist dimension of English power in that age, Cronin's dominant focal space in this regard being the British Isles—"the practices of translation and interpreting in sixteenth- and early seventeenth-century England and Ireland and their role in the political and military conflicts opposing the two islands in the period." Cronin is especially alert to the fact that, parallel to England's territorial expansion, Shakespeare was extending the scope of the English language, and this allows him to emphasize "the crucial connection between translation, eloquence, and empire in Shakespeare's drama." The dramatist was hardly unaware of the extent to which language skills are imbricated with notions of political loyalty and deviance. And Cronin's inquiry combines an attention to the real-time enactment of duplicity as embodied in interpreters on the scene of power, with the ex post facto political validation provided by texts that are dislocated for the sake of endowing their new contexts with a legitimizing narrative: "the forging of a new national identity implies the forgery of translation, the reading of the translation as if it was the original."

Whether "art [needs] a nation" is the query raised at the very end of Dominique Goy-Blanquet's contribution. Her article largely centers on the vast process of reception and translation that characterizes textual production in Shakespeare's age, and especially the extent to which that includes numerous instances of "covert translation." She also highlights the reservations that an austere Protestant ethics causes to emerge in Elizabethan commentary as regards foreign influence in the domains of the arts, letters, and manners, and combines a general assessment of such intellectual attitudes with a discussion of specific instances of texts appropriated into Elizabethan English, identifying and detailing some of the strategies that can be discerned behind the constitution of those textual debts.

An attention to the specifics of translation is also a feature of the other two articles in this section, otherwise markedly distinct in their respective objects and approaches. Ángel-Luis Pujante and Keith Gregor offer a contribution to the study of Shakespeare's reception in the form of a disquisition on a segment of *Hamlet*'s Spanish afterlife. As Pujante and Gregor duly explain, the four translations of *Hamlet* considered here were not based directly upon Shakespeare's text, but upon Ducis's epoch-making French version (like many translations into other European languages, in fact). These four Spanish *Hamlets* are read against a background of historico-political upheaval in eighteenth- and early nineteenth-century Spain. However, Pujante and Gregor offer no linear cause-and-effect relationship between context and text: on the contrary, their conclusions are based on an attentive assessment of the political contradictions evinced by their textual objects when considered in their respective circumstances.

Karen Bennett also examines a particular translation of Shakespeare—only in this case the rendering is not interlingual, but rather intersemiotic, since it is a ballet score, Prokofiev's *Romeo and Juliet.* Bennett reads the composer's piece against a backdrop dominated by the expectations regarding art and literature that were proper to socialist realism in the Soviet Union of the 1930s, and she delineates the case for and against an understanding of Prokofiev's re-creation of Shakespeare's love tragedy as conforming to those expectations. A significant aspect of Bennett's contribution is the fact that her study is grounded not only on a literary-dramatic consideration of structural differences between Shakespeare's play and Prokofiev's reworking of the dramatist's plot, but also on the score's internal evidence for the composer's strategies, from the perspective of musical analysis. No clear-cut conclusion can be reached regarding Prokofiev's positioning vis-à-vis the ideological struggles of his day, but the combination of approaches and methodologies that characterizes this article allows some of the complexities of this intersemiotic rendering to emerge vividly.

Together, the five pieces collected in this section combine a common purpose—to shed some light on the intersections of translation and politics with regard to the work of Shakespeare—with the variety of approaches briefly suggested in these introductory lines. And that combination forcefully argues the case for translation as a fundamental dimension of the volume's overall theme and scope.

Notes

1. Cf. Lawrence Venuti, ed., *Translation and Minority,* special issue of *The Translator* 4.2 (Manchester: St. Jerome, 1998); Sherry Simon, *Gender in Translation: Cul-*

tural Identity and the Politics of Transmission (London: Routledge, 1996); Susan Bassnett and Harish Trivedi, eds., *Post-colonial Translation: Theory and Practice* (London: Routledge, 1999); Homi K. Bhabha, *The Location of Culture* (London: Routledge, 1994), 38–39; Wolfgang Iser, "On Translatability: Variables of Interpretation," *European English Messenger* 4.1 (Spring 1995): 30–38; Mary Snell Hornby et al., eds., *Translation Studies: An Interdiscipline* (Amsterdam: John Benjamins, 1994); Theo Hermans, ed., "Introduction: Translation Studies and a New Paradigm," in *The Manipulation of Literature: Studies in Literary Translation* (London: Croom Helm, 1985), 7–15.

2. The phrase is famously employed in Harold Bloom, *The Western Canon* (1994; London: Macmillan, 1995), 45.

3. These have broadly been characteristic strategies of the so-called "new contextualisms" that from their "alternative" beginnings two decades ago have become mainstream in Shakespeare studies. For the phrase "new contextualisms," I am indebted to Howard Felperin, *The Uses of the Canon: Elizabethan Literature and Contemporary Theory* (Oxford: Clarendon, 1990). Relevant references from (American) New Historicism and (British) cultural materialism would be legion, but one may be historically justified in citing the following: John Drakakis, ed., *Alternative Shakespeares* (London and New York: Routledge, 1985); Stephen Greenblatt, *Shakespearean Negotiations: The Circulation of Social Energy in Renaissance England* (Oxford: Clarendon, 1988); Terence Hawkes, ed., *Alternative Shakespeares,* vol. 2 (London: Routledge, 1996).

Translating Europe into Your England
Dominique Goy-Blanquet

WHEN PRINCESS KATHERINE TELLS HENRY V, "YOUR MAJESTY SHALL mock at me. I cannot speak your England," she has in fact already begun to practice the invader's idiom. Her decision to learn English shows quite extraordinary foresight, as well as a practical turn of mind: she takes her first lesson before the battle has even started, and it is a battle that everyone else in France believes will be won. Henry's courtship, a plain soldier's as he likes to call it, turns French "courtoisie" into an all-conquering war machine, and a French princess into "the better Englishwoman." But she is not so easily fooled: "the tongues of men are full of deceits," Shakespeare warns us in three different languages.[1] The poet shows amazing intuition in these scenes, or fine historical knowledge. At a time when all aristocratic England still spoke French, Henry V was the first monarch to impose the use of English in peace negotiations, a fact that none of Shakespeare's familiar chroniclers cared to mention.

This strange linguistic object "your England" could also be spelled "Eurengland," as in "EURO," to highlight a mode of *translatio* commonly practiced under the Tudors: "Englishing" Europe, absorbing and naturalizing foreign goods so strenuously that their origin gets lost in the process. Many passages drawn from foreign works are unacknowledged as such to this day in their editors' otherwise learned footnotes, for instance, in these few examples: the Petrarchan sonnet inserted by Chaucer into *Troylus and Criseyde;* the fragments of Aristotle's *Poetics* in Sidney's *Apology for Poetrie;* Spenser's *Ruins of Rome,* which critics often fail to identify as a translation of Du Bellay's *Antiquités;* Samuel Daniel's *Delia* and its debt to Maurice Scève; and so on. Some historians even fail to tell their readers that North's *Lives* was translated from Jacques Amyot's version and not directly from Plutarch. How innocent this naturalizing may be, that is the question. Borrowers like Sidney do it naturally, convinced that their readers will recognize the quotations. In several cases, erasure of the sources seems deliberate, when covert translation simply denies debts as if they were slurs on the national genius. Where Shakespeare is concerned, despite his known habits of wide reading and borrowing, the claim to national independence can grow frantic, reaching such heights of amnesia that it creates odd gaps in source studies. *Timeo Danaos et dona ferentes:*[2] to most Anglophone critics, "foreign Shakespeare" remains largely a one-way trade, an appraisal of his gifts to the world at large rather than dubious foreigners' gifts to a trueborn, purebred Englishman.

For beginners interested in basic Eurengland, the best account of its love and war with alien idioms is to be found in the reminiscences of the nineteenth-century critic John A. Symonds. Just before Shakespeare's birth, Symonds writes, "when men of culture turned their attention to the stage, a determined effort was made to impose the canons of classical art, as they were then received in Southern Europe, on our playwrights."[3] England not yet having fashioned her own forms of art, "there was a danger lest invention should be crushed by imitation at the outset."[4] Indeed, affluent young men "visited the South and returned with the arts, accomplishments, and follies of Italian capitals,"[5] and the London bookshops were "flooded with translations of loose Italian novels, to such an extent that Ascham trembled for the morals of his countrymen."[6] Still, Symonds is happy to note, "the core of the nation remained sound and wholesome": "The native genius of the English people, though menaced by these diverse dangers, was so vigorous, the race itself was so isolated and so full of a robust tempestuous vitality, the language was so copious and vivid in its spoken strength, the poetic impulse was so powerful, that all efforts to domesticate alien styles ... ended in the assimilation of congenial and the rejection of repugnant elements."[7] The mention of Roger Ascham at the roots of Eurengland is appropriate. The Elizabethan humanist was one of the earliest supporters of the native idiom. In his dedication of *Toxophilus* (1545) to Henry VIII, he claims he would have found it easier to use Latin or Greek, but he chose to write "this English matter in the English tongue for Englishmen." He probably wrote the work in Latin, though, before translating it into Englishmen's English.[8] *The Scholemaster,* on which Ascham started work in 1563 at the request of Sir Richard Sackville, expresses a general disgust with foreign trash: "Now, let Italian, and Latin itself, Spanishe, French, Douch, and Englishe bring forth their lerning, and recite their Authors, Cicero onelie excepted, and one or two moe in Latin, they be all patched cloutes and ragges, in comparison of faire wouen broade clothes."[9] Having himself briefly visited Italy ten years before, Ascham strongly advises parents against sending their sons there. Venice, "Circe's court," is a nest of vices. As for Rome, it used to be the best breeder of worthy men, but that time is gone, and "though the place remayne, yet the olde and present maners, do differ as farre, as blacke and white, as vertue and vice. Vertue once made that contrie Mistres ouer all the worlde. Vice now maketh that contrie slaue to them." In short, Italy is no longer fit to teach us anything: "For surelie, they will make other but bad Scholers, that be so ill Masters to them selues."

In Symonds's opinion, the best to be said in favor of travel is that these foolish youngsters brought back the sonnet and blank verse to England. Across the Atlantic, at much the same time, the American poet Sidney Lanier (1842–81) supported a very similar view of Eurengland. His posthumously published *Shakspere and His Forerunners* spends four chapters on the Tudor sonnet-makers, drawing a straight line from Chaucer to the "bright-colored, vivacious tongue of Wyatt and Surrey," and wasting just one sentence on their foreign sources: "It is perfectly true that Petrarch made Sonnets a long time before Wyatt and Surrey imported them from Italy: but the moment they commenced to write, the sonnet acquired a new life with its English idiom, and became just as purely an English form as the words with which we enriched our language out of their tongues."[10] To illustrate his point, Lanier borrows Samuel Daniel's image of an English vessel ravaging the French coast, to "take that wealth wherein they gloried most, / And make it ours by such a gallant prey."[11]

Translating Conquerors

Elizabethan translators are justly famed for a wealth of works that are regarded as creations in their own right. Daniel's image of their conquering labors made adepts. Philemon Holland, who won the nickname of "Translator Generall in his age," introduced his translation of Pliny as an endeavor "by all means to triumph now over the Romans in subduing their literature under the dent of the English pen, in requitall of the conquest some time over this Island, atchieved by the edge of their sword."[12] Rather than a wedding of cultures, then, Eurengland was a fight of North against South. To Symonds, "[w]hat rendered the [English] people superior to Italians and Spaniards was the firmness of their moral fibre, the sweetness of their humanity, a more masculine temper, less vitiated instincts and sophisticated intellects . . . They were coarse, but not vicious; pleasure-loving, but not licentious; violent, but not cruel; luxurious, but not effeminate. Machiavelli was a name of loathing to them."[13] Raw energy, alert Protestant curiosity, national interest, popular tastes and entertainments, clean if somewhat brutal customs *versus* decadent Catholic Southerners exhausted by their three centuries' advance in learning and literature. The denouement to this dramatic conflict was a happy one: the native pen triumphed over the courtly muses of Europe. Despite their efforts, Symonds is pleased to write, the English "courtly makers" were unable to stem the tide of popular inclination. A born playwright knew by instinct that "the path of Shakspere and the people was the only path to walk in," and the playgoers chose "the stirring melodrama and varied scenes of the romantic poets" in preference to classical rhetoric.[14]

The fight in its early phases was staged at the Inns of Court, whose well-traveled young bloods were torn between love of the classics and love of the nation. When Ascham embarked on his manifesto, Sackville's son had just presented England with its first tragedy in the native tongue, *Gorboduc,* and two of his fellows were about to produce a fabulous piece of Eurengland, *Jocasta,* originally presented as "[a] Tragedie written in Greeke by *Euripides,* translated and digested into Acte by George Gascoygne and Francis Kinwelmershe of Grayes Inne, and there by them presented, 1566."[15] "Digested" is the operative word, for in actual fact this *Jocasta* is a close rendering of an Italian version of Euripides' *Phoenissae,* published in 1549, by one Lodovico Dolce.[16] And, not being a great scholar himself, Dolce had probably not translated his *Giocasta* from the Greek either, but adapted a Latin version of Euripides' play.[17] The English *Jocasta* enjoyed a measure of success in its time, attested by several reissues during the reign of Elizabeth.[18] Gabriel Harvey praised it in the margin of his own copy as "[a]n excellent Tragedie: full of many discreet, wise and deep considerations," in line with *Gorboduc* and *The Mirror for Magistrates.* It was, most recent critics would argue, the only Greek play available in English under the reign of Elizabeth, a point one would expect to stir some interest but, strangely enough, that is about all they have to say on the subject. For further light, one needs to return to the older generation of scholars.

Dolce's part in *Jocasta* remained unacknowledged for three centuries. The first to point out the debt was the classical scholar John P. Mahaffy in 1879, followed by Symonds in 1884. Mahaffy expressed surprise it should have remained unspotted for so long, despite obvious clues like the intrusion in the English cast of the name *Bailo*—the Venetian word for "pedagogue"—for Antigone's tutor.[19] Dolce's rights having been restored by these learned critics, in 1906 John W. Cunliffe gave the first and only Italian/English edition of the play.[20] But after this short break, Dolce faded away again. When Cunliffe's edition of the *Complete Works of George Gascoigne* was published the following year, it was without his explanatory introduction, notes, or Italian text: all mention of Dolce's part or name had disappeared. The various reprints, down to the 1992 facsimile, all reproduce Gascoigne's original title page, committing Dolce to oblivion. Charles Prouty does not mention him either in his edition of *A Hundreth Sundrie Flowres,* and suppresses *Jocasta,* because he believes it was not part of Gascoigne's original plan to include "the Tragedie translated out of Euripides" in this collection of his earlier works.[21] Even Pigman's 2000 edition, though its endnotes make ample reference to the Italian original, sticks to the 1573 edition and leaves Dolce out of the title pages.[22]

The first responsibility for this persistent obliteration of Dolce goes, of course, to his English translators, who omitted all reference to him as if they had "digested" him along with Euripides. And yet Harvey, for one, was fully aware of their debt, as appears from his handwritten note on "*La Giocasta* d'Euripide, Dolce, et Gascoigno."[23] Dolce as a writer was quite well known to the Elizabethans. His *Didone* inspired the prologue of *Gismond of Salerne,* which was performed at the Inner Temple the year following *Jocasta,* and some of his sonnets were translated by Thomas Lodge.[24] Dolce had studied with Castelvetro at the University of Padua, the birthplace of neoclassical tragedy, where a number of young English aristocrats went to complete their education,[25] and where he often returned from his hometown Venice between his labors for the publisher Giotoli. Dolce's catalog of publications is a full library by itself. An enormously active polygraph, he edited a crowd of famous Italian writers (those whose "loose novels" were also "flooding" the London bookshops), he adapted or translated Homer, Virgil, Horace, Cicero, Ovid, Plautus, Euripides (four plays), and Seneca (all ten tragedies), and he wrote a few plays himself.[26] This was not enough, apparently, to ensure his lasting fame. Cunliffe, recounting how classical and native elements combined to "bring about the emergence of popular tragedy" in England, notes that Dolce "exercised some influence on our early drama" thanks to his *Giocasta,* and considers this to be his best title to even so much attention.[27]

Despite their better knowledge, none of our old scholars has much time for *Jocasta.* They note scattered similarities with Shakespeare, but do not dwell on them. Francis James Child in *Four Old Plays* records one between Bailo's speech to Antigone, "It standes not with the honor of your state . . ." and Laertes' to Ophelia, "Then weigh what loss your honour may sustain."[28] Cunliffe praises Gascoigne for having translated Ariosto's *Suppositi,* but thinks he was less happy in his choice of a tragedy. Mahaffy dismisses *Jocasta* as "a motley and incongruous piece": "Its chief literary interest lies in the loose paraphrase of Eteocles' piece, which appears to have suggested directly to Shakspeare the speech of Hotspur in *1 Henry IV:* 'By heavens, methinks it were an easy leap / To pluck bright honour from the pale-faced moon...'"

"So far as I know," the footnote goes, "this is the only direct contact with, or rather direct obligation to, the Greek tragedy in Shakspeare," and after quoting Gascoigne's corresponding lines, he concludes: "the likeness is but slight, yet it is real."[29]

There is also a likeness, slight but real, in this same speech with *3 Henry VI.* Eteocles' admission that

> If lawe of right may any way be broke,
> "Desire of rule within a climbing brest
> To breake a vow may beare the buckler best"
>
> (2.1.391–93)

is echoed by Edward of York:

> But for a kingdom any oath may be broken.
> I would break a thousand oaths to reign one year.
> (*3 Henry VI,* 1.2.15–16)[30]

T. W. Baldwin spotted but did not explore this similarity: he was not sure that *3 Henry VI* was wholly Shakespeare's work, and he thought that the playwright, whoever he was, got the quotation from Cicero's *De Officiis.*[31] Gascoigne does note in the margin at this point "Tullyes opinion," although Cicero reports it as Caesar's opinion. In Nicolas Grimald's translation of 1556, it goes like this:

> he [Caesar] had alwaies in his mouthe Euripides greke verses of the Phenisians: which I will expresse, as well as I can: perchaunce without their grace, but yet so as the meaning may be conceiued.
>
> > If breach of lawes, a man shall vndertake:
> > He must them boldly breake, for kingdoms sake:
> > In eche thing els, looke you regarde the right.
>
> Hainous was that Eteocles, or rather Euripides: who excepted only this, which was most detestable.[32]

Between Euripides, Cicero, Dolce, or Gascoigne, it is hard to decide where Edward of York's cue found its punch:[33] it is inimitably Shakespearean, and here there is no denying the poet's successful domestication of alien styles. It is harder to understand the general lack of interest for *Jocasta* and *Phoenissae,* which some Elizabethans at least found interesting enough to translate, perform, publish, and read. No piece was more copied or quoted than the *Phoenissae,* claims Mahaffy, along with Erasmus's rendering of *Hecuba,* while Baldwin notes that it was part of Johann Sturm's curriculum in Strasbourg. Between them, Johann Sturm and Erasmus provided models for grammar schools all over Europe: Euripides in various shapes was on most school programs.[34] His extant tragedies were all available in Latin versions,[35] but according to Charles and Michelle Martindale, "if Shakespeare read them he gained little from the experience." However, the Martindales ignore *Henry VI* and, like most critics, they tend to dismiss Euripides on the ground that the Elizabethans much preferred Seneca.[36] In Prouty's opinion, "[t]o Gascoigne and Kinwelmarshe the principal charm of *Giocasta* probably lay in its close resemblance to the ideals of Seneca, with which they were familiar." He goes one step further with this politically incorrect gem: "The carefully etched rhetoric of Seneca possessed a surface glitter that was as joyfully accepted by the Elizabethans as are bright beads sparkling in the sunlight by primitive peoples today."[37]

It is true that the neoclassical school did not greatly admire Euripides. He was apt to introduce comic elements in his plays, and give active parts to lowborn characters, features strongly disapproved of by the Italian theoreticians. Cinthio, for one, thought his works were marred by a natural diction unsuited to the dignity of tragedy, although he was quite tolerant of other irregularities like *intermedii,* and found pedantic arguments to justify violent deaths onstage.[38] To complicate matters further, the text of *Phoenissae* raises more problems than most, inducing doubts as to its integrity.[39] The arguments for or against interpolations and multiple authorship are very similar to those touching the Shakespeare canon, and they are likewise often based on views of what is "right" or "wrong" in dramatic composition. A recent French translator of *Phoenissae* complains that it suffers from an excess of characters, and of dead bodies: too many people run around and too many things happen, while its inconclusive ending makes it "a mongrel play."[40]

Symonds has no quarrel with Euripides, quite the reverse. Predictably enough, it is the "Senecasters" who are to him the source of all evil: "Applying rules of Aristotle and Horace, travestying Sophocles and Euripides, copying the worst faults of Seneca, patching, boggling, rehandling, misconceiving ... they produced the dreariest *caput mortuum* of unintelligent industry which it is the melancholy duty of historians to chronicle."[41] The classical models adopted by the English "courtly makers" belonged to a decadent period of art, Neronian Rome, viewed through the prism of the no less corrupt society of sixteenth-century Italy, which shared similar tastes, and therefore must be condemned as "pernicious models for incipient literature." As to Gascoigne, who followed Dolce, he "must be denied the originality of having adapted a tragedy from the Greek." The sad truth is that "like the rest of the classical drama of the period, *Jocasta* had an Italian derivation."[42] Having crushed classicism with his pithy demonstration, Symonds abandons *Jocasta* without further analysis.

Cunliffe, who holds similar, if less virulent, views, further explains the rapid decline of Cinquecento tragedy by the fact that "it was always either court tragedy or closet tragedy—never a national form of art, for there was no Italian nation to appeal to, and it was never popular." It succeeded and failed with the English neoclassicists for the same reason: "The very fact that Senecan tragedy was not a truly national drama gave it greater universality of appeal, and its strongly marked characteristics made it easier to imitate, even if those characteristics were defects and exaggerations."[43] T. S. Eliot alone takes the opposite view—he has to be contrary: "When all reserves have been made, there is still much to be said for Seneca as a dramatist," so he blames it all on the Italians. Take blood and corpses, for instance, they are not so much Senecan as Italian: "The French drama is from the beginning restrained and decorous . . . The Italian is bloodthirsty in the extreme."[44] Cunliffe's work on Senecan trends earns praise in typical Eliot manner: it is the most useful of all books, within its limits. Eliot mentions *Jocasta* twice, but does not discuss it, and once refers to *3 Henry VI*, or rather the *True Tragedy of Richard Duke of York*, only to note the deep influence of Seneca on its language.

Theban Dames

Cunliffe's bilingual edition of *Jocasta* is a rare jewel. As the editor writes with legitimate pride, "the closeness with which the English translators stuck to their Italian text (except in the choruses) is made clear for the first time in the parallel text and notes following. The translators of Dolce, it will be seen, added practically nothing to their original."[45] The translators certainly owe little, if anything, directly to *Phoenissae*. Euripides' plot emulates *The Seven Against Thebes,* with some helpings of Sophocles' *Antigone* and *Oedipus at Colonus*. A good deal is his own invention, like the sacrifice of Creon's son, Meneceus, which saves the town from destruction but does not prevent the final massacre. Euripides shows no more reverence than Shakespeare for his predecessors. Instead of listening to the catalog of leaders made famous by Aeschylus, Eteocles declares this would be a waste of time, with the enemy at the gate: he works with his arm, not his tongue. The brothers' fatal struggle for power is both the result of their father's curse and of Ares' anger against the distant ancestor of the Thebans, Cadmos. It takes place under the eyes of a helpless Jocasta who, against tradition, has survived the revelation of her incest and begs in vain for peace. The play is overcast by the shadow of Oedipus, an "airy ghost" (*aitherophanes*) in the background, who enters after the fight to hear the report of his wife's and sons' deaths, to be sentenced to exile, and to leave under the guidance of Antigone.

Dolce divided the play into acts, cut all references to Cadmos and the vengeance of Ares, otherwise keeping to its main design, and added approximately a thousand lines to the Greek original. He also added several anonymous characters (Servo, Sacerdote—identified by their function like the former *Paidagógos,* Bailo), gave a name (Manto) to the mute daughter of Tiresias, turned the Greek gods into Latin ones, and the chorus of foreign visitors into "Donne Tebane" (with a more passionate concern for their homeland than Euripides' Phoenicians), all of whom found their way into the cast of Gascoigne and Kinwelmersh. Jocasta's original soliloquy on the history of her cursed family is reshaped into a dialogue between the Queen and the faithful Servo—Dolce's main concession to the demands of neoclassical theoreticians—and here too he is followed by the English team. The other major alteration is to the character of Creon, who has intermittent fits of tyranny: he rejoices when the death of his son leaves the way to the throne open for him, then sheds heartrending tears a few pages later, when Dolce returns to Euripides.[46]

The only Greek touch present in the English text but not in Dolce is the names of the Theban gates, specified many times in the stage directions, but not at places where Euripides mentions them, which means the English translators probably found the information elsewhere and used it for a touch of local color. Otherwise they stuck to Dolce's plot quite faithfully, adopted all his innovations, and added in turn an opening argument (done by Gascoigne), an epilogue (by Christopher Yelverton), and dumb shows before every act. Gascoigne translated acts 2, 3, and 5, Kinwelmersh acts 1 and 4, with only occasional misunderstandings. One of their so-called mistakes, the rendering of "L'equità" by "Equalitie," is due in fact to Cunliffe's having selected the wrong edition of the source text. The translators used the original 1549 edition, which actually has "Egualità" (in conformity with Euripides, where Jocasta advocates equality between the brothers).⁴⁷ The additions to the choruses pointed by Cunliffe are expansions: same matter, with more words.

Jocasta was performed on a scaffold, as *Gorboduc* had been.⁴⁸ Perhaps its authors aimed to outdo this precedent with more mute characters, more musical instruments, still more elaborate dumb shows, marches, and processions. After the first dialogue, the chorus *"take their place, where they continue to the end of the tragedie,"* keeping the action continuous. If the stage directions do describe what was shown, it must have been a memorable evening. The play began by "a dolefull and straunge noyse of violles, cythren, bandurion, and such like," after which "there came in uppon the stage a king with an imperial crown upon his head, . . . sitting in a chariote very richly furnished, drawne in by foure kinges in their dublettes and hosen, with crownes also upon their heades," probably the model of Tamburlaine's. The second dumb show was striking enough to have lent notes not only for the emblem of civil war in *3 Henry VI* ("*Enter a Sonne that hath kill'd his Father, at one doore: and a Father that hath kill'd his Sonne at another doore*"), but also for Ophelia's burial in *Hamlet:* accompanied by "a very dolefull noise of flutes," "there came in uppon the stage two coffins covered with hearclothes," attended by sixteen mourners, "and after they had caried the coffins about the stage, there opened and appeared a grave, wherin they buried the coffins, and put fire to them, but the flames did sever and parte in twaine, signifying discord by the history of two brethren . . . After the funerals were ended and the fire consumed, the grave was closed up again . . ." This striking visual image perfectly illustrates the transfers from antiquity to the gorgeous spectacles for which the gentlemen of Gray's Inn were renowned. In Euripides, the priests use more conventional devices to foretell the outcome of the battle: slaughtering sheep and observing the bent of the sacrificial flame, all of which are reported to Jocasta by a messenger rather than shown. From this report, Dolce drew the sacrifice performed onstage in act 3, scene 1, "la fiamma di color diversi," foretelling murderous division, which in turn inspired the all-consuming grave of the English dumb show.

Alliterative Fireworks

These theatrical delights were further enhanced by a fine display of alliterative fireworks, mostly in the parts that Gascoigne translated. For example:

> . . . this minde of mine
> Doth fleete full farre from that farfetch of his . . .

(2.1.356–57)

> That, as the tracke of trustlesse time hath taught . . .
>
> (2.1.398)

Along with the dumb shows, the verse technique entails the most significant departures from the Italian source. Where Dolce alternates *settenai* and *endecasillabi* to interpret the varying meters of Euripides, the English team alternate blank verse and rhyme royal, but keep a rigidly regular pentameter, even when it means elongating Dolce's heptasyllabic lines to decasyllabic ones. Compare the duet of mother and daughter, for instance:

> Figliuola, i tuoi fratelli,
> Sangue del sangue mio
>
> (4.2.13–14)

> O, deare daughter, thy most unhappie brethren,
> That sometimes lodgde within these wretched loynes
>
> (4.2.12–13),

or the following lines:

> Ma che potremo noi,
> Voi debol vecchia, et io
> Impotente fanciulla?
>
> (4.2.47–49)

> But what shall we be able for to doe—
> You a weake old woman forworne with yeares
> And I, God knows, a silly simple mayde?
>
> (4.2.36–38)

The demands of the pentameter often lead the translators very far from the naturalness of Dolce's (and Euripides') diction:

> Padre io debbo morir, non voi.
>
> (3.2.63)

> I father ought, so ought not you, to die.
>
> (3.2.64)

The need to fill in the line is met with various padding devices of the "God wot" kind, or doubled vocatives, "Beholde, O queene, beholde, O worthie queene." Where Dolce uses run-on lines boldly and often successfully, the team of translators seldom allow themselves this facility, thus accentuating the monotony of the beat.

In his later "Notes of Instruction,"⁴⁹ an account of English versification, Gascoigne advises the poet to "holde the same measure wherwith you begin, whether it be in a verse of six syllables, eight, ten, twelve, &c.," and defends his own prosodic choices, alliterative tastes, and rhythmical uniformity. But he does not discuss blank verse, the one feature that elicits praise from Symonds: if blank verse must be saluted as the foreigners' best gift, "dramatic blank verse was certainly the discovery of Norton, Sackville, Hughes, and Gascoigne."⁵⁰ Well, yes and no. The Italian playwrights had established *endecasillabi sciolti*, unrhymed verse, on the tragic stage since 1515, with Trissino's *Sofonisba*.⁵¹ Dolce simply followed their lead, using blank verse for the dialogues of *Giocasta*, and rhymed couplets for the chorus, and the English team followed Dolce: blank verse in the dialogue, couplets or rhyme royal for the chorus. The Italians were also pioneers in the use of *intermedii*, which Cinzio and Dolce defended against the purists as moments of recreation for the spectators, while admitting there was no classical authority for them.⁵² "There can be little doubt," Cunliffe recognizes, "that we owe to the Italian *intermedii* the English dumb shows, which are of the same general character and serve the same purpose."⁵³ Gascoigne must have had some knowledge of Italian stage practices because in the third dumb show, he uses the story of Curtius, one of the stock figures of Italian *intermedii*.⁵⁴

What John Symonds likes to interpret as "native woodnotes wild" has in all cases really a distant Euripidean (or "Euritalian") background. *Jocasta* innovates in other fruitful directions, all distinctly Euripidean, which Symonds fails to mention. As Eteocles points out:

>If what to some seemes honest, good, and just,
>Could seeme even so in every doubtfull mind,
>No dark debate nor quarrel could arise:
>But looke! How many men so many mindes,
>And that, that one man judgeth good and just,
>Some other deemes as deeply to be wrong,⁵⁵

multiple viewpoints are the very matter of the play's agon, and the play in all three versions offers a good show of it with abundant use of stichomythia, which makes its first entrance here on the English stage. There is nothing in the ponderous exchanges of *Gorboduc* to compare with the slanging match between brothers:

>*Po.* O holy temples of the heavenly gods.
>*Ete.* That for thy wicked deedes do hate thy name
>*Po.* Out of my kingdome am I driven by force.
>*Ete.* Out of the which thou camst me for to drive.

> *Po.* Punish, O gods, this wicked tyrant here.
> *Ete.* Pray to the gods in Greece and not in Thebes.
> *Po.* No savage beast so cruell nor unjust.
> *Ete.* Not cruel to my countrie like to thee.
> *Po.* Since from my right I am with wrong deprived.
> *Ete.* Eke from thy life, if long thou tarie here
>
> (2.1.554–63)

or with Antigone's moving plea for equity against state law, or with Creon's dispute with Tiresias about divine justice:

> *Cre.* Unjust is he condemnes the innocent.
> *Tyr.* A fole is he accuseth heavens above.
>
> (3.1.213–14)

Nor does *Jocasta* lend itself to the kind of overt didacticism found in *Gorboduc*. True, we do hear some traditional lessons on the versatility of fortune, evil ambition, vain royal pomp, and civic duties, but these are challenged by less orthodox notes. Thus, the characters' sufferings are not the deserved punishment for misdeeds, as they tend to be in the so-called Elizabethan tragedies. There is much ground for Antigone's complaint at the end that "Justice lyes on sleepe": ill stars and harsh, possibly malevolent gods, loom above, while Jocasta shows a clearer understanding of hamartia than most Elizabethan characters outside Shakespeare:

> So deeply faulteth none, the which unwares
> Doth fall into the crime he can not shunne.
>
> (1.1.134–35)

Many features of the original *Phoenissae*, the very ones that lay it open to censorious criticism, made it intractable to Senecan reduction: its episodic structure, wealth of incidents, open conclusion, lack of a central hero, numerous characters, and distinct skepticism. Gabriel Harvey aptly defined it as *"Quasi Synopsis Tragoediarum Omnium,"* a summary of all tragedies. If Shakespeare had access in his youth to half a dozen English tragedies at best, then this would have been the one closest to his leanings. *Jocasta* may or may not have played a decisive part in the orientation of the Elizabethan stage, it does have many elements that Shakespeare was to cultivate and refine in his histories, most prominently in *3 Henry VI:* fatal curses, revenge, ghosts, and stichomythia (all of these were Greek before they turned Senecan), oath breaking, prophecies and soothsayers, and strong feminine figures (Jocasta, like Queen Margaret, survives her husband's fall). The servant's speech on "[t]he glittering mace, the pompe of swarming traine" paid for by heavy cares anticipates Shakespeare's sleepless kings. Creon and his son competing to die for their country herald the Talbots. The other characters express equally patriotic feelings: they love the common weal, resent the violation of their homeland by foreign troops, and cannot bear to live in exile. Blood-drawing scenes alternate with tear-drawing scenes, as the protagonists move from violent anger to violent sorrow. The fratricidal war induces symmetries of construction, duels, normative images of a cosmos ruled by the regular division of day and night, the same lost world evoked by Henry VI's nostalgic dream of harmony in the midst of battle.[56]

Gascoigne clearly advertised his early practice of Eurengland in the 1573 reedition, under the title *A Hundreth Sundrie Flowres,* of works "Gathered partely by Translation in the fyne outlandish Gardins of Euripides, Ovid, Petrarke, Ariosto, and others, and partly by invention out of our owne fruitfull orchardes in England." But the poet ended by repudiating his youthful flirtation with foreign styles, symbolized by the monstrous figures shown in his verse satire *The Steele Glass* (1576):

> What be they? women? masking in men's weeds?
> With Dutchkin doublets, and with jerkins jagg'd?
> With Spanish spangs, and ruffs fet out of France,
> With high-copp'd hats, and feathers flaunt-a-flaunt?
>
> (ll. 1160–63)

In another one of Gascoigne's late works, his essay on prosody, Chaucer is his reference, not the Latin poets. He recommends avoiding polysyllables in verse, for many reasons: "first the most aunciient English wordes are of one sillable, so that the more monasyllables that you use, the truer Englishman you shall seeme, and the lesse you shall smell of the Inkehorne."[57]

The aging Shakespeare went the opposite way. True, *Cymbeline,* written in the late autumn of his career, offers with Iachimo a suitably villainous Italian to popular prejudice, but the play ends up owning Shakespeare's debt to ancient Rome when the protagonist freely agrees to pay Rome his "wonted tribute" (*Cymbeline,* 5.5.463). To be sure, this was a far more subtle diplomacy than Philemon Holland's triumphant war with Latin roots. Our old scholars in their archaeological quest put their knowledge of foreign idioms to a nationalistic cause. They followed the path of Gascoigne's reformed xenophobia and turned a blind eye on Shakespeare's link with the decadent South, which more recent critics, lacking their erudition, have buried altogether. As a joint creation of Renaissance England and Europe, Shakespeare is the best incitement to brush up Eurengland and address this central issue: does art, more especially poetry, need a nation?

NOTES

1. *King Henry V,* 5.2.102–3, 3.4.1–5, 5.2.115–20. All references to Shakespeare's plays are to the Arden Shakespeare, 3rd series.
2. Virgil, *Aeneid,* book 2, 49 ("I distrust the Greeks, even when they are generous"—the reference is to the Trojan horse).
3. John A. Symonds, *Shakespere's Predecessors in the English Drama* (London: Smith, Elder, 1884), 212.
4. Ibid., 4.
5. Ibid., 34.
6. Ibid., 216 and n. Symonds refers to John E. B. Mayor's edition of Ascham's *Schoolmaster* (S.l.: Bell, 1863).
7. Symonds, 4–5.
8. Like More and other humanists, Ascham was an adept of double translation, which held a large place in the influential educational program of Johann Sturm of Strasbourg. See T. W. Baldwin, *William Shakspere's Small Latine and Lesse Greeke,* 2 vols. (Urbana: University of Illinois Press, 1944).
9. Roger Ascham, *The Scholemaster,* London 1570, facsimile (Amsterdam: Theatrum Orbis Terrarum; New York: Da Capo Press, 1968), 17vo.
10. Sidney Lanier, *Shakspere and His Forerunners: Studies in Elizabethan Poetry and its Development from Early English,* 2 vols. (New York: Doubleday, 1902), 1:166–68.
11. Ibid., 224. Daniel's poem goes on less aggressively to stress mutual interest in "The glory of the worke, that we may boast / Much to have wonne, and others nothing lost," since the treasure is made "by thy taking greater than before."
12. Philemon Holland, preface to *The Historie of the World, commonly called, the Naturall Historie of C. Plinius Secundus* (London: Adam Islip, 1601).
13. Symonds, *Shakespere's Predecessors,* 33.
14. Ibid., 223, 244.
15. *Supposes; and Jocasta: Two plays translated from the Italian the first by Geo. Gascoigne, the second by Geo. Gascoigne and F. Kinwelmersh,* ed. John W. Cunliffe (Boston: D. C. Heath, 1906).
16. *Giocasta,* tragedia di M. Lodovico Dolce (Vinegia: Figliuoli d'Aldo, Aldi filii, 1549). On Dolce's considerable production, see Ronnie H. Terpening, *Lodovico Dolce: Renaissance Man of Letters* (Toronto: University of Toronto Press, 1997).
17. Cunliffe thinks he used the Latin translation of Rudolf Ambühl (Dorotheus Camillus), published at Basel in 1541 by Robert Winter, on the evidence of one misspelling common to both this Latin version and Dolce's rendering. Critics like Emanuele Antonio Cigogna, Cunliffe, or more recently Terpening (*Lodovico Dolce,* 93) actually think that Dolce had little or no Greek, and note many serious departures from the original in his *Odyssey,* for instance.
18. *Jocasta* was published on its own in 1566, then as part of *A Hundreth Sundrie Flowres* in 1573 (London: Richard Smith), which came out in a revised edition as *The Posies of George Gascoigne Esquire* (London: Richard Smith) in 1575, and it was fi-

nally included in the posthumous *The Whole woorkes of George Gascoigne* from 1587 (London: Abell Ieffes). Pigman's edition—George Gascoigne, *A Hundreth Sundrie Flowres,* ed. G. W. Pigman III (Oxford: Clarendon Press, 2000)—is based on the 1573 *Flowers,* with the 1566 and 1575 variants in footnotes, but it does not record "87's many errors," referring the curious to Cunliffe's textual appendix (textual introduction, l).

19. John P. Mahaffy, *Euripides,* Classical Writers (New York: D. Appleton, 1879), 134–35.

20. Gascoigne never mentions his Italian source, contrary to Terpening's assertion (*Lodovico Dolce,* 94) that *Jocasta* "appeared in print in the translation of George Gascoigne and Francis Kinwelmarsh, along with Ariosto's *I Suppositi,* with Italian and English on facing pages, in 1573." The only bilingual edition is Cunliffe's from 1906.

21. Prouty makes no allusion to Dolce when he discusses *Jocasta* in his introduction to *A Hundreth Sundrie Flowres* (Columbia: University of Missouri Press, 1942), though he does mention him in his biography of Gascoigne, *George Gascoigne: Elizabethan Courtier, Soldier, and Poet* (New York: Columbia University Press, 1942).

22. Pigman's biographical introduction to *A Hundreth Sundrie Flowres,* xxiii, describes *Jocasta* as "the earliest version of a Greek tragedy in English," and duly explains in the first footnote that it "is not as it claims on its title-page, a translation of Euripides' *Phoenissae* but rather Lodovico Dolce's adaptation of Euripides, *Giocasta.*" Dolce does not appear in Pigman's textual introduction (xlv–lxv), nor anywhere in the section of the volume (29–140) reprinting the text of *Jocasta,* which is based on the 1573 edition. However, Dolce reappears on p. 465, in the endnotes, where his *Giocasta* is abundantly quoted and discussed.

23. In his copy of *Medea Tragedia,* Venice, 1566, sig. A1v. See Pigman, ed., *A Hundreth Sundrie Flowres,* 517.

24. On Lodge's translation, see Sidney Lee, *Elizabethan Sonnets, Newly Arranged and Indexed,* 2 vols. (Westminster: Archibald Constable, 1904), 1:lxv, lxxiii.

25. See Jonathan Woolfson, *Padua and the Tudors: English Students in Italy, 1485–1603* (Cambridge: James Clark, 1999). This revival began in the early fourteenth century with an original Latin tragedy by Albertino Mussato, *Ecerinis,* and it spread to Ferrara (where Plautus's *Menaechmi* was performed in 1486 before ten thousand people), Mantua (which held a dramatic festival in 1501), and at a later stage Rome (under the papacy of Leo X).

26. Dolce can boast 216 items on the British Library Catalogue. Apart from his translations, he edited or prefaced Dante, Petrarch, Boccaccio, Tasso, Bembo, Castiglione, Ariosto, Aretino, and Sannazzaro's *Arcadia,* among other English favorites.

27. John W. Cunliffe, *Early English Classical Tragedies* (Oxford: Clarendon Press, 1912), xxxvii, lxvii.

28. *Four Old Plays. Three interludes: Thersytes, Jack Jugler, and Heywood's Pardoner and Frere: and Jocasta, a tragedy by Gascoigne and Kinwelmarsh,* introd. by Francis J. Child (Cambridge, MA: George Nichols, 1848).

29. *1 Henry VI,* 1.3.199–205. Cf. *Jocasta:* "If I could rule or reigne in heaven above, / And eke commaund in depth of darksome hell . . ." John P. Mahaffy, *A History of Classical Greek Literature,* 2 vols. (London: Longmans, Green, 1880), 1:365–66. Mahaffy (ibid., 326) also finds "a strange external resemblance" between the concluding scenes of *Alcestis* and the heroine's return from the dead in *The Winter's Tale,* and furthermore he quotes the French critic Henri Patin (author of a series of *Études sur les tragiques grecs,* 1877–81), who had compared Hecuba to Margaret in *Richard III.*

30. All references are to Cunliffe's 1906 bilingual edition, which added scene divisions to the originals.

31. T. W. Baldwin, *William Shakespere's Small Latine*, 2:596–97, quoting *De Officiis*, 3, 21.

32. *Marcus Tullius Ciceroes Thre Bokes of Duties*, ed. Gerald O'Gorman (London: Associated University Presses / Washington: Folger Shakespeare Library, 1990), 3, 1140–49, p. 176, and sidenote in first edition, p. 220: "C. Iulius Cesar delited much to reherse these verses of Euripides." Nicolas Grimald's translation, published by Richard Tottel in 1556, had seven editions in the next forty-five years. The Loeb Latin and English translation by Arthur S. Way, 3, xxi, 354–57, suppresses Cicero's opinion of Euripides, "vel potius Euripides": "Our tyrant deserved his death for having made an exception of the one thing that was the blackest crime of all."

33. On the notoriety of these lines since antiquity, see Donald J. Mastronarde, ed., *Euripides: Phoenissae* (Cambridge: Cambridge University Press, 1994), notes to 524–25, and Pigman, ed., *A Hundreth Sundrie Flowres*, 531. Cf. "For a kingdom any law may be broken": Morris P. Tilley, *A Dictionary of the Proverbs in England in the Sixteenth and Seventeenth Centuries* (Ann Arbor: University of Michigan Press, 1950), K90.

34. Sturm, who inspired Ascham's program of studies for young Edward VI, laid great emphasis on the declamation and acting of plays. Colet's school of Saint Paul's took its lead from Erasmus and served as model for most of the new grammar schools like the renowned Merchant Taylors', where an impressive number of playwrights were educated.

35. Desiderius Erasmus, *Euripidis tragici poete nobilissimi Hecuba et Iphigenia: latine facte, Erasmo interprete* (Paris: Ex officina Ascensiana, 1506).

36. Charles and Michelle Martindale, *Shakespeare and the Uses of Antiquity: An Introductory Essay* (London: Routledge, 1990), 41–44, disagree with Emrys Jones's conclusions in *The Origins of Shakespeare* (Oxford: Clarendon Press, 1977), chapters 3 and 4. "In the background to Seneca are the tragedies of Euripides," John Jowett notes in his edition of *Richard III* (Oxford: Oxford University Press, 2000), 23, though he doubts Shakespeare knew them. John Kerrigan, *Revenge Tragedy: Aeschylus to Armageddon* (Oxford: Clarendon Press, 1994), has many references to Euripides, but none to *Jocasta*.

37. Prouty, *George Gascoigne: Elizabethan Courtier, Soldier, and Poet*, 145–46.

38. Cinzio, *Discorsi di M. Giovanbattista Giraldi Cinthio ... intorno al comporre dei romanzi, delle comedie, e delle tragedie, e di altre maniere di poesie*, 1554 (Paris: BnF microfilm, 1995).

39. The Greek text of *Phoenissae*, printed in 1503 by Aldus Manutius was the basis of most subsequent editions.

40. "Une pièce un peu bâtarde à nos yeux," Victor-Henry Debidour, *Les Tragiques grecs: Théâtre complet* (Paris: Livre de Poche, 1999), 1461. In contrast with this French "classicism," Donald Mastronarde, ed., *Euripides: Phoenissae*, defends and reattributes most contested scenes to Euripides, though he does admit to some spurious lines, especially in the tailpiece.

41. John A. Symonds, *Renaissance in Italy: Italian Literature*, 2 vols. (London: Smith Elder, 1904), 2:116–17.

42. Symonds, *Shakespere's Predecessors*, 219, 222.

43. Cunliffe, *Early English Classical Tragedies*, xxxviii, viii.

44. T. S. Eliot, "Seneca in Elizabethan Translation," in *Elizabethan Dramatists* (London: Faber, 1963), 32.

45. Introduction, xxix–xxx. The French *Catalogue Collectif* records only one copy of this unique bilingual edition, located at the University Library of Rennes.

46. *Giocasta*, 4.3.55–73; *Jocasta*, 4.3.57–78 and 5.1.

47. *Phoenissae*, l. 537. *Giocasta*, 2.1.390; *Jocasta*, 2.1.415, pp. 226–27. Cunliffe's Italian text is based on the 1560 edition, which has *L'equità*.

48. Cunliffe, *Early English Classical Tragedies*, lxxxv.

49. *Certayne notes of Instruction concerning the making of verse or ryme in English, written at the request of Master Edouardo Donati*, published in Gascoigne, *The Posies*, 1575.

50. Symonds, *Shakespere's Predecessors*, 245. Surrey's book 4 of the *Aeneid* was published in 1554, and book 2 in 1557.

51. Trissino's *Sofonisba*, written in 1515, established it on the tragic stage, imitated by Rucellai in *Rosmunda* (1524). See Michel Paoli, "Alberti, Trissino, Algarotti: Le vers blanc italien entre modèle antique et génie du toscan," in *Invisibilité du vers blanc*, special issue of *In'hui*, no. 55, guest-edited by Jacques Darras (Bruxelles: Le Cri, 2000), 16–25.

52. There are no details known on the 1549 performance of *Giocasta*, but it was revived in 1570 at the Academy of Viterbo with spectacular *intermedii*. Dolce used *intermedii* in his *Troiane*. Cunliffe, *Early English Classical Tragedies*, xl, notes that dumb shows may have arisen from native pageants, but finds the coincidence with *intermedii* too marked to be ignored.

53. Michael Hattaway, *Elizabethan Popular Theatre* (London: Routledge & Kegan Paul, 1982), 65, notes that Tamburlaine's chariot in scene 5.3 of *2 Tamburlaine* may have derived from Italian *trionfi*. The triumph of death is also evoked by the Talbots in *1 Henry VI*.

54. The story of Curtius is reported by Livy, but Gascoigne took it from Valerius Maximus, and translated it in *The Glasse of Government*, 31: "Curtius the Romayne, when there apeared a greate gulfe in the market place . . ."

55. *Phoenissae*, ll. 499–502; *Giocasta*, 2.1.328–33; *Jocasta*, 3.1.350–55. Each makes the same point with increasing length.

56. *3 Henry VI*, 2.5.1–40.

57. Gascoigne, *Certayne notes of Instruction*, 468, §5.

Conservatism and Liberalism in the Four Spanish Renderings of Ducis's *Hamlet*

Ángel-Luis Pujante and Keith Gregor

SHAKESPEARE FIRST REACHED THE SPANISH STAGE IN A TRANSLATION from Jean-François Ducis's neoclassical rewriting of *Hamlet*, not in a rendering or adaptation from the English original. It was the first translation of this *Hamlet* into another European language and was used on the stage in 1772, that is, three years after the play's premiere in France, and two years after it was first published there in 1770. The fortunes of Ducis's *Hamlet* in Europe—and of his other Shakespearean versions—were notable. Leaving aside France (where it was performed 203 times between 1769 and 1851), his *Hamlet* was, in turn, translated or adapted, not only in Spain, but also in Italy, the Low Countries, Russia, and Poland.[1] In the Low Countries it was translated three times, the third rendering being now lost. However, the case of Ducis's *Hamlet* in Spain is unique, as (1) there are no fewer than four different translations of the play; (2) the first two are based on the 1770 edition, whereas the original of the last two is a much later revised version; (3) at least the last two were written after the publication in 1798 of the first Spanish translation of Shakespeare's *Hamlet* by playwright Leandro Fernández de Moratín, which was not used on the stage; and (4) the last of the four was written as late as 1825.

Rather than being an alternative for European playgoers at the time, derivative plays like Ducis's *Hamlet* and further versions of the play in other languages were the usual, if not only, form of access to "Shakespeare."[2] They therefore bear witness to the evolution of the Hamlet myth and the way it contributed to the reception of Shakespeare in Spain and Europe as a whole. More specifically, the four Spanish translations of Ducis's *Hamlet* show the extent to which Spanish and European history and politics could be a concern of the translators, leading to tampered-with versions of an already refashioned story.

The Four Neoclassical Spanish *Hamlet*s

The first of the translations, attributed to playwright Ramón de la Cruz, was played on the Madrid stage in October and December 1772, but it was not published till 1900.[3] We shall refer to this first translation as "Cruz." There are no records as to stagings or publication of the other three, and consequently these are only available in manuscript form. Admittedly, they are cases of literary production without reception, but they give evidence for the growing importance of the Hamlet myth in Spain in a period that spans more than fifty years.

The second translation, anonymous and undated, cannot have been written much later than 1800, as it is based on the 1770 French edition, and probably not earlier than 1793, as we shall propose later on. We shall refer to it as "Santander," after the city where the only manuscript is kept.[4] The third, by lawyer, translator, and playwright Antonio de Saviñón, is also undated, though it must have been written before 1814, which was the year of Saviñón's death.[5] The text appears in two manuscripts with some minor verbal differences and, as we shall see, the odd significant line omission.[6] We shall refer to it as "Saviñón." The fourth and last, written by journalist and man of letters José María de Carnerero and dated 1825, is also based on the "definitive" version of the play. One of the two manuscripts contains all the necessary authorizations for performance, but no theater records have been found to suggest the play was ever staged.[7] We shall refer to it as "Carnerero."

All of the translations were composed in verse as theatrical texts, that is, not in informative prose translations only to be read. The connection of the first and fourth with the theater is obvious, but even the Santander and the Saviñón versions could be said to have been rendered for some intended or hoped-for performance. The Santander translation is preceded by a brief note, at the end of which, right after the remarks about the moral qualities of the play, the translator adds, "De que resulta que el público podría sacar utilidad de su representación" (Whence the possible usefulness of its performance for the audience),[8] obviously endorsing the eighteenth-century didactic view of the theater, but also expressing the hope or possibility of performance with this translation. As for the Saviñón rendering, no such note accompanies his manuscripts, though the specificity of the stage directions in at least one of the manuscripts (268), together with Saviñón's track record as a performance author, point in the direction of a probable, or at least intended, production.

Ramón de la Cruz

In Ducis the Hamlet story has become a court-intrigue in which Claudius and his party attempt to overthrow the new young king Hamlet. However slightly or inexplicitly, this subject involves questions of loyalty, rebellion, legitimacy, usurpation, and regicide. Ducis's *Hamlet* did not have to fear the risk of censorship, since, unlike other tragedies of the period, it punishes rebellion instead of celebrating it. Perhaps because the play deals with other themes, too, such as filial tenderness (Romy Heylen points out that it is bourgeois domestic drama under neoclassical garb[9]), it does not emphasize or insist upon the political issues involved. This, however, is one of the aspects in which at least three of the Spanish translators differ from the original, as in their renderings they tend to emphasize the status quo of the ancien régime and the evils of rebellion, usurpation, and regicide.

Thus, when there is nothing in the original that justifies it, the Cruz translation stresses the subjects' loyalty to their king and uses the word "vasallo" at least seven times. When Ducis refers to a king's subject specifically, he uses "sujet" instead of the more feudal "vassal," but Cruz avoids the Spanish equivalent "súbdito" and sticks to "vasallo." This tendency becomes obvious when "vasallo(s)" translates the impersonal French "on" (1.2), when "un devoir pour moi" (a duty for me) is rendered "obligación de amigo y de vasallo" (the obligation of a friend and vassal) (2.6), or when, in rendering the image of a "main perfide" (treacherous hand) lifting a dagger against kings, the subject of the action becomes a "vasallo rebelado" (rebellious vassal) (5.6).

But it is in some of the translator's amplifications that this tendency is more evident. In act 5, scene 4 of the Ducis original, when the rebellion is already under way, Polonius (here Claudius's fellow conspirator) advises to make haste, for he fears that Norceste (the counterpart of Shakespeare's Horatio) will discover them and they will then miss their opportunity and be arrested. In Cruz everything becomes more politically specific:

> [Norceste] al rey defenderá con los leales
> y nosotros seremos destruidos.
> Los rebeldes se turban fácilmente
> y, viendo que los cargan, ni el camino
> hallan para la fuga. Creedme, Claudio:
> mientras dura el furor en sus caprichos
> quitémosles el tiempo de que puedan
> reflexionar su culpa y su castigo.

> [(Norceste) will defend the king with his loyal supporters
> and we shall be destroyed.
> The rebels are easily alarmed
> and, if they see they are under attack, cannot
> even find the way to escape. Believe me, Claudio,
> as long as they are fired by their caprices
> let us leave them not a second
> to reflect upon their crime and punishment.]

In Ducis there are no specific French words that lead to "leales" or "rebeldes," less so to the rebels' actions being referred to as "caprichos." If they are found out, they will be arrested "tremblants, déconcertés" (trembling, disconcerted). Cruz makes their basic cowardice more explicit: if the loyals attack them, they will not even find the way to escape. Toward the end, Polonius advises haste, lest they should think of the "grandeur du crime" (the enormity of the crime). Cruz adds the punishment to their crime. Politics aside, one also wonders if this is a likely vocabulary for rebels to use when discussing themselves and their actions.

When Hamlet has killed Claudius and stopped the conspiracy, the conspirators are addressed by him with a vague and laconic "Rentrez dans le devoir, réparez votre offense" (Accept your obligations and make atonement for your offense), which leaves open the possibility that they may have to make amends by some sort of punishment. In the Cruz translation this possibility is ruled out by making Hamlet a king who pardons them in exchange for the loyalty they must ensure him and whose "example" and "pity" are enough, according to Norceste, to discourage future traitors. In other words, the young king achieves his revenge, but shows himself to be very generous with his loyal subjects in a far more explicit way than in the vague Ducis:

> Y vosotros, daneses, convencidos
> de vuestro error, venid donde os enseñe
> en la benignidad con que os recibo
> la lealtad que debéis asegurarme.
> . . . .
> ¿Quién podrá ser traidor con este ejemplo
> y con esta piedad?
>
> [And, Danes, those amongst you
> who are convinced of your error, come that I may teach you,
> with the kindness that I receive you,
> the loyalty which you must vow.
> . . . .
> Who, when shown such an example and such pity,
> could possibly turn to treachery?]

The way in which the translator adapted and manipulated the Ducis original should leave little doubt about the translator's political sympathies. These may be explained as the mere conservatism of a law-abiding person,[10] or perhaps his political feelings had been awakened or further enhanced by a specific historical situation that he had witnessed. In effect, his *Hamleto* was staged only six years after one of the most widely known political upheavals in eighteenth-century Spain, the so-called "motín de Esquilache" in 1766, in which the people of Madrid rebelled against the minister Leopoldo de Gregorio Esquilache, sacked his house, and caused public disorders. King Charles III had to accept the conditions imposed by an angry mob standing just outside the Royal Palace. The disturbances were renewed a month later in some other towns and villages. Things came back to normal after the minister was replaced, but this was surely the worst political convulsion Spain had had to suffer after the end of the War of Succession in 1713. Ironically, this happened under the reign of a king who has always been regarded as the most efficient of the century and one who gained for himself a fair amount of popularity and respect. Obviously, there can be no certainty about the influence of this revolt on the translator, but we believe that the facts are evident enough to consider it as a reasonable hypothesis.

The Santander Translation

The Santander translation follows Cruz's linguistic manipulations with a vengeance. It also renders the "sujet" as "vasallo" instead of the less feudal "súbdito," and it stresses the bond of loyalty by using "vasallo" when the original does not require it, at least as significantly as the Cruz translation. Thus, "prince" in Ducis (referring to Claudius) becomes "un vasallo del primer orden" (a first-rate vassal) (2.5), and a line like "T'aimer & t'obéir, voilà notre partage" (To love and obey you, such is our lot) is significantly translated as "Prestaste la obediencia, / y amarte siempre toca a tus leales / y felices vasallos" (You showed obedience, / and to love you is ever the lot of your loyal / and happy vassals) (3.1), in which three points (loyalty, vassalage, and happiness of the vassals) are made significantly specific when they are not so in the original.

But the most remarkable case of lexico-political tampering in the Santander rendering is to be found in its treatment of the intended assassination of the king (5.2), when Ophelia condemns the conspiracy of Claudius, who in Ducis's version is her father. The original "coups" (blows) that Hamlet may suffer will be given in the translation specifically by a "puñal rebelde" (rebel dagger). In Ducis the assassination is referred to by Ophelia as an "affreux parricide," a term that she is using in the now-archaic sense of "régicide" but that in Spanish (and in its English equivalent) demands "regicidio," since, apart from its narrow legal sense, the victim of a "parricidio" is normally taken to be either of one's parents. This is the way the Cruz and the Santander translations put the original. However, the Santander rendering uses this very specific concept also when the original does not require it: "coupables mains" (guilty hands) becomes "manos regicidas" (regicidal hands), and "regicidas" will be used at the end of the play in lines that have no correspondence with the original. Later in the same scene, Ophelia's reference to the projected killing of the king as "une action si noire" (so dark an act) becomes "hecho tan sacrílego" (so sacrilegious a deed), which obviously emphasizes the medieval doctrine of the divine origin of kings.

This lexical manipulation can be said to pave the way for the ending of the play, which in the Santander translation (5.6) differs significantly from the original. In Ducis Hamlet kills Claudius and stops the other conspirators by showing them the dead body and by rebuking them. Besides, in Ducis there is only a brief stage direction here ("*Montrant le corps de Claudius*") (Showing the body of Claudius), but in the translation the action is significantly amplified:

> *Cae Claudio. Consternados los rebeldes con tan inesperado suceso, se postran ante el rey, rindiéndole las armas, con ademán de arrepentidos.*
>
> [Claudio dies. Dismayed by such an unexpected turn of events, the rebels prostrate themselves before the king, offering up their arms in a gesture of repentance.]

This sounds almost as if the translator were tacitly reproaching Ducis for leaving out here what must be done in such cases: not only the dismay of the "rebeldes," but their public self-humiliation, their gesture of repentance, and their yielding of their arms. Now, since in his version the dead man is Ophelia's father, Ducis made his play end, as we mentioned earlier, with Ophelia apparently turning against Hamlet when she sees the body, and the uncertainty about their future relationship. All this disappears in the Santander translation. Here Ophelia does not come onstage, and the play ends abruptly with Hamlet's upbraiding the conspirators in a way that finds no correspondence in Ducis, except for a brief reference to the "justice des Dieux":

> ¡Vosotros, almas bajas y venales
> cuyas divisas son "Viva quien venza,"

> mirad como escarmienta a regicidas
> de las deidades la justicia eterna!
>
> [You low and venal souls
> whose emblems are "Long live he who conquers,"
> see how regicides are punished
> by the eternal justice of the gods!]

This obsession with punishing "regicidas" and humiliating the conspirators to the extent of dispensing with Ophelia's presence at this point clearly goes beyond Ducis and also shows a contrast with Cruz's image of an explicitly benevolent king capable of pardoning his enemies. This contrast could have been deliberate if the Santander translator had seen the play performed, or had read the Cruz translation in manuscript (which is not impossible, if we consider that manuscript copies were often sold).[11] If we now consider that the Santander translation amplifies the original much less than the Cruz and that its vocabulary and style is more stilted and neoclassical, we could say, using Jorge Luis Borges's phrase, that this is another case of one translator translating *against another*.[12]

But let us return to the translator's political attitude, particularly as shown in the concern with the killing of a king and the treatment of the play's ending. As is known, certain words are not much used until events put them into circulation. One of them is "regicide," which was applied to the English parliamentarians who endorsed the death sentence of Charles I Stuart, and in the eighteenth century to the members of the Directory who voted the execution of Louis XVI in 1793 (and even nowadays "régicide" immediately calls to French people's minds the killing of this king). The execution of Louis XVI was the turning point of a historical process, bent on abolishing absolutist monarchy and the ancien régime, which was hailed throughout Europe by many, but also hated and feared by old monarchists and traditionalists. Spain was no exception, and we should not be surprised to find that the Santander translator was such a supporter of the old order and so hated the French Revolution as to carry his or her political concerns over to the rendering of this play beyond the letter of the original. As before with the Cruz translation, there is no evidence to support these suggestions, but the impact of historical events should render them a reasonable hypothesis.

Antonio de Saviñón

The source text of the last two translations to be dealt with was the so-called "definitive" Ducis version of 1809, with subsequent (mainly verbal) revisions in 1815, 1816, and 1818. In this later text, as well as some important adjustments to the action that involved a radical rewriting of act 5, Ducis is said to have taken the actor Talma's tip and made Hamlet the central figure. "Furthermore," as John Golder has noted, "the original concentration on the private concerns of love, duty and remorse were offset by giving more attention to the public questions of the Prince's impending coronation and Claudius's conspiracy."[13]

When Antonio de Saviñón wrote his translation of *Hamlet*, these last concerns could hardly have been more relevant. Spain's Central Junta, hemmed in in the southern city of Cádiz by an alliance of French troops and so-called "afrancesados" (Frenchified supporters of the regime loyal to Joseph Bonaparte), was in the process of deciding the future of the Spanish monarchy. In a draft constitution that, among other measures, provided for a democratically elected government and an end to ministerial despotism, unprecedented emphasis was laid on the sovereignty of the people. For the liberal lawyer Saviñón, whose adaptation of a work by Vittorio Alfieri, pointedly entitled *Roma libre,* had been played in 1812 to mark the publication of the constitution, Ducis's play must have stood as a vindication of the idea of legitimate monarchy strengthened by popular support, as well as a sobering lesson in the ever-present threat of usurpation by scheming, hawkish Machiavels.

As if to draw more attention to this fact, one of the very few cuts in Saviñón's virtual line-for-line rendering of the play occurs at the very end of act 4. In what is plainly the text intended for performance, Saviñón edits out Claudius's response to Polonius's reservations concerning the popular reaction to Hamlet's overthrow (4.7). A desire to shorten the role of Claudius by a writer who generally omits nothing seems unlikely. Rather, Saviñón's likely intention is revealed by the *effect* one has from reading through the scene. By slashing the speech, Saviñón appears to have wanted to avoid detailing the extent of Claudius's callousness ("Je ne crains plus les cris d'une mère éperdue; / Je fais saisir Hamlet" [I fear no more the cries of a desperate mother; / I shall have Hamlet arrested]), while concentrating the audience's attention on the purely political implications of ruling with or without the support of the populace. This stroke seems to reveal Saviñón's willingness, in a performance at least, to play down the insight into Claudius's "psychological" development in exchange for a fairly blunt rendering of the political reflexions of the unscrupulous tyrant.

On the other hand, and perhaps surprisingly for the radical liberal he appears to have been, Saviñón's translation is steeped in the moral discourse of a church whose institutions were under serious threat in the anticlerical climate of the Napoleonic years and the three-year period of the national government at Cádiz. We are thinking particularly of the foregrounding of elements such as the sacralization of Hamlet's revenge "en nombre del Autor Supremo" (in the name of the Supreme Creator) (2.5)—a divine sanction for the killing unthinkable in Ducis—or the nature of the oath Hamlet obliges his mother to swear in 5.4, not, as in Ducis, before her son but before the ultimate Arbiter: "juro y atesto al Cielo mi inocencia" (I swear and attest my innocence before Heaven). Despite the apparent radicalism of many of Spain's nineteenth-century liberals and the Cádiz government's adoption of anticlerical measures such as the abolition of the Inquisition in 1813, the notion of a godless state would have been anathema to all but a handful of those who backed the constitution, and Saviñón was no exception.

It was just such an appropriation of the genre of drama, either for political or religious ends or even both, together with an excessive concern with the emotional impact of the play and the dependence on spectacular effects, especially in the "free zones" such as Cádiz, where Saviñón almost certainly wrote the piece, that is assumed to have spelled the end of the neoclassical project of theatrical reform. "Of the neoclassical project," it has been claimed, "there remained but one idea: the *use-value* of drama as a *school,* but not one in which to learn good manners but where the *citizen* is given lessons in how to face the new political situation."[14] The War of Independence had left the country deeply divided between, on the one hand, radical liberals like Saviñón who had pressed for independence from French occupation and for the urgent reform of Spain's outmoded social and political structure, and on the other, conservatives who demanded a firm hand to purge the country of the pernicious presence of the "afrancesados" and, at the same time, to restore to the Church both its influence and its lands. The triumph of the latter tendency, embodied in the accession to the throne of Ferdinand VII in 1814, was the prelude to a later period of repression and ruthless elimination of the vestiges of French rule. For if there was anything truly remarkable in the first few years of Ferdinand's reign, it was, as Guillermo Carnero has shown, the ease with which terms like "neoclásico" were used as synonyms for "afrancesado," "liberal," or "revolucionario."[15] Among the victims of the purge that began with the accession were Saviñón, whose arrest and trial were based on his authorship of the "revolutionary" *Roma libre,* and in general the neoclassical project with which he and many other writers of the period were, often wrongly, associated.

José María de Carnerero

Following an uprising of liberals anxious to restore the 1812 constitution, the formation of an absolutist "apostolic" regency in Urgell, and the restoration of Ferdinand by the "Cien mil hijos de San Luis," all between the years 1820 and 1823, the semantic confusions mentioned by Carnero gave way to a full-blown political purge. The "década ominosa" (shameful decade), as the period 1823–33 would become known, saw the enforced exile and, in many cases, execution of the Crown's liberal opponents. Among the most ardent defenders of the "new" old regime was the journalist and littérateur José María de Carnerero, whose career is a testimony to the persistence of a dramatic model whose very raison d'être had been called into question. A former liberal whose open support for Joseph Bonaparte had earned him a post as subeditor of the *Gaceta de Madrid* and, on Ferdinand's accession to the throne, a seven-year exile in France, Carnerero successfully wed his activities as a professional journalist to those as translator of foreign, mainly French plays. And though most of these were, in the words of one critic, nothing more than "mediocres piececillas" (second-rate little plays), Carnerero's status as reactionary born-again monarchist and self-appointed laureate to the court of Ferdinand and María Cristina soon got the plays a billing at Madrid's theater venues.[16]

Hamlet (1825) seems to have been written in the midst of Carnerero's metamorphosis from Frenchified liberal to die-hard conservative. Carnerero, who had already aired his intentions two years earlier in the one-act *La noticia feliz* (*The happy news*), which had celebrated "la restauración de la paz y del orden, y la solidez del trono legítimo" (the restoration of peace and order, the solidity of the legitimate throne), clearly found in Ducis's play, then running into its eleventh single-text edition in France, the perfect vehicle for his own hard-line monarchist views.

These views are especially apparent in his translation of *Hamlet*. If from the outset of both Ducis's play and Carnerero's translation the menace of a foreign power sweeping an already divided kingdom is a rhetorical ploy used by Claudius to beguile the populace, in the Spanish version "la guerra horrible / que amenaza el Imperio" (the dreadful war / which threatens the Empire) (3.4.), as Polonius calls it, is compounded at home by the uprising of Claudius and his "revolucionarios" (revolutionaries) (5.7), a striking use of the term which, given its novelty, could not help but identify Claudius and his followers with the French protagonists of 1789. The extent of the threat of Claudius and his followers, together with the extreme heroism of the defenders of legitimacy, described by Voltimán (Ducis's Voltimand, a rough equivalent to Shakespeare's Marcellus) in 5.5 has no precedent in either Ducis or any of the texts here mentioned:

> El grito alzando
> jefe se muestra del rebelde bando;
> y sin pudor, librándose a su encono,
> conspira contra vos y vuestro trono.
> Ah . . . sí . . . No lo dudéis . . . Este recinto
> verse amenaza con la sangre tinto
> de súbditos leales, que al despecho
> de los traidores, oponiendo el pecho,
> y peligros sin término venciendo,
> la furia arrostran del combate horrendo.
> A la muerte . . . o al triunfo . . . que en tal suerte
> es morir con honor, dichosa muerte.
>
> [Raising a cry
> he proclaims himself leader of the rebel band;
> while, shamelessly, allowing himself to be swept away by fury
> he conspires against you and your throne.
> Oh . . . yes . . . be in no doubt . . . These grounds
> threaten to run red with the blood
> of loyal subjects, who scorning
> the traitors, baring their breasts
> and braving endless dangers,
> face the fury of horrible combat.
> To death . . . or to triumph . . . for to die like this
> is to die with honor. Oh happy death.]

In such a hostile climate, which to many must have evoked the turmoil of the liberal uprising and the Urgell regency, it was indeed reassuring that Hamlet's apparent madness could (still) be punctuated by moments of genuine self-possession, moments in which he could address the upstart Claudius with words that carry the weight of authority and legitimacy: "¿O habéis creído por desgracia vuestra / que, aunque Hamlet triste y lánguido se muestra, / sus derechos legítimos descuida . . . ?" (Or were you foolish enough to believe / that Hamlet, even though he seems so sad and languid, / neglects his lawful rights?) (4.4). Hamlet's victory, though pyrrhic, is, it is suggested, a victory for legitimacy over the lawless rebel and his followers, a confirmation of ancien régime rights over the illicit aspirations of the "revolutionary" pretender Claudius. In a burst of populism in 5.9 worthy of one of his leaders in *La revista española,* Carnerero duly rewrites Ducis's closing lines to render Hamlet not the lonely "homme et roi: réservé pour souffrir" (A man and king: doomed to suffer), but the natural leader of men:

> ¡Vivamos, pues! . . . ¡Obligación es mía
> dar a mis pueblos mi existencia entera!
> ¡A ellos consagro mi mortal carrera!
> Y ¡ojalá logre en aflicción tan dura
> mi alivio ser la general ventura!
>
> [Let us choose life, then! . . . I am duty-bound
> to give my people my whole existence!
> To them I owe my mortal course!
> And being as I am so sorely grieved,
> may the general happiness be my only respite!]

Thus ends the play, not on the note of personal resignation that sounds at the close of Ducis's revised text, but with Hamlet's almost Christlike dedication to his people, generously identifying his own fate with theirs.

Conclusion

The notion of the translator as a neutral filter belongs to olden times or to naïveté. Far from being a carbon copy of the original, his or her work is usually a combination of additions, omissions, emphases, and understatements, particularly when the text deals with such sensitive issues as politics. The translations discussed here are no exception. They were written over a crucial and eventful period of Spanish and European political history. Both in their language and in their significant departures from the original, they show the political sympathies, conservative or liberal, of the translators, and reveal the uses to which they intended their texts to be put.

From a literary viewpoint, theatrical adaptations of Shakespeare's plays in Europe have often been valued with regard to their originals or alongside more or less faithful translations of them. In consequence, they have been thought of as poor alternatives, been underrated and considered as peripheral, when they have received any attention at all. However, in the world of the theater and in a period when "the real Shakespeare" was usually absent from the European stages, these rewritings were central rather than peripheral and cannot, therefore, be overlooked in the study of the spread and reception of Shakespeare's works. Moreover, if they were further manipulated with a political intention, they have an added historical and political interest. The four Spanish renderings of Ducis's *Hamlet*, composed as performable plays, are very much a case in point, and should take their place, however modest, in the history of the European reception of Shakespeare.

Notes

This paper is part of Research Project BFF2002–02019, financed by the Spanish Ministry of Science and Technology and FEDER. In preparing it we have benefited from specific information and comments provided by Dirk Delabastita, Isabelle Schwartz-Gastine, Gunnar Sorelius, and Marta Gibińska. Our warmest thanks are due to them all.

1. Paul Benchettrit, "*Hamlet* at the Comédie Française: 1769–1896," *Shakespeare Survey* 9 (1956): 60. Benchettrit points out that Ducis's *Hamlet* was played on sixty-five nights between 1831 and 1840, that is, "at the peak of the Romantic movement" (ibid.). The Italian translation, by Francesco Gritti, was staged and published in 1774, as documented by Gaby Petrone Fresco in her *Shakespeare's Reception in 18th Century Italy: The Case of Hamlet* (Bern: Peter Lang, 1993), 169–79, and not in 1772, as stated by Paul Van Tieghem in his *Le Préromantisme* (Paris: Sfelt, 1947), 3:246, and by those who follow him on this point, including Mary B. Vanderhoof, "Hamlet: A Tragedy Adapted from Shakespeare (1770) by Jean-François Ducis," *Proceedings of the American Philosophical Society* 97, no. 1 (February 1953): 88, and Romy Heylen, *Translation, Poetics and the Stage: Six French* Hamlets (London and New York: Routledge, 1993), 29. Also, Heylen misquotes Van Tieghem in suggesting that there was a Swedish translation of Ducis's *Hamlet*, when Van Tieghem only says (247) that Ducis's Shakespearean adaptations were acted at the Swedish court by a famous French actor, in French. There was, however, a *Hamlet* production in Göteborg in 1787, though there is no information available about the adaptation or its author; see Wilhelm Berg, *Anteckningar om Göteborgs Äldre Teatrar* 1 (Göteborg: Zachrissons boktryckeri, 1896), 1:342. For the translations of Ducis's *Hamlet* in the Low Countries and in Russia, see Dirk Delabastita and Lieven D'hulst, eds., *European Shakespeares: Translating Shakespeare in the Romantic Age* (Philadelphia: John Benjamins, 1993), 219–32 and 75–76, respectively. Finally, there appears to have been a Polish translation of Ducis's *Hamlet* by Andrzej Horodyski used in a 1799 production in Warsaw, but it was never published and the manuscript is now lost. See Andrzej Żurowski, *Szekspiriady Polskie* (Warszawa: Pax, 1976), 189–90.

2. Let us remind ourselves that even in England Shakespeare was adapted, sometimes beyond recognition, from the Restoration till close to the mid-nineteenth century; see Gary Taylor, *Reinventing Shakespeare: A Cultural History from the Restoration to the Present* (London: Vintage, 1991), 200–201. Similarly, audiences in Germany, where Ducis's versions were not used, had to rely on severely eviscerated or adapted versions of the plays, as in the case of the "first" *Hamlet*, Friedrich Ludwig Schröder's "domesticated" versions of 1776 and 1777; see Simon Williams, *Shakespeare on the German Stage, vol. 1, 1586–1914* (Cambridge: Cambridge University Press, 1990), 67–68 and 72–81.

3. In the *Revista Contemporánea* 120 (1900): 142–58, 273–91, 379–91, 500–12, and 640–51. The edition, prepared by Carlos Cambronero, is based on one of the two rather similar manuscripts kept at the Madrid Archivo de la Villa (Tea 1–118–1, A and Tea 1–118–1, B); a third one, kept at the Biblioteca Nacional (MS 16095), dif-

fers from the other two on some significant points (see note 11 below). For dates and also the performance venue, see René Andioc and Mireille Coulon, *Cartelera teatral madrileña del siglo XVIII: 1708–1808* (Madrid: Anejos de Criticón, 1996), 312.

4. At the local Biblioteca de Menéndez Pelayo, Ms. 277.

5. This leaves unresolved the "mystery" of how the ending of Saviñón's translation (from 5.7 to the close) coincides with a version of Ducis's denouement not published till 1815. Could Saviñón possibly have had access to an unpublished manuscript of the original? Till new hard evidence comes to light we can only speculate. The question is, in any case, immaterial here.

6. At the Biblioteca de la Real Academia Española, Mss. 268 and 275. There is also a very rough version (Ms. 312) that includes various translations from other authors.

7. The "performance" text is kept at the Archivo de la Villa in Madrid (Tea 1–36–10), while there is another ms., with no official authorizations, at the Biblioteca Nacional (Ms. 16238).

8. Most of the note is actually a translation of Ducis's own note to the 1770 edition of his *Hamlet*. This and all subsequent translations from the Spanish and French are our own.

9. Romy Heylen, *Translation, Poetics and the Stage*, 28.

10. If the translator was, according to the accepted attribution, the playwright Ramón de la Cruz, he was certainly a traditionalist.

11. If so, it would be a copy of the Biblioteca Nacional manuscript, in which the ending is even happier, not only than in Ducis but also than in the performed text. In this manuscript nine lines are added at the end, in which Ophelia and Hamlet are explicitly reconciled and the noble audience's indulgence is sought for the actors' errors.

12. "Los traductores de las *1001 Noches*" (The translators of the *Arabian Nights*), in his *Historia de la eternidad* (Buenos Aires and Barcelona: Emecé, 1968 [1936]). Though few, there are some verbal parallels suggesting that the Santander translator may have known the Cruz text.

13. John Golder, *Shakespeare for the Age of Reason: The Earliest Stage Adaptations of Jean-François Ducis, 1769–1792* (Oxford: Voltaire Foundation, 1992), 64.

14. Ana Freire, "El definitivo escollo del proyecto neoclásico de reforma del teatro (Panorama teatral de la Guerra de la Independencia)," in J. M. Sala Valldaura, ed., *El teatro español del siglo XVIII* (Lleida: Universitat, 1996), 1:395–96.

15. Guillermo Carnero, "El teatro de Calderón como arma ideolológica en el origen del romanticismo conservador español," *Estudios sobre teatro español del siglo XVIII* (Zaragoza: Prensas Universitarias de Zaragoza, 1997), 246.

16. Consider his "melodramatic poem" *Las glorias de España* (The glories of Spain) (1829) and his "allegorical melodrama" *Los festejos olímpicos ó el triunfo de Citeréa* (The Olympic Festivities or The Triumph of Cytherea) (1830), or the vociferous leaders he wrote for the two publications he headed in the early thirties, *Cartas españolas* and *La revista española*. For Carnerero's part in a virtual "intellectual dictatorship" in the Spain of the 1820s and '30s, a regime that included the Italian-born impresario Grimaldi, who would go on to run the Teatro del Príncipe, see Gloria Rokiski Lázaro, "Apuntes bio-bibliográficos de José María de Carnerero," *Cuadernos bibliográficos* 47 (1987): 142–43.

Prokofiev's *Romeo and Juliet* and Socialist Realism: A Case Study in Intersemiotic Translation

Karen Bennett

IN THE GREAT SOCIAL EXPERIMENT THAT WAS THE SOVIET UNION OF the 1930s, a very important role was accorded, as we know, to the writers, artists, and composers of the regime. These were expected to be the prophets and guides of socialism, engineering human souls in the task of "ideological reformation and education of the working masses,"[1] and from around 1934, proclamations began to appear about how this should best be achieved. Andrei Zhdanov, the secretary of the Central Committee of the All-Russian Communist Party, announced to the Union of Soviet Writers that literature was expected to "organise the working masses and the oppressed in a struggle for the ultimate demolition of all exploitation and of the yoke of hired slavery."[2] Consequently, literature had to be permeated with enthusiasm and heroic optimism, focusing on heroes that were actively engaged in the construction of a new way of life. The non-literary arts, too, were expected to contain a clearly identifiable ideological content and deal with humanistic themes that were edifying and inspiring for the people. But just how this was to be achieved in a medium like music was not made explicit. Indeed, it is perhaps only in retrospect that the notion of socialist realism as applied to music has gained any sort of coherence; for during the 1930s, when it was effectively being defined, composers had to work on a trial and error basis, never knowing what the official reaction would be.

Another aspect of Soviet policy urged by Zhdanov in his 1934 speech to the Union of Soviet Writers was the systematic appropriation of canonical works from the past, with the dual objective of affirming the veracity of official ideology while simultaneously establishing Soviet artists as the culmination of a tradition that stretched back into the mists of time. Shakespeare was one of the most appreciated of these "Great Precursors of Communism" and his works were frequently adapted to the new politics. This typically involved the introduction of more crowd scenes to represent the proletarian element and the expansion of the comic parts of the tragedies to give them a more optimistic tone, with a sharpening of the contrast between good and evil characters in order to reflect the antagonism between the progressive and archaic elements of society.

Romeo and Juliet, along with *Hamlet*, was a particular favorite and there were several productions of the play during the Soviet era. However, Prokofiev's decision to compose a ballet score based on it was almost certainly not ideologically inspired. Indeed, the idea for the ballet did not in fact come from the composer himself; it was Sergey Radlov, artistic director of the Leningrad State Academic Theater of Opera and Ballet, who first approached the composer with the idea in December 1934.

Before it could come to fruition, however, the project suffered a number of setbacks that have never been fully explained. Shortly after work had begun on it, in 1935, it was abandoned, when Radlov was forced to leave the Leningrad State Academic Theater as part of an administrative reshuffle in the wake of the assassination of Kirov. Then, early the following year, having been taken up by the Bolshoi Company, it was dropped for a second time, despite the fact that the piano score had been approved and performance was scheduled for the spring. Whether this reflects some uncertainty on the part of the authorities about its ideological soundness, as Jaffé suggests, is not clear.[3] It was, however, a very difficult time politically for Soviet composers, because a crisis had just erupted over Shostakovitch's opera *Lady Macbeth of Mzensk*, and all sorts of works were being condemned as "formalistic" in a frenzy of denunciations. *Romeo and Juliet* may just have been too ill defined to risk being offered to the public at such a sensitive time.

Indeed, although the first of the three orchestral suites based on material from the ballet was premiered in Moscow at the Bolshoi in November 1936, the ballet itself was not performed in Russia until 1940, after it had already become a success abroad. Even then, things did not run smoothly. The dancers, who were unused to the syncopated rhythms and unusual orchestration, deemed it "undanceable," and Prokofiev was requested to make alterations. Finally on January 11, 1940, the ballet was presented at the Kirov, with the leading roles danced by Galina Ulanova and Konstantin Sergeyev, a production that remained the work of reference for some time.

The Form of the Ballet

It may have been the tense political climate at the time that almost led to the implementation of one of the most controversial changes that could have been made in relation to this play, namely, the decision to give the ballet a happy ending, with Romeo returning a minute sooner, and finding Juliet alive. This was eventually revoked, however, and the final version is largely faithful to the Shakespeare play. Of course, owing to the particular requirements of ballet dramaturgy, the play had to be abridged, and Shakespeare's five acts of twenty-four scenes were divided into (originally) fifty-eight short episodes with a descriptive title for each, allowing the possibility of creating sharply contrasting moods in a short period. Scenes are presented in almost the same order as the original, although they are grouped differently, with act 2 beginning only after the balcony scene in the ballet, for example; interestingly, the whole of the final scene in the tomb is presented as the epilogue. Scenes that lend themselves particularly well to dance have been considerably extended (the fights and the ball scene, notably) and a number of folk dances have been included in order to allow the chorus to demonstrate its virtuosity.

Narrative structure is created musically through the use of leitmotif, a technique developed by Wagner for opera. This involves the allocation of musical themes to characters and to dramatic ideas, basic melodies that are then altered (rhythmically, harmonically, melodically, and through orchestration) to reflect shifting interactions and emotional states. Most of the characters in *Romeo and Juliet* are identified by at least one portrait theme, and there is a clear division between those that develop musically and those that do not, suggesting an interesting comparison with the realist novel. There are also abstract themes like Love, Death, and Strife, which in many cases develop out of the character themes, thus providing an interesting musical illustration of the Romantic notion that plot develops out of character.

Perhaps also owing to the influence of Romanticism, which was of course still a dominant force in the ballet tradition, Prokofiev's version of *Romeo and Juliet* introduces a significant shift in focus in relation to Shakespeare's play. This manifests itself from the outset. In Shakespeare's prologue, it is the feud between the two families that is presented as the theme of the play, visibly reinforced and illustrated by the extended brawl in the opening scene. Prokofiev's overture, on the other hand, does not speak of enmity. He could have used bellicose passages such as the Knight's Theme, elements from "The Fight," or even the ominous episode known as "The Duke's Order," to create a sense of conflict and tragic premonition; instead it is the lyrical Romeo and Juliet Theme that has precedence, interspersed with fragments from Juliet's B Theme and the Love Theme. The overwhelming tone is thus romantic and poignant, unequivocally summarizing the work as a tale of love. Thus, its scope is reduced from the broad social plane to the private domain of the psyche, and the panoramic vision is narrowed down to the partial perspective of one individual soul.

Romeo is also given more prominence in the ballet. While in Shakespeare, he is introduced to us only at the end of scene 1, after the fight and the Prince's warning, in Prokofiev's version he is the first figure to appear upon the stage. Across the ballet as a whole, he is present in over 70 percent of the musical episodes, which gives him a much more centralized role than he has in the original play.

This dramatic prominence is reflected musically by the enormous development undergone by Romeo's Theme. When he first appears onstage in the ballet, he is a very different character than the lovesick young romantic of Shakespeare. The first rendition of his theme (no. 2) portrays him as foolish, gauche, even bawdy, and it is contact with Juliet and with the Courtly Theme associated with Paris that causes it to mutate and evolve, until it eventually blossoms into the graceful Love Theme. Thus, we have a kind of Ugly Duckling story superimposed onto Shakespeare's *Romeo and Juliet,* and it is significant that the transformation is attributed to the alchemy of love.

There is no other character in the ballet whose theme changes so dramatically. Juliet is presented in a fragmented way, with three themes, each representing a different facet of her nature; Mercutio has his own portrait theme but is also associated closely with two group themes; the Nurse and Friar Laurence are no more than caricatures, with static simple themes that highlight a single trait; and most of the other characters disappear into an undifferentiated mass. Thus, Prokofiev has managed to achieve musically the kind of characterization that nineteenth-century novelists strove for in words. He has drawn a rounded psychological portrait of the central protagonist who develops and grows throughout the course of the action, introduced secondary developing characters who are perceived in relation to the protagonist and are therefore fragmentary, and peopled the background with a series of static minor characters who serve only to personify some particular characteristic that is of interest to the protagonist at the moment.

One of the most important changes introduced by Prokofiev into Shakespeare's play is the minimization of Tybalt. Curiously, this character, who has such a pivotal role in Shakespeare's play, is not even given his own portrait theme but instead is subsumed into the general theme of clan enmity. We can only speculate as to his reasons for this. One answer might be that Prokofiev did in fact intend this ballet to have a happy ending (which is also suggested by the restructuring of scene boundaries and by the absence of strife imagery in the overture). Tybalt, as Susan Snyder has pointed out,[4] is the only truly tragic character in Shakespeare's play; it is essentially his intervention that transforms *Romeo and Juliet* from a romantic comedy into a tragedy, since, up to the death of Mercutio, the action could have developed in a completely benign direction. Thus, diminishing this character's importance would automatically diminish the tragic potential of the play and make a happy ending all the more plausible, if that were in fact the composer's intention.

On the other hand, there could be ideological reasons for the reduction of Tybalt's role. Since he is effectively the catalyst of the tragic action, the character has frequently been interpreted as the devilish agent of a dark Fate (and indeed, there are several hints in the play that its final catastrophe is somehow preordained). Reducing Tybalt's role thus effectively de-activates fatalistic or supernatural interpretations of the tragedy and returns the action to the merely social plane. By not allowing him a theme of his own, his potential as freethinking individual and satanic provocateur is dramatically reduced. Instead, the role of villain is taken over musically by the whole clan, or rather, by the feudal society that propagates such tribal strife. Thus, it is these that become the tragic forces in the ballet, a transformation of Shakespeare's vision that is perhaps significant in the light of the regime under which Prokofiev lived.

Ideological Underlay

On the broader plane, however, determining the ideology underlying the musical discourse of Prokofiev's *Romeo and Juliet,* and indeed the composer's relationship with the regime generally, is not at all an easy matter. For despite the celebration of the work by the Soviet authorities following its great success abroad, it is by no means clear that it does in fact abide by the norms of socialist realism; indeed, the early fortunes of the ballet would indicate that perhaps the authorities themselves were uncertain about its status, as I have suggested.

Prokofiev himself has in fact been appropriated by both sides of the ideological divide. Two Russian biographies published in English in the 1960s are in sharp contradiction as to his politics: *Prokofiev,* by Israel V. Nestyev, the official Soviet version, paints him unequivocally as a son of the regime, and attempts to prove through detailed interpretations of his works that these are exemplary cases of socialist realism; while *Sergei Prokofiev: A Soviet Tragedy* by Victor Seroff takes the opposite line, seeing him essentially as a nonconformist who was co-opted against his will.[5] Other more recent non-Russian biographies, such as those by Claude Samuel (1971), David Gutman (1988), and Daniel Jaffé (1998) wisely shy away from simplistic interpretations, preferring to reserve judgment on most of the politically delicate issues.[6]

Neither is it easy to determine Prokofiev's political attitudes from the events of his life. The fact that he clearly enjoyed a privileged status and was showered with honors at a time when so many other composers were undergoing persecution would support Nestyev's argument. On the other hand, we cannot forget that, as early as 1936, his ballet *Le Pas d'Acier* was rejected as a "flat and vulgar anti-Soviet anecdote, a counter-revolutionary composition bordering on Fascism,"[7] while ten years later, he was officially accused of formalism and sacked from the directorate of the Union of Soviet Composers.

Musically, the composer is equally difficult to pin down and never so much as in *Romeo and Juliet*. Nestyev describes the composer's return to traditional tonality, upon his return to the Soviet Union in 1929, as a blossoming, brought about by his dawning awareness of the Truth residing in socialism; Seroff, on the other hand, claims that Prokofiev's musical idiom is far from conformist, and that, according to the definition of "formalism" given by Nikolai Chelyapov to the Union of Soviet Composers in 1932, most of the composer's works "obviously should have been scrapped."[8] Jaffé takes a different line again. He points out that, following the undermining of the very infrastructure of tonality by avant-garde experimentalism, composers of the late 1920s were faced with a stark choice between finding "new ways of structuring their music" or somehow renovating past practices, and attributes Prokofiev's return to lyricism to the influence of Schopenhauer, whom the composer was reading at the time. He also claims that Prokofiev systematically used the semiotic potential inherent in tonality to provide an ironic subtext to even his most apparently conformist works (such as the infamous *October Cantata*), thus ultimately refusing to submit to the demands of the regime.[9]

Whatever his reasons, however, Prokofiev's decision to make use of traditional tonality in this work was effectively an ideological act, since it represented conformism to Soviet aesthetics and a rejection of the alternative approaches to musical composition that were being developed elsewhere at the time. The decision to use this discourse in a representational way also aligned the composer with official cultural policy, since *Romeo and Juliet* is undoubtedly "realism," both in the sense that it aims to draw a faithful portrait of some extramusical world, and also in its use of centralized perspective, which connects it firmly with realism in painting and literature. At a time when abstraction was in the ascendancy in all arts, this appears a very conservative approach and made it easy for Nestyev to imply that the ballet's greatness resulted from the fact that it was "done under new conditions, after the composer had joined his fate with the humanist Soviet culture."[10]

The specifically Russian elements in *Romeo and Juliet* would also have ingratiated Prokofiev with the authorities. Renaissance Italy was evoked in the ballet only occasionally and unsystematically, and the dominant tone is distinctly Russian, evidence, for Nestyev, of the composer's talent "for projecting images derived from foreign sources through the spectrum of his own national sensibilities" (460).

There are aspects of the musical idiom of *Romeo and Juliet* that are less assimilable to the official line, however. Although the overall harmonic structure is clearly diatonic, the work does contain a great deal of dissonance that verges on atonality in places. This is used to create dramatic effects of anguish and foreboding so powerful that they would seem to entirely contradict the requirement that the tone be optimistic and edifying. It is interesting to note that one episode, which uses dissonance to express a foreboding of cosmic proportions, has been bathetically entitled "The Duke's Order" (no. 7). Could this verbal tag be an attempt by the composer to constrain interpretations of this episode, playing down any possible references to a malignant Fate by making the feudal overlord into the source of dread instead?

The ending of the ballet also contains hints of unresolved harmonic tensions that contradict glibly optimistic interpretations. The melodic balance of Juliet's dignified C Theme, which finally reaches its full expression as she prepares herself to die, is distinctly undermined by the insertion of a discordant ninth between each rendering, a chord not considered legitimate in traditional tonality. Could this be interpreted as the kind of ironic subtext of the kind that Jaffé identified in the *October Cantata*? Certainly it is impossible to read anything heroic or triumphant into such an ending, even if we allow for the equilibrium suggested melodically by the fulfillment of Juliet's C Theme.

It is interesting to see how Nestyev has dealt with these aspects in the official biography. Insisting upon the composer's loyalty to tonality, he implies that his use of dissonance merely serves as a foil to enhance the beauty of traditional harmonies (467). The "eerie-sounding interval" of the ninth is justified on the grounds that it connotes "grief and despair" (475), and Nestyev takes it for granted that this is appropriate in contexts such as death. However, he does not seem aware that admitting these emotions into the final bars of this ballet makes it impossible to argue that the work displays the kind of heroic optimism demanded by socialist realism. Consequently, this musicologist, in his anxiety to appropriate Prokofiev for the regime, has unwittingly argued himself into a knot, and we are left with the feeling that perhaps this work is not quite as neatly categorizable as he would have us think.

Elsewhere in the same chapter, Nestyev attributes Prokofiev's harmonic nonconformism to a desire to "revitalize the expressive means of music" (466), and later suggests that it reveals "a more specific and meaningful purpose: to expose the enemies of mankind, the misanthropes who murder and destroy" (471). Among the list of "enemies of mankind" that follows this extract, Nestyev specifically mentions the "haughty, vengeful knights" of *Romeo and Juliet.* Here, as in the rest of his critical assessment of the ballet, he seems determined to demonstrate that Prokofiev has adequately polarized the characters into progressive and reactionary forces in required socialist-realist fashion. Hence, we are told that "Romeo corresponds completely to Shakespeare's conception of the hero, seized at first with romantic yearning and later displaying the flaming passion of a lover and the valor of a warrior"; Juliet develops into "a strong, selfless and loving woman"; Friar Laurence is a "humanist"; and Tybalt is "the personification of evil, arrogance, and class haughtiness." As for Mercutio, he is full of "bitter jests" that are, we understand, directed toward the overthrow of "medieval bigotry" (269–70).

I would argue that there is much to take issue with in this characterization. For one, the opposing forces are not musically polarized in such a clear-cut fashion as Nestyev would have us believe; instead, characters are foregrounded or backgrounded from a centralized perspective, and the protagonists display a much greater internal complexity than would be permitted by the simple allegory suggested here. There are also points where the characterization seems actively to contradict the official line. Paris, for example, considered to be a highly reactionary figure in socialist commentary, is given a particularly harmonious and balanced portrait theme that actively influences Romeo's in a positive way. Nor are the "people" idealized in the required fashion. Although there is a suitable abundance of crowd scenes (providing plentiful opportunities for the corps de ballet, of course), these subjects are not noticeably oppressed by the feudal strife; instead they enthusiastically participate in it, as we see in the gradual transformation of the two initial folk dances, "The Street

Awakens" (no. 3) and "Dance in the Morning" (no. 4), into "The Quarrel" (no. 5) and then "The Fight" (no. 6).

In some cases the musical semiotic is just not subtle enough to support Nestyev's interpretations. For example, he claims that, in the characterization of Friar Laurence, "there is neither churchly sanctity nor mystical remoteness; the music underscores the Friar's wisdom, spiritual nobility and kindly love of people" (269–70), but just how the music manages to depict a spirituality that is specifically non-churchly, nonmystical, and proletarian, he does not explain. Similarly, it is not clear exactly when or how Mercutio's humor actually becomes "bitter"; my own analysis would suggest that this character is mostly drawn playful and light, in order to provide a more marked contrast with Tybalt's rigidity.

The extent to which Romeo may be considered a socialist hero is worthy of some attention. Clearly, the character has been foregrounded far more than in Shakespeare, and his theme undergoes an unprecedented development. But could he be said to be an "active participant in the proletarian struggle, idealized to the point of superhuman perfection, and displaying the internal coherence, courage, and love of life necessary to enable him to overthrow the forces of feudal prejudice"?[11] I would say not. On his first appearance, he is portrayed as something of a buffoon, with a gauche, disjointed theme executed on that most comical instrument, the bassoon; and as we have seen, it is the acquisition of courtly graces (not proletarian virtues) that enables him to become worthy of Juliet's love. Even after his blossoming, he is associated with tunes that are above all sentimental and romantic, not heroic or militant. To my mind, therefore, Romeo's complexities align him with heroes of the bildungsroman, rather than those of the socialist kind, types that are quite clearly distinguished by the ideologues.

Finally, what of the requirement that socialist realism be above all optimistic? To what extent has Prokofiev managed to turn Shakespeare's tragedy into a triumph for the forces of progress and light in the required Soviet manner? Let us turn first to the question of the happy ending that was to be given to the tragedy at one point, but was later revoked. Could this have been an attempt by Prokofiev and Radlov to pander to the authorities on this issue? After all, the doctrine of socialist realism was still being defined at this time, and the Popov version of *Romeo and Juliet*,[12] which became the production of reference for many years, had not yet appeared. Could it be that, in the political climate of 1934–35, it just seemed too risky to stage a full-blown tragedy, and the authors took the only measures that occurred to them to bring their work into line with official decrees?

Prokofiev's officially sanctioned autobiography claims otherwise. "The reason for taking such a barbarous liberty with Shakespeare's play was purely choreographic," he wrote, "live people can dance, but the dying can hardly be expected to dance in bed,"[13] justified on the grounds that Shakespeare himself was said to have been uncertain about the endings of his plays. Although this argument interestingly anticipates the case put forward by Susan Snyder that Shakespeare's *Romeo and Juliet* is structurally a comedy until the death of Mercutio,[14] the decision was apparently not popular with Shakespearean scholars who protested vehemently against the travesty.

What can the musical text itself tell us about all this? For, of course, in a well-formed work of art the ending is not arbitrary, but is present at the very beginning, indeed is *determined* by artistic choices inherent to the structure. If Prokofiev had intended the ballet to be a romantic comedy, then surely there would be some musical indication of that from the outset.

There is indeed some evidence of this. First, there is the matter of the overture, which sets the tone for a tale of romance and not a tale of conflict or anguish; and second, there is the scenic restructuring, by means of which all the tragic material occurs in the epilogue as if it were hurriedly tagged on the end following a change of plan. These might be vestiges of that earlier draft of the work. On the other hand, it is also true that the music does not sound like "true happiness," as Prokofiev himself acknowledged in the quotation above. Many of the themes associated with the lovers (such as the main Romeo and Juliet Theme, the Love Theme, and Juliet's C Theme) contain strong overtones of pathos or yearning that clearly would be inappropriate in a comedy. Could it be then that the composer himself was divided on this issue, emotionally committed to a tale of thwarted love, even while he was structuring the work as comedy?

Of course, we will never know what Prokofiev's intentions truly were when he composed *Romeo and Juliet*. But perhaps this does not matter. What is more interesting in the end is the effect that the work has had upon different contexts of reception. For, while it did not comply totally with the dominant paradigm of the local cultural system (socialist realism), it clearly found resonance on the wider stage, going on to become one of the best-loved and most performed ballets of the twentieth century.

Notes

1. From the constitution of the Union of Soviet Writers. Quoted from Alexander Shurbanov and Boika Sokolova, *Painting Shakespeare Red: An East-European Appropriation* (Newark: University of Delaware Press, 2001), 96.

2. Ibid.

3. Daniel Jaffé, *Sergey Prokofiev* (London: Phaidon Press, 1998), 141.

4. Susan Snyder, "The Comic Matrix of *Romeo and Juliet*" [1979], in *Shakespeare's Early Tragedies,* Casebook Series, ed. Neil Taylor and Bryan Loughrey, 168–79 (Basingstoke: Macmillan, 1991).

5. Israel V. Nestyev, *Prokofiev,* trans. Florence Jones (Stanford, CA: Stanford University Press, 1960); Victor Seroff, *Sergei Prokofiev: A Soviet Tragedy* (London: Leslie Frewin, 1969).

6. Claude Samuel, *Prokofiev,* trans. Miriam John (London: Calder and Boyars, 1971); David Gutman, *Prokofiev* (London: Alderman Press, 1988); and Jaffé, *Sergey Prokofiev.*

7. Jaffé, *Sergey Prokofiev,* 118.

8. Nestyev, *Prokofiev,* 454; Seroff, *Sergei Prokofiev,* 216.

9. Jaffé, *Sergey Prokofiev,* 149.

10. Nestyev, *Prokofiev,* 268. Further references to this book will be given parenthetically by page number in the text.

11. For a detailed description of the socialist hero, see Shurbanov and Sokolova, *Painting Shakespeare Red,* 99.

12. Ibid., 101–4. This 1935 production finished with a brightening blue sky showing through the window of the charnel house, indicating that, spiritually at least, the characters had all got what they deserved.

13. Seroff, *Sergei Prokofiev,* 202–3, and Gutman, *Prokofiev,* 111–13.

14. Snyder, "The Comic Matrix of *Romeo and Juliet,*" 170.

The Smithy of the Soul: Shakespeare, Translation, and Identity
Michael Cronin

In an ambitious survey of the history of the English language, the novelist Melvyn Bragg does not shy clear of hyperbole when recruiting Shakespeare to the seraphim of the language's elect: "He is not only thought to be the greatest writer the world has seen but the most written-about writer the world has ever known for his chroniclers and commentators spill over global tongues, German, Italian, Spanish, French, Dutch, Russian, Japanese, Hindi: unroll the map. He is in more than fifty languages. He was not for an age but for all time, was the boast and the prophecy, and so far it has been fulfilled."[1] Bragg's comment can be seen at one level as a rather excitable proof of the Derridean intuition in *Tours de Babel* that originals owe their prestige to the existence of translations.[2] As Derrida argued, an elegant paradox of literature is that it is those authors who are famously "untranslatable" (Joyce, Proust, Shakespeare) who attract the most assiduous translation attention, their very untranslatability a prime motive for their translatability. However, my concern in this essay will not be what happens to Shakespeare in translation but what happens to translation in Shakespeare. More specifically, I will be tracking an intratextual translation presence to show how Shakespearean drama through the conduit of translation articulates English and more broadly European concerns with language, power, representation, metamorphosis, proximity, and control. The question of translation will be bound up with the way in which the "unique" island of Britain will translate itself around the globe, its translatability both articulated and foreshadowed in the work of the world's most translated dramatist. A primary framework for the exploration of these issues will be the practices of translation and interpreting in sixteenth- and early seventeenth-century England and Ireland and their role in the political and military conflicts opposing the two islands in the period. The essay will begin by sketching out the background to classical and Renaissance theories of eloquence and then proceed to examine the relationship between translation and English nationalism and imperialism as it emerges in different plays by Shakespeare.

Eloquence

An abiding preoccupation of the European Renaissance was the notion of civility. It was civility that admitted one to the community of the civilized and made one a worthy citizen of the polis.[3] Not surprisingly, a great deal of polemical and pedagogical energy would go into defining what exactly constituted civility, who had it, and what was the best way of passing it on to the next generation. Few commentators disagreed, however, about the centrality of language to the construction and representation of civility. The consensus lay in the perceived link between language and eloquence. Eloquence not only took place in the world, but it had the power to change the world. Thus, an essential part of the transformative vision of the Renaissance resided in the belief that words properly ordered possessed a power that changed the minds, habits, and dispositions of those who heard them.

An illustrative example of this credo can be found in Pier Paolo Vergerio *De Ingenius Moribus et Liberalibus Adulescentiae* (The Character and Studies Befitting a Free-Born Youth) from 1402–3. Vergerio lists those objects of study most likely to promote the cultivation of civility in a young man of means and social standing. He advocates the study of history and moral philosophy, but to these subjects he adds a third, eloquence: "Through philosophy we can acquire correct views, which is of first importance in everything; through eloquence we can speak with weight and polish, which is the one skill that most effectively wins over the minds of the masses."[4] Vergerio is not innovating here but drawing on the models from antiquity that would animate so much of Renaissance thinking. Cicero in his *De Inventione* presents a scene of what might be described as primal colonization where the rude and uncouth savage is converted to civility through eloquence. In his *De optimo genere oratorum*, he makes explicit the connection between using language and winning friends and influencing people: "The supreme orator, then, is one whose speech instructs, delights and moves the minds of his audience ... For as eloquence consists of language and thought, we must manage while keeping our diction faultless and pure—that is in good Latin—to achieve a choice of words both proper and figurative. Of 'proper words' we should choose the most elegant, and in the case of figurative language we should be modest in our use of metaphors and careful to avoid far-fetched comparisons."[5] Underlying Cicero's pedagogy is the classical tradition of topical rhetoric. Arguments are won when the speaker takes hold of the topos, the place of argument. The successful orator becomes sole owner and all others are driven from that place that is no longer rightfully theirs and that they have forfeited through defective eloquence. Eloquence in this sense is agonistic and proprietorial. It is Quintilian who will ask what the resources are that the orator might draw on and who establishes a link between translation and eloquence: "For the Greek authors excel in copiousness of matter, and have introduced a vast deal of art into the study of eloquence; and, in translating them, we may use the very best words, for all that we use may be our own. As to [verbal] figures, by which language is principally ornamented we may be under the necessity of inventing a great number and variety of them, because the Roman tongue differs greatly from that of the Greeks."[6] If eloquence is related to the exercise of power, then translation is related to power in that it is a mechanism which allows politically stronger cultures to appropriate the "copiousness of matter" that is to be found in cultures annexed by or subordinate to empire. For Quintilian the power of the eloquent orator lies not in the proud isolation of imperial autonomy but in the careful exploitation of translation heteronymy whereby "all that we use may be our own." Classical antecedents and Renaissance reappropriation make of the eloquent orator one of the most significant authorization voices in the Western tradition. Those who speak well not only move their audiences to action, but they also move others out of places previously occupied, and expropriation through eloquence further enhances the power and position of the speaker.

Expansion

In tracing the crucial connection between translation, eloquence, and empire in Shakespeare's drama, it is necessary to consider first an internal shift in Shakespeare's history plays. Jean-Marc Chadelat in his discussion of Shakespeare's history plays describes the key transition from the world of *Richard II* to that of *Henry V, Julius Caesar,* and *Coriolanus* as follows: "To the closed and defensive nature of societies concerned with the past correspond by a similar inversion the opening of a space made expandable by the expansionist nature of power acting on itself."[7] What we have, in effect, is the movement from the heteronomous world of *Richard II*, structured by a theological order and guided by a set of metaphysical beliefs, to the one we find in *Henry V, Julius Caesar,* and *Coriolanus,* where an autonomous society legislates for itself and politics becomes a real and symbolic site of transformation.

Implicit in this transformation is the notion that power can extend itself indefinitely in space and that space can be extended as far as the reach of power. If Shakespeare will notably expand the resources of the English language and English dramatic expression, this development will take place alongside the territorial expansion of England itself overseas. It is no accident therefore that it should be precisely at that moment when England begins to consolidate (monarchy) internally and expand externally (empire) that it should seek to consolidate the internal legitimacy of English and expand the external use of the language. The coincidence of the two projects can be observed in the linguistic interests of a number of notable military adventurers and propagandists involved in the Tudor and Elizabethan campaigns in Ireland. Fynes Moryson, for example, who was a zealous defender of the English cause in Ireland, was equally preoccupied with the defense of the English language. Determined to pursue the claims of the vernacular he claimed: "they are confuted who traduce the English tounge to be like a beggers patched Cloke, which they should rather compayre to a Posey of sweetest flowers, because by the sayd meanes, it hath been in late ages excellently refyned and made perfitt for ready and brief deliuery both in prose and verse."[8] Humphrey Gilbert, who used extreme violence in suppressing the rebellion in Munster in the southwest of Ireland in 1579, was similarly preoccupied with the future status of English. His proposal was for the establishment of a university in London, to be called Queen Elizabeth's Academy, which would be in a sense the capital's answer to Oxbridge. The Academy would offer extensive oratorical training but would differ from the established universities in one crucial respect: the training would be through the medium of the vernacular, English, rather than through Latin. In addition, Gilbert recommended that each language teacher in the Academy should "printe some Translation into the English tongue of some good worke" every three years.[9]

The more eloquent the English language, the better it was fitted to be the language of empire and the more flowers in the bouquet, the more becoming the conquest itself. Like a latter-day Quintilian, Gilbert realizes that no imperial language can do this all by itself and hence the requirement that the trainers of his orators also be translators. Gilbert as soldier and educational theorist was by no means unusual in his interest in translation. As Patricia Palmer points out in *Language and Conquest in Early Modern Ireland,* "[t]he fact that so many leading translators of the age—Bryskett, Fenton, Googe, Harrington—were also players in the conquest of Ireland confirms the uncanny incongruity between pushing back the frontiers of English and expanding the geopolitical boundaries in which it operated."[10] It is therefore in a larger context of linguistic and territorial expansion attended by the good offices or otherwise of translation that Shakespeare is working as a writer. What I would like to suggest is that what we find in his work is a recognition that the construction of nation and by extension the beginning of empire is among other things an exercise in translation, and moreover, that it is translation that becomes an exemplary figure for many of the anxieties attending the nation in its expansionary moment. I will consider Shakespeare's political engagement with the question of translation as it relates to French and Irish Gaelic, and concentrate on two of Shakespeare's history plays, *2 Henry VI* and *Henry V*, which provides particularly fruitful insights into the doubts and uncertainties besetting the Tudor and Elizabethan mind around the necessary but troubled exchange of translation.

Double Dealing

In *2 Henry VI*, the rebel leader Jack Cade enters into dialogue with Stafford and sets out the grounds for his suspicion of the trustworthiness of Lord Say. Cade's attitude to Say is primarily dictated by questions of language and more specifically by Say's role as a translator, as a linguistic broker in the Franco-English translation space:

Cade. . . . Fellow kings, I tell you that Lord Say hath gelded the commonwealth and made it a eunuch; and more than that, he can speak French; and therefore he is a traitor.
Stafford. O gross and miserable ignorance!
Cade. Nay, answer, if you can: The Frenchmen are our enemies; go to then, I ask you but this, can he that speaks with the tongue of an enemy be a good counsellor, or no?

(4.2.178–86)[11]

Cade's sentiments cannot simply be dismissed as Stafford would have us believe as "gross and miserable ignorance." Cade, in effect, was simply articulating a belief that was widely held in Elizabethan England, namely that language knowledge potentially compromised political fealty. Edmund Spenser in his *A View of the Present State of Ireland* advances a broadly similar argument to that of Cade when he advocates the radical elimination of the Irish language, "the speech being Irish, the heart must needs be Irish for out of the abundance of the heart, the tongue speaketh."[12] When Say is captured by the rebels and brought before Cade, he mounts a defense of his linguistic brokerage claiming:

> This tongue hath parley'd unto foreign kings
> For your behoof.
>
> (4.7.82–83)

The argument advanced by Say on the necessary, strategic importance of translation in times of conflict is the standard defense of linguistic mediation. Its merits are, however, lost on Cade, and Say is unable to save his life. Cade's indifference to Say's defense is all the more surprising in that Cade is a mirror image of Say, not so much in his pretensions to political power as in his past experience of translatorial intervention. We know of this because of the portrait of Cade that York first presents to us when he outlines the former's military prowess in the Irish wars. York focuses initially on the valor and indomitable energy of Cade:

> In Ireland I have seen this stubborn Cade
> Oppose himself against a troop of kerns,
> And fought so long, till that his thighs with darts
> Were almost like a sharp-quill'd porpentine:
> And, in the end being rescued, I have seen
> Him caper upright like a wild Morisco,
> Shaking the bloody darts as he his bells.
>
> (3.1.360–66)

But then York reveals information that is arguably crucial to our understanding of Cade:

> Full often, like a shag-hair'd crafty kern,
> Hath he conversed with the enemy,
> And undiscover'd come to me again,
> And given me notice of their villainies.
>
> (3.1.367–70)

The implication in York's account is that Cade was able to act as a translator/interpreter from Irish Gaelic to English and this accounts in part for the inestimable worth of Cade as a soldier and ally. Indeed, if Cade had not mastered Irish Gaelic, he would have been perfectly unable to communicate with the overwhelmingly Irish-speaking infantry, the "kerns," and his Irish would have to be very good if he was somehow to go "undiscover'd." The rebel Cade like the loyal Say has acted as a linguistic double agent and both have found themselves thrust into the role of translator by the expansionist drive of the English Crown.

That both France and Ireland are linked in the political ambitions of the English Crown is made apparent in the presentation of York. York himself is explicit in proclaiming his attachment to the "realms of England, France and Ireland," and we are told by Salisbury that what makes York feared and honored of the people is "thy acts in Ireland, / In bringing them to civil discipline" and "[t]hy late exploits done in the heart of France" (1.1.195–96 and 197). Both the realms of Ireland and France involve an engagement with language and translation, an engagement that is seen to be fraught with danger not only at the level of actual practice in the field (away) but in terms of perception in the (home) country from which the translators come.

It is interesting to note that the motif of translation is not only expressed in the direct accounts of interpreting practice but is also variously indicated in more oblique ways in the play. A feature of Cade's language in 2 Henry VI is his relentless punning. Both in his soliloquies and his exchanges with others, Cade is drawn irresistibly toward wordplay so that it becomes a characteristic marker of his speech. Cade's obsessive fondness for the pun could be seen as indicative of a social unease, a slightly frantic and undisciplined imitation of the corrosive wit of his erstwhile aristocratic masters, or as the comic signature tune of the Shakespearean low-life character. However, it is also possible to see punning itself as a form of double language so that the double language of interlingual translation (Cade as Gaelic-English translator) is mirrored by the double language of intralingual translation in the form of punning.[13] Not only has Cade spoken a "double language" in Ireland in his role as interpreter, but in England he continues to speak a double language as punster and usurper.

A further echo of Cade's activity as translator is to be found in the metaphor used to describe Cade's political ambitions and his activities in Ireland. When York tells us of Cade's work as an informant in Ireland, we are told that he was in disguise, he went "undiscover'd" because he presumably wore the distinctive dress of "shag-hair'd crafty kern." If he had not, such were the disparities between native Gaelic and Tudor dress, he would have been found out instantly.[14] Not only is Cade himself a clothier by profession, but when his follower George Beavis looks for an image to describe the political project of Cade, he takes his metaphor from the professional occupation of the rebel leader: "Jack Cade the clothier means to dress the commonwealth, and turn it, and set a new nap upon it" (4.2.6–8). Theo Hermans has commented on the prevalence of the "garment metaphor" in Renaissance discourse on translation and it is significant that it is Cade the Clothier who also ends up as Cade the Translator.[15] The attraction of dress as metaphor is that like metaphor itself, dress both reveals and conceals. If Cade dresses to disguise his true intentions from the native Irish, his dress in England reveals his social standing in the eyes of both his aristocratic allies and enemies, useful as a tool or feared as a rabble-rouser, but ultimately outside any hierarchy of inclusion. His position as interpreter gives him power in the field, but it is when he seeks to enlarge this power to the court that his cover is in a sense blown.

If Matthiessen sees translation as a quintessentially Elizabethan art and part of the literary effervescence of sixteenth- and early seventeenth-century England, it is because it takes place in the context of and influences other developments in English society at the time.[16] When Cade lists off the charges that he believes warrant the execution of Lord Say, he includes Say's role in the promotion of the printing press ("thou hast caused printing to be used," 4.6.39–40) and in the heightening of language awareness ("thou hast men about thee that usually talk of a noun and a verb, and such abominable words as no Christian ear can endure to hear," 4.6.43–45). Cade in his indictment of a fellow translator shows himself to be remarkably aware of the context and consequences of translation, even if the egregious nature of the justification for the killing of Say is doubtless intended to alienate any possible sympathy for Cade among the audience. The printing press was of course crucial to the dissemination of translations in Tudor and Elizabethan England, and the fortunes of the English Bible in particular are bound up with the revolutionary possibilities of the new technology.[17] As we saw earlier, a constant preoccupation of the period was with the legitimacy of the vernacular language as an adequate means of expression. One effect of translation in many different cultures and historical periods has been an enhanced linguistic self-awareness. As languages, both modern and classical, come into sustained and continuous contact with English, it is inevitable that there will be more and more "talk of a noun and a verb" as the English language becomes increasingly aware of its own specificity but also through philological study of its relationship to other languages. Cade in singling out the printing press and grammatical self-knowledge has perhaps unwittingly identified crucial elements in the elaboration of the "civilizing" mission of empire, where propaganda, proselytism, and printing are conjoined in the workshops of translation.

This primary role for translation is not, of course, without its drawbacks, as Cade's subsequent career shows. General anxieties around expansion of empire and consequent vulnerability are manifold in the period and not infrequently cluster around translation. An example is to be found in a letter to the poet John Donne written by his close friend, Sir Henry Wotton, one of the most distinguished English diplomats of the period. At one stage in his career Wotton was secretary to the Earl of Essex, who was at that time in negotiations with Hugh O'Neill, the leader of the Gaelic Irish. Wotton is less than charitable about interpreters in Ireland whose loyalty he finds more than questionable: "Whatsoever we have done, or mean to do, we know what will become of it, when it comes among our worst enemies, which are interpreters. I would there were more O'Neales and Macguiers and O'Donnells and Mac-Mahons and fewer of them."[18] The central problem of translation in general and interpreting in particular, is the problem of control. Anderson says of the interpreter that "his position in the middle has the advantage of power inherent in all positions which control scarce resources."[19] The proximity is both desired, and dreaded. The desire comes from a clear wish to control and manipulate a situation. The dread results from the fear of being misled either by the native interpreter or by the nonnative interpreter changing sides and going native.

The difficulty for the imperial agent is dealing with this monstrous doubleness, the potential duplicity of interpreters. William Jones in his *Grammar of the Persian Language* (1771) stated that for British officials, "[i]t was found highly dangerous to employ the natives as interpreters, upon whose fidelity they could not depend."[20] The choice for the architects of empire was between what might be termed *heteronomous* and *autonomous* systems of interpreting. A heteronomous system involves the recruitment of local interpreters and teaching them the imperial language. The interpreters may be recruited either by force or through inducements. An autonomous system is one where colonizers train their own subjects in the language or languages of the colonized. The conflicting merits of both systems are vividly illustrated in a letter of Pedro Vaz de Carminha, dated May 1, 1500. In this letter we find an account of a Portuguese admiral asking whether two Tupis should be taken by force to act as interpreters-informants. A majority of Portuguese officers are reported as claiming that "it was not necessary to take men by force, since those taken anywhere by force usually say of everything that they are asked about that they have it in their country. If we left two of the exiles there, they would give better, very much better information than those men if we took them; for nobody can understand them, nor would it be a speedy matter for them to learn to speak well enough to be able to tell us nearly so much about that country as the exiles will when your

Majesty sends them here."[21] The "exiles" were those Portuguese whose punishment for breaking the law took the form of banishment to live among the indigenous peoples in Portugal's newly discovered colonies.

The Portuguese officers might have added that the return of the native is rarely comforting. Return offers the promise of closure, the synthesis of retrospection, the gathering in after the voyage out. However, the Prodigal Son is a figure of disquiet and Ulysses' arrival in Ithaca is marked by a bloodbath. The Bible and Homer intimate that return usually unsettles, disturbing the settled community. The dilemma for interpreters in colonial contexts is whether they can return as *native*. In other words, what is apparent in Wotton's letter to Donne is his unhappiness with having recourse to heteronomous interpreters and the questions this raises for control of situations of conflict. However, the autonomous interpreters too are dogged by suspicions around the tension between linguistic agility and political fidelity. So when Cade, for example, returns to England from Ireland, he is both unsettled and unsettling. The one who has conversed with the enemy has now become the enemy. Cade has with respect to his allegiance to the Crown gone native and behaved like the kerns he affected to deceive. Lord Say, who also performs as an autonomous interpreter, falls foul too of the image of the translator/interpreter as duplicitous double and is condemned in the eyes of Cade and his followers for his linguistic fraternizing with the French enemy.

Forging the Nation

If we move to consider another play in Shakespeare's history cycle, *Henry V*, it is possible to see the relationship between translation, nation, and empire play itself out in a different context. In a famous scene from the play, which I have commented on in other terms elsewhere, soldiers from the various nations that will go on to constitute the United Kingdom engage in a series of sharp exchanges:[22]

> *Fluellen.* Captain Macmorris, I think, look you, under your correction, there is not many of your nation–
> *Macmorris.* Of my nation! What ish my nation? Ish a villain, and a bastard, and a knave, and a rascal? What ish my nation? Who talks of my nation?
> *Fluellen.* Look you, if you take the matter otherwise than is meant, Captain Macmorris, peradventure I shall think you do not use me with that affability as in discretion you ought to use me, look you; being as

good a man as yourself, both in the disciplines of wars, and in the derivation of my birth, and in other particularities.
Macmorris. I do not know you so good as myself: so Chrish save me, I will cut off your head.
Gowan. Gentlemen both, you will mistake each other.
Jamy. A! that's a foul fault.

(3.2.136–52).

In this scene Fluellen, Jamy, and Macmorris (the Welsh, Scottish, and Irish soldiers) are busy translating themselves into the new language and political order of (Great) Britain, the Irish language ghosting the final "s" in Macmorris's famous question, "What ish my nation," so that Macmorris, like so many stage Irishmen after him, will become the emblematic figure of translation or mistranslation. However, what I would like to consider here is the relationship between translation and artifice and the significance of that relationship for the construction of nation. To take translation itself, is there something about this activity that is vaguely fraudulent? Translation history indeed has many examples of fictitious translation from Macpherson's eighteenth-century Ossianic forgeries to a number of nineteenth-century "translations" from the German by the Irish poet James Clarence Mangan, who attributed the original poems to the German poets "Selber" and "Drechsler," who did not, of course, exist.[23] One question that might be asked is whether students of literary or indeed any kind of translation are training to be master forgers? If we take Jean-René Ladmiral's definition of the function of translation, "ça sert à nous dispenser de la lecture du texte original" (it saves us having to read the original), we could argue that the end user of a novel, who has no access to or knowledge of the other language, has a copy that is as good as the original, in other words a successful forgery.[24] Translators may object that this analogy belittles their expertise, but good forgers are enormously skillful, and bad translation bears all the hallmarks of shoddy imitation.

Staying with this idea it is arguable that there is a crucial link between *translation and forgery* and *translation and the forging of the nation*. It is an observation frequently made that what Tudor and Elizabethan England, classical France, and Romantic Germany had in common was a desire to provide cultural legitimacy for the emerging nation and a close and unstinting involvement in the activity of translation.[25] What translations and translators were doing in the critical period of political consolidation and national expansion was *forging* the language, the vernacular that would be appropriate and adequate to the ambitions of the new body politic. In other words, the forging of a new national identity implies the forgery of translation, the reading of the translation as if it was the original. Put another way, these translated subjects, Fluellen, Jamy, and Macmorris, must now be presented as English or, more properly, British originals. The drama of their encounter is that they must now behave as if they were always, already English speakers. Their identity forged in the military alliance of the conquering nation must be seen as their original condition, because if they, in the words of the Englishman Gowan, continue to "mistake each other" and revert to their original condition and language, the national and imperial project is threatened by dissent and disaffection. *"What ish my nation?"* will of course be the language-haunted question that will dominate European politics throughout the Age of Empire and its alter ego in the form of a rising cultural nationalism that will seek to expose the "forgery" of empire through a return to the "originals" of the constituent languages and cultures of empire. In the Irish case, for example, as the nineteenth century draws to a close, the translation traces become not the residue of shame (an imperfect original) but the kernel of the new language (Hiberno-English) of the Irish Literary Renaissance.

In Shakespeare's presentation of the transactions of translation and their consequences in periods of political conflict, we are offered an insight into both the genesis and the decline of empire. The intrinsic duality of the translation exchange means that the eloquence of civility is always vulnerable to the return of the originals, always potentially destabilized by new forms of forgery (irredentism) that draw their power from claiming to be closer to and more "faithful" to the original. If Shakespeare reminds us in different ways just how fraught the translation process is and how it is not only knaves but their masters who double their tongues, it is Joyce, that great student of Shakespeare who was closer than he perhaps realized to an important political and translation truth when Stephen Dedalus famously declared, "I go to encounter for the millionth time the reality of experience and to forge in the smithy of my soul the uncreated conscience of my race."[26] Bragg's contention that the supreme fiction of translation has meant that Shakespeare is truly a writer not for an age but for all time must be qualified by Shakespeare's own awareness that in forging the uncreated conscience of his own race, both age and time would watch over the handiwork of the translator as forger of nation and empire.

Notes

1. Melvyn Bragg, *The Adventure of English: 500 AD to 2000; The Biography of a Language* (London: Hodder & Stoughton, 2003), 141.

2. Jacques Derrida, "Des Tours de Babel," trans. by Joseph Graham, in *Difference in Translation*, ed. by Joseph Graham (Ithaca: Cornell University Press, 1985), 165–248.

3. Anna Bryson, *From Courtesy to Civility: Changing Codes of Conduct in Early Modern England* (Oxford: Clarendon Press, 1998).

4. Pier Paolo Vergerio, "The Character and Studies Befitting a Free-Born Youth," in *Humanist Educational Treatises*, ed. and trans. by Craig W. Wallendorf (Cambridge, MA: Harvard University Press, 2002), 40. The original: Per philosophiam quidem possumus recte sentire quod est in omni re primum; per eloquentiam graviter ornatque dicere qua una re maxime conciliantur multitudinis animi.

5. Cicero, "De optimo genere oratorum," in *Western Translation Theory from Herodotus to Nietzsche*, ed. Douglas Robinson (Manchester: St. Jerome, 1997), 7–8.

6. Quintillian, "Institutio oratoria," in Robinson, *Western Translation Theory*, 20.

7. Jean-Marc Chadelat, "Le désenchantement du monde: De *Richard II* à *Coriolan*," in *Formes littéraires du Théologico-Politique de la Renaissance au XVIIIe siècle: Angleterre et Europe*, ed. Jacques Pironon and Jacques Wagner (Clermont-Ferrand: Presses Universitaires Blaise Pascal, 2003), 244. The original: À l'espace clos et défensif des sociétés passéistes correspond par une inversion analogue l'ouverture d'un espace rendu extensible par la nature expansionniste de la puissance d'action sur soi-même.

8. *Shakespeare's Europe, Unpublished Chapters of Fynes Moryson's Itinerary, with an Introduction and Account of Fynes Moryson's Career*, ed. Charles Hughes (London: Sherratt & Hughes, 1903), 437–38.

9. Humphrey Gilbert, *Queene Elizabethes Academy*, ed. F. J. Furnivall (*EETS* e.s., 8, 1869), 1–12.

10. Patricia Palmer, *Language and Conquest in Early Modern Ireland* (Cambridge: Cambridge University Press, 2001), 111.

11. This reference and all subsequent references to Shakespeare's plays are taken from William Shakespeare, *The Complete Works*, ed. W. J. Craig (Oxford: Oxford University Press, 1974) and appear in the text.

12. Edmund Spenser, *A View of the Present State of Ireland*, ed. W. L. Renwick (Oxford: Clarendon Press, 1970), 68.

13. For a discussion of translation and puns, see Dirk Delabastita, *There's a Double Tongue: An Investigation into the Translation of Shakespeare's Wordplay, with special reference to "Hamlet"* (Amsterdam and Atlanta, GA: Rodopi, 1993).

14. Mairéad Dunlevy, *Dress in Ireland* (London: Batsford, 1989), 43–64.

15. Theo Hermans, "Images of Translation: Metaphor and Imagery in the Renaissance Discourse on Translation," in *The Manipulation of Literature: Studies in Literary Translation*, ed. Theo Hermans (London: Croom Helm, 1985), 106.

16. F. O. Matthiessen, *Translation: An Elizabethan Art* (Cambridge, MA: Harvard University Press, 1931).

17. See Alister McGrath, *In the Beginning: The Story of the King James Bible and how it changed a Nation, a Language and a Culture* (London: Hodder and Stoughton, 2001).

18. L. Pearsall Smith, *The Life and Letters of Sir Henry Wotton*, 2 vols. (Oxford: Clarendon Press, 1907), 1:308.

19. R. B. W. Anderson, "Perspectives on the Role of Interpreter," in *Translation: Applications and Research*, ed. by R. W. Brislin (New York: Gardner Press, 1976), 218.

20. Tejaswini Niranjana, *Siting Translation: History, Poststructuralism and the Postcolonial Context* (Berkeley: University of California Press, 1992), 16.

21. Pedro Vaz de Caminha, "The Discovery of Brazil," in *Portuguese Voyages*, ed. Charles David Ley (London: J. M. Dent, 1947), 49.

22. Michael Cronin, "Rug-Headed Kerns Speaking Tongues: Shakespeare, Translation and the Irish Language," in *Shakespeare and Ireland: History, Politics, Culture*, ed. Mark Thornton Burnett and Ramona Wray, 193–212 (London: Macmillan, 1997).

23. James Clarence Mangan, "Anthologia Germanica," *Dublin University Magazine* 7, no. 39 (1836): 278–302.

24. Jean-René Ladmiral, "Traduire, c'est-à-dire... Phénoménologies d'un concept pluriel," *Meta* 40, no. 3 (1995): 418.

25. Jean Delisle and Judith Woodsworth, eds., *Les Traducteurs dans l'histoire* (Ottawa: Les Presses de l'Université d'Ottawa, 1995), 39–76.

26. James Joyce, *A Portrait of the Artist as a Young Man* (London: Panther, 1977), 228.

Anthologies, Translations, and European Identities
Dirk Delabastita

THE TITLE OF THIS VOLUME, *SHAKESPEARE AND EUROPEAN POLITICS*, lends itself to two possible readings: "Shakespeare and politics *in Europe*" or "Shakespeare and *the* politics *of Europe.*" The former one is much wider and less focused. "Politics in Europe" concerns the problems associated with government and nationhood in Europe and possibly its former colonial extensions, and it also includes gender, race, class, language, religion, and other principles existing within the European space, founding social groups and cultural identities, and thus inspiring in-group loyalties and intergroup conflicts. But it does not necessarily engage the European dimension as such. The second reading of the title does precisely that and thereby considerably narrows down the scope of investigation. The phrase "the politics of Europe" calls up specific images of a shared European cultural identity, perhaps even of the European Union and its many historical and imagined predecessors. Our main theme now becomes that of the identity-building and nation-building that takes place specifically on the European scale, as distinct from the global context and as opposed to the national boundaries and divisive nationalisms that many European projects have wanted to counterbalance or transcend.

The second reading may seem to reduce the semantic range of the word "politics" to the narrower sense it has in traditional political philosophy or history, as opposed to the comprehensive sense that contemporary cultural studies has given to the term. But that need not be so. Even when viewed from a transnational angle, issues of government and nationhood are intertwined with "cultural" categories such as gender, race, class, language, or religion. It will be remembered, for instance, that Shakespeare in *Henry V* patriotically endows England with "manly" virtues and describes the French as "effeminate," or that Europe itself is often gendered as a woman, in accordance with its supposed origin in Greek mythology or with its later role as "mother" to all European nations. In the end, what differentiates the second reading of the title from the first is its concern with territory and its focus on Europe as a fluctuating intermediate entity between world politics and local or national politics within Europe.

This essay intends to develop the second perspective: Shakespeare and the politics of Europe. We shall look into the elusive reality of Europeanness and its partly hidden conceptual logic and wonder how Shakespeare fits into the picture. To what extent could he be called a "typical" European author, besides many other identities that have been claimed for him?

Aspects of Nationalism

It might be useful to start by recalling a few aspects of nationalism, which was an increasingly strong force in the Renaissance world of Shakespeare and even more so in the post-Renaissance world of Shakespeare's afterlife. No straightforward, unproblematic, or universally valid definition of nation and nationalism seems to be readily available,[1] but let us agree to accept the following four assumptions as helpful working hypotheses within the context of Renaissance and post-Renaissance Europe.

First, nation is a concept of social identity that may coexist peacefully or conflictingly with other social identities. Thus, an ardent patriot may simultaneously be a committed member of his or her local village community, a zealous citizen of the world, and several other things besides.

Second, whereas the human impulse to belong to a larger group is probably driven by a universal instinct for survival through mutual protection, nations as such should be seen as historical constructs rather than unchanging essences. Being "imagined communities,"[2] they exist in the minds of people in the form of value-laden representations of the world, and they typically find expression in linguistic and cultural behavior and in the creation of institutions.

Third, there is a dynamic interplay between national identities and the formation of institutions such as the state. Nationalist feelings may precede and prompt the creation of a state, and, conversely, state structures will tend to foster national feelings. Either way, national attachments usually originate first in the intellectual classes (artists, authors, scholars, teachers, politicians, etc.), who then try to mobilize the lower classes.

Last but not least, the media (from writing and print to today's digital media) play a crucial role in these processes by networking people in specific configurations, by permitting the rapid spread of new models or ideas, by promoting processes of linguistic and cultural standardization, and thus by enabling group attachments to be channeled or even engineered more efficiently.

Furthermore, it is worth bearing in mind three typical constituents of nationalist ideologies: common origin, common identity, and common language. The belief in a common origin holds that, despite their current diversity, the members of a nation share the same history and are bound together by a continuity of common experiences and by memories of a glorious past. That golden age may have been followed by a decline, but the mission of the community today is to build a new future together on the basis of its past achievements.

Having the same roots, the members of a nation also believe that, deep down, they share the same true nature. This self-defined common identity may be characterized in positive terms (i.e., defining values and traits, also typical behavior following from these traits and values) and in negative terms (i.e., what the nation is *not* or refuses to be and to do). In other words, the idea of the nation depends on both what it stands for and what it rejects as "other" or "different," so that inclusion and exclusion go hand in hand. Relations with outsiders are guided by "sentiments which vary from complete indifference to the most bitter antipathy, and are subject to swift changes within that range."[3] Of course, the notion of a common identity necessarily implies a certain degree of unity and conformity, possibly requiring the erasure of inner differences or the suppression of local identities, especially those that could threaten the supremacy of those holding the reins. Furthermore, the unique character of a nation's common identity is usually understood to entitle that nation to an autonomous territory and to political sovereignty. After all, like an individual person, a nation wants a home to live in and claims the right to follow its own inner voice.

The use of a standardized common language greatly facilitates the practical administration and government of the nation insofar as it can assert itself as a state, and, moreover, it shapes common perceptions, understandings, and valuations of the world. No less importantly, a national language is also a key symbolical marker of the group's collective identity.[4] Language is visibly or audibly present in virtually all forms of human interaction, and linguistic origin is very hard to either hide or simulate. Functioning as a foundational metonymy of the community, language and accent both symbolize and cement the community's oneness.[5]

The importance of literature—more specifically, of the national literary canon—in these processes of nation-building is well documented. After all, the canonized authors are expert users of the common language and become exemplars of its excellence; their works embody and stabilize the nation's common identity both through positive self-affirmation and by suitably casting "foreigners" or alleged "subversive" groups (e.g., Gypsies, Jews, outlaws, criminals, anarchists, etc.) as untrustworthy outsiders; and their epics and historical tales invent or reproduce appropriate myths of common origin and present inspiring examples of national heroism.

Here, as always, one should beware of rash conclusions and deterministic models, but there is no denying the correlation between the rise of nationalisms in Europe and the development of Europe's various national literary canons. Both the authors themselves and the mechanisms of patronage have played their part in these processes, but so has the system of literary criticism and, in conjunction with it, the education system from the nineteenth century onward. Philologists and critics are the acknowledged legislators who determine what is "good" literature and why. The teaching system inculcates such beliefs in the young minds of the elite and increasingly of the lower social strata as well. Among its most powerful instruments is the anthology, which selects and configures the "best" and the most "representative" literary pieces of the past and thus either constructs or perpetuates a national literary patrimony, making it available in a portable and easily teachable format.[6]

The nineteenth century was of course the heyday of nationalism in Europe. Not surprisingly, this period also witnessed the birth of the various national philologies, which gave scientific backing and thus lent credibility to the rediscovery and revaluation of the nation's literary origins, both by confirming their antiquity and authenticity, and by presenting them as the wellspring of an autonomous and continuous national literature. But even today, the practices of studying and teaching literature often follow the nationalistic model, thereby showing a partial blindness both to wider international contexts and to literary facts allegedly situated below the benchmark of national importance. The enormous sway of the national model shows itself even in the very types of academic literary research that were meant to complement or correct the national bias, for instance, in comparative literature, where the international perspective has indeed occasionally been used to serve a national agenda. Let me quote the French scholar and chief inspector of schools Gustave Vapereau, who concluded the preface to his *Dictionnaire Universel des Littératures* (1884) with the pious wish that the many years he spent working on this project would turn out to be fruitful:[7]

> Puisse cet emploi d'une partie notable de la vie d'un homme n'être pas jugé inutile à l'enseignement, aux lettres et à mon pays!

[May this employment of a notable part of a man's life be judged to be useful to education, to letters, and to my country!]

Note the curious linking of the author's "universal" literary aspirations with the triad *enseignement, lettres,* and *mon pays.*

Nationalistic thinking may also, less overtly perhaps, drive research into the international afterlife of Shakespeare. Think of studies of the popular type "Shakespeare in Holland," "Shakespeare in Russia," and so on, whose very titles suggest a tendency to define the reception of Shakespeare in terms of a creative dialogue between two national cultures operating in a binary or bilateral relationship. The hidden motive of this may be to show that the researcher's native culture was quick enough to respond to Shakespeare's genius, and that in due course and despite many obstacles it developed a tradition of Shakespearean reception as "rich" and "authentic," or perhaps as "creative" and "original," as that of any other nation. With ambassadorial zeal, the scholar wants to make sure that his or her nation is given due recognition for its part in the international history of Shakespeare's reception.

Such research tends to result in the production of well-documented, but separate national histories of Shakespeare's afterlife, which may then be compiled and compared. But it might be more profitable to strive for an approach that, while recognizing the vital importance of national traditions, refuses to be hamstrung by them. What we need is an X-ray type of vision that reveals the relevant subnational, supranational, and cross-national phenomena as well as those to which national significance is ascribed in a given setting. Insofar as it is the permanent interplay between multiple social identities, ideological constructs, and their conflicting interests at various levels—from local to global—which is the stuff of history, little could be more relevant for our purpose than studying the implications of that complex interplay for the ways in which we read, think, and rewrite Shakespeare.

International Shakespeares

What is gained by dropping our national blinkers is a less restricted view of the various channels through which Shakespeare has managed to permeate our modern world. This may be illustrated by figure 1, which presents an overview of the various flows of people (i.e. producers and/or carriers of texts) and texts (i.e. verbal texts, but also

	England and Its Colonial Extensions		
17th century	**1** London, England the "authentic" Shakespeare nationalized		
18th century	Britain and the American Colonies,		
	the British Empire, and the United States of America		
19th century	*nontranslation* the "authentic" Shakespeare exported		
20th century pre–WW II	*linguistic and cultural translation* Shakespeare imported by noncolonized non-Western cultures		
post–WW II	**2** postcolonial nationalisms worldwide *domesticating translation into local vernacular or into local english* Shakespeare cannibalized	**3** expansive capitalism modern media style and free choice *translation into more accessible English* Shakespeare Hollywoodized	**4** countertraditional cultures at home Shakespeare (post)modernized
post-Communist	**5** Increased Physical and Intellectual Mobility; Globalization; The Spread of English		

performance texts, music, film, and so on) that have given such extraordinary scope and depth to the cultural presence of Shakespeare. Being a survey of worldwide Shakespeare across four centuries in a mere two-hundred words, the diagram may be forgiven for not being exhaustive. Nor can a rigid structure of boxes hope to do visual justice to patterns of transition or to areas of tension and contestation, important as these have certainly been. In this crucial respect, our own intellectual toil shall have to mend what misses in the diagram. Let us

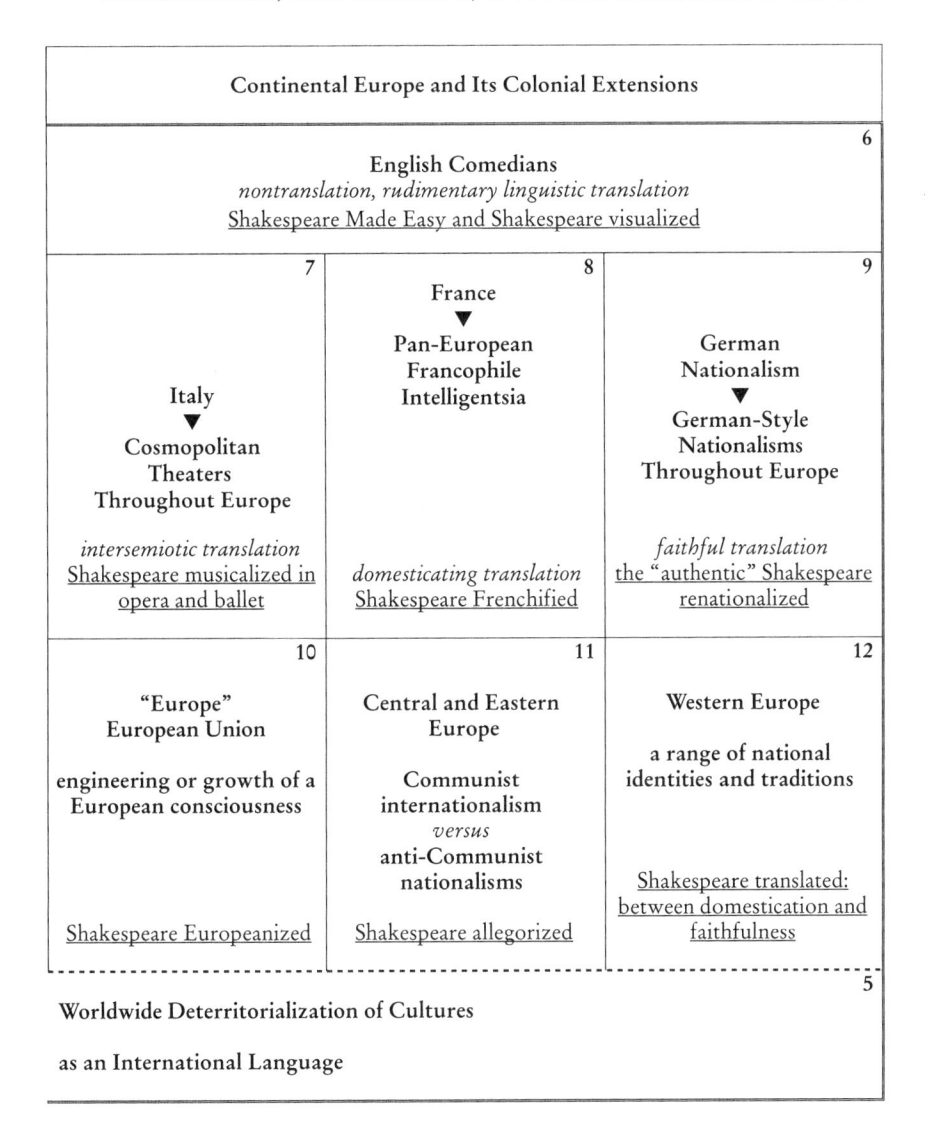

Continental Europe and Its Colonial Extensions		
English Comedians *nontranslation, rudimentary linguistic translation* <u>Shakespeare Made Easy and Shakespeare visualized</u>			6
7 Italy ▼ Cosmopolitan Theaters Throughout Europe *intersemiotic translation* <u>Shakespeare musicalized in opera and ballet</u>	8 France ▼ Pan-European Francophile Intelligentsia *domesticating translation* <u>Shakespeare Frenchified</u>	9 German Nationalism ▼ German-Style Nationalisms Throughout Europe *faithful translation* <u>the "authentic" Shakespeare renationalized</u>
10 "Europe" European Union engineering or growth of a European consciousness <u>Shakespeare Europeanized</u>	11 Central and Eastern Europe Communist internationalism *versus* anti-Communist nationalisms <u>Shakespeare allegorized</u>	12 Western Europe a range of national identities and traditions <u>Shakespeare translated: between domestication and faithfulness</u>
Worldwide Deterritorialization of Cultures as an International Language			5

now run through the table, roughly following the numbering of the various boxes.

Box 1 refers to England emerging from the Renaissance as an early and powerful prototype of the European nation-state and soon enlisting literature for the purpose of nation-building. In that process Shakespeare got established as England's national poet (e.g., David Garrick).[8] As efforts continued to forge a British union and with England's overseas colonial ventures faring well, Shakespeare also became a major cultural export product closely following the imperial flag. This happened mostly in untranslated form. After their independence, the United States, as well as other English-speaking settler colonies, developed their own Shakespeare tradition, also essentially untranslated. But beyond the immediate sphere of British and American imperialism, too, the massive presence of English-language trade and culture was later to promote Shakespeare as an icon of high culture abroad. In these cases the unforced importation of Shakespeare often did require linguistic translation and even forms of cultural translation (e.g., Kabuki-style Shakespeare, or the Kurosawa films in Japan). Sometimes, such interpretations have been made to serve a local postcolonial agenda, for instance in Quebec (where Shakespeare translations have been used to take a stand against both Parisian French and American English),[9] or in places like Mexico (where some translations have expressed a resistance to Iberian, i.e., European, Spanish).[10]

The next three cells in the diagram indicate further developments within the English-speaking world that have had a massive impact on the international afterlife of Shakespeare. Box 2 encapsulates the fact that, as the British Empire fell apart and gave way to the pressures of postcolonial nationalisms arising worldwide, the "authentic" British Shakespeare formerly taught at school in the imperial context was increasingly rejected, and the local cultures began to recycle him for their own purposes. This happened either in the local vernacular or in a hybridized English, in what some critics have termed a cannibalizing form of translation (e.g. Welcome Msomi with his Zulu *Macbeth*). Interestingly, a similar process occurred in Britain's Celtic fringe (e.g., two *Macbeth*s came out in Scots in 1992).[11] Box 3 hints at another postwar phenomenon in the English-speaking world, further pushing Shakespeare into the international arena, namely, the expansion of the modern media and of Western-style capitalism, which brought commercialized forms of Shakespeare to television sets, cinema theaters, and now also computer screens all over the world. This has happened either in English versions (more or less modernized and edited, with or without subtitled translation) or in dubbed ones. Meanwhile, as is suggested by box 4, at home modernist and postmodernist avant-gardism caused directors to abandon the search for historical authenticity and to look for contemporary styles in an increasingly cosmopolitan dialogue with overseas colleagues (e.g., Peter Brook, Ariane Mnouchkine). Box 5 is there to remind us that, at the same time, English was, of course, growing into a world language, becoming at once the vehicle and a symbol of a globalized economy and culture, and with enhanced mobility eroding the importance of territorially based cultural identities.

It should be remembered, though, that the international fortunes of Shakespeare had really started during his own lifetime with the activities of the English Comedians, who, as box 6 reminds us, brought simplified versions to the Continent in English or in rudimentary translation. The later seventeenth and the eighteenth centuries, partly also the nineteenth, witnessed the cultural supremacy of the French language and literary taste across most of continental Europe (box 8), reaching out as far as Russia and Turkey, while, via Spain and Portugal, this French influence extended to Central and South America as well. The neoclassical taste of the French caused a deeply ambivalent reaction to Shakespeare (e.g., Voltaire), generating a series of strongly Frenchified, domesticated translations for both the stage (e.g., Ducis) and the page (e.g., La Place, Le Tourneur). These were bought, read, discussed in *salons littéraires,* translated further as intermediary texts, and, in Ducis's case, performed throughout Europe and in places as far away from Paris as Buenos Aires or Rio de Janeiro.

Italy (box 7), too, belonged to the Pan-European sphere of Francophile influence, but, while typically using French translations as intertexts, in the nineteenth century it also developed two traditions of its own, which gave a major boost to the international spread of Shakespeare. First, Italian or Italian-style ballets and operas (e.g., Verdi) brought musical forms of Shakespeare to theaters across Europe and in the colonies as well. Second, the invention of the "star" system in the theaters catapulted actors like Ernesto Rossi to worldwide prominence. International tours often had these star actors performing in Italian with the rest of the cast being local actors who spoke their own tongue.

By that time Germany (box 9) had long rejected the belief in the universal and timeless perfection of French-language neoclassical culture. Replacing it by a Romantic affirmation of its own national heritage, it adopted Shakespeare as an anticlassical and prohistoricist model (e.g., Herder, Goethe, Schiller).[12] In translation, a more faithful approach to the "authentic" Shakespeare was promoted (e.g., Eschenburg, Schlegel-Tieck) as a reaction against the French tradition of translational domestication (*les belles infidèles*) and simply to enable Shakespeare to function as a genuinely new model. Germany's example was soon followed by other aspiring nations and Shakespeare became a catalyst and a high-value cultural asset for nationalistic movements throughout Europe. This often happened in conscious imitation of the German models (with, for example, Eschenburg or Schlegel-Tieck now replacing Ducis and Le Tourneur as intertexts for secondhand translation), but the German mode inevitably ended up inspiring translators and critics to turn to the English sources directly. In other cases, the integration of Shakespeare into the young or would-be nation's cultural repertoire took place quite independently from Germany's example (e.g., the more recent translations into Catalan or Basque).

If this pattern of recycling Shakespeare for nationalistic purposes evokes analogies with the trend we signaled in box 2, there are important differences, too. The continental-European nationalisms just referred to have used the Shakespearean model as a strategic weapon in their struggle against what was seen as an oppressive foreign hegemony (e.g., French neoclassicism or, later, Napoleonic expansionism; or the Castilian-Spanish dominance for the Catalans); the emancipatory value associated with the English originals explains why there was an overall preference for source-oriented translation. The national cultures emerging from the British Empire, on the other hand, have a different relationship with Shakespeare and the English language; actually being a powerful educational tool and symbol of the resented foreign hegemony, Shakespeare could for its opponents become a weapon against it only through more subversive or transgressive forms of rewriting and translation.

Box 12 sums up the fact that postwar Europe saw a broad range of Shakespeares that had developed out of this complex mix of models, with translations of various types serving as the textual basis for national Shakespeare cults. Meanwhile (box 11), Central and Eastern Europe had become subject to the homogenizing impact of an aggressive socialist internationalism that employed allegorical reading and staging techniques applied to fairly faithful translations in order to "paint Shakespeare red."[13] Interestingly, dissident artists used quite similar methods to elude censorship and convey their coded message of protest to the masses.

As we know from recent history, the collapse of Communist internationalism unleashed the sometimes violent forces of local nationalisms, at a time when, like the rest of the world, Europe was swept along by the mounting wave of globalization (box 5 again). And at the same time, the political unification of Europe got under way (box 10), bolstering the possibility of a distinctly European identity for Shakespeare. As I write, ten new member states coming mostly from the former Communist bloc have just entered the European Union, and several others are queuing up, raising the question of Europeanness with unprecedented urgency and unease.

Shakespeare a European?

Most of the phenomena just listed have been amply documented and studied separately. My aim in bringing them together in a single survey is to highlight the most extraordinary combination of successive and/or competing nationalisms and internationalisms that the history of Shakespeare's reception soon got entangled in. But the empirical data summarized in our survey may also provide us with the beginning of an answer to the question if Shakespeare may be called a truly European author. In terms of Shakespeare's afterlife, how much literary, theatrical, or cultural substance is there to the somewhat mysterious tenth cell in the table? Quite regardless of the fact that the settings of his plays cover much of Europe's history and geocultural space,[14] Shakespeare's massive presence in Europe does indeed seem to offer reasons for regarding him as a European author par excellence and for placing him in the same European "champions league" as Dante, Petrarch, Calderón, Corneille, Cervantes, Voltaire, Goethe, and a few more.

But then, the only period in which Shakespeare's European reception showed a relatively uniform pattern was that of the Pan-European cultural dominance of France, which, as we all know, was superseded by the Romantic nationalisms of the nineteenth century and is now essentially a thing of the past.[15] It might at this point be argued that the pattern of these nationalistic, anti-French appropriations of Shakespeare, first in Germany and later elsewhere, also looks fairly consistent, strengthening in this roundabout manner the case for a common European Shakespeare. But this consistency may be a deceptive appearance. Rather than being a banner under which distinct nationalistic revivals united and revolted collectively against the French cultural hegemony, Shakespeare was more of a pawn in a highly competitive game in which each respective nationalism tried to claim him for its own self-assertive purposes. In other words, for much of Europe's cultural history, Shakespeare was an apple of discord as much as a symbol of harmony. Like the Bible, Shakespearean texts and references may be present everywhere in European culture, but more as a site of confessional struggle than as a basis for ecumenical unity; in either case translation and commentary (criticism, exegesis) can be said to constitute the main textual battlefields. If in the Renaissance period, the issue of the true ownership and orthodox reading of the Scriptures divided Europe along religious and political lines, the post-Renaissance period saw how the ownership and orthodox reading of Shakespeare divided Europe along aesthetic and political lines.

At the same time, various factors had elevated Shakespeare to the position of a world author. One of these is definitely the wide range and lasting relevance of his themes and his undogmatic, dialogical approach (as has often been argued, the copresence of many ideological positions and the balancing of voices and countervoices give Shakespeare's works an unusual protean character, so that they can be made to fit the ideological and imaginative needs of socialism as easily as those of Christian humanism, or of the Hollywood film industry, and so on). Another factor, of course, is the sheer fact that he wrote in English, progressively more the world's lingua franca. It should be noted, incidentally, that the latter fact has surely made Shakespeare rather less of a European for those continentals who feel ill at ease with the steady rise of English in Europe or with the closeness of Anglo-American political bonds.[16]

Summing up, Shakespeare has a very high profile *above* the European level, as a world author, as well as *below* the European level, being both the epitome of Englishness and a key actor in a history of divisive nationalisms and annexations abroad. This state of affairs does not necessarily bar him from also becoming an icon of a European identity. All depends on how one defines that European identity. For instance, if diversity, Englishness, and/or global cosmopolitanism are believed to be part of such an identity, nothing is lost for the case of the European Bard. But it does follow that it is to the vexed notion of the cultural identity of Europe that we now have to direct our attention.

European Identities

Rather than firmly arguing some thesis about the existence of a definite European cultural and literary identity, or about the centrality of Shakespeare to such an identity, I really want to encourage further research into the notion of a European literature in the late twentieth and early twenty-first century, into the historical circumstances that have accompanied its flickering existence from the Middle Ages to the present, and into its fascinating conceptual and ideological implications. For the sake of analysis, I will develop the hypothesis that Europe today is a state "in-the-making," involved in the elaboration of political, economic, and defense structures (traditional appurtenances of the state) but also trying to build a sense of Euronational identity as a justification for itself.

Like other state structures, Europe is not a natural or transcendental given, but a result of human history. The European Union was born out of a range of considerations of an economic nature (the convenience of larger markets and fewer trade barriers) and a political nature (the determination to avoid another debacle after two traumatic world wars). Thus, the Union typically shows the top-down mechanism whereby state structures precede and try to foster feelings of identification and attachment. This massive endeavor has not prevented many people at the grassroots level from reacting with indifference or even downright skepticism ("Euroscepticism") to the "artificial" and "bureaucratic" project that they perceive Europe to be. Dissatisfaction about the erosion of national sovereignty that the Union entails has occasionally even led to an upsurge of nationalistic sentiment,[17] further implicating the European Union in the dialectic process whereby internationalist projects are envisaged in order to absorb or control aggressive nationalisms but may in their turn become the midwife of nationalistic fervor. The perceived failures of international structures beget nationalisms; the perceived failures of nationalisms call for new international structures; and so on.

European officials and Europe-minded intellectuals have had recourse to various policies and social-engineering techniques (via public education and the culture industry) to strengthen not only European unity but also the public perception of such a unity, ranging from the introduction of symbols, such as a European flag and anthem, to the adoption of a common currency. In 2006 a European Museum is to be opened in a new wing of the European Parliament in Brussels, providing the European equivalent of the many national monuments and museums erected during the nineteenth century. Nor should we underrate the symbolical impact of certain highly visible day-to-day realities, such as European number plates for cars, Champions League football, song contests, educational exchange schemes, and so on.

Inevitably, literature too has become part of this partly conscious and partly unconscious process of Euronation-building. One cannot help being struck by the flood of self-styled "European" literary publications in the late 1980s and 1990s, that is, the crucial period of the German reunification and the Maastricht "Treaty on European Union," and afterward. In the French-language area, from which my examples will be taken, we may note, among others, the following reference works, histories, and other scholarly publications:

Backès, Jean-Louis, *La littérature européenne* (Paris: Belin, 1996).
Benoît-Dusausoy, Annick, and Guy Fontaine, eds., *Lettres européennes: Histoire de la littérature européenne* (Bruxelles: De Boeck, 1992).

Benoît-Dusausoy, Annick, and Guy Fontaine, eds., *Dictionnaire des auteurs européens* (Paris: Hachette, 1995).
Didier, Béatrice, ed., *Précis de littérature européenne* (Paris: PUF, 1998).
Fumaroli, Marc et al., eds., *Identité littéraire de l'Europe* (Paris: PUF, 2000).
Moretti, Franco (trans. Jérôme Nicolas), *Atlas du roman européen, 1800–1900* (Paris: Seuil, 2000).
Polet, Jean-Claude, ed., *Patrimoine littéraire européen: Actes du colloque international, Namur 26, 27 et 28 novembre 1998* (Bruxelles: De Boeck, 2000).

as well as the following anthologies:

Bersani, Jacques, ed., *Anthologie des littératures européennes du XIe au XXe siècle* (Paris: Hachette, 1995).
Biet, Christian, and Jean-Paul Brighelli, eds., *Mémoires d'Europe: Anthologie des littératures européennes*, 3 vols. (Paris: Gallimard, 1993).
Polet, Jean-Claude, ed., *Patrimoine littéraire européen*, 15 vols. (Bruxelles: De Boeck Université, 1992–2000).
Valette, Bernard et al., eds., *Anthologie de la littérature française et européenne* (Paris: Nathan, 1992).

Several of these works make explicit references to the political construction of Europe, and, indeed, some have even been produced under the aegis of official European agencies.[18]

Identity, Roots, Language

The creation of a European identity is definitely an uphill task. There is, first of all, the problem of Europe's fluid boundaries. Which of the former Warsaw Pact countries can it accommodate? Does Turkey belong to Europe? Is the UK fully part of it? Needless to say, such geopolitical questions cannot be separated from the ideological concept of what Europe wants to stand for, and, more pointedly perhaps, what it refuses to be. Who or what is Europe's "other"? Different visions of Europe will generate different answers to that question, but here is a list of some "others" that are often invoked: separate European nationalisms (which pursue their own ends sometimes to the point of cherishing hegemonic ambitions at the peril of the international community); the Third World and the Orient (whose inhabitants are alienated by perceptions of exoticism and cultural inferiority); international Communism (the major international threat until the 1990s); aggressive Philistine liberalism and vulgar capitalism (a bête noire which is not always differentiated from the spread of English as an international language or from the supremacy of the United States as a world power);[19] the Muslim world (including the many Muslim communities living within the heartlands of Europe's geographical space);[20] and the Orthodox Eastern world (including Russia).

When it comes to defining Europe's cultural (and literary) identity in a positive rather than negative manner by identifying its characteristic traits, values, and corresponding behavioral patterns, one has to grapple with two difficulties at least: first, that of making sure that the alleged typical and unifying traits do not also characterize non-European cultures. Logically speaking, features lose their defining quality if they possess no differential value. This difficulty is often "resolved" by avoiding systematic comparisons and thus simply evading the issue altogether. But the second problem is much harder to sweep under the rug. Any concept of a common European culture flies in the face of the obvious reality of the cultural (ethnic, linguistic, religious, etc.) diversity within Europe. This diversity is actually bound to remain on the increase for as long as the official European space keeps expanding, and it is reflected most visibly—and very problematically—by Europe's great variety of languages. This is a major difficulty indeed, and upon closer inspection we see that two discursive strategies are often turned to in order to take care of it.

The first is to promote the notion of a unity-in-diversity (to be sure, the ultimate European catchphrase!), without, however, specifying what exactly the unity consists in, where the diversity begins, and how far diversity may be allowed to go. At best, topographical metaphors are used to suggest vaguely that while the diversity is visible at the "surface" level, the unity is to be found at "deeper" levels of experience.

A second discursive strategy is to turn the argument away from our rather muddled present to a safer past in which the European unity was supposedly more evident and beyond controversy. Hence, the many references to the common "roots" of Europe, which are usually taken to include Greek and Roman antiquity, Christianity, humanism, and/or the Enlightenment. Interestingly, this shift from a synchronic viewpoint (what is European culture today) to a diachronic one (the alleged common roots of Europe) often takes place almost silently and thus without awkward critical questions being asked such as: How well were the supposed textual roots of Europeanness known beyond a very small cultural elite?[21] Was there a continuous consensus about the "correct" meanings of Europe's fundamental texts (or, as with Shakespeare, was their reception process characterized by discontinuities and difference)? Exactly through what kind of semiotic process can age-old texts (many of which predate modernity and embody the very things—dependence on the classics, on Christianity, on the ruling classes—that modern literature has tried to emancipate itself from) become constitutive of meanings and cultural identities today?

Both discursive strategies resolutely affirm the reality of a European identity, implicitly also endowing it with moral authority (for who would not be happy to embrace the ethics of unity-within-difference, reconciling as it does togetherness with respect for singularity?) as well as with cultural authority (for, if luminaries like Aristotle, Dante, Cervantes, or indeed Shakespeare are said to embody European culture, how much room is left for dissent?). But neither strategy is very good at matching the force of its assertion of a European identity with a precise description of what this identity consists in. Conceptually speaking, that identity remains a fairly vague notion.[22]

In reality there is, of course, not one but many different Europeanist discourses, with each tending to reconcile or combine "unity" and "diversity" in different admixtures. A more careful logical analysis enables us to map these different concepts between two extreme positions that are in themselves so radical that they can exist as utopian visions at best.

One of these extremes would be the utopia of a fully integrated and no longer differentiated Europe that entirely sacrifices diversity to unity. The radical unity of this one European identity would require a single common language to be used by all.[23] Thus, this vision projects the alluring effect of delivering all Europeans from the curse of Babel and restoring them to a linguistic state of original purity, directness, and unity. Translation may be done away with simply because there is no longer any need for it.

The other extreme would be to categorically deny not just the existence, or the desirability, but even the very possibility of a common Europeanness, and to proclaim instead the model of multiple cultural identities within Europe in the most extreme terms of plurality and mutual incommensurability. Like its opposite, the model of total integration, such a particularist and culturally solipsistic refusal of even the logical possibility of a Pan-European identity does away with translation, but it does so for altogether different reasons. Babel is not overcome here but decisively vindicated. The radicality of linguistic and cultural difference is here seen as making impossible, or at least invalidating, cross-language communication at the European level. No (real) translation and thus no (real) Pan-European communication is possible because the scattering and confusion of languages lies beyond human remedy.

These absolutes of European integrationism and anti-European particularism are both imaginary extremes, of course, and most definitions of Europeanness exist at some point along the cline between them. But while avoiding the absolute extremes, many definitions do tend toward either a "maximalist" or a "minimalist" position.[24] Maximalist definitions of Europe posit the existence of a European essence and thus make the case for a profound unity at the expense of diversity. Minimalist definitions sacrifice unity to diversity, arguing that the commitment to the latter (creating possibilities for dialogue, complementarity, and mutual enrichment) is in the final analysis the one and only unifying factor that makes up the European identity.

It may be hypothesized that opinions regarding language planning and translation policies will vary accordingly. Thus, the more one positions oneself on the side of cultural diversity in Europe, the more one is likely to resist the pull toward a common lingua franca; the more one is likely to promote minority languages and multilingualism, as well as to accept the ensuing need for massive amounts of translating; and the more one is likely, furthermore, to favor a "literalist" or "foreignizing" poetics of translation that wants translations to be visible *as such* and to preserve the "difference" and the "strangeness" of the original text, language, and culture. Conversely, the more one believes in a common European identity, the more one will perhaps gravitate toward a "domesticating" mode of translation that effaces difference and subtly obscures the foreign origin of the text by rewriting it according to the stylistic norms and cultural canon of the receptor culture; furthermore, adherents of such a maximalist position (especially those belonging to a hegemonic culture themselves) are also likely to have somewhat less patience with the claims of minority languages, and they may be more sympathetic to the idea of a common European lingua franca (preferably their own!) as an alternative to translation.[25]

Anthologizing European Literature?

Keeping the above distinctions in mind, what would an anthology of European literature have to look like? Those who adopt a minimalist and hence a plural approach to the issue of Europe's cultural identity are sure to prefer juxtaposition and contrast over seamless integration as their principal editorial strategy. In terms of language policy, for instance, they might prefer to quote Shakespearean fragments in English, Dante in Italian, and Goethe in German, defending a multilingual anthology as the only possible *authentic* European anthology. If translations have to be added, or indeed, if a monolingual European anthology is preferred after all (e.g., for the sake of comprehension and marketability), no special efforts should be expected here to hide the translated origin of the selections. On the contrary, "literal" and "foreignizing" techniques may prevail, inasmuch as they underscore the foreign origin of the texts and expose the processes of cross-cultural, cross-lingual, and cross-temporal transmission, and their inevitable effects of semantic dislocation. The irreducible differences between the languages and cultures of Europe *need* to be put on display, because they reflect the diversity that is Europe's true nature.

But the more one positions oneself toward the maximalist view of Europeanness, the more the anthologist and the translator may see themselves as being entrusted with the task of creating unity out of difference. The careful selection of originals to be included in the anthology may help to suggest patterns of continuity through space and time, thus avoiding impressions of incoherence or eclecticism. Also, and crucially, the ontological difference between the translations in the anthology and the originals that they represent will need to be papered over. The project of an integrated European literature is doomed if the anthology reads like a patchwork of translations each of which advertises its translated status—its historicity and its partiality as a representation of the original—and thus its failure to really *be* the original. The impression of equivalence must override linguistic and cultural difference for the illusion of an essential, timeless Europeanness in literature to stand. Hence the expected preference for translations that use domesticating techniques and thus efface their translatedness from the reader's consciousness.[26]

These are all fairly speculative hypotheses that cry out for empirical testing, but in the present essay there is room for a limited case study only. Let us compare two of the European anthologies listed above: Jean-Claude Polet's impressive *Patrimoine littéraire européen* (which tends toward the maximum, essentialist, or integrationist side of the spectrum), and Christian Biet and Jean-Paul Brighelli's *Mémoires d'Europe: Anthologie des littératures européennes* (which appears to adopt a more minimalistic and pragmatic concept of Europeanness).[27]

An analysis of the sheer bibliographic data is already revealing. Consider the editors' programmatic use of the singular and the plural in their respective titles: Polet's *Patrimoine littéraire européen* has the singular throughout, whereas Biet and Brighelli's *Mémoires d'Europe: Anthologie des littératures européennes* grammatically expresses a belief in plurality. Consider also their choice of metaphors. While the titles of both anthologies (*patrimoine* on the one hand, *mémoires d'Europe* on the other) recognize the importance of the past for present identities, the metaphor *mémoires* allows for the selectiveness, waywardness, and presentness of cultural memories, whereas Polet's *patrimoine* evokes images of a nonnegotiable wholeness handed down to us from the past in an unbroken continuity and commanding a respectful guardianship. Not surprisingly, the Biet and Brighelli project, published in three volumes, takes the beginning of the Renaissance as its terminus a quo, that is, the period where Europe's linguistic and cultural divergence became manifest, whereas Polet devotes almost half of its fourteen massive volumes to the Jewish, Christian, Greek, Latin, medieval, and other "roots" of Renaissance and post-Renaissance European literature, retracing and anchoring diachronic patterns of continuity to a number of absolute beginnings.

In their programmatic texts (blurb, preface), Biet and Brighelli refer several times to the symbolical date 1993 (when the Maastricht Treaty came into force) and to pioneering European politicians such as Jean Monnet. The anthology's alleged purpose is to strengthen the cultural basis for the new political edifice of Europe. In contradistinction, the programmatic texts in Polet use the larger timescale of human civilization. The key date here is 2000, the project's planned completion having been made to coincide with the new millennium. Correspondingly, the anthology's mission is defined less by a political and more by an ethically colored discourse, illustrated by the following fragment from the editor's preface (reprinted in each volume):

> Au seuil du troisième millénaire de son ère, l'Europe, soucieuse d'assumer les responsabilités de sa culture, que l'histoire des deux derniers siècles a répandue dans le monde entier, se doit de procurer aux générations du nouvel âge un ensemble cohérent des valeurs qui l'illustrent et la constituent.

> [On the threshold of its third millennium, Europe, anxious to assume the responsibilities of its culture, which the history of the past two centuries has spread to the entire world, has a duty to provide the generations of the new age with a coherent set of the values which illustrate it and constitute it.]

Interestingly and somewhat surprisingly, the Polet anthology deliberately emphasizes linguistic diversity. Thus, it takes on board Europe's "minority" languages and "marginal" literatures, and it makes laudable editorial efforts to make translation visible (e.g., by the decision to use translations from different periods or by the *Répertoire des traducteurs*). By my own analysis, this may appear to be at odds with what I perceive to be the anthology's Pan-European, integrationist tendency. This openness toward Europe's plurality of "smaller" languages is indeed a fairly surprising phenomenon here, as it would be in many other French-language publications, given France's proverbial tradition of cultural centralism and linguistic homogeneity, and its strong belief in the "universality" of the French language.[28] But there might be a deeper cultural strategy at work here.

The idea of promoting linguistic democracy and diversity would have been utterly alien to France's international language policies for as long as the world status of authority and prestige of French was safe. But in the 1950s, French came within a single vote from the ultimate humiliation of losing its status as a working language at the United Nations,[29] showing the alarming speed with which French was being overtaken by another, more successful lingua franca: English. This new context changed everything. The principle of linguistic plurality stopped being an insult or a threat to the proud supremacy of French: it now had to be positively invoked and upheld in the name of an ethics of difference and mutual respect in order to stem the rising tide of English. If indeed, as was also noted by the sociolinguist Florian Coulmas, "the Francophonie movement has begun to paint a picture of itself as the guarantor of linguistic pluralism,"[30] its ethics of difference and its principled commitment to cultural and linguistic diversity serves at least partly as a firewall against the further globalization of English. Béatrice Didier makes the point quite clearly in her *Précis de littérature européenne:*

> le respect des langues est capital dans l'affirmation des diversités. Une Europe réduite à employer un américain ramené à cinq cent mots ne pourra plus avoir une littérature, partant une importance culturelle, et même économique dans le monde de demain.[32]

> [the respect for languages is crucial in the affirmation of the diversities. A Europe which is reduced to using an American English diminished to five hundred words will no longer be able to have a literature, and thus no cultural importance and even no economic importance in the world of tomorrow.]

As it happens, the cultural openness of the Polet anthology reflects an agenda that not only (subtly) opposes the spread of English but that is also (rather less subtly) pro-French. The policy of cultural openness and equal linguistic rights is never pursued to the point where one would have to lower one's cultural standards. The anthology implicitly presents French as the true heir of Greek and Latin and thus as the perfect and natural medium for anything that is worth saying in Europe. French culture is nostalgically presented as *une des références et un des dynamismes majeurs de la civilisation en Europe* (one of the standards and major forces of civilization in Europe); French is cast as the *langue culturelle de l'Europe* (the cultural language of Europe) or *la langue de référence* within *une Europe de la culture* (the prime language of European culture).[32] The anthology as a whole is meant to demonstrate *la mission historique de l'Europe dans le monde et de la langue française en Europe* (the historical mission of Europe in the world and of the French language in Europe). It would seem that in this respect the anthology has moved little beyond the position of Philarète Chasles, one of the nineteenth-century fathers of French *littérature comparée,* who said that "what Europe is to the world, France is to Europe."[33]

Consequently, the *Patrimoine* anthology makes translation "visible" only from a certain angle. Translators and translations are historicized in the sense of being inserted in a diachronic series, but the bothersome question as to what extent they may have manipulated the style and content of the source texts is hardly asked. The essential equivalence between original and translation is taken for granted by the ease with which French perceptions and rewritings of European texts—some of them very biased and selective (*belles infidèles*)—are passed off as the real thing. Historically based variations in the spelling, style, or language of the translations are duly highlighted, but this does little more than suggest that even in its earlier stages French was a perfect medium for Europe's best writers and that this remained one of its permanent characteristics. The historicity of the translations concerns the diachronic evolution of the target language, not the nature or the validity of the relationship between source texts and target texts.

Concluding Remark

There are so many Shakespeares because each time we "frame" him anew and in a different manner. It takes as little effort to make Shakespeare into a Romantic author (anachronism) as into a German classic (anatopism), showing that not even the most basic parameters of human existence—space and time—are beyond redefinition. To understand these processes, we have to be ready to leave Shakespeare alone for a while to study such relevant frames before returning to our Shakespearean documents with opportunities for a fresh understanding. Thus, building on the copious research literature already available in political science, sociology, and history,[34] we need further efforts to understand the cultural, literary, and linguistic politics of Europe as another frame for Shakespeare's afterlife. What can "European" literary discourses (e.g., anthologies, journals, literary histories) and nonliterary discourses (e.g., political, educational, academic, commercial ones) tell us about the deeper *logique identitaire* underlying the wide range of pro-European or anti-European positions? Which individuals or groups have attempted to raise the European consciousness in the cultural field, and beyond it, these last two or three centuries? What were their overt agendas and their tacit values, their rhetorical strategies, their conceptual metaphors, and their positions with respect to other nationalist and internationalist projects? And how does all of this tally with the various outside perceptions and understandings of Europe?

Research of this type necessarily has to span different disciplines (including sociolinguistics, translation studies, and imagology). It will have to look hard at the historical evidence, moving not only beyond sheer speculation but beyond the somewhat facile practice of "anecdotal empiricism"[35] as well. Unfortunately, the only thing I have left to conclude this essay with is precisely that, another anecdote. In June 2003 the press reported a stunning archaeological find in Creswell, Derbyshire, where twelve-thousand-year-old engravings came to light in a cave, representing the oldest example of prehistoric cave art in Britain. The *Guardian* (June 15, 2003) identified the artists as "ancient Britons" and appeared pleased to note that even in those early days Britain was not lagging behind its old rivals Spain (the Altamira caves!) or France (the Lascaux caves!), but confidently spearheading the progress of civilization. A few weeks later, the Flemish-Belgian newspaper *De Morgen* (July 4, 2003) also reported the event, but the article's headline gave the story a somewhat different spin: "Perhaps Belgians brought prehistoric art to England" (*Belgen brachten misschien prehistorische kunst naar Engeland*). After all, one of the animals depicted was the ibex, an animal that was unknown in Britain but that did live in one of Belgium's regions. To be fair to the Belgian journalist, we also have to quote his midarticle heading, which graciously foregrounds the European dimension: "this find demonstrates that something like a European Union existed, a homogeneous European culture" (*deze vondst toont aan dat er zoiets als een Europese Unie bestond, een homogene Europese cultuur*).

Whether inspired by national pride or by the search for an ancestral homeland for the European Union, there is mythmaking and rootdigging all around here, and one could hardly dig much deeper than prehistory. Incidentally, the Belgian region where, in one version of the story, the cave artists honed their art before exporting it to bar-

baric Britain was none other than les Ardennes—in English sometimes called Arden.

Notes

1. For an insightful survey, see John Hutchinson and Anthony D. Smith, eds., *Nationalism*, Oxford Readers (Oxford and New York: Oxford University Press, 1994).
2. Benedict Anderson, *Imagined Communities: Reflections on the Origins and Spread of Nationalism* (London: Verso, 1991).
3. Hans Kohn, *The Idea of Nationalism* (New York: Macmillan, 1945), excerpted in Hutchinson and Smith, *Nationalism*, 163.
4. Florian Coulmas, ed., *A Language Policy for the European Community: Prospects and Quandaries* (Berlin and New York: Mouton de Gruyter, 1991); see especially pp. 103–19.
5. As several scholars have pointed out, it is profoundly ironic that a rigid policy of linguistic centralism and standardization soon had to be imposed to enable the democratic and freedom-loving ideals of the French Revolution to be put into practice. See, for example, Coulmas, *A Language Policy,* 21.
6. Emmanuel Fraisse, *Les Anthologies en France* (Paris: Presses Universitaires de France, 1997), 131 and 153. Literary history, too, is such an important instrument. See, for example, the critical discussion by Theo D'haen of Michael Alexander's *History of English Literature* (Houndmills: Palgrave Macmillan, 2000), in his "Pound Wise, Euro Foolish? On English Literature, Euroliterature, and World Literature," *European English Messenger* 10, no. 1 (2001): 60–63.
7. Gustave Vapereau, *Dictionnaire Universel des Littératures,* 2nd ed. (Paris: Hachette, 1884), xvi.
8. See, among others, Michael Dobson, *The Making of the National Poet: Shakespeare, Adaptation, and Authorship, 1660–1769* (Oxford and New York: Oxford University Press, 1992).
9. See Annie Brisset, *A Sociocritique of Translation: Theatre and Alterity in Quebec* (Toronto: University of Toronto Press, 1996) and Leanore Lieblein, "'Cette Belle Langue': The 'Tradaptation' of Shakespeare in Quebec," in *Shakespeare and the Language of Translation,* the Arden Shakespeare, ed. Ton Hoenselaars, 255–69 (London: Thomson Learning, 2004).
10. Alfredo Michel Modenessi, "'A Double Tongue Within Your Mask': Translating Shakespeare In/to Spanish-speaking Latin America," in *Shakespeare and the Language of Translation,* the Arden Shakespeare, ed. Ton Hoenselaars, 240–54 (London: Thomson Learning, 2004).
11. See David Kinloch, "*Macbeth* in Québécois and Scots," *Translator* 8, no. 1 (2002): 73–100. Also J. Derrick McClure, "Scots for Shakespeare," in *Shakespeare and the Language of Translation,* the Arden Shakespeare, ed. Ton Hoenselaars, 217–39 (London: Thomson Learning, 2004).
12. Pascale Casanova, *La République Mondiale des Lettres* (Paris: Éditions du Seuil, 1999), 110–18, as well as Marc Fumaroli et al., eds., *Identité Littéraire de l'Europe* (Paris: PUF, 2000), 65–66.
13. As Martin Hilský put it in his essay "Shakespeare in Czech: An Essay in Cultural Semantics," in *Shakespeare in the New Europe,* ed. Michael Hattaway, Boika Sokolova, and Derek Roper, 150–58 (Sheffield: Sheffield Academic Press, 1994): "It

is surprising to see how little refashioning Shakespeare needed to be integrated into the official Marxist doctrine . . . no major tampering with the texts of the tragedies, comedies or histories was required" (151). Also see Alexander Shurbanov and Boika Sokolova, *Painting Shakespeare Red: An East-European Appropriation* (Newark: University of Delaware Press, 2001).

14. For this aspect of Shakespeare's Europeanness, see, among others, Neil Forsyth, "Shakespeare the European," in *Translating Traduire Tradurre Shakespeare,* ed. Irene Weber Henking (Lausanne: Centre de traduction littéraire, 2001), 5–21.

15. The earliest stage of Shakespeare's continental European reception may also have shown a fairly uniform shape (the English Comedians), but these early performances took place in circumstances that barely allowed a common European consciousness to be formed.

16. There is a further complication. The fact that the now-archaic nature of Shakespeare's English makes his works "difficult," to the point of giving them a "foreign" character for native speakers of English no less than for continental Europeans and other nonnative speakers, again creates more of a level playing field for all. Could this be said to strengthen his perception as a global writer?

17. The picture is in some cases more intricate. A number of cultural minorities formerly suppressed within established nation-states have seen the European Union as an ally in their struggle for greater emancipation through a process of devolution. This has caused the authority of those nation-states to be eroded at both supranational and subnational levels, with powers moving either upward to the European level or downward toward the autonomy-craving regions.

18. For example, the *Dictionnaire des auteurs européens,* ed. Annick Benoît-Dusausoy and Guy Fontaine (Paris: Hachette, 1995) was partly funded by various "institutions particulièrement sensibilisées à l'idée européenne," including the "Commission des Communautés européennes: Direction générale XXII—Éducation." The same editors also managed to secure funding for their *Histoire de la littérature européenne* (Bruxelles: De Boeck, 1992) through inter alia the "Commission des communautés européennes: Task Force Ressources humaines, éducation, formation et jeunesse" and the French "Ministère des affaires européennes" (6).

19. Reflecting widely held stereotypes, René Étiemble in the early 1960s compared American and French culture in terms of the difference between Coca-Cola and a good *mise en bouteille au château:* see Clem Robyns, "Defending the National Identity: Franglais and Francophony," in *Literaturkanon—Medienereignis—Kultureller Text,* ed. Andreas Poltermann (Berlin: Erich Schmidt, 1995), 179–207. Robyns (199) also quotes Xavier Deniau, who gave us the following comparison in his book *La francophonie* (Paris: PUF, 1983): "l'anglais c'est le téléphone, le français c'est un système culturel de référence."

20. Nezar AlSayyad and Manuel Castells, eds., *Muslim Europe or Euro-Islam: Politics, Culture, and Citizenship in the Age of Globalization* (Lanham, MD: Lexington Books, 2002).

21. One may recall the study of Eugen Weber, *Peasants into Frenchmen: The Modernization of Rural France, 1870–1914* (London: Chatto & Windus, 1979), whose main thesis is that peasants and small-town dwellers within France did not see themselves as members of the French nation until 1870 at least and often regarded French as a foreign language as opposed to their native patois.

22. This may also be illustrated by the occasional use of the following three models of definition: *family relationships* (as between members of a family, European cultures variously share some but not all substantive traits between them), *contact and exchange of goods* (European history is a chain of intercultural encounters, with ma-

terial and cultural goods becoming shared property through patterns of import and export), and *analogous experiences* (even European cultures sharing few or no traits or goods between them may be united by a history of independent but analogous experiences).

23. For an analogy, consider the myth of the monolingual nature of the Greek and then the Latin empire. In reality, both were, of course, polyglot worlds; see J. N. Adams, *Bilingualism and the Latin Language* (Cambridge: Cambridge University Press, 2003). Or, in a more recent past, consider the abortive attempt to impose Russian as the main and ultimately the only language of communication within the former USSR; see Coulmas, *A Language Policy for the European Unity,* 108.

24. In more narrowly "political" terms, these tendencies correspond roughly to what is usually called the federalist position (favoring a strong supranational Union) and the intergovernmentalist position (insisting on the sovereignty of member states) respectively.

25. It has been argued that language protection measures in Europe designed to preserve linguistic diversity represent an illegal (!) barrier to free trade and that adopting a single language (English, of course) would help to create a unified Europe. For this example I am indebted to Robert Phillipson's excellent *English-Only Europe? Challenging Language Policy* (London and New York: Routledge, 2003), 79.

26. An example of such an anthology is Oswald LeWinter's *Shakespeare in Europe* (repr., Harmondsworth: Penguin, 1970), whose editorial policy might create the illusion that Victor Hugo, Tolstoy, and Ungaretti were really English writers. Non-Shakespearean examples might typically include American anthologies of (world) literature such as *An Introduction to Literature: Fiction, Poetry, Drama,* ed. Sylvan Barnet et al. (Boston: Little, Brown, 1977, 6th edition); such anthologies quote "masterpieces" from a variety of periods and languages but remain almost entirely silent on issues of cross-temporal and crosslinguistic text mediation. Texts are dehistoricized by the editorial blandness of their presentation and are thus abstracted from the history of their contexts and their transmission, in order to serve as timeless witnesses of "general" categories of literature.

27. It so happens that I personally prepared the entry on Shakespeare for Professor Polet's anthology, but my focus here is obviously on overall editorial policies and their underlying ideology.

28. See the famous dissertation by Antoine de Rivarol, *Discours sur l'universalité de la langue française* from 1784. Among other points, Rivarol argues that a text written in a foreign language will only reveal its true sense when it is translated into French.

29. René Étiemble, *Parlez-vous franglais?* (Paris: Gallimard, 1964), 239–40. As Étiemble notes with horror, French not only lost much of its former status on the international scene, but English was seen as positively "invading" the French language within its own natural territories, resulting in a hybrid franglais. See also Robyns, "Defending the National Identity: Franglais and Francophony."

30. Coulmas, *A Language Policy,* 21.

31. Béatrice Didier, "Étudier la littérature européenne?" in *Précis de littérature européenne,* ed. Béatrice Didier (Paris: PUF, 1998), 8.

32. Quotations from the editor's introduction to the proceedings of a conference devoted to the anthology: *Patrimoine littéraire européen: Actes du colloque international, Namur 26, 27 et 28 novembre 1998,* ed. Jean-Claude Polet (Bruxelles: De Boeck, 2000), 7–9.

33. Chasles also added that he had "complete contempt for narrow-minded and blind patriotism." Quotations from Susan Bassnett, *Comparative Literature: A Comparative Introduction* (Oxford: Blackwell, 1993), 20.

34. For example, Peter Rietbergen, *Europe: A Cultural History* (London and New York: Routledge, 1998) or Anthony Pagden, ed., *The Idea of Europe: From Antiquity to the European Union* (Cambridge: Cambridge University Press / Washington: Woodrow Wilson Center Press, 2002).

35. I am borrowing this phrase from Joep Leerssen, "The Rhetoric of National Character: a Programmatic Survey," *Poetics Today* 21, no. 2 (2000): 267–92.

Notes on Contributors

KAREN BENNETT is a member of the research team at the Centre for Comparative Studies, University of Lisbon. Her main interests are translation studies (especially intersemiotic translation) and comparative literature. Her articles include "The Seven Veils of Salomé: Wilde's Play in Portuguese Translation" (*The Translator*, 2003), "The Recurrent Quest: Demeter and Persephone in Modern Ireland" (*Classical and Modern Literature*, 2003), and "The Duende in England: Lorca's *Blood Wedding* in Translation" (*Translation and Literature*, 2002).

BETTINA BOECKER studied English, German, and history in Constance, Glasgow, and Heidelberg. In 2004 she completed her doctoral dissertation, entitled *Shakespeares elisabethanisches Publikum: Formen und Funktionen einer Fiktion der Shakespearekritik* (Shakespeare's Elizabethan Audience: Forms and Functions of a Critical Fiction). She now teaches at the University of Munich.

CLARA CALVO is reader in English literature at the University of Murcia. She has coauthored, with Jean Jacques Weber, *The Literature Workbook* (1998) and has published articles on the pronouns of address in Shakespeare and the reception of Shakespeare in Spain during the Romantic period and the 1916 tercentenary celebrations.

RUI CARVALHO HOMEM is associate professor of English at the University of Oporto. His research interests include Irish studies, early modern English drama, and translation. He has published annotated translations of *Antony and Cleopatra* (2001) and *Love's Labour's Lost* (2005). He is also coeditor (with Ton Hoenselaars) of *Translating Shakespeare for the Twenty-First Century* (2004). He is the coordinator of a research project on the intersections of literature and the visual arts and is currently editing a volume to be titled *Writing and Seeing: Essays on Literature and the Visual Arts*.

JANET CLARE is senior lecturer in English at University College Dublin. She has written extensively on Shakespeare and dramatists of the English Renaissance, censorship, New Historicism, women writers of the Renaissance, and the drama performed during the English Republic. Publications include "*Art Made Tongue-tied by Authority*": *Elizabethan and Jacobean Censorship* (1991; 1999), *Drama of the English Republic, 1649–1660* (2002), and *Revenge Tragedies of the Renaissance* (2005).

MICHAEL CRONIN is director of the Centre for Translation Studies, Dublin City University. He is the author of *Translating Ireland: Translation, Languages, Identities* (1996); *Across the Lines: Travel, Language and Translation* (2000); *Translation and Globalization* (2003); and *Time Tracks: Scenes from the Irish Everyday* (2003). He is coeditor of *Tourism in Ireland: A Critical Analysis* (1993); *Nouvelles d'Irlande* (1997); *Unity in Diversity: Current Trends in Translation Studies* (1998); *Reinventing Ireland:*

Culture, Society and the Global Economy (2002); *Irish Tourism: Image, Culture, Identity* (2003); and *The Languages of Ireland* (2003).

DIRK DELABASTITA teaches English literature and literary theory at the University of Namur. His *There's a Double Tongue* (1993) deals with Shakespeare's wordplay and its translation. He coauthored a Dutch *Lexicon van Literaire Termen,* translated into French as *Dictionnaire des termes littéraires* (2001). Edited volumes include *European Shakespeares* (with Lieven D'hulst, 1993); *Wordplay and Translation* (1996); *Traductio: Essays on Punning and Translation* (1997); and *Fictionalizing Translation and Multilingualism* (with Rainier Grutman, 2005).

JOZEF DE VOS teaches English literature and theater history at Ghent University. He is vice president of the Shakespeare Society of the Low Countries and editor of the Ghent-based theater journal *Documenta.* He has published on the reception of Shakespeare in the Low Countries, on modern English drama, and on Shakespeare in performance in journals such as *Theatre Research International, Shakespeare Jahrbuch, Shakespeare Quarterly,* and *Folio.* Recent contributions on Shakespeare adaptations appeared in *Four Hundred Years of Shakespeare in Europe* (ed. Ángel-Luis Pujante and Ton Hoenselaars, UDP, 2003) and *The Globalization of Shakespeare in the Nineteenth Century* (ed. K. Kujawinska Courtney and John Mercer).

JOHN DRAKAKIS is professor of English Studies at the University of Stirling. He is also the director of the Scottish Institute for Renaissance Studies. He is the editor of *Shakespearean Tragedy* (1992), the New Casebook on *Antony and Cleopatra* (1994), *Alternative Shakespeares* (second edition, 2002), and *Arden 3: The Merchant of Venice* (forthcoming). He has contributed widely to international journals in the area of Shakespeare studies, literary theory, and popular culture, and is currently the general editor of the *Routledge New Critical Idiom Series.* His next project is the completion of a book entitled *Shakespearean Discourses.*

PAUL FRANSSEN teaches British literature at the English Department of Utrecht University. He has published various articles on English literature, mainly of the early modern period. He has coedited, with Ton Hoenselaars, *The Author as Character: Representing Historical Writers in Western Literature* (1999), and edits *Folio,* the journal of the Shakespeare Society of the Low Countries.

DOMINIQUE GOY-BLANQUET, professor of Elizabethan theater at the University of Picardie, is a regular contributor of the *TLS* and *La Quinzaine Littéraire.* Her latest works include *Shakespeare's Early History Plays: From Chronicle to Stage* (2003), *Shakespeare et l'invention de l'histoire* (2004), the edition of *Joan of Arc, A Saint for All Reasons: Studies in Myth and Politics* (2003), and essays for *Shakespeare Survey, Arden 3, Cambridge Companion,* and a French translation of W. H. Auden's *Lectures on Shakespeare* (2003).

KEITH GREGOR lectures in English and Irish literature at the University of Murcia. The coeditor of *Teatro clásico en traducción* (1996) and of a special issue of *Cuadernos de Filología Inglesa* (2001) devoted to Shakespeare in Europe, he has written extensively on the question of Shakespeare's reception on the Spanish stage and is currently preparing a book-length study of twentieth- and twenty-first-century Spanish productions of his work. He is also a contributor to the *Oxford Encyclopedia of Theatre and Performance* (2003).

LAWRENCE GUNTNER teaches English and American literature, cultural studies, and media studies at the Technical University in Braunschweig. Among his publications are *Redefining Shakespeare: Literary Theory and Theater Practice in the German Democratic Republic* with Andrew McLean (UDP, 1997), and *Negotiations with Hal: Multi-Media Perceptions of (Shakespeare's) Henry the Fifth* together with Peter Drexler (1995). He has published various articles on non-Anglophone Shakespeare performance and Shakespeare on film.

TERENCE HAWKES is emeritus professor of English at Cardiff University. He is the author of *Metaphor* (1972) and *Structuralism and Semiotics* (1977, 2003), as well as a number of books on Shakespeare, including *Shakespeare and the Reason* (1964), *Shakespeare's Talking Animals* (1973), *That Shakespeherian Rag* (1986), *Meaning By Shakespeare* (1992), and *Shakespeare in the Present* (2002). He is also general editor of the *Accents on Shakespeare* series published by Routledge.

TON HOENSELAARS is senior lecturer in the English Department of Utrecht University. He is the author of *Images of Englishmen and Foreigners in the Drama of Shakespeare and His Contemporaries* (1992). He has edited, alone or with others, *Shakespeare's Italy* (1993), *The Italian World of English Renaissance Drama* (1997), *English Literature and the Other Languages* (1999), *The Author as Character* (1999), *Four Hundred Years of Shakespeare in Europe* (UDP, 2003), *Shakespeare and the Language of Translation* (2004), and *Shakespeare's History Plays* (2004). He is also the founding chairman of the Shakespeare Society of the Low Countries, and managing editor of its journal *Folio*. He is currently writing a monograph on Shakespeare and Richard Wagner.

ANDREAS HÖFELE is professor of English at the University of Munich and currently president of the German Shakespeare Society. His publications include books on Shakespeare's stagecraft, late nineteenth-century parody, and on Malcolm Lowry, as well as numerous articles on Renaissance and twentieth-century themes. He has also published five novels.

WILHELM HORTMANN studied English and German literature at the University of Cologne, sociology at Fordham University, New York, and taught English literature and drama at the universities of Frankfurt, Duisburg, and Santa Barbara. His main work, *Shakespeare on the German Stage: The Twentieth Century*, was published in 1998. A revised and extended edition in German, *Shakespeare und das deutsche Theater im XX. Jahrhundert*, came out in 2001.

RAPHAËL INGELBIEN is a lecturer in English at the University of Leuven, where he teaches a module on Shakespeare. He is the author of *Misreading England: Poetry and Nationhood since the Second World War* (2002), and has published various articles on modern poetry, perceptions of national identity in literature, and Anglo-Irish writing.

NANCY ISENBERG is a member of the Comparative Literature Department at the Università di Roma Tre. Her interests concern early modern theater, literature and ballet, and eighteenth-century Anglo-Italian connections. Among her recent publications are *La posa eroica di Ofelia: Saggi sul personaggio femminile nel teatro elisabettiano* (ed. with Viola Papetti, 2003), and articles on ballet versions of Virginia Woolf's *Orlando* and Bram Stoker's *Dracula*. Her "Accommodating Shakespeare to Ballet: John

Cranko's *Romeo and Juliet* (Venice, 1958)" appeared in *Shifting the Scene: Shakespeare in European Culture* (ed. Ladina Bezzola Lambert and Balz Engler, 2004).

DENNIS KENNEDY is Samuel Beckett Professor of Drama at Trinity College Dublin. His books include *The Oxford Encyclopedia of Theatre and Performance, Looking at Shakespeare, Foreign Shakespeare,* and *Granville Barker and the Dream of Theatre*. A second volume of *Foreign Shakespeare* is in progress, on performance in Asia, coedited with Yong Li Lan. He also works in the theater, recently directing *Pericles* in Dublin and *As You Like It* in Beijing.

JOEP LEERSSEN is professor of Modern European Literature and director of the Huizinga-Instituut (Dutch national research institute for cultural history). Author of *Mere Irish and Fíor-Ghael, Remembrance and Imagination,* and *Nationaal Denken in Europa*, he works chiefly on the role of literature and of critics/philologists in the articulation of national prejudice and national thought in nineteenth-century Europe.

RODERICK J. LYALL is emeritus professor of Literatures in English at the Vrije Universiteit Amsterdam, having previously taught English at Massey University, New Zealand, and Scottish literature at the University of Glasgow. He has edited several early modern Scottish texts and published numerous articles in the field. His critical study of Alexander Montgomerie will shortly appear in the *Arizona Medieval and Renaissance Texts and Studies* series. He is currently editing John Ireland's *Meroure of Wysdome* for the Scottish Text Society and working on a study of Henryson's *Morall Fabillis.*

ZOLTÁN MÁRKUS is assistant professor of English at Vassar College, New York. His main fields of research are early modern English literature, especially drama; Shakespeare studies; European drama and theater; and cultural, literary, and performance theory. His current project, *Shakespeares at War: Cultural Appropriations of Shakespeare in London, Berlin, and Budapest during World War II*, is a comparative study of Shakespeare's cultural reception in these three European cities during the Second World War.

MANFRED PFISTER is professor of English at the Freie Universität Berlin. He is coeditor of the *Shakespeare Jahrbuch* and *Poetica* and author of *Das Drama: Theorie und Analyse* (1982, English translation, 1988; Chinese translation, 2004). Among his recent book publications are *"The Fatal Gift of Beauty": The Italies of British Travellers* (1996), *Venetian Views, Venetian Blinds: English Fantasies of Venice* (1999), *Laurence Sterne* (2001), and *A History of English Laughter* (2002).

ANTONELLA PIAZZA teaches English literature at the University of Salerno. Her area of research is mainly early modernity. She has published a book on the Elizabethan stage and the rise of the modern nuclear family: *"IV: Honour Thy Father"; Domestic Tragedies on the Elizabethan Stage* (2000). She has edited a collection of essays on D. H. Lawrence (*Lawrence: Arte e Mito*, 2000) and another on Shakespeare (*Shakespeare in Europa,* 2004).

ÁNGEL-LUIS PUJANTE is professor of English at the University of Murcia. He is the author of *El Manuscrito Shakespeariano de Manuel Herrera Bustamante* (2001), and has edited, with Keith Gregor, *Teatro Clásico en Traducción* (1996) and *More European Shakespeares* (2001), as well as, with Ton Hoenselaars, *Four Hundred Years of*

Shakespeare in Europe (UDP, 2003). He has published annotated translations of nineteen of Shakespeare's plays to date, and of Middleton's *A Game at Chess* (1983), as well as critical essays on English Renaissance drama and literary translation. He is the head of a research project on Shakespeare's presence in Spain in the framework of European culture.

VERONIKA SCHANDL graduated from Pázmány Péter Catholic University in 1999, and in the same year she started the Renaissance and Baroque Literature PhD Programme of Eötvös Loránd University, Budapest. She has written her PhD dissertation on the reception and stage history of the Shakespearean problem plays during the Kádár regime in Hungary. Her major research interests include Renaissance and contemporary drama as well as the Shakespearean apocrypha.

ISABELLE SCHWARTZ-GASTINE is associate professor of English literature and Renaissance drama at the University of Caen, Basse-Normandie. She is an associate researcher at the French Centre National de la Recherche Scientifique. She specializes in Renaissance theater on the French stage, past and present, and has published a good number of articles on the subject, including those in *The Oxford Companion to Shakespeare, Four Hundred Years of Shakespeare in Europe,* and the CNRS volume on *Amateur Theatre.* She has published a volume on *A Midsummer Night's Dream* (2002) and has edited one on *Richard II* (2005).

Index

Abend-David, Dror, 16–17, 26 n. 6, 143, 154 n. 1
Adams, J. N., 367 n. 23
Adams, John Quincy, 58
Adenauer, Konrad, 269
Adorno, Theodor W., 275 n. 58
Aeschylus, 238, 294
Agate, James, 144, 146, 155 n. 2 and 3
Albee, Edward, 166
Alexander, Michael, 365 n. 6
Alexander, Peter, 170
Alexandre (actor), 131, 133
Alfieri, Vittorio, 311
AlSayyad, Nezar, 366 n. 20
Altrincham (Lord), 68
Amyot, Jacques, 141 n. 1, 286
Anderson, Benedict, 32, 365 n. 2
Anderson, Duncan, 81
Anderson, Jack, 176 n. 5
Anderson, R. B. W., 337, 341 n. 19
Andioc, René, 317 n. 3
Angelet, Christian, 52 n. 7
Angoulême, Duke of, 110
Annan, Noel, 72 n. 28
Anouilh, Jean, 259
Antal, Gábor, 168 n. 41
Aquinas, Thomas, 84
Arcimboldo, Giuseppe, 197
Aretino, Pietro, 301 n.
Ariel, Brigitte, 142 n. 25
Ariosto, Ludovico, 290, 299, 301 n. 20
Aristophanes, 215
Aristotle, 282, 286, 292, 358
Arminius the Cheruscan, 47
Armstrong, Karen, 71 n. 15
Arndt, Ernst Moritz, 45
Arnim, Ludwig Joachim, 47
Arnold, Matthew, 50, 55 n. 33
Ascham, Roger, 287, 289, 300 n. 6, 302 n. 34
Aspinall, Dana, 176 n. 3

Atkins, Robert, 145
Atlee, Clement, 67
Augustine (Saint), 84
Austen, Jane, 263

Babarczy, László, 164
Backès, Jean-Louis, 355
Bahn, Eugene H., 271 n. 12
Baker, David J., 101 n. 6
Bakhtin, Michail, 173, 199
Baldick, Chris, 237, 245 n. 10
Baldwin, Stanley, 59, 64
Baldwin, T. W., 291–92, 302 n. 31
Balfour, Arthur, 67
Balfour, Michael, 257, 270 n. 6, 272 n. 22
Bance, Alan, 271 n. 14
Banes, Sally, 177 n. 8
Bánffy, György, 160
Banham, Martin, 201
Barnet, Sylvan, 367 n. 26
Barthes, Roland, 187
Bassnett, Susan, 285 n. 1, 367 n. 33
Bate, Jonathan, 216, 219 n. 5
Beaumont, Francis, 227, 229, 232 n. 26
Beckett, Samuel, 201
Beier, Karin, 205
Bellini, Vincenzo, 116
Bembo, Pietro, 301 n. 26
Ben Gurion, David, 67
Benchettrit, Paul, 316 n. 1
Benedek, Marcell, 151, 157 n. 31
Benjamin, Walter, 266
Bennett, H. S., 225, 232 n. 14
Bennett, Karen, 21, 23, 284
Benoît-Dusausoy, Annick, 355, 356, 366 n. 18
Beowulf, 46, 48, 49
Berg, Wilhelm, 316 n. 1
Bergsträsser, Arnold, 272 n. 21
Bersani, Jacques, 356
Besson, Benno, 189

INDEX OF NAMES

Bethlen, Gabor, 77
Bevin, Ernest, 72–73 n. 38
Beyer, Hermann, 188
Bhabha, Homi K., 285 n. 1
Bharucha, Rustom, 201
Biet, Christian, 356, 360–63
Bireley, Robert, 88 n. 12
Blair, Hugh, 41
Blake, William, 62, 71 n. 19
Bloom, Harold, 99, 100, 102 n. 34, 282, 285 n. 2
Blotius, Hugo, 79, 82, 83
Boccaccio, Giovanni, 301 n. 26
Bock, Gisela, 176 n. 2
Bocskai, Istvan, 88 n. 6
Boecker, Bettina, 18, 217
Bolingbroke, Henry, 71 n. 18
Boll, André, 127
Bonaparte, Joseph, 114, 311, 313
Bondy, François, 273 n. 31
Boose, Lynda E., 177 n. 11
Booth, Michael R., 232 n. 11
Borges, Jorge Luis, 41, 53 n. 10, 310
Bosch, Hieronymus, 197
Both, Béla, 150
Bower, Tom, 272 n. 17
Bowyer, J. W., 211 n. 4
Brace, Catherine, 55 n. 35
Bradley, A. C., 222–23, 231 n. 8 and 9
Bragg, Melvyn, 329, 340 n. 1
Braidotti, Rosi, 177 n. 7
Brandes, Georg, 98
Braun, Alfred, 181–82
Brecht, Bertolt, 22, 106, 107, 108 n. 3, 134, 140, 142 n. 23, 179–95, 206, 260
Brentano, Clemens, 47
Breth, Andrea, 205
Brickner, Richard M., 275 n. 49
Bridges, Robert, 223, 228, 232 n. 10
Bridges-Adams, William, 106, 108 n. 2
Brighelli, Jean-Paul, 356, 360–63
Brinson, Charmian, 274 n. 43
Brislin, R. W., 341 n. 19
Brisset, Annie, 365 n. 9
Bristol, Michael D., 33, 35 n. 2
Brock, Susan, 88 n. 5
Broich, Margarete, 190
Brook, Peter, 350
Brooks, J. L., 211 n. 4
Brown, Allison, 176 n. 2
Brown, Ivor, 145, 155 n. 7

Brown, John Russell, 201
Brown, Marshall, 73 n. 44
Brown, Richard, 102 n. 29
Browning, Robert, 199
Bryskett, Lodowick, 332
Bryson, Anna, 341 n. 3
Bucer, Martin, 84
Budgen, Frank, 101 n. 26
Buffet, Cyril, 273 n. 33
Burbage, Richard, 183
Burnacini, Ottavio, 199
Burnett, Mark Thornton, 101 n. 6, 273 n. 35, 342 n. 22
Burns, Rob, 177 n. 7
Burt, Richard, 177 n. 11
Burton, Richard, 172
Butler, Christopher, 219 n. 7
Butler, Martin, 233 n. 30
Butler, Rohan, 273 n. 29

Caesar, Julius, 124
Calderón de la Barca, Don Pedro, 44, 47, 353
Calvo, Clara, 20, 24, 105
Cambronero, Carlos, 316 n. 3
Camões, Luís Vaz de, 32
Caputo, John, 252
Carlson, Marvin, 201
Carlyle, Thomas, 50, 51, 55 nn. 32 and 34, 199
Carminha, Pedro Vaz de, 337, 342
Carnerero, José María de, 113, 305, 313, 317 n. 16
Carnero, Guillermo, 122 n. 18, 312
Carter, Alexandra, 178 n. 15
Carvalho Homem, Rui, 16
Casanova, Pascale, 365 n. 12
Castells, Manuel, 366 n. 20
Castelvetro, Lodovico, 290
Castiglione, Baldassare, 301 n. 26
Castorf, Frank, 205, 206
Cecil, William, 79, 82
Cervantes, Miguel de, 32, 37, 41, 44, 51, 282, 353, 358
Chadelat, Jean-Marc, 331, 341 n. 7
Champion, Édouard, 141 n. 18
Chanson de Roland, 46, 49
Chapman, George, 216
Chardigni, Signor, 24
Charles (Prince of Wales), 58
Charles I (King of England), 310

INDEX OF NAMES

Charles III (King of Spain), 308
Charters, David A., 73 n. 41
Chasles, Philarète, 363
Chateaubriand, François-René de, 100
Chaucer, Geoffrey, 286, 288, 299
Chelyapov, Nikolai, 323
Cheng, Vincent, 101 n. 9
Chesterton, A. K., 70
Child, Francis James, 290, 301 n. 28
Church, Esmé, 145–46
Churchill, Sir Winston, 72 n. 23, 271 n. 9
Cicero, Marcus Tullius, 287, 290–91, 302 n. 32, 331, 341 n. 5
Cigogna, Emanuele Antonio, 300 n. 17
Cinthio, Giovanbattista Giraldi, 78, 192, 297, 302 n. 38
Clare, Janet, 21, 218
Claudianus, 215
Clayton, Tom, 88 n. 5
Clemen, Wolfgang, 277 n. 72
Clemens, Gabriele, 272 n. 25
Coghill, Nevill, 170
Cohen, Walter, 233 n. 30
Colao, Alberto, 121 n. 1
Coleridge, Samuel Taylor, 95, 221–22, 231 n. 6, 236
Cook, Ann Jennalie, 217, 230, 231 n. 1, 232 n. 21, 233 n. 29
Cook, E. T., 211 n. 4
Coors, J. G., 211 n. 7
Copeau, Jacques, 141 n. 18, 274 n. 46
Coriolanus, 124
Corneille, Pierre, 353
Coulmas, Florian, 362, 365 n. 4, 367 n. 23
Coulon, Mireille, 317 n. 3
Cowler, Rosemary, 231 n. 4
Cox, John D., 232 n. 21, 233 n. 31
Cragun, Richard, 170
Craig, W. J., 341 n. 11
Cranko, John, 22–23, 107, 169–78
Crato, Johannes, 83
Cresswell, Peter, 71 n. 13
Cripps, Stafford, 255
Cronin, Michael, 19, 283, 342 n. 22
Cruz, Ramón de la, 305–17
Csapó, György, 167 n. 15
Cserhalmi, György, 163
Cumming, John, 275 n. 58
Cunliffe, John W., 289–90, 293–94, 297, 300 n. 17, 301 n. 18
Cunningham-Reid, Captain, 270 n. 6

Curtius, Ernst Robert, 297, 303 n. 54
Cyril, 36

Daladier, Edouard, 131
Daly, Ann, 177 n. 15
Daniel, Samuel, 216, 286, 288, 300 n. 11
Dante, Alighieri, 41, 51, 95, 96, 100, 282, 301 n. 26, 353, 358, 360
Dargel, F. A., 149, 156 n. 24
Darras, Jacques, 303 n. 51
Davenant, William, 199
David, Jacques Louis, 125
Dávidházi, Péter, 111, 122 n. 11
De Gaulle, Charles, 100, 135
De Valois, Marguerite, 75
De Vane, Dean William, 71 n. 10
Deane, Seamus, 93, 94, 100 n. 3, 101 n. 8
Debidour, Victor-Henry, 302 n. 40
Debussy, Claude, 107
DeGroot, Angéla, 273 n. 32
Deighton, Anne, 273 n. 30, 276 n. 69
Delabastita, Dirk, 23–24, 25 n. 3, 123 n. 29, 282, 316 n. 1, 341 n. 13
Delisle, Jean, 342 n. 25
Deniau, Xavier, 366 n. 19
Derrida, Jacques, 251–52, 276 n. 61, 329, 341 n. 2
Desmond, Jane C., 177 n. 15
Devereux, Robert, 89 n. 20
D'haen, Theo, 365 n. 6
d'Hourville, Gérard, 141 n. 17
D'hulst, Lieven, 25 n. 3, 123 n. 29, 316 n. 1
Dickens, Charles, 39, 264
Didier, Béatrice, 356, 362, 367 n. 31
Dobai, Vilmos, 160
Dobson, Michael, 177 n. 10, 365 n. 8
Dolce, Lodovico, 19, 289–95, 300 n. 6
Dollimore, Jonathan, 193 n. 22, 219 n. 4, 233 n. 32
Donaldson, Frances, 272 n. 26
Donat, Robert, 146
Donne, John, 82, 337–38
Donnison, Frank S. V., 272 n. 24
Dorril, Stephen, 68, 73 n. 4
Dort, Bernard, 134, 141 n. 21
Dove, Richard, 274 n. 43
Drakakis, John, 19, 201, 219 n. 4, 285 n. 3
Draudt, Manfred, 78, 88 n. 9
Drayton, Michael, 216
Dresen, Adolf, 189, 194 n. 36

INDEX OF NAMES

Drewniak, Boguslaw, 273 n. 36, 275 n. 51
Drexler, Peter, 194 n. 32
Dryden, John, 39, 199
Du Bellay, Joachim, 286
Du Bled, Victor, 141 n. 3
Ducis, Jean-François, 20, 24, 109–16, 284, 304–17, 351
Duff, William, 53 n. 12
Duffett, Thomas, 199
Düllmann, Susanne, 187
Duncan, Isadora, 176 n. 1
Dunlevy, Mairéad, 341 n. 14
Duval, Alexandre, 110–12
Duvick, Donald N., 211 n. 7
Dyserinck, Hugo, 52 n. 6, 52–53 n. 8

Eade, Charles, 271 n. 9
Eagleton, Terry, 219 n. 7
Easthope, Anthony, 268, 276 n. 65
Echtermeyer, Theodor, 55 n. 31
Eckermann, Johann Peter, 54 n. 26
Eckhart, Ludwig, 40
Edda, 36
Edelman, Charles, 155 n. 15
Edward (Lord Zouche), 82
Edward VIII (King of England), 33, 57, 63, 65, 69
Edwards, Gale, 177 n. 12
Edwards, Philip, 242, 245 n. 28
Eicher, Thomas, 155–56 n. 21, 157 n. 35
Eksteins, Modris, 273 n. 35
Elgar, Sir Edward, 261
Eliot, George, 51
Eliot, T. S., 90, 94, 95, 100 n. 1, 101 n. 21, 218, 224, 232 n. 17, 234–45, 259, 293, 302 n. 44
Ellis, Ruth, 71 n. 14
Ellison, James, 88 n. 16
Ellmann, Richard, 98, 100 n. 2
Emerson, Ralph Waldo, 33
Engler, Balz, 25 n. 2, 115, 123 n. 28, 219 n. 3, 253 n. 1
Erasmus, Desiderius, 292, 302 n. 35
Eschenburg, Johann Joachim, 351
Esslin, Martin, 274 n. 41
Étiemble, René, 366 n. 19, 367 n. 29
Ettmüller, Ludwig, 48, 55 n. 28
Euripides, 201, 238, 289–99
Evans, R. J. W., 88 n. 12

Fabre, Émile, 127, 131–32, 141 n. 7
Fairbanks, Douglas, 175

Farias, Victor, 275 n. 61
Farquharson, John E., 271 n. 14
Felperin, Howard, 285 n. 3
Fenton, Ferrar, 332
Ferdinand II (Emperor of Austria), 80, 82, 88 n. 12
Ferdinand VII (King of Spain), 110–11, 114, 122 n. 23, 312–13
Fernández de Moratín, Leandro, 304
Fernie, Ewan, 73 n. 44
Feuchtwanger, Leon, 180
Fichte, Johann Gottlieb, 45
Firchow, Peter E., 52
Fischer, Gerhard, 194 n. 31
Fischer-Lichte, Erika, 201
Flaubert, Gustave, 94
Foakes, Reginald A., 231 n. 6
Fodor, Géza, 160, 167 n. 10
Fontaine, Guy, 355, 356, 366 n. 18
Fonteyn, Margot, 169
Forés, Vicente, 88 n. 5
Forsyth, Neil, 366 n. 14
Fraisse, Emmanuel, 365 n. 6
Franssen, Paul, 25 n. 1
Freire, Ana M[a.], 122 n. 24, 317 n. 14
Frenz, Horst, 276 n. 70
Fresco, Gaby Petrone, 316 n. 1
Freud, Sigmund, 183, 193 n. 16
Friedan, Betty, 170
Friedesheim, von (Baron), 82
Fry, Christopher, 275 n. 56
Fuegi, John, 193 n. 13
Fumaroli, Marc, 356, 365 n. 12
Fürbeth, Frank, 54 n. 24
Furnivall, F. J., 341 n. 9
Fussell, Paul, 276 n. 70

Gadamer, Hans-Georg, 246
Gaddis, John Lewis, 276 n. 69
Gál, Péter Molnár, 160, 167 n. 13
Ganzl, Serge, 135–36, 142 n. 25
Garbo, Greta, 66
García Garrosa, María Jesús, 122 n. 18
Garnett, Richard, 211 n. 4
Garran, Gabriel, 134–40, 142 n. 25
Garrick, David, 349
Gascoigne, George, 19
Gash, Anthony, 84, 89 n. 27
Gaskill, Howard, 53 n. 11
Gehring, Hansjörg, 271 n. 10
Genette, Gérard, 53 n. 16

INDEX OF NAMES

Genton, Bernard, 273 n. 32
George V (King of England), 64
George VI (King of England), 64
George, Heinrich, 151
Gerhard, Ute, 177 n. 7
Gerhardt, Uta, 275 n. 49
Gervais, David, 268, 276 n. 68
Gibinska, Marta, 316 n.
Gielgud, John, 66, 146
Gies, David Thatcher, 116, 121–22 n. 6, 122 n. 7, 123 n. 30
Gilbert, Humphrey, 332, 341 n. 9
Gilbert, Stuart, 97
Gillies, John, 34, 74, 87 n. 1, 87–88 n. 2
Glaser, Hermann, 273 n. 37
Glyndwr, Owain, 72 n. 28
Goddard, Harold, 170
Goebbels, Joseph, 148, 152, 256, 259, 266
Goerres, Joseph, 46
Goethe, Johann Wolfgang von, 43, 44, 47, 51, 95, 100, 183, 196, 219, 236, 266, 351, 353, 360
Golder, John, 311, 317 n. 13
Googe, Barnabe, 332
Goring, Marius, 261–70, 274 n. 46
Gosse, Edmund, 226, 232 n. 19
Gotscheff, Dimiter, 179
Goy-Blanquet, Dominique, 19, 283
Grady, Hugh, 73 n. 43, 219 n. 5, 232 n. 13, 241, 244 n. 1, 248, 254 n. 4, 276 n. 67
Graham, Joseph, 341 n. 2
Graham, Martha, 176 n. 1
Granville-Barker, Harley, 147, 153, 155 n. 17, 157 n. 36
Greenaway, Peter, 198
Greenblatt, Stephen, 219 n. 1, 243, 245 n. 33, 285 n. 3
Greene, Graham, 274 n. 42
Greene, Hugh Carleton, 274 n. 42
Greer, Germaine, 170, 175, 178 n. 18
Greg, W. W., 225, 232 nn. 14, 15, and 16
Gregor, Keith, 20, 24, 25–26 n. 3, 111–12, 121 n. 2, 122 n. 10, 284
Gregorio Esquilache, Leopoldo de, 308
Greiner, Bernhard, 193 n. 29, 194 n. 36
Griffin, Gabriele, 177 n. 7
Grimald, Nicolas, 291, 302 n. 32
Grimaldi, Jean-Marie, 109–23, 317 n. 16
Grimm, Jacob, 45–48, 50
Grimm, Wilhelm, 46
Gritti, Francesco, 316 n. 1

Grofain, Phyllis, 101 n. 10
Gross, John, 26 n. 7
Gründgens, Gustaf, 196, 210 n. 1, 260, 274 n. 39
Grundschöttel, Wilhelm, 156 n. 23
Gudzuhn, Jörg, 191
Gundolf, Friedrich, 37, 38, 55 n. 34
Guntner, Lawrence, 22, 106–7, 194 n. 32, 195 n. 42
Gurr, Andrew, 233 n. 30
Gutman, David, 323, 328 n. 6
Gwisdek, Michael, 188

Haarder, Andreas, 55 n. 27
Haas, Azisa, 195 n. 43
Habart, Michel, 134, 142 n. 22
Habermas, Jürgen, 42, 53 n. 15
Habicht, Werner, 270 n. 5, 273 n. 35, 275 n. 47, 277 n. 74
Hall, Peter, 106
Halpern, Richard, 232 n. 17
Hamburger, Maik, 189, 194 n. 36, 195 n. 42
Hammer, Paul E. J., 82, 89 n. 20
Hammerschmidt, Hildegard, 273 n. 35
Handke, Peter, 39
Hanna, Judith Lynne, 177 n. 15
Harbage, Alfred, 217, 227–30, 232 n. 20
Hardy, Thomas, 51
Hargreaves, Raymond, 244 n.
Harington, John, 333
Hartman, Geoffrey, 276 n. 63
Harvey, Gabriel, 289–90, 298
Harwood, Ronald, 155 n. 3
Hattaway, Michael, 25 n. 3, 219 n. 6, 303 n. 53, 365 n. 13
Hauptmann, Gerhart, 37–39, 255, 270 n. 4
Hauschild, Jan-Christoph, 194 n. 37
Hausmann, W. A., 239, 245 n. 16
Hawkes, Terence, 20, 23, 24, 31–33, 219 n. 4, 244, 245 n. 36, 285 n. 3
Haydee, Marcia, 171
Hazlitt, William, 222, 231 n. 7
Hecht, Werner, 192 n. 9
Heidegger, Martin, 266, 275 n. 61
Heilman, Robert, 170, 176 n. 3
Heine, Heinrich, 45, 47
Heinemann, Margot, 184, 193 n. 22
Heinrichs, Heinz-Dieter, 157 n. 37
Helgerson, Richard, 101 n. 10

INDEX OF NAMES

Hemingway, Ernest, 259
Henderson, Diana, 177 n. 11
Henking, Irene Weber, 366 n. 14
Henry IV (King of England), 66
Henry IV (King of France), 75
Henry V (King of England), 64, 286
Henry VIII (King of England), 287
Henschel, Ludwig, 55 n. 31
Henß, Rudolf, 54 n. 24
Herder, Johann Gottfried, 41, 43, 351
Hermans, Theo, 285 n. 1, 335, 341 n. 15
Hermon, Michel, 136, 140
Herreros, Bretón de los, 111
Hesiod, 215
Heylen, Romy, 306, 316 n. 1, 317 n. 9
Hibbard, G. R., 75, 88 n. 3
Hilský, Martin, 365 n. 13
Himmler, Heinrich, 266
Hinz, Hans-Martin, 273 n. 32
Hitler, Adolf, 105, 131, 261, 266, 269
Hodgdon, Barbara, 176 n. 3
Hoenselaars, Ton, 25, 121 n. 2, 142 n. 24, 194 n. 36, 365 n. 10
Höfele, Andreas, 22, 195 n. 42, 218, 273 n. 37
Hölderlin, Friedrich, 39, 204
Holderness, Graham, 87–88 n. 2, 172–73, 177 n. 10, 233 n. 27
Holland, Philemon, 288, 300 n. 12
Hollí, Ján, 51
Hollingdale, R. J., 254 n. 7
Holzman, Michael, 71 n. 10
Holzwarth, Pit, 203
Homer, 41, 42, 46, 51, 90, 95, 97, 215, 290, 338
Homolka, Oskar, 182
Honigmann, E. A. J., 89 n. 23
Horace, 290, 292
Horkheimer, Max, 275 n. 58
Hörnigk, Frank, 194 n. 38, 195 n. 41
Horodyski, Andrzej, 316 n. 1
Hortmann, Wilhelm, 23, 52 n. 2, 107, 148, 155 n. 20, 195 n. 42, 260, 273 n. 35, 274 n. 38
Houben, H. H., 54 n. 26
Howe, P. P., 231 n. 7
Howes, Janet, 177 n. 9
Hughes, Charles, 341 n. 8
Hughes, Thomas, 297
Hugo, François-Victor, 134
Hugo, Victor, 367 n. 26
Hutchinson, John, 365 n. 3

Ibsen, Henrik, 94
Iglódi, István, 162
Ihering, Herbert, 180, 192 n. 7
Ingelbien, Raphaël, 19, 21, 31, 34
Ingram, Martin, 89 n. 29
Irigaray, Luce, 175, 178 n. 17
Isenberg, Nancy, 22–23, 107, 178 n. 15
Iser, Wolfgang, 285 n. 1
Isham, Gyles, 33, 65, 68, 69, 72 n. 27
Isham, John, 66
Isham, Justinian, 66
Isham, Thomas, 66
Isham, Sir Vere, 65
Izquierdo, Lucio, 113, 122 n. 19

Jackson, Ken, 218, 251–53, 254 n. 14
Jacquot, Jean, 141 n. 20
Jaffé, Daniel, 319, 323, 328 n. 3
Jahn, Friedrich, 45
James VI (King of England), 82
Jardin, Pierre, 273 n. 32
Jarry, Alfred, 166
Jefferson, Thomas, 66
Jellicoe, G. A., 70 n. 3
Jessner, Leopold, 193 n. 13, 260
John, Miriam, 328 n. 6
Johnson, Samuel, 197
Jones, Emrys, 302 n. 36
Jones, Ernest, 193 n. 16
Jones, Florence, 328 n. 5
Jones, Henry Arthur, 255, 262, 270 n. 5
Jones, William, 337
Jonson, Ben, 200, 216
Jordan, Ulrike, 270 n. 2, 271 n. 13
Joughin, John J., 246, 253 n. 2
Jowett, John, 77, 78, 86, 87, 88 n. 8, 302 n. 36
Joyce, James, 16, 19, 21, 34, 35, 90–102, 224, 234, 329, 340, 342 n. 26
Junker, Detlef, 273 n. 37
Jürgensen, Kurt, 271 n. 9, 272 n. 18

Kádár, János, 161–64
Kahn, Coppélia, 251, 254 n. 13
Kalb, Jonathan, 193 n. 28, 194 n. 36
Kállay, Ferenc, 162
Kaplan, Gisela, 176 n. 2
Karusseit, Ursula, 187–88
Kastan, David Scott, 232 n. 21, 233 n. 31
Kaufmann, Walter, 254 n. 7
Kearney, Richard, 102 n. 35
Kemble, John Philip, 124

Kemp, Will, 92
Kennedy, Dennis, 16, 26 n. 4, 142 n. 24, 195 n. 42, 202
Kerrigan, John, 243, 245 n. 33, 302 n. 36
Kéry, László, 159, 167 n. 5
Kettenacker, Lothar, 270 n. 1, 271 n. 15
Khlesl, Melchior, 80, 83, 88 n. 13
Kibert, Declan, 92, 101 n. 7
King, Ros, 25 n. 1
Kinloch, David, 365 n. 11
Kinwelmersh, Francis, 289, 292, 294
Kipp, Heide, 188
Kirov, Sergej, 319
Kiss, Sándor Köröspataki, 168 n. 50
Klein, J. L., 236
Kleist, Heinrich von, 47, 50
Klett, Renate, 209
Knapp, Peggy A., 276 n. 67
Knight, G. Wilson, 19, 21, 248–51, 254 n. 6
Knopf, Jan, 192 n. 9
Knowles, Ronald, 89 n. 27, 101 n. 10
Koch, Georg August, 149, 156 n. 28
Koeppler, Heinz, 271 n. 13
Kögl, Martina, 274 n. 41
Kohn, Hans, 365 n.
Koltay, Tamás, 165, 167 n. 19, 168 n. 36
König, H.-J., 272 n. 21
Körtner, Fritz, 182
Kott, Jan, 106, 134, 189, 193 n. 19
Kranz, Dieter, 194 n. 32
Kraus, Karl, 179, 200
Kroepelin, Hermann, 152–53
Kruse, Jürgen, 204
Kuberski, Angela, 194 n. 32
Kun, Vilmos, 164
Kurosawa, Akira, 350
Kushner, Tony, 152, 157 n. 33
Kyd, Thomas, 182, 191

La Harpe, Jean-François de, 125
La Place, P.-A. de, 351
Lacalle, Teodoro, 113
Lacoue-Labarthe, Philippe, 276 n. 61
Ladmiral, Jean-René, 339, 342 n. 24
Laforgue, Jules, 95, 101 n. 21
Lambert, José, 52, 115, 123 n. 29
Lambert, Ladina Bezzola, 25 n. 2, 219 n. 3, 253 n. 1
Lamormaini, William, 80
Langhoff, Matthias, 189, 194 n. 36

Lanier, Sidney, 288, 300 n. 10
Larson, Kenneth E., 52 n. 2, 54 n. 20
Latorre, Carlos, 122 n. 9
Laugier, Émile, 141 n. 4
Le Tourneur, P., 351
Lean, David, 273 n. 32
Léandre, Joëlle, 142 n. 27
Leavis, F. R., 268
Leavis, Q. D., 225–26, 232 n. 18
Leday, Annette, 202
Ledebur, Ruth von (Freifrau), 273 n. 35, 277 n. 74
Leder, Lily, 194 n. 32
Lee, Robert E., 66
Lee, Sidney, 301 n. 24
Leerssen, Joep, 19, 23, 31, 368 n. 35
Lehmann, Hans-Thies, 186
Lehmkuhl, Ursula, 272 n. 21
Leo X (Pope), 301 n. 25
Leopold I (of Vienna), 199
Lesieur, Stephen, 81
Leskó, László, 168 n. 37
Lessing, Gotthold Ephraim, 33, 38–40, 42, 43
Létay, Vera, 168 n. 27
Lever, J. W., 168 n. 20
Levin, Harry, 100 n. 4
Levith, Murray J., 87–88 n. 2
Levy, Oscar, 245 n. 16
Lewes, George Henry, 220–21, 231 n. 2
LeWinter, Oswald, 367 n. 26
Ley, Charles David, 342 n. 21
Lieblein, Leanore, 365 n. 9
Linzer, Martin, 194 n. 39
Livy, 303 n. 54
Lodge, Thomas, 290, 301 n. 24
Loomba, Ania, 71 n. 17, 201
Lord, Andrew, 209
Loughrey, Bryan, 328 n. 4
Louis XVI (King of France), 310
Louis XVIII (King of France), 110
Louthan, Howard, 83, 89 n. 24
Lovejoy, A. O., 266, 275 n. 60
Loyon, René, 142 n. 26
Lutter, Tibor, 167 n. 7
Lyall, Roderick, 18, 31, 34
Lyotard, Francois, 276 n. 61
Lyubimov, Yuri, 106

MacCabe, Colin, 102 n. 31
MacCarthy, Lillah, 57

INDEX OF NAMES

Macdonald, Ramsay, 65
Machiavelli, Niccolò, 288
Macpherson, James, 41–44, 339
Magyar, Bálint, 156 n. 29
Mahaffy, John P., 289–90, 292, 301 n. 19
Máiquez, Isidoro, 109, 111, 113
Maistre, Joseph-Marie de, 46
Major, Tamás, 151–52, 156 n. 27, 157 n. 32, 160–63, 165
Makaryk, Irena, 195 n. 42
Malpas, S., 254 n. 2
Mangan, James Clarence, 339, 342 n. 23
Mann, Klaus, 196, 274 n. 39
Mann, Thomas, 101 n. 15
Mannheim, Lucie, 275 n. 46
Manning, John, 273 n. 35
Manuce, Aldo, 302 n. 39
Manzoni, Alessandro, 51
March, Fredric, 66
Margolies, David, 229, 233 nn. 27 and 30
María Cristina (Queen Regent of Spain), 122 n. 23, 313
Marie de France, 40
Márkus, Zoltán, 16–17, 19, 21, 106
Marlowe, Christopher, 148, 216
Marrapodi, Michele, 87–88 n. 2
Marston, John, 78
Martin, Randy, 178 n. 15
Martindale, Charles and Michelle, 292, 302 n. 36
Marx, Karl, 218, 247, 254 n. 3
Masefield, John, 57
Mason, Ellsworth, 101 n. 13
Mastronarde, Donald J., 302 n. 40
Matless, David, 55 n. 33
Mátrai-Betegh, Béla, 167 n. 14
Matthiessen, F. O., 336, 341 n. 16
Maugham, William Somerset, 259
Maximilian II (Emperor), 79, 83
Maximus, Valerius, 303 n. 54
Mayfield, Les, 31
Mayhew, Henry, 223
Mayor, John E. B., 300 n. 6
McCarthy, Suzanne, 177 n. 5
McClure, J. Derrick, 365 n. 11
McGinn, D. J., 84, 89 n. 26
McGrath, Alister, 341 n. 17
McLaine, Ian, 147, 155 n. 19
Mead, Margaret, 275 n. 49
Mecenseffy, Grete, 88 n. 11
Meisel, Edmund, 181

Mellon, Andrew, 71 n. 12
Mélykuti, Ilona, 156 n. 28, 156–57 n. 30
Mendelssohn, Felix, 264, 268
Meres, Francis, 215–16
Mészáros, Tamás, 164, 168 n. 37
Meyer, Jean, 141 n. 20
Meyer, Michael, 146, 155 n. 10
Middleton, Thomas, 76–78, 86
Mihályi, Gábor, 168 n. 28
Millet, Kate, 170
Milner, Alfred, 72 n. 33
Mittenzwei, Werner, 192 n. 9
Mnouchkine, Ariane, 107, 196
Modenessi, Alfredo Michel, 365 n. 10
Molière, 133
Monk, Samuel H., 53 n. 13
Monnet, Jean, 361
Montag, Dieter, 188
Moore, Helen, 73 n. 44
More, Thomas, 300 n. 8
Moretti, Franco, 32, 35 nn. 1 and 3, 356
Moryson, Fynes, 332
Moyne, Lord, 72 n. 37
Mrožek, Slawomir, 166
Msomi, Welcome, 350
Mühe, Ulrich, 190
Müller, Heiner, 22, 106–7, 179–95, 206
Müller, Klaus-Detlef, 193 n. 9
Mussato, Albertino, 301 n. 25

Nagy, Judit, 168 n. 32
Napoleon, 20, 24, 109–23
Nashe, Thomas, 215
Neill, Michael, 243, 245 n. 33
Németh, Antal, 151
Nestyev, Israel V., 322–25
Nibelungenlied, 56
Nicholls, Anthony J., 270 n. 2
Nietzsche, Friedrich, 21, 218, 235, 238–40, 249–50, 254 n. 7
Ninagawa, Yukio, 201
Niranjana, Tejaswini, 341 n. 20
Nolan, Emer, 100 n. 3
North, Thomas, 141 n. 1, 286
Norton, Thomas, 297
Novák, Mária, 168 n. 54
Nureyev, Rudolf, 169

O'Gorman, Gerald, 302 n. 32
O'Neill, Con, 271 n. 11
O'Neill, Hugh, 337
Okhlopkov, Nikolai, 106

Oliver, H. J., 253 n. 1
Olivier, Laurence, 146
Orgel, Stephen, 176 n. 3
Örkény, István, 164
Orkin, Martin, 71 n. 17, 201
Országh, László, 167 n. 7
Ossian. *See* Macpherson, James
Ostendorf, Berndt, 272 n. 21
Ovendale, Ritchie, 72 n. 33
Ovid, 215, 290, 299
Owen, W. J. B., 231 n. 5
Oz, Avraham, 61, 71 n. 17

Paál, István, 158, 166
Pagden, Anthony, 368 n. 34
Pakschies, Günter, 272 n. 19
Palmer, Patricia, 332, 341 n. 10
Pandey, S., 211 n. 7
Panse, Barbara, 155 n. 21
Paoli, Michel, 303 n. 51
Papp, Antal, 168 n. 25
Par, Alfonso, 112–14, 121 n. 3
Parsons, Talcott, 275 n. 49
Partridge, Eric, 70 n. 1
Patin, Henri, 301 n. 29
Paulin, Roger, 273 n. 35
Pavis, Patrice, 201
Pearce, Roy Harvey, 53 n. 12
Pechter, Edward, 73 n. 44
Pelly, M. E., 273 n. 29
Percival, John, 176 n. 4
Pereszlenyi, J., 274 n. *See also* Esslin, Martin
Petersohn, Roland, 192, 194 n. 32
Petrarch (Francesco Petrarca), 286, 299, 301 n. 26, 353
Pfister, Manfred, 16, 246, 253 n. 1, 273 n. 35
Phillipson, Robert, 367 n. 25
Piachaud, René-Louis, 126–27, 134, 137, 141 n. 6
Piazza, Antonella, 19, 21, 218, 253 n. 1
Pickford, Mary, 175
Pieller, Jacques, 141 n. 26
Pigman, G. W., 290, 301 n. 22, 302 n. 33
Piñal, Francisco Aguilar, 112, 116, 122 n. 17, 123 n. 32
Pironon, Jacques, 341 n. 7
Piscator, Erwin, 181, 193 n. 13, 260
Planchon, Roger, 106
Platt, Len, 101 n. 16

Plautus, 216, 290, 301 n. 25
Pliny, 288
Plutarch, 124, 138, 286
Polanski, Roman, 189
Polet, Jean-Claude, 356, 360–63, 367 n. 27
Polhemus, Ted, 178 n. 15
Polo, Marco, 40
Poltermann, Andreas, 366 n. 19
Pope, Alexander, 26 n. 8, 143, 221, 228, 231 n. 4
Popov, Gavriil Nikolayevich, 326
Popovic, Jovan Sterija, 51
Potter, Nick, 87–88 n. 1
Pound, Ezra, 94, 224
Poussin, Nicolas, 141 n. 19
Price, Joseph, 195 n. 42
Priestley, Joseph, 259
Prokofiev, Sergej, 21, 23, 107, 284, 318–28
Pronay, Nicholas, 270 n. 6, 271 n. 9
Proust, Marcel, 329
Prouty, Charles, 290, 292, 301 n. 21, 302 n. 37
Pujante, Ángel Luis, 20, 24, 25–26 n. 3, 26 n. , 112, 116, 122 n. 20, 123 n. 28, 142 n. 24, 284
Pushkin, Alexander S., 51

Quiller-Couch, Sir Arthur, 236
Quintilian, 331, 341 n. 6

Radlov, Sergey, 319, 326
Rainer, Yvonne, 171
Rákosi, Matyas, 161
Ralph, Edgar, 155 n. 11
Rapin, René, 53 n. 16
Redgrave, Michael, 146
Reich, Bernhard, 181, 192 n. 8
Renwick, W. L., 341 n. 12
Reynard the Fox, 36, 49
Richard II (King of England), 64, 92
Richardson, Charles, 261–70
Richardson, Ralph, 146
Richmond, Hugh M., 88 n. 3
Riego, Rafael de, 110
Rietbergen, Peter, 368 n. 34
Rinke, Stefan, 272 n. 21
Rischbieter, Henning, 156 n. 21
Rivarol, Antoine de, 367 n. 28
Robertson, J. M., 235–37, 244 n. 5
Robinson, Douglas, 341 n. 5

INDEX OF NAMES

Robyns, Clem, 366 n. 19
Rodríguez, Concepción, 112
Rokiski Lázaro, Gloria, 317 n. 16
Romano, Colonna, 133
Romanos, Mesoneros, 121–22 n. 6
Romsics, Ignác, 167 n. 17, 168 n. 33
Róna, Éva, 167 n. 7
Roper, Derek, 25 n. 3, 219 n. 6, 365 n.
Rose, Paul, 149, 153, 156 n. 23
Rossi, Ernesto, 351
Roth, Philip, 17, 18
Rubel, Margaret Mary, 53 n. 12
Rucellai, Giovanni, 303 n. 51
Rudolf II (Emperor), 79, 83
Rühle, Günther, 210 n. 1
Rushdie, Salman, 207, 270, 277 n. 73
Ruskin, John, 199
Ruszt, József, 160

Sackville, Richard, 287, 289, 297
Sala Valldaura, Josep Maria, 122 n. 18, 317 n. 14
Samuel, Claude, 323, 328 n. 6
Sándor, Iván, 167 n. 18
Sándor, János, 163
Sandys, Edwin, 81–82, 88 n. 17
Sankey, John, 177 n. 13
Sannazzaro, Jacopo, 301 n. 26
Santucci, L. Falzon, 87 n. 2
Saroyan, William, 146
Sartre, Jean-Paul, 259
Saunders, Frances S., 273 n. 31
Saviñón, Antonio de, 305, 311–12, 317 n. 5
Scève, Maurice, 286
Schabert, Ina, 211 n. 5
Schandl, Veronika, 22, 106
Scharf, Claus, 272 n. 20
Schechner, Richard, 201
Scheemakers, Peter, 66
Schelle, Hansjoerg R., 52 n. 2
Schiller, Friedrich, 39, 43, 46, 47, 51, 53–54 n. 17, 179, 196, 219, 351
Schlegel, August Wilhelm, 44, 50
Schlegel, Friedrich, 35, 46
Schlegel-Tieck (translation), 194 n. 36, 200, 262, 351
Schlingensief, Christoph, 205
Schlösser, Anselm, 194 n. 36
Schlösser, Rainer, 148, 152
Schmidt, Wolf Gerhard, 43, 54 n. 19

Schneider, Irmela, 210 n. 2
Schneider, Stefanie, 272 n. 21
Schnittke, Alfred, 207
Schnoor, Rainer, 194 n. 32
Scholz, Gunter, 52
Schopenhauer, Arthur, 323
Schröder, Friedrich Ludwig, 316 n. 2
Schröder, Hans-Jürgen, 272 n. 21
Schubert, Franz, 264
Schuchard, Ron, 101 n. 21
Schumacher, Frank, 272 n. 21
Schutte, William, 100, 102 n. 30
Schwartz, Robert, 232 n. 24
Schwartz-Gastine, Isabelle, 21, 105, 112, 121 n. 5, 316 n.
Schwarzschild, Leopold, 270 n. 7
Schwendi, Lazarus von, 83
Scott, Elizabeth, 57
Sehrt, Ernst Theodor, 269, 277 n. 72
Seneca, 216, 290, 292
Sergeyev, Konstantin, 319
Seroff, Victor, 323, 328 n. 13
Sever, Frentin, 163
Seymour, Charles, 71 n. 10
Shadwell, Thomas, 199
Shakespeare, William. Works:
  All's Well that Ends Well, 74, 159; *Antony and Cleopatra*, 95, 223; *As You Like It*, 81, 105, 179; *Coriolanus*, 21, 95, 105, 106, 124–42, 331; *Cymbeline*, 299; *Hamlet*, 16, 20, 21, 24, 34, 74, 90, 106, 107, 144, 155 n. 6, 179, 182, 185, 200, 205–7, 218, 223, 225–26, 229, 234–45, 284, 304–17, 319; *Henry IV*, 33, 60–64, 66, 69, 106, 229; *Henry V*, 19, 50, 223, 274 n. 41, 331, 333, 338–39, 343; *Henry VI*, 19, 215, 291–93, 298, 301 n. 29, 333–36; *Henry VIII*, 134; *Julius Caesar*, 249, 331; *King Lear*, 209–10, 223, 231 n. 9; *Love's Labours Lost*, 31, 74, 75, 264; *Macbeth*, 179, 210, 231 n. 9, 255, 274 n. 41, 276 n. 71, 350; *Measure for Measure*, 18, 22, 34, 75–89, 106, 158–68, 180; *The Merchant of Venice*, 16–17, 21, 74, 106, 143–57, 263, 267; *A Midsummer Night's Dream*, 84, 144, 146, 155 n. 6, 205; *Much Ado About Nothing*, 274 n. 41; *Othello*, 79, 88 n. 10, 92, 207; *Richard II*, 62, 180, 267, 331; *Richard III*, 180, 261, 301 n. 29, 302 n. 36; *Romeo*

and Juliet, 107, 161, 249, 284, 318–28; *The Taming of the Shrew*, 107, 169–78; *The Tempest*, 17, 92, 107, 202–4, 209, 264, 268; *Timon of Athens*, 21, 218, 246–54; *Titus Andronicus*, 95, 179; *Troilus and Cressida*, 159; *Twelfth Night*, 75, 144, 147, 205; *Wars of the Roses*, 106; *The Winter's Tale*, 74
Shaw, George Bernard, 273 n. 36
Shepherd, Simon, 232 n. 12, 233 n. 28
Shippey, Thomas A., 55 n. 27
Shostakovitch, Dmitri, 319
Shuger, Debora Kuller, 84, 89 nn. 28, 29, and 30
Shurbanov, Alexander, 327 n. 1, 328 n. 11, 366 n. 13
Siddons, Sarah, 124
Sidney, Mary, 36
Sidney, Philip, 215, 286
Simón Díaz, José, 123 n.
Simon, Sherry, 284 n. 1
Simpson, Wallis, 64
Simrock, Karl, 49, 50, 55 n. 29
Sinfield, Alan, 193 n. 22, 219 n. 4, 233 n. 32
Sjögren, Gunnar, 78, 88 n. 9
Smith, Anthony D., 365 n. 1
Smith, Logan Pearsall, 82, 89 n. 19, 341 n. 18
Snell-Hornby, Mary, 285 n. 1
Snyder, Susan, 322, 327, 328 n. 4
Sokolova, Boika, 25 n. 3, 219 n. 6, 327 n. 1, 328 n. 11, 365 n. 13
Solís, Dionisio, 113, 116
Sophocles, 292–93
Sorelius, Gunnar, 316 n. 1
Spender, Stephen, 273 n. 31
Spengler, Oswald, 250
Spenser, Edmund, 215–16, 286, 333, 341 n. 12
Spiel, Hilde, 275 n. 56
Spitzer, Leo, 266, 275 n. 60
Stalin, Joseph, 185
Steenbergh, Kristine, 25
Steiner, George, 100, 102 n. 35
Stern, Avraham, 72 n. 36
Strada, Jacopo, 83
Strauss, Johan, 187
Strehler, Giorgio, 134
Sturm, Johann, 292, 300 n. 8, 302 n. 34
Surrey, Henry Howard (Earl of), 288

Suzuki, Tadashi, 201
Symington, Rodney, 192 n. 5
Symonds, John A., 287–88, 292–93, 297, 300 n. 6, 302 n. 41
Szabados, Tamás, 168 n. 43
Szabó, László Cs., 168 n. 45
Szabó, Miklós, 167 n. 17
Szántó, Erika, 168 n. 21
Szántó, Judit, 159, 167 n. 4, 168 n. 49
Szekrényessy, Júlia, 167 n. 3, 168 n. 52
Szenczi, Miklós, 167 n. 7
Színház, Nemzeti, 156 n. 29
Szirtes, Ádám, 158

Taïeb, Michèle, 142 n. 28
Tallents, Stephen, 258, 264
Talma, François-Joseph, 20, 109–10, 112, 116, 124, 133, 311
Tasso, Torquato, 41, 301 n. 26
Taylor, Edward, 221, 231 n. 4
Taylor, Elizabeth, 172
Taylor, Gary, 76, 77, 79, 81, 86, 87, 88 n. 5, 216, 219 n. 5, 265, 275 n. 57, 316 n. 2
Taylor, Neil, 328 n. 4
Taylor, Philip M., 265, 272 n. 27, 275 n. 53
Taylor, Sam, 177 n. 11
Tenschert, Joachim, 134
Terpening, Ronnie H., 301 n. 20
Thiery, Árpád, 167 n. 12
Thies, Jochen, 272 n. 20
Thomas, T. V., 88 n. 12
Thompson, Ann, 176 n. 3
Thomsen, Christian W., 210 n. 2
Tieck, Ludwig, 44, 46. *See also* Schlegel-Tieck
Tilley, Morris P., 302 n. 33
Tillyard, E. M. W., 268, 276 n. 67
Tolstoy, Leo, 367 n. 26
Tooke, Benjamin, 89 n. 19
Tottel, Richard, 302 n. 32
Trissino, Gian Giorgio, 303 n. 51
Trivedi, Harish, 285 n. 1
Tscholakowa, Ginka, 186–87
Turner, Ian, 271 n. 17
Turner, John, 87–88 n. 2

Uhland, Ludwig, 46
Ulanova, Galina, 319
Ullrich, Peter, 194 n. 39
Ulric, Duke of Holstein, 88 n. 6

INDEX OF NAMES

Ulrici, Hermann, 84
Ungaretti, Giuseppe, 367 n. 26

Valette, Bernard, 356
Valk, Diana, 146, 155 n. 9
Valk, Frederick, 146, 152
Valk, Fritz, 145
Valuch, Tibor, 167 n. 17
Vanderhoof Mary B., 316 n. 1
Vansittart, Robert, 256, 270 n. 8
Van Tieghem, Paul, 316 n. 1
Van Veldeke, Henric, 40
Vapereau, Gustave, 346, 365 n. 7
Vaughan, Henry, 72 n. 28
Vega, Ventura de la, 111–12, 122 n. 9
Venturi, Franco, 53–54 n. 17
Venuti, Lawrence, 284 n. 1
Verdi, Giuseppi, 351
Vergerio, Pier Paolo, 339, 341 n. 4
Vickers, Brian, 231 n. 4
Vico, Giambattista, 34, 41, 74
Vilanova, Antonio, 122 n. 9
Virgil, 51, 215, 290, 300 n. 2
Viroli, Maurizio, 53–54 n. 17
Voltaire, 109, 124, 351, 353
Von der Hagen, Friedrich, 46, 47, 50
Vondung, Klaus, 52 n. 4
Von Wiese, Benno, 54 n. 24

Wagner, Jacques, 341 n. 7
Wagner, Richard, 47, 49, 320
Walden, Jeff, 277 n. 74
Wallace, Henry, 270 n. 7
Wallendorf, Craig W., 341 n. 4
Warburton, William, 221
Wardetzky, Jutta, 273 n. 36
Warner, William, 216
Warren, Austin, 277 n. 72
Waterson, Simon, 81
Watt, Donald C., 272 n. 23
Way, Arthur S., 302 n. 32
Wearing, J. P., 155 n. 6
Weber, Carl, 193 n. 20
Weber, Eugen, 366 n. 21
Webster, Margaret, 170
Wedderburn, Alexander, 211 n. 4
Weichart, Carl, 149, 156 n. 25
Weidmann, Helga, 54 n. 22
Weigel, Helene, 179
Weimann, Robert, 105, 108 n. 1, 191, 193 n. 21, 217, 228–29, 232 n. 24, 233 n. 26

Weise, Klaus, 207
Wekwerth, Manfred, 134, 194 n. 34
Welch, David, 271 n. 13
Wellek, René, 277 n. 72
Welles, Orson, 182
Wellington, Duke of, 114
Wells, R. Headlam, 73 n. 44
Wells, Stanley, 200, 210 n. 3
Welsh, Alexander, 102 n. 33
Werder, Karl, 236
West, Nigel, 72 n. 30, 73 n. 40
Whetstone, George, 79
Whitehead, John W., 26 n. 11
Whitgift (Archbishop), 81, 84
Wiener, Martin J., 265, 275 n. 55
Wiesner-Hanks, Merry E., 88 n. 14
Wilder, Thornton, 259, 269, 276 n. 70
Wilhelm V of Bavaria (Duke), 80, 88 n. 13
Willey, Basil, 245 n. 7
Williams, Simon, 52 n. 2, 273 n. 35, 316 n. 2
Wilson, John Dover, 191, 195 n. 44, 218, 221, 225, 231 n. 3, 234–45
Wilson, Keith, 270 n. 6, 271 n. 9
Wilson, Woodrow, 72 n. 33
Winter, Robert, 300 n. 17
Wolfe, Robert, 271 n. 10
Wolff, F. A., 46
Wolfit, Donald, 144, 145
Wolin, Richard, 276 n. 61
Womack, Peter, 232 n. 12, 233 n. 28
Wood, Michael, 275 n. 57
Woodsworth, Judith, 342 n. 25
Woolf, Virginia, 234
Wordsworth, William, 221, 231 n. 5
Wotton, Henry, 82, 83, 89 n. 19, 337–38
Woudhuysen, Henry, 75, 88 n. 3
Wray, Ramona, 101 n. 6, 342 n. 22
Wulf, Joseph, 149, 156 n. 22
Wyss, Ulrich, 54 n. 24

Yeats, William Butler, 92
Yelverton, Christopher, 294

Zadek, Peter, 207
Zappe, László, 167 n. 2, 168 n. 5
Zeffirelli, Franco, 172–73
Zhdanov, Andrei, 318
Zimmerman, Heiner O., 273 n. 35
Żurowski, Andrzej, 316 n. 1